DATE DUE

DEC 1 1 1997			
GAYLORD			PRINTED IN U.S.A.

The Baseball Chronicles

The Baseball Chronicles

A Decade-by-Decade History of the All-American Pastime

Larry Burke

SMITHMARK

A FRIEDMAN GROUP BOOK

This edition published in 1995 by SMITHMARK Publishers Inc.
16 East 32nd Street, New York, NY 10016.

SMITHMARK Books are available for bulk purchase for sales
promotion and premium use. For details write or call the manager of special sales, SMITHMARK Publishers Inc., 16 East 32nd
Street, New York, NY 10016; (212) 532-6600.

ISBN 0-8317-0680-5

THE BASEBALL CHRONICLES
A Decade-by-Decade History of the All-American Pastime
was prepared and produced by
Michael Friedman Publishing Group, Inc.
15 West 26th Street
New York, NY 10010

Editors: Susan Lauzau and Karla Olson
Art Director: Jeff Batzli
Designer: Kevin Ullrich
Photography Editors: Susan Mettler and Wendy Missan

Color separations by Ocean Graphic (International) Co. Ltd.
Printed in China by Leefung-Asco Printers Ltd.

10 9 8 7 6 5 4 3 2 1

Dedication

For Beth, the MVP, and Casey, our rookie of the year.

Acknowledgments

Many thanks to Greg Garber, of the *Hartford Courant*, ESPN, and countless other affiliations, who threw out the first ball, came on in relief to put out the fire in the bottom of the ninth, and was a valuable player throughout the writing of this book. The research staff at the National Baseball Library and Archive provided a wealth of information and was always happy to assist. Thanks also to the Michael Friedman Publishing Group, especially editors Karla Olson and Susan Lauzau, designer Kevin Ullrich, and photo editors Susan Mettler and Wendy Missan, for lending their talents; to writer/editor David Craft for his input; and to photo researchers Patricia Kelly, Darci Harrington, and Bill Burdick of the National Baseball Library and Archive, and Paul Harrington of FPG International for their assistance. Finally, thanks to Beth for taking care of everything else in our lives while I was immersed in this book—and still finding time to research and proofread—and to Dad for taking me to my first game.

CONT

ENTS

Introduction

[Baseball is] the exponent of American Courage, Confidence, Combativeness; American Dash, Discipline, Determination; American Energy, Eagerness, Enthusiasm; American Pluck, Persistency, Performance; American Spirit, Sagacity, Success; American Vim, Vigor, Virility.

—Albert Spalding, as quoted in the *Baseball Research Journal*

Whoever wants to know the heart and mind of America had better learn baseball, the rules and realities of the game.

—Jacques Barzun, philosophy professor, Columbia University

Baseball? It's just a game—as simple as a ball and a bat. Yet, as complex as the American spirit it symbolizes. It's a sport, business—and sometimes even a religion.

—Ernie Harwell, from the essay "The Game for All America"

Baseball is continuous, like nothing else among American things, an endless game of repeated summers, joining the long generations of all the fathers and all the sons.

—Donald Hall, from the book *Fathers Playing Catch With Sons*

Baseball's inherent rhythm, minutes and minutes of passivity erupting into seconds of frenzied action, matches an attribute of the American character. But no existential proclamation, or any tortured neo-Freudianism, or any outburst of popular sociology, not even—or least of all— my own, explains baseball's lock on the American heart.

You learn to let some mysteries alone, and when you do, you find they sing themselves.

—Roger Kahn, from the *Sports Illustrated* article "Still a Grand Old Game"

We could list page after page of such quotes, but we trust that these, culled from volumes that encompass about a century of baseball men talking and writing about the game, have made our point clear: baseball, more than any other sport, is America's game.

Sure, other games have their moments of excitement and drama, but none can match baseball's ebbs and flows, its unique combination of thrilling moments with the simple pleasures of a sun-drenched, breezy afternoon at the ballpark. As Roger Kahn wrote in a 1957 article in *The American Scholar*: "Football is violence and cold weather and sex and college rye. Horse racing is animated roulette. Boxing is smoky halls and kidneys battered until they bleed. Tennis and golf are best played, not watched. Basketball, hockey and track meets are action heaped upon action, climax upon climax, until the onlooker's responses become deadened. Baseball is for the leisurely afternoons of summer and for the unchanging dreams."

To that we would add that baseball and America share a common past that no other sport will ever know. No other game is so finely woven into the fabric of this country's history. Baseball is our national pastime for one simple reason: the game and the nation grew up together. The first organized baseball game was played seventeen years before Abraham Lincoln delivered the Emancipation Proclamation; forty-five years before basketball's inventor, Dr. James Naismith, hung up his first peach baskets for hoops; and forty-six years before two Pittsburgh athletic clubs hooked up for the first professional football game. On April 22, 1876, Boston defeated Philadelphia 6–5 in the first game for baseball's National League; two months later, in the Battle of the Little Bighorn, Colonel George Custer and the 7th Cavalry suffered a considerably more lopsided defeat at the hands of the Sioux Indians. The debut of professional leagues for football and basketball came even later: the National Football League formed in 1922, the National Basketball Association in 1949.

As an army captain, Abner Doubleday fired the first shot for Union forces in the Civil War. Twentieth-century historians have concluded that his contribution to baseball history was considerably less significant.

The Generation X sports fan might counter that this is yesterday's news and that times have changed. Well, to a baseball fan, tradition and history mean a great deal—and they always will. This book is a tribute to those things.

Baseball's Origin and the Early Years

So when—and how—did baseball begin? Well, do you prefer a popular legend based largely on the testimony of one person, or a more plausible story with considerably more evidence to support it? The legend, as reported by the Mills Commission (a panel of experts commissioned in 1905 to determine the origin of baseball, or "base ball," as the game was originally known) and as testified to by Adam Graves, has it that Abner Doubleday, a friend of Graves' and an army captain who served in the Mexican and U.S. Civil Wars and fired the first shot for Union troops at Fort Sumter, South Carolina, was the game's founder. Graves claimed that Doubleday modified the American game of "town ball," which derived from the English game of rounders, by drawing a field in the shape of a diamond, adding bases, limiting the number of players, and putting

in a pitcher and a catcher. Former National League President A.G. Mills, the chairman of the committee that bore his name, stated in his report (which was not signed by any of the other committee members) that in Cooperstown, New York, in 1839, Doubleday had drawn a diagram of the first baseball field and had outlined the basic rules of play. The problem was, no copy of the diagram or rules could be found, and no one in or around Cooperstown, save for Graves, knew anything about it. Nonetheless, Albert Spalding, the sporting goods magnate and former baseball player and manager who had commissioned Mills and company to research baseball's origins, accepted Mills' report. The name of Doubleday, the year 1839, and the city of Cooperstown, where baseball subsequently erected its Hall of Fame, thus all became fixed in the lore of the game.

As for the more plausible version, those historians who dismissed the popular legend and based their conclusions on more tangible evidence contend that Doubleday probably never even played the game. They claim that baseball's roots go back to the early 1800s and that although the game is uniquely American, it may have evolved as a loose variation of English games such as rounders and cricket. Baseball, much like the country in which it was born, probably was developed as a "melting pot" of several other games. The first "Base Ball Diagram," a sketch of a playing field that provided for twelve players and asymmetrical distances between the bases, was drawn in New York in 1842. The fact that the game was becoming more popular with young men as opposed to young

This could be the start of something big: an artist's rendering of the Elysian Fields in Hoboken, New Jersey, where the first organized baseball game was played. Skyboxes, fireworks, and the wave were not yet in vogue.

boys was further proven by the formation of the Knickerbocker Base Ball Club of New York in 1845.

That organization, the first of its kind, appointed a committee headed by surveyor Alexander Cartwright to compose a standardized list of baseball rules. Cartwright designed a square playing field which, except for a few minor changes in positioning of fielders, is the same baseball diamond used today. His committee submitted this diagram and a list of baseball rules to the Knickerbocker club in 1846. The Knickerbockers voted in favor of Cartwright's plan and preparations were made for the first organized baseball game, which took place on June 19, 1846, on the Elysian Fields in Hoboken, New Jersey, between the Knickerbockers and the New York Nine. Cartwright, a player for the Knickerbockers, chose to umpire the game instead. The New York Nine won 23–1 in 4 innings. Obviously disheartened by the defeat, the Knickerbockers confined themselves to intrasquad games until June 3, 1851, when they defeated the Washington Base Ball Club of New York 21–11 in 8 innings. The Knickerbockers emerged as a powerful force and the game's popularity continued to grow on the club level. The Civil War slowed the progress of baseball in the 1860s but also helped spread the game to the South, as soldiers on both sides learned to play as campsite recreation.

The first all-professional team, the Cincinnati Red Stockings, was formed in 1869. For an eight-month season of barnstorming, players' salaries ranged from six hundred dollars for a reserve to twelve hundred dollars for manager and left fielder Harry Wright to fourteen hundred dollars for the Reds' captain and star shortstop, Wright's brother, George. The total team payroll for the season was $9,300, less than a quarter of what today's highest-paid players earn per game. In 57 games in 1869, before an estimated total of 200,000 fans, the Red Stockings won 56 and tied 1. They suffered their first loss on June 14, 1870, at the hands of the Brooklyn Atlantics, who scored 3 runs in the bottom of the eleventh inning to win 8–7. Subsequent losses—both on the field and on the balance sheet—led to the demise of the Cincinnati club after the 1870 season.

Other cities nonetheless had taken notice of the national notoriety that the Red Stockings had brought to Cincinnati, so the future of baseball as a professional enterprise was solidified. The National Association of Base Ball Players, which had been organized in 1858 to govern the game as an amateur sport at the club level, had all but died out by 1871. In its place stepped the National Association of Professional Base Ball Players, formed in March of 1871. The National Association, the first professional baseball league, began its inaugural season with ten teams: Boston Red Stockings, Chicago White

Above: They were a dapper group, but the 1889 Philadelphia Phillies finished 20½ games out of first place and were still twenty-six years away from their first National League pennant. Right: An 1892 view of a New York Giants game at the Polo Grounds, which held only 16,000 fans, 5,500 of them in the grandstand. After the grandstand was destroyed by fire in 1911, the park was rebuilt as a larger, concrete-and-steel stadium.

Stockings, Cleveland Forest Citys, Fort Wayne Kekiongas, New York Mutuals, Philadelphia Athletics, Rockford Forest Citys, Troy Haymakers, Washington Nationals, and Washington Olympics. Judging the venture too risky, the Brooklyn Eckfords opted not to pay the ten-dollar initiation fee; they later replaced Fort Wayne, which dropped out of the league in midseason. Philadelphia won 22 of 29 games to take the first championship, and Boston claimed the next four titles. Those two teams, along with New York, were the only franchises to compete in each of the National Association's five seasons; more than twenty-five different teams were members at one time or another during the league's brief existence. By the end of the 1875 season, amid financial losses, competitive imbalance, and allegations of gambling and game-fixing, the National Association was in serious trouble.

Chicago White Stockings owner William A. Hulbert figured that professional baseball still could be a money-maker, but he wanted a league that was better managed. With the support of the National Association's three other western teams—Cincinnati, Louisville, and St. Louis—Hulbert was able to persuade four other National Association teams—Boston, Hartford, New York, and Philadelphia—to pull the plug on the National Association and join his new National League of Professional Base Ball Clubs, the same National League that exists today. Hartford President M.G. Bulkeley was elected president, and the league adopted a no-nonsense, business-minded approach, instituting strict player contracts and banning gambling, Sunday play, and liquor sales at games. The National League debuted on April 22, 1876, with Boston beating Philadelphia 6–5 before three thousand spectators. The basic game was the same as that played today, but there were some major differences: most fielders played bare-handed; the catcher stood directly behind the plate only when there was a runner on base and hitters were permitted to request a high or low pitch.

The National League struggled through the 1870s, and faced challenges from three other leagues in its first fifteen years of existence. The most serious came from the American Association of Base Ball Clubs (1882–1891), which cut ticket prices from fifty cents to twenty-five cents, permitted liquor sales, and played Sunday games. Bitter rivals at first, the National League and American Association signed the National Agreement of 1883, which provided for the mutual observance of the reserve clause and a post-season championship series between the two leagues. The Union Association of Base Ball Clubs, which tried to entice players from the other two leagues by proclaiming its opposition to the reserve clause, played only the 1884 season. The Players League, formed in 1890 by the Brotherhood of Professional Base Ball Players because of the players' objections to the reserve clause and owners' threats to institute a ceiling on salaries, lasted only one year.

Soon after the Players League's demise, the National League and American Association were at war again, and this time the latter did not survive. Out of the ashes emerged the twelve-team National League and American Association of Professional Base Ball Clubs, which added the American Association teams from Baltimore, Louisville, St. Louis, and Washington to the National League's existing franchises in Boston, Brooklyn, Chicago, Cincinnati, Cleveland, New York, Philadelphia, and Pittsburgh, and served as the game's sole major league from 1892 until the end of the century. Though not a financial success, the league was at least stable during this period, putting an end to the merry-go-round of teams, cities, and circuits that had existed in the previous two decades.

The 1900s
"America's Game" Catches On

Growth, optimism, and innovation were the buzz-words in America as the twentieth century began—and baseball was no exception. While the United States was experiencing an industrial boom, unprecedented European immigration, and the benefits of such technological innovations as automobiles, motion picture cameras, and wireless radios, the first decade of the 1900s saw the birth of baseball's second major league and the construction of the game's first concrete-and-steel stadiums. America—like its national pastime—was entering a new era.

Ushering in this new era in baseball was the birth of an American institution. The first World Series, a best-of-nine contest, was played from October 1 to October 13, 1903. Despite heavy feuding between the leagues during the season, the champions of the National League, the Pittsburgh Pirates, met the Boston Pilgrims of the American League for Game One on the field of Boston's Huntington Avenue Grounds before a crowd of more than sixteen thousand, large for the day. The Pirates won that first game and two of the next three, but the Pilgrims regrouped and won the next four, taking the Series, much to the chagrin of the National League. There has been a great deal of speculation about the upset, but indeed, the Pirates were hindered by the loss of pitchers Jesse Tannehill and Jack Chesbro, who had signed with the American League. In addition, Sam Leever's arm injury left him unable to play, and, most tragically, left-handed pitcher Ed Doheny suffered a mental breakdown the night before the first game of the Series. Conversely, it was the strength of pitchers Cy Young and Bill Dineen that ensured the Pilgrims' victory.

The next year's NL champions, the New York Giants, firmly refused the honor of playing in the Series, but by the autumn of 1905 the Giants, again the pennant winners, reconsidered. This time the National League entry

Albert Spalding earned notoriety—and a 1939 Hall of Fame induction—as one of the game's pioneers, but he was also a pretty fair pitcher. He was baseball's first 20-game winner, and he fashioned a 205–55 record with Boston of the National Association from 1871 to 1875.

prevailed, defeating the Philadelphia Athletics 4 games to 1 in the Series' new best-of-seven format.

The popularity of baseball was growing by leaps and bounds. Ban Johnson's American League led the way in getting its players to curb their rowdy behavior on the field, and when it was clear that the fans approved, the National League followed suit. Intense on-field competition—some classic down-to-the-wire pennant races and the novelty of the World Series—also spurred more fan interest. The major leagues drew more than fifty million fans in the decade, and total attendance in 1909 was more than double the 1901 figure.

More fan interest naturally meant more media coverage for the game. Fans found that following baseball was an enjoyable release from the labors of the work week. Newspapers—especially those in the urban centers, where the teams were based and the population was greatest—capitalized on baseball coverage as a way to boost their circulation. By the end of the decade, Western Union was telegraphing baseball games on a consistent basis. The 1908 World Series was the first captured in motion pictures.

Baseball clearly had assumed a special place in the hearts and minds of Americans. "Every city, town and village in America has its team," noted the *St. Louis Globe and Commercial Advertiser* in 1905. But was baseball truly "America's game"? Or, as many experts—including the sport's most respected historian, Henry Chadwick—asserted, had baseball evolved from the English game of rounders?

Major League Teams in the 1900s

Note: team nicknames in this period were not as standardized as they are today, when each club has one nickname and essentially sticks with it. Many teams of the early 1900s were known by several nicknames, and some names went in and out of vogue in just a few years. Teams in the American League were sometimes called "Americans," and likewise National League clubs were sometimes referred to as "Nationals"—the exception being the Washington team, which, despite being an American League entry, opted to call itself the Nationals for a time. The list below includes each team's most common nickname(s) of the period:

NATIONAL LEAGUE
Boston Nationals/Doves/Braves
Brooklyn Superbas/Dodgers
Chicago Colts/Orphans/Cubs
Cincinnati Reds
New York Giants
Philadelphia Phillies
Pittsburgh Pirates
St. Louis Cardinals

AMERICAN LEAGUE
(Teams played 1901–1909 unless otherwise noted)
Baltimore Orioles (became New York Highlanders in 1903)
Boston Americans/Pilgrims/Puritans/Plymouth Rocks/Somersets/Red Sox
Chicago White Stockings/White Sox
Cleveland Blues/Bronchos/Naps
Detroit Tigers
Milwaukee Brewers (became St. Louis Browns/Ravens in 1902)
Philadelphia Athletics
Washington Senators/Nationals

Infielder/outfielder Bob Hall models the road uniform of the 1905 world champion New York Giants. Like many uniforms of the period, New York's featured a loose-fitting, long-sleeved shirt with a high collar (most players wore it turned up), a wide belt that was buckled on the side (most pants had a belt loop in the front), and a cap without a team insignia.

Sporting goods magnate Albert G. Spalding decided in 1905 to try to settle the question once and for all, organizing a panel of seven baseball experts, including two U.S. senators, to determine baseball's origins. The commission was chaired by Abraham G. Mills, the former NL president who sixteen years earlier had publicly stated that "patriotism and research" had proved that baseball was purely an American sport. It therefore came as no surprise that after two years of research the commission rejected the rounders theory. What was a bit of a surprise, though, was the commission's final conclusion: baseball was invented by one man, a former Civil War hero named Abner Doubleday, on a field in Cooperstown, New York. Even though subsequent research has strongly supported baseball's link to the English game, the Doubleday legend has remained the prevalent tale of how baseball was born. Cooperstown remains the game's most revered city and the home of its Hall of Fame.

On the field, meanwhile, strategy was at a premium. The home run was a rarity—the 1902 Pittsburgh Pirates won the pennant and led the league with only 19 round-trippers; the 1906 Chicago White Sox won the World Series despite hitting just 7 homers in the regular season. So rather than sit back and wait for the long ball, managers relied on speed, defense, pitching, teamwork, and sound tactical moves.

In 1900, Boston's Herman Long led the National League with 12 home runs. Long, a 5-foot-8½-inch (174cm), 160-pound (72.6kg) shortstop, was not exactly cut from the cloth of the larger-than-life sluggers that would follow him. In 1909, Red Murray of the New York Giants led the National League with merely 7 home runs, while the American League champion, Detroit's Ty Cobb, had 9. It was the only time in twenty-four seasons that Cobb led in homers; on six occasions he led in stolen bases, including 1909, when he swiped 76. Stolen bases, as a rule, were far more frequent. And it wasn't just speed that prevailed on the base paths; in the era before the long ball, intelligence could sometimes overcome age. In 1900, St. Louis manager and right fielder Patsy Donovan—at the age of thirty-five—and New York center fielder George Van Haltren—thirty-four years old—led the league in stolen bases, with 45 each.

Off the field, the game was dominated by some strong personalities—who invariably clashed. One of the most pivotal conflicts of the late 1800s was between

In 1909 New York Giants outfielder Red Murray (above) *led the National League in home runs with just 7, which tied his career high (set in each of the previous two seasons). Soon Yankee star Babe Ruth would come along and hit that many in about a week's time.*

Spalding, president of the Chicago White Stockings and the voice of management, and John Montgomery "Monte" Ward, a player with the New York Giants who tried to lead his brethren out of indentured servitude to baseball owners by forming a separate league. The early 1900s, meanwhile, turned on the clashes between Johnson, the AL president, and his rivals in the National League, principally Giants Manager John McGraw, whose hard-nosed, pugnacious style had angered Johnson when McGraw played for the AL's Baltimore Orioles. In the decade ahead, though, the National League and American League would unite to promote the sport and fight common adversaries.

1900: National League franchises in Baltimore, Cleveland, Louisville, and Washington are dropped, bringing the NL down to eight teams.

1900: Rules change: home plate is changed from a 12-inch (30.4cm) square to a five-sided figure 17 inches (43.1cm) wide.

1900: A new players union, called the Protective Association of Professional Baseball Players, is formed; Charles "Chief" Zimmer is president.

January 29, 1900: The Western League is renamed the American League and reorganized, planting franchises in Chicago, Cleveland, Baltimore, and Washington. The AL's request to the National League for recognition as a major league is refused.

October 1900: NL champion Brooklyn defeats runner-up Pittsburgh in a postseason series.

The American League Declares War December 1900: AL President Ban Johnson, planning to plant a team in Boston for the 1901 season, is granted an audience to discuss the move with NL executives at their winter meetings. But the NL men stand Johnson up—slipping out a side door while the AL president sits waiting for hours outside the meeting room. Furious, Johnson goes forward with his plans for a Boston team to compete with the NL's Braves—making Boston the third city, along with Chicago and Philadelphia, where the two leagues will compete head-to-head—and promises a fight "to the finish." By offering significantly higher salaries, the American League attracts about thirty NL regulars, including Nap Lajoie, Cy Young, Clark Griffith, John McGraw, Joe McGinnity, and Jimmy Collins.

Aptly nicknamed "Iron Man," Joe McGinnity (above) set modern major league records by throwing 434 innings in the 1903 season (one of five years in which he eclipsed the 400-inning mark) and by pitching 2 games on the same day five times. **Below:** *As was the custom of the period, spectators crowd the outfield at Manhattan's Polo Grounds to watch the May 30, 1901, game between the New York Giants and the St. Louis Cardinals.*

September 6, 1901: *U.S. President McKinley is shot by anarchist Leon Czolgosz at the Pan-American Exposition in Buffalo. When McKinley dies eight days later, Theodore Roosevelt takes the oath of office and becomes the country's youngest president at the age of forty-two.*

October 1901: By the end of the season, NL owners are in disagreement over who should lead the league in its war against the American League. Four owners support incumbent president Nick Young; the other four want Albert Spalding to assume the presidency. The confusion leads to the formation of a three-man Executive Committee of club owners John T. Brush of New York, Arthur Soden of Boston, and James Hart of Chicago.

November 28, 1901: *Alabama's new state constitution disenfranchises African Americans by requiring property and literacy tests and by including a grandfather clause.*

1901: New parks: Boston's Huntington Avenue Grounds (Red Sox), Chicago's South Side Park (White Sox), Philadelphia's Columbia Avenue Grounds (Athletics), Detroit's Bennett Park, and Washington's American League Park.

1901: The National Association of Minor Leagues is organized.

1901: Rules change: in the National League, a foul ball not caught on the fly is counted as a strike unless the batter already has 2 strikes. (The American League adopts this rule in 1903.) The infield fly rule applies with no outs as well as one.

1901: Nap Lajoie of the Philadelphia Athletics hits .426, still the highest figure in AL history. He adds 14 homers and 125 runs batted in to win the Triple Crown.

August 1901: AL President Ban Johnson suspends Chicago shortstop Frank Shugart for striking an umpire. Shugart never plays in the majors again.

John McGraw's career as a major league player ended in 1906 with the New York Giants, a team he later managed to ten NL pennants and three world championships.

1902: The AL's Milwaukee Brewers move to St. Louis and are renamed the Browns. Jesse Burkett, Bobby Wallace, Dick Padden, Emmet Heidrick, Jack Harper, and Jack Powell join the Browns from the NL's St. Louis Cardinals.

1902: Colombia native Louis Castro, the first Latin player in the majors, hits .245 in 42 games for the Athletics.

April 1902: Cincinnati's newly renovated League Park, now known as the Palace of the Fans, opens.

April 1902: Nap Lajoie and Bill Bernhard, who had jumped from the NL's Philadelphia Phillies to the AL's Athletics, are transferred to the AL's Cleveland Blues to circumvent a Pennsylvania Supreme Court ruling that the players must return to the Phillies. Chick Fraser, who also jumped to the Athletics, returns to the Phillies.

July 17, 1902: The AL's Orioles, who were purchased and stripped of star players by NL Executive Committee Chairman John T. Brush, are unable to field a team for their scheduled game against St. Louis. They are therefore forced to forfeit the contest, which, under league rules, allows AL President Ban Johnson to take control of the franchise with league funds. Johnson appoints Wilbert Robinson manager and sets up a plan for restocking the Orioles roster with players from other AL ball clubs.

December 1902: Harry Pulliam is elected president of the National League, replacing the three-man Executive Committee.

The AL Comes to New York

1903: The American League drops its final bomb in the great baseball war by unveiling its plans to move the Orioles from Baltimore to New York and rename them the Highlanders. The direct competition in the nation's biggest market is bad enough—the AL had already outdrawn the National League in all four "head-to-head" cities in 1902—but the Highlanders, who will play their games in newly built Hilltop Park, also begin immediate raids on NL rosters; Brooklyn's Willie Keeler and Pittsburgh's Jack Chesbro and Jesse Tannehill are the big names to jump to New York.

1903: Rules change: the height of the pitcher's mound is limited to 15 inches (38.1cm) above the baselines and home plate.

January 5, 1903: In a meeting between representatives of the two major leagues, the NL representatives propose an NL-AL merger into one twelve-team league. The AL representatives refuse and walk out of the meeting.

The National Agreement Is Signed

January 9, 1903: As part of a peace agreement ending a two-year war between the National League and American League, the AL gains recognition as a major circuit and the National Commission is formed to oversee all of "organized baseball," which consists of the NL, the AL, and the National Association of Minor Leagues. Original members of the commission are Cincinnati owner August "Garry" Herrmann, NL President Harry Pulliam, and AL President Ban Johnson. The AL also agrees to cancel its plan to move the

financially struggling Detroit franchise to Pittsburgh, thus finalizing a geographic setup of sixteen clubs that will remain intact for the next fifty years. The two sides establish territorial rights, agree on a common body of rules, and draw up a list of seven players that the AL will return to the NL: Christy Mathewson, Sam Mertes, Rudy Hulswitt, Frank Bowerman, Tommy Leach, Vic Willis, and Harry Smith. The negotiated settlement is regarded as a victory for the AL on all counts.

Left: *An 1898 photo of National League President Harry Pulliam, an original member of baseball's National Commission.* Below: *Hall of Fame outfielder "Wee Willie" Keeler stood just 5 foot 4½ (163.8 cm) and weighed only 140 pounds (63.5 kg), but he hit .345 in his nineteen-year major league career.*

Senators Star Delahanty Dies

July 2, 1903: Eddie Delahanty, a future Hall of Famer who won two batting titles and broke the .400 mark three times, dies mysteriously at age thirty-six. Delahanty is reportedly suffering from an illness and leaves the club in Detroit to go back east by train to recuperate. At Niagara, Ontario, Delahanty is ordered off the train because he is drunk and disorderly. He apparently tumbles into the river and is swept over Niagara Falls; his body is found in the currents at the base of the falls a few days later.

August 6, 1903: Twelve people are killed and two hundred injured when a left-field balcony collapses at Philadelphia's National League Park during a Phillies game.

The First World Series Opens

October 1, 1903: A crowd of 16,242 is on hand at Boston's Huntington Avenue Grounds to watch the AL champion Pilgrims play the NL pennant-winning Pirates in the first World Series game. Deacon Phillippe outduels Cy Young and Pittsburgh's Jimmy Sebring hits the first Series homer as the Pirates win 7–3. The Pilgrims go on to win the Series.

1904: Both leagues increase their teams' regular-season schedules from 140 games to 154.

1904: Rules change: two coaches, one at first and one at third, are permitted on the field at a time. Third base coaches are prohibited from running toward home plate in an attempt to draw a throw from a fielder.

1904: Jack Chesbro of the Highlanders wins 41 games in 51 starts with 48 complete games, all modern-era records that still stand.

May 5, 1904: Cy Young of the Boston Red Sox pitches the first perfect game in AL history to beat the Athletics 3–0.

Giants Pass on Series

October 1904: Calling the American League "a minor organization"—ironic considering the AL's victory in the previous year's World Series—Giants owner John T. Brush and Manager John McGraw decline to have their NL champs play the

Boston's Huntington Avenue Grounds on the day of the first World Series game in 1903. The site is now occupied by Northeastern University's Geoffrey Lowell Cabot Physical Education Center.

Denton True (Cy) Young, whose name is now used to honor pitching greatness, won a major league record 511 games in his career.

AL pennant winners and defending Series champions, the Pilgrims, in a post-season series. McGraw later admits the decision was largely his, based on his dislike for AL President Ban Johnson.

1905: Two teams change nicknames. The Cleveland Blues become the Napoleans, or Naps, in honor of star player–manager Napolean Lajoie. The Washington Senators rename themselves the Nationals.

1905: Giants owner John T. Brush works tirelessly with the National Commission to establish official guidelines for the

World Series as a best-of-seven championship in which both leagues share gate receipts.

1905: As a result of a spike injury suffered by Cleveland's Nap Lajoie, all players begin wearing sanitary socks under their woolen outerwear. Roger Bresnahan experiments with a batting helmet in spring training but discards it as too cumbersome.

1905: Vic Willis of the Braves, who had lost 25 games the year before, suffers an all-time record 29 losses.

September 5, 1905: *Assisted by President Roosevelt's mediation, delegates from Russia and Japan sign a treaty in Portsmouth, New Hampshire, ending the Russo-Japanese War.*

October 9, 1905: After a one-year interruption, the tradition of the World Series resumes. The Giants, wearing controversial all-black uniforms, defeat the Athletics in 5 games—each one a shutout. New York's pitching ace Christy Mathewson throws a record 3 shutouts in 3 starts, and he allows only 14 hits in 27 innings.

1906: The Browns christen themselves the Ravens. The new name never really catches on, and by the end of the decade they are back to the Browns.

1906: Chicago wins a major league record 116 games on its way to the NL pennant. The Boston Braves lose a record 20 straight games.

November 9, 1906: *President Roosevelt leaves for Panama to observe the progress on the Panama Canal project. He is the first president to travel abroad.*

1907: George Dovey purchases Boston's NL club and mandates a change to all-white uniforms. The club becomes known as the Doves. Chicago's NL club, known as the Colts or Orphans, officially adopts the nickname Cubs.

1907: Rules change: in the American League, all appearances by a player in an official game count as a game played. Before the change, pinch hitters, pinch runners, and defensive substitutes were usually not credited with a game played. A runner will be called out for passing a teammate on the base paths.

April 1907: Roger Bresnahan of the Giants employs the first pair of catcher's shin guards. Their use is slow to spread among catchers, who are concerned about compromising the "manly" nature of their position.

October 1, 1907: *The public panics because of the continual downturn of the stock market and makes a run on banks, starting the depression of 1907–1908.*

Mills Commission: Baseball Is America's Game

December 30, 1907: The Mills Commission, assembled by sporting goods magnate and baseball patriarch Albert G. Spalding to determine the origin of baseball and chaired by former NL President Abraham G. Mills, reveals its findings: the game was invented by Abner Doubleday in 1839 at Cooperstown, New York.

1908: Rules change: pitchers are prohibited from soiling or scuffing a new ball. A batter is credited with a sacrifice fly and not charged with a time at bat if he hits a fly ball that is caught, but a runner tags up and scores after the catch.

1908: *Baseball* magazine publishes its first issue.

1908: Jack Norworth (lyrics) and Albert von Tilzer (music) write "Take Me Out to the Ball Game." Norworth, ironically, won't see his first major league game until more than thirty years later.

1908: Starting regularly on two days' rest and even making relief appearances between starts, White Sox spitballer Ed Walsh pitches a record 464 innings, still the most of the post-1900 era, and goes 40–15 with a 1.42 earned-run average. Christy Mathewson of the Giants wins an NL-record 37 games and leads the league in complete games with 34, innings pitched with 391, strikeouts with 259—walking just 42—shutouts with 11, and ERA with 1.43. He also saves 5 games.

April 20, 1908: Henry Chadwick, who published the first baseball guide book in 1860 and later ran *Spalding's Official Baseball Guide,* dies of pneumonia at age eighty-three. He had worked to promote baseball for more than forty years.

Below left: Roger Bresnahan, a baseball equipment pioneer and a versatile player who started his career as a pitcher, moved to the outfield, and later developed into one of the game's best all-around catchers, earned a spot in the Hall of Fame in 1945. Below right: First baseman Fred Merkle, on the other hand, wound up in the hall of shame after his infamous baserunning blunder cost the New York Giants a victory in a crucial game against the Chicago Cubs on September 23, 1908.

His opponents—and even many of his teammates—disliked Ty Cobb, but all respected the imense talent that brought him twelve batting titles, 4,191 hits, a .367 lifetime batting average, and 892 stolen bases.

June 9, 1908: In the fifth inning of their game against Boston, the Naps set a record when all nine batters get a hit and score a run.

"Merkle's Boner" Costs Giants
September 23, 1908: New York rookie Fred Merkle's infamous baserunning blunder—he fails to touch second base after Al Bridwell's apparent game-winning single—costs the Giants a victory in a crucial game against the Cubs. In the ensuing mayhem after Bridwell's hit, the game is called and declared a draw instead of a win for New York. When the teams meet on October 8 to replay the contest, Chicago wins and takes the pennant. Merkle's play will be known ever after as the classic baseball boner.

October 1908: The Baseball Writers Association of America is formed at the World Series.

October 1, 1908: *Henry Ford introduces the Model T.*

October 2, 1908: Addie Joss' perfect game for the Naps beats the White Sox by a score of 1–0.

1909: Rules change: a foul bunt with 2 strikes is a strikeout. A pitcher or catcher is charged with an error if a wild pitch or a passed ball on the third strike allows the batter to reach first base. A stolen base is not credited to any runner on an attempted double-steal if either runner is thrown out.

1909: Giants Manager John McGraw makes Arlie Latham Major League Baseball's first paid coach. Latham serves as third base coach and tutors the Giants in baserunning skills.

1909: St. Louis' Sportsman's Park, home of the Browns, is rebuilt and reoriented so that home plate is where first base used to be.

1909: The cork-center ball, also known as the "jack-rabbit" ball, is introduced for occasional play. Invented by Athletics owner and president Benjamin F. Shibe, the ball is used regularly beginning with the 1910 season.

Shibe Park Opens
April 12, 1909: Ushering in what *Sporting Life* calls "a new era in baseball," the Athletics play their first game in front of 30,162 fans in Shibe Park (later known as Connie Mack Stadium), baseball's first concrete-and-steel stadium. Named for Athletics owner Ben Shibe, the park is one of four larger stadiums constructed in 1909 (Pittsburgh got a new stadium and St. Louis' Sportsman's Park and Cleveland's League Park were renovated), as small, wooden ballparks become a thing of the past.

June 18, 1909: Cincinnati's Palace of the Fans is host to an experimental night baseball game (not involving major league clubs). The results were disappointing, and the idea was deemed unworkable for the major leagues.

June 30, 1909: Pittsburgh's Forbes Field opens. It will close its doors sixty-one years later as the only park never to have a no-hitter pitched within its walls.

Pulliam Commits Suicide
July 29, 1909: The baseball world is stunned by the news that NL President Harry Pulliam, suffering a nervous breakdown, has died at the age of forty from a self-inflicted gunshot wound in New York. Pulliam, whose six-and-a-half-year term was wrought with tension and frustration, is replaced on an interim basis by John Heydler and in December by Tom Lynch, a former umpire.

October 1909: Detroit's Ty Cobb wins the Triple Crown with a .377 average, 9 homers, and 107 RBI.

Man of the Decade: Ban Johnson

It's ironic that many NL owners initially shrugged off the threat of Ban Johnson and his upstart American League. In fact, Johnson, a Cincinnati sportswriter from 1887 to 1894, was in every way their equal—if not their superior—as a businessman, an administrator, and a baseball man. He quickly proved that when he took over as president of the revived Western League in 1894 and in just seven years guided the circuit from minor league status to its current position as baseball's second major league.

Most Memorable Games

1. September 23, 1908, at the Polo Grounds; New York Giants 1, Chicago Cubs 1. Nineteen-year-old Fred Merkle, in the Giants' lineup only because starting first baseman Fred Tenney is suffering a lumbago attack, commits the most famous blunder in baseball history. In the ninth inning of a key game between the Giants and Cubs, Merkle is on first and Moose McCormick is on third with 2 out. Al Bridwell singles to center, and Merkle, having seen the winning run score, heads for the clubhouse—without ever touching second base. Amid a melee of players and fans on the field, Cubs shortstop Johnny Evers grabs a ball—it may or may not be the *right* ball—and tags second, claiming that Merkle is out for not touching second and that the winning run doesn't count. Umpire Hank O'Day concurs, and with night falling and the crowd on the field, the game is called a 1–1 tie. New York's appeals are refused and after both clubs finish the season with 99 wins, the replay of the game becomes a virtual 1-game pennant playoff. Chicago wins it 4–2 and Merkle earns a spot in baseball's hall of shame.

2. October 2, 1908, at League Park; Cleveland Naps 1, Chicago White Sox 0. In the thick of the pennant race, Chicago's Ed Walsh and Cleveland's Addie Joss lock horns in one of the greatest pitching duels the game has ever seen. Walsh goes the distance and gives up just 1 unearned run on 4 hits, striking out 15. But Joss is perfect, retiring all 27 hitters he faces.

3. October 10, 1904, at Hilltop Park; Boston Pilgrims 3, New York Highlanders 2. In the first game of a

As a baseball player at Ohio's Marietta College, Ban Johnson distinguished himself as a tough catcher who—without a glove, mask, or chest protector— would stand on the receiving end of even the hardest-throwing pitchers; he later showed that same toughness as the AL's first president.

doubleheader on the season's final day, defending AL champion Boston wins the game and the pennant as Lou Criger scores the winning run in the ninth inning on a wild pitch by Highlander ace Jack Chesbro, who is 41–12 for the season.

4. 1903 World Series, Game One, October 1 at Huntington Avenue Grounds; Pittsburgh Pirates 7, Boston Pilgrims 3. A crowd of 16,242—large for the time—is on hand as Jimmy Sebring drives in 4 runs and Deacon Phillippe strikes out 10 and gives up just 6 hits and 2 earned runs to beat Cy Young in the first World Series game.

5. May 5, 1904, at Huntington Avenue Grounds; Boston Pilgrims 3, Philadelphia Athletics 0. Boston's Cy Young pitches the first perfect game in modern major league history and the only one of his twenty-four-year, Hall of Fame career.

Best Pennant Races

1. 1908 National League: Chicago Cubs–New York Giants–Pittsburgh Pirates. One of the wildest pennant races the game has ever seen goes down to the season's final day: a replay of the September 23 "Merkle's Boner" game that had been ruled a tie. The Cubs' Three Finger Brown comes on in relief to beat the Giants' Christy Mathewson in Chicago's come-from-behind 4–2 win, while Pittsburgh loses and, like New York, finishes 1 game off the pace.

2. 1904 American League: Boston Pilgrims–New York Highlanders. Five teams hang in the race for most of the season, but down the stretch only Boston and New York remain. With the Pilgrims ahead by a scant half-game, the two clubs square off in a 5-game series on the season's final weekend. New York wins the opener, but drops a doubleheader the next day. Needing to sweep a twin bill on the final day to claim the flag, the Highlanders lose the opener 3–2 as the winning run scores on a wild pitch by 41-game winner Jack Chesbro.

In his first eight years with the Cubs (1904–1911), Mordecai "Three Finger" Brown had a 181–76 record, 48 shutouts, 199 complete games, and a 1.72 ERA; he also led the league in saves from 1908 to 1911.

3. 1908 American League: Detroit Tigers–Cleveland Naps–Chicago White Sox. Only 2½ games separate the top four teams on September 1. St. Louis falls off the pace, but the other three clubs battle down to the final day, with Detroit beating Chicago to win by the narrowest margin in history: 1 half-game. The Tigers and Naps both win 90 games, but Detroit loses 1 fewer—63—and, under the rules of the day, does not have to make up the game it had rained out.

Best Teams

1. 1907 Chicago Cubs, 107–45; player-manager: Frank Chance. The Cubs had won a record 116 games the year before but were upset in the World Series by their South Side rivals, the White Sox. The 1907 Cubs did not lead the league outright in any major offensive category, were without a .300 hitter (there were only four in the league that year), and had no player who hit more than 2 home runs, but a strong pitching staff carried them to another pennant and a Series sweep of Detroit. Orvie Overall (23–8), Three Finger Brown (20–6), and Carl Lundgren (18–7) led a group of five starters with at least 15 victories; Ed Reulbach had the highest ERA of the five: 1.69.

2. 1905 New York Giants, 105–48; manager: John McGraw. The repeat NL champions sported an offense that led the league in runs scored, home runs, batting average, and stolen bases, and a pitching staff that led in strikeouts and saves. Mike Donlin (.356 batting average, league-leading 124 runs), Roger Bresnahan (.302), and Sam Mertes (108 RBI) led a balanced attack, and Christy Mathewson (32–8, 1.27 ERA, 206 strikeouts, all NL highs), Red Ames (22–8), and Joe McGinnity (22–16) were the mound aces for the Giants, who beat the Athletics in 5 games in the World Series.

3. 1902 Pittsburgh Pirates, 103–36; player-manager: Fred Clarke. Unlike its NL rivals, Pittsburgh managed to avoid having its roster ravaged by AL player raids. With an offense led by Ginger Beaumont (league-leading .357 batting average), Honus Wagner (.329), and Clarke (.321), and a pitching staff that featured three 20-game winners in Jack Chesbro (28–6), Jesse Tannehill (20–6), and Deacon Phillippe (20–9), the Pirates set a league record for victories and rolled to the pennant by a 27½-game margin. An NL championship was all they could claim, however—the World Series wasn't born until the following year.

Best World Series

1. 1909, Pittsburgh Pirates over Detroit Tigers, 4 games to 3. The focus of the Series is on the matchup between each club's hitting star, each of whom is playing in his final Series: Pittsburgh shortstop Honus Wagner, a fan favorite, and Boston center fielder Ty Cobb, the player fans love to hate. Wagner wins the battle with a .333 average and 6 stolen bases as compared with Cobb's .231 and 2 steals, but the Series hero is Pittsburgh's Babe Adams, who allows only 4 earned runs in 27 innings and wins all 3 of his starts, including a shutout in Game Seven.

WHAT'S IN/WHAT'S OUT IN THE 1900s

In

Competition between the NL and AL
Players jumping leagues
Strikeouts
Defensive hitting
Trick pitches
Larger, better fielding gloves
Conservative strategy
Two umpires
Liquor and beer sales at games
Ban Johnson vs. John McGraw
Unruly fans
Clean-shaven players
Treating umpires with respect
Billboards on the outfield walls
Action photos with newspaper coverage
Colorful nicknames like "Piano Legs," "Noodles," and "Brickyard"

Out

The NL's monopoly
Players held hostage by the reserve clause
High batting averages
Power-hitting
Consistent offense
Rampant errors
Aggressive play
One umpire with his hands full
Prohibition at the park
Albert Spalding vs. Monte Ward
Unruly players
Handlebar mustaches
Verbal—even physical—abuse of umpires
Bare fences
No photos
Given names

Mike Donlin is pictured in 1914, the last of his twelve major league seasons. "Turkey Mike" had his best year in 1905, when he hit .356 and scored 124 runs to help the New York Giants take the Series.

DECADE PITCHING LEADERS

	National League			American League		
YEAR	PLAYER	TEAM	ERA	PLAYER	TEAM	ERA
1900	Rube Waddell	Pittsburgh	2.37			
1901	Jesse Tannehill	Pittsburgh	2.18	Cy Young	Boston	1.62
1902	Jack Taylor	Chicago	1.33	Ed Siever	Detroit	1.91
1903	Sam Leever	Pittsburgh	2.06	Earl Moore	Cleveland	1.77
1904	Joe McGinnity	New York	1.61	Addie Joss	Cleveland	1.59
1905	Christy Mathewson	New York	1.27	Rube Waddell	Philadelphia	1.48
1906	Three Finger Brown	Chicago	1.04	Doc White	Chicago	1.52
1907	Jack Pfiester	Chicago	1.15	Ed Walsh	Chicago	1.60
1908	Christy Mathewson	New York	1.43	Addie Joss	Cleveland	1.16
1909	Christy Mathewson	New York	1.14	Harry Krause	Philadelphia	1.39

Cy Young wasn't an overpowering pitcher; his greatest assets were his control (he averaged just 1.5 walks per 9 innings during his twenty-two-year career, compared to 3.4 strikeouts per 9), his durability (he pitched 751 complete games in his career), and his endurance (he was still going strong in 1907, when, at age forty, he threw 343 innings and won 22 games; in fact, Young won 76 games after his fortieth birthday).

2. 1903, Boston Pilgrims over Pittsburgh Pirates, 5 games to 3. Pittsburgh wins 3 of the first 4 games in the first World Series—one of only four played under a best-of-nine format—but that's all the Bucs get. Cy Young and Bill Dinneen, who combine to pitch 69 of 71 Series innings for Boston, each win 2 games as the Pilgrims sweep the next 4 contests to give the upstart American Leaguers bragging rights over their more established NL counterparts.

3. 1906, Chicago White Sox over Chicago Cubs, 4 games to 2. Known as "the hitless wonders," the White Sox are the American League's worst-hitting team, with a .230 average. They enter the Series as overwhelming underdogs to the powerful Cubs, but hold their West Side rivals to a .196 average in the Series to pull off the upset. Ed Walsh wins 2 games, and the White Sox even display a little offense, banging out 26 hits in their wins in Games Five and Six.

Worth Remembering

The Deal of a Lifetime. After the 1900 season, the Cincinnati Reds traded a twenty-year-old rookie pitcher named Christy Mathewson, who had an 0–3 record in the major leagues, to the Giants for twenty-nine-year-old Amos Rusie, nicknamed "The Hoosier Thunderbolt," a future Hall of Famer who had won 243 games. Rusie never won another game in his career, while Mathewson went on to win 373 games; his last win, ironically, came with the Reds, who reacquired him as a player-manager in July

M. BROWN. J. PFEISTER A. HOFMAN C.G. WILLIAMS O. OVERALL. E. REULBACH. J. KLING.
H. GESSLER. J. TAYLOR. H. STEINFELDT. J. McCORMICK. F. CHANCE. J. SHECKARD. P. MORAN. F. SCHULTE
C. LUNDGREN. T. WALSH. J. EVERS. J. SLAGLE. J. TINKER.

1916, his final season as a player. The Reds got revenge, though—when they reacquired Mathewson they also got outfielder Edd Roush, a future Hall of Famer who hit .320 or better for the next ten years.

Shooting for the Bull. Because every club was looking for ways to generate extra revenue, billboards on the outfield wall, advertising everything from cigarettes and shoes to political candidates, were a common sight in ballparks of the early 1900s. Players were often offered cash or merchandise prizes if they could drive a ball into or over a particular billboard. The most popular such promotion, which popped up in most parks by the end of the decade, was Bull Durham Tobacco's trademark bull sign. Any player who could hit the "bullboard" on the fly received fifty dollars, tobacco samples, and a spot in a national Bull Durham ad. It wasn't easy money, though: the bulls were always in the outer reaches of the park; for example, the sign in New York's Hilltop Park was in deep center field.

Putting Something on It. Elmer Stricklett, Major League Baseball's first spitball pitcher, reportedly picked up the

Above: The 1906 Chicago Cubs won a record 116 games but were up-set in the World Series by their downtown rivals, the White Sox. The Cubs' roster featured four Hall of Famers: Three Finger Brown, Frank Chance, Johnny Evers, and Joe Tinker. Right: Among Christy Mathewson's many accomplishments are his three consecutive 30-vic-tory seasons (1903–1905), his 3 shutouts of the Philadelphia Athletics in the 1905 World Series, and his National League record 37 wins in 1908.

DECADE BATTING LEADERS

		National League			American League		
YEAR	PLAYER	TEAM	AVG.	PLAYER	TEAM	AVG.
1900	Honus Wagner	Pittsburgh	.381			
1901	Jesse Burkett	St. Louis	.382	Nap Lajoie	Philadelphia	.422
1902	Ginger Beaumont	Pittsburgh	.357	Ed Delahanty	Washington	.376
1903	Honus Wagner	Pittsburgh	.355	Nap Lajoie	Cleveland	.355
1904	Honus Wagner	Pittsburgh	.349	Nap Lajoie	Cleveland	.381
1905	Cy Seymour	Cincinnati	.377	Elmer Flick	Cleveland	.306
1906	Honus Wagner	Pittsburgh	.339	George Stone	St. Louis	.358
1907	Honus Wagner	Pittsburgh	.350	Ty Cobb	Detroit	.350
1908	Honus Wagner	Pittsburgh	.354	Ty Cobb	Detroit	.324
1909	Honus Wagner	Pittsburgh	.339	Ty Cobb	Detroit	.377

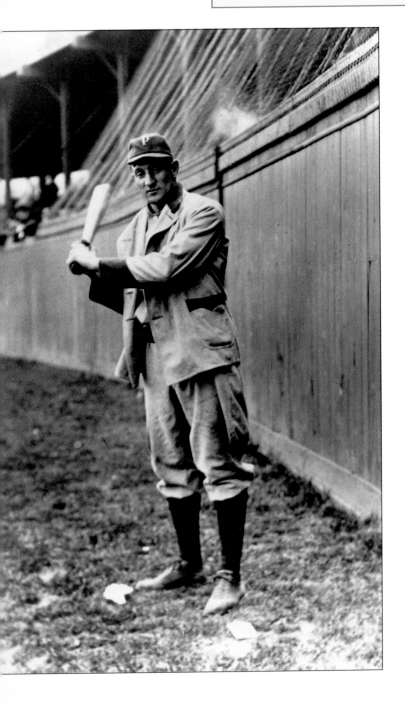

Below: *Nicknamed the Flying Dutchman, Hall of Famer Honus Wagner hit .300 or better seventeen straight years (1897–1913), set a National League record with 252 triples, and led the league in stolen bases five times.*

pitch in the Pacific Coast League from George Hildebrand, who went on to become an umpire in the American League. Hildebrand, legend has it, came upon the idea while playing catch in the rain; he later found he could get the same effect by using his saliva without having to wait for a cloudburst. The spitter would help a lot of pitchers win a lot of games, but Stricklett wasn't one of them; he lasted only four years in the majors and had a 35–51 record.

A Court Jester of All Trades. Germany Schaefer, whose real first name was Herman, was the leader in a decade that had its share of cutups. Schaefer, who played all four infield positions and the outfield, and even pitched in 2 games in his fifteen-year career, was popular for his pregame juggling act and his antics as a base coach. His trademark stunt, however, was "stealing" first base when he was the runner on second with a man on third. The idea was that the opposition would be so thoroughly confused watching Schaefer running in reverse that the runner on third would be able to score.

Arrogance in Uniform. The Giants, who already had put their noses in the air when they refused to play the "minor league" AL champs from Boston in the World Series after they won the 1904 NL pennant, and then wore controversial black uniforms during their 5-game Series victory over Philadelphia the next year, did themselves one better at the start of the 1906 season. Manager John McGraw ordered up new home and away uniforms for his charges, with the words "World's Champions" emblazoned across the front. The Giants couldn't live up to their boast, though: they finished 20 games behind the Cubs that year.

Decade Spotlight

Dummy Taylor: His Nickname Was a Misnomer

Luther Haden Taylor may have been deaf, but he certainly wasn't dumb. Taylor, the first deaf-mute pitcher to play in the major leagues, graduated with honors from the Kansas School for the Deaf at Olathe. "Dummy" Taylor, as he was known, was smart, quick-witted, and loved a good practical joke. He was also a pretty fair pitcher; the master of the "drop ball," he fashioned a 115–106 record and a 2.75 ERA in nine big-league seasons and helped the Giants win two NL pennants.

As a teenager, the strong-armed Taylor wanted to be a boxer, but turned to baseball instead when his parents objected to a career in the ring. Taylor pitched five years of semipro and minor league ball before he made it to the majors with the Giants in July of 1900. At the time, there was already a noteworthy deaf player in the majors: William E. Hoy, also nicknamed "Dummy," an outfielder with the Chicago White Stockings. Hoy went over to the NL's Cincinnati Reds two years later, and on May 16, 1902, the two played in a game against each other—the first and only time two deaf baseball players have opposed each other in the majors. Hoy got 2 hits off Taylor, but Taylor pitched 8 strong innings and won the game by a score of 5–3.

There were better pitchers than Taylor, but few better bench jockeys. Opposing players dreaded the sight of Taylor perched in the other dugout or, worse yet, heading for the coach's box. Unable to speak except for two-syllable sounds, Taylor nonetheless kept up a steady stream of noise that drove the opposition crazy.

Taylor also enjoyed riding opposing players and umpires with sign language. That way he could "say" anything he wanted without fear of retribution—or so he thought. One afternoon he signed a stream of insults at umpire Hank O'Day, and was shocked to see O'Day sign back: "You go to the clubhouse. Pay twenty-five dollars." It turned out O'Day had a deaf relative who had taught him sign language.

Taylor's good sense of humor made him a target of practical jokes. His teammates pulled one favorite prank whenever a deaf friend visited Taylor on the road. While Taylor and his friend sat in Taylor's hotel room conversing in sign language, a teammate would sneak into the room (Taylor always left his door open so visitors could come in without knocking) and shut off the lights. In the darkened room, the conversation was over.

Giants players also got a laugh by paging Taylor in the hotel lobby, then pointing him out to the confused bellboy. But Taylor got his revenge: on the team train he would dump one handful of salt and one of ice in the berth of the perpetrators of a recent prank.

Popular legend has it that a deaf player—most such stories name Hoy—was responsible for umpires using hand signals to convey their calls. But an article in the 1909 edition of *Spalding's Official Baseball Guide*, the preeminent source of the day, says that hand signals were first proposed in 1906 or 1907 and adopted soon thereafter for the benefit of spectators who were out of earshot. "If an umpire did not use hand signals," the article reasoned, "two-thirds of the spectators…would be wholly at sea as to what was transpiring on the field, except as they might guess successfully." No mention is made of signs being of any benefit to a deaf player, although they obviously would have been.

Following his retirement from the major leagues after the 1908 season, Taylor took a coaching job at the Kansas School for the Deaf, where the Luther Taylor Gym was named in his honor. He later worked as a house father at the Illinois School for the Deaf. He died in 1958 at the age of eighty-two.

Luther Taylor didn't let his handicap hold him back; he won 115 games in nine major league seasons, including 21 in 1904.

The 1910s
Coming of Age—the Hard Way

For the world of baseball, the second decade of the twentieth century started with promise. It ended with the game on the brink of disaster. And what transpired in the intervening years was anything but tranquil.

By 1910, baseball, like the United States, was coming of age. Two major leagues were firmly entrenched and spacious, new, concrete-and-steel parks were rapidly replacing the small,

Charley Hall went 15–8 in 1912, including a league-high 6 relief wins, to help the Red Sox to the first of what would be four world championships in the decade.

wooden structures that had a temporary feel. By 1916 every major league club would be in a concrete-and-steel stadium that had been built in the last ten years. The growth curve looked promising—but it soon began to level out. Overall attendance, which had reached a record level of more than seven million in 1909 and had still remained at better than six million for the next four years, fell dramatically in 1914 to less than 4.5 million. One major cause was competition from a third major league, the Federal League, which made its debut in 1914. James A. Gilmore, a Chicago iron manufacturer and the Federal League president, had convinced his investors that there was great money to be made in baseball. He was right—but he and his backers were trying to grab a slice of what was at this time a shrinking pie. Baseball did experience a boom in popularity, but not in this decade.

The specter of the Federal League brought the same reaction from major league owners that Ban Johnson and the American League had thirteen years earlier and the

Players League a decade before that: they braced for battle, coerced their players to stay put with threats of blacklisting and promises of more money or both, and turned to the courts for help. There they had an ally in Judge Kenesaw Mountain Landis, who later became the game's first commissioner. It was Landis who delayed making a ruling on the Federal League's antitrust suit against Major League Baseball and helped urge the two sides toward a settlement. With World War I looming and the Federal League's losses mounting after just two seasons, the settlement finally came, but the battle with the Federal League cost the NL and AL an estimated five million dollars.

There were more problems to come. The U.S. war effort was in full swing by the spring of 1917, but baseball owners still hoped they could keep their players out of mandatory military service. They were wrong. By the following spring, Provost Marshall Gen. Enoch H. Crowder issued a "work or fight" order, forcing all draft-eligible men into either the military or "an essential industry." Secretary of War Newton D. Baker specifically rejected baseball's claim that it was "essential." As a result, Major League Baseball lost more than 220 players, including Jack Barry and Duffy Lewis of the Boston Red Sox; Red Faber, Swede Risberg, Joe Jackson, Happy Felsch, and Lefty Williams of the Chicago White Sox; Grover "Pete" Alexander of the Chicago Cubs; and Benny Kauff, Rube Benton, Jeff

Tesreau, and Walter Holke of the New York Giants. The 1918 season was shortened to fewer than 130 games.

Still, there was much to marvel at when the players performed between the foul lines; a number of individual feats transcended the game's gray landscape.

After losing the 1910 batting title to Cleveland's Nap Lajoie on the season's final day, Detroit's Ty Cobb had the best season of his twenty-four-year career in 1911. He led the American League in every offensive department except home runs (he was tied for second with Boston's Tris Speaker, behind Philadelphia's Home Run Baker). A year later, Chicago Cubs third baseman Heinie Zimmerman won the National League's Triple Crown with a .372 average, 103 runs batted in, and 14 home runs. He never again challenged for a batting title. Teammate Larry Cheney, a rookie pitcher, won 26 games to tie New York's Rube Marquard for the league lead, but never approached that mark again. Pittsburgh's Owen Wilson hit 36 triples, setting a new record.

In Boston, a powerful young pitcher emerged. His name was George Herman Ruth, but they called the 6-foot-2 (187.9cm), 215-pounder (97.6kg) "Babe." He played for the Red Sox in only 5 games in 1914 at the age of nineteen, but in 1915 he appeared in 32 games and was 18–8. The left-hander was also something of a hitter. In a modest 92 at bats he managed to hit 4 home runs; league-leader Braggo Roth needed 384 at bats to clout 7. Ruth

Major League Teams in the 1910s

NATIONAL LEAGUE
Boston Braves
Brooklyn Dodgers
Chicago Cubs
Cincinnati Reds
New York Giants
Philadelphia Phillies
Pittsburgh Pirates
St. Louis Cardinals

AMERICAN LEAGUE
Boston Red Sox
Chicago White Sox
Cleveland Naps/Indians
Detroit Tigers
New York Highlanders/Yankees
Philadelphia Athletics
St. Louis Browns
Washington Senators

FEDERAL LEAGUE (1914–1915)
Baltimore Terrapins
Brooklyn Tip-Tops/Brookfeds
Buffalo Buffeds
Chicago Whales/Chifeds
Indianapolis Hoosiers/Federals (became Newark Peps in 1915)
Kansas City Packers
Pittsburgh Rebels
St. Louis Terriers

Joe Agler was one of the many players who got a shot in the "major leagues," thanks to the birth of the Federal League in 1914. Agler, a first baseman/outfielder with Buffalo and Baltimore, was not one of the lucky Federal League players who later jumped to the established major leagues, however; his big-league career ended when the FL folded after the 1915 season.

made only a single appearance in the 1915 World Series against Philadelphia—as a pinch hitter—but in 1916, he crafted an American League–leading earned-run average of 1.75 and pitched 9 shutouts. In the 1916 and 1918 World Series, Ruth won 3 games and pitched 29⅔ consecutive scoreless innings. It was in 1918 that Ruth first played more games in the field (59) than as a pitcher (20). For their vision, the Red Sox were rewarded with a league-leading 11 home runs. That transformation, from pitcher to hitter, would drastically alter the way the game was played—and received by a sporting nation.

Baseball got through the FL crisis and World War I with a unified front, but dissension in and around the National Commission grew in the 1910s. Team owners had clashes with league presidents on several occasions—most notably over which teams should have the rights to players Scott Perry and Carl Mays—but the root of the problem was the unhappiness of the players themselves. With the threat of the Federal League as a backdrop, the Players Fraternity won a few concessions from ownership, such as the right for ten-year major league veterans to negotiate with the club of their choice, but once the competition of another, high-paying league was removed, the players found they had little bargaining power. The plight of the Philadelphia Athletics' "$100,000 infield" was typical of the players' sense of helplessness. They were the best in the baseball business, but in 1914 second baseman Eddie Collins was sold to Chicago to prevent him from jumping to the Federal League. The following year shortstop Jack Barry was dealt to Boston, and three seasons later first baseman Stuffy McInnis joined Barry in a Red Sox uniform. Philadelphia's Home Run Baker wanted to renegotiate his three-year contract, but

was refused by Manager Connie Mack. The third baseman sat out the entire 1915 season and returned a year later—as a New York Yankee. Similarly, Boston slugger Tris Speaker was shipped to Cleveland in 1916 after the Red Sox asked him to take a 25 percent cut even though he had hit .322 (tied for third in the American League) in 1915.

Many players grew resentful of the tight-fisted owners, which served to create a climate for the unthinkable: a group of players throwing the World Series for money. When that prospect became reality, baseball had a far greater problem on its hands than any it had faced before.

Above: *Babe Ruth was the greatest two-way threat the game has ever known. His hitting accomplishments are well-documented, but he also compiled a 65–33 record and 16 shutouts in his three seasons as a regular pitcher for the Red Sox (1915–1917).* **Left:** *Before Ruth emerged as baseball's premier power hitter, that honor belonged to Frank "Home Run" Baker of the Athletics, who led the AL in homers four straight years (1911–1914).*

1910: New NL President Tom Lynch announces that photographers will be banned from the playing field during games. Newspapers vehemently protest.

President Taft Makes It "Official"

April 14, 1910: Before the Washington Senators play the Athletics on Opening Day, William H. Taft becomes the first U.S. president to throw out the first ball, marking baseball as the "official" national pastime. Washington's Walter Johnson throws a 1-hitter and wins 1–0.

July 1, 1910: Chicago's Comiskey Park opens.

Drive for the Batting Title

October 9, 1910: How much is Detroit's Ty Cobb disliked by his fellow players? Heading into the season's final day, Cobb has seemingly clinched the AL batting title—and the automobile that the Chalmers Motor Company has put up for the winner. But in a doubleheader on the last day Cleveland's Nap Lajoie is credited with 8 hits in 8 at bats—7 of them on bunt singles while St. Louis Browns rookie third baseman Red Corriden plays 10 feet (3m) behind the bag—and finishes a point ahead of Cobb. In the ensuing controversy AL President Ban Johnson adds a couple of hits to Cobb's total and declares him the champion, .385 to .384. Chalmers awards a car to both players.

March 1911: While the Senators are at spring training, Washington's National Park, which would become Griffith Stadium in 1920, is severely damaged by fire. However, the park is rebuilt in eighteen days and the Senators open the season on schedule.

March 7, 1911: *The United States orders twenty thousand troops to the Mexican border to protect its interests during a rebellion against Mexican dictator Porfirio Diaz, who has ruled since 1876.*

April 14, 1911: The Polo Grounds, home of the Giants, is severely damaged by a fire. The Giants play their home games in the New York Highlanders' Hilltop Park until September, when reconstruction at the Polo Grounds is complete.

The single-season stolen base record of 96, set by Detroit's Ty Cobb (above right) *in 1915, stood for forty-seven years, until Maury Wills of the Los Angeles Dodgers broke it with 104 in 1962.*

Cy Young broke the 20-victory mark sixteen times—but he only pitched in one World Series in his career (in 1903, when he won 2 games to help the Pilgrims beat the Pirates).

April 14, 1911: Popular Cleveland Indians pitcher Addie Joss dies of tubercular meningitis at the age of thirty-one. Later in the season the Indians organize what is essentially the first All-Star Game—a benefit contest pitting a team of AL all-stars against the Indians. The AL stars win 7–2, and approximately thirteen thousand dollars is raised for Joss's widow.

October 1911: Ty Cobb wins the fifth of his twelve career batting titles with a .420 average—the second-best average in history to that point—and leads the American League with 147 runs, 141 runs batted in, 47 doubles, 24 triples, and 83 stolen bases; all but the last figure is a career high. In his first full season, Cleveland's Joe Jackson sets a rookie batting record with a .408 average; it is his career high but not good enough for a batting title, thanks to Cobb. Jackson, in fact, will never win a batting title in his career, even though he finishes with the third-highest career average in history (.356).

1912: Cy Young retires with a career record of 511–313 in twenty-two seasons.

1912: Rules change: a pitcher is charged with an earned run each time a runner

Boston's Fenway Park (above) and Detroit's Tiger Stadium, both of which opened in 1912 when concrete-and-steel ballparks were replacing wooden structures, are the oldest baseball stadiums in the major leagues and two of the last remaining links to the early twentieth-century roots of the game.

scores by the aid of a hit, sacrifice, walk, hit batter, wild pitch, or balk before enough fielding chances have been offered to retire the side. Earned-run average becomes an official NL statistic; the American League adopts it the following year. In the National League, all appearances by a player in an official game count as a game played (prior to this, pinch hitters, pinch runners, and defensive replacements were often not credited with a game played).

1912: Pittsburgh's Owen Wilson hits a record 36 triples; his total of 14 triples the following year is the next-highest of his nine-year career. Smoky Joe Wood, the Red Sox's twenty-two-year-old right-hander, goes 34–5 with a 1.91 earned-run average and 10 shutouts, and wins 3 more games in the World Series; he never again tops the 15-victory mark.

April 11, 1912: Cincinnati's reconstructed Redland Field (later renamed Crosley Field), damaged by fire in 1911, reopens.

April 15, 1912: *The steamship* Titanic *strikes an iceberg in the Atlantic Ocean and approximately fifteen hundred lives are lost at sea because there are not enough lifeboats for all passengers.*

April 20, 1912: After two days of rain-induced postponements, the Red Sox play their inaugural game in Fenway Park. On the same day, the Tigers play their first game in reconstructed Bennett Park. The following year concrete stands are constructed and the park is dedicated as Navin Field in honor of team president Frank Navin. It is renamed Tiger Stadium in 1961.

Cobb Suspension Sparks Insurrection
May 15, 1912: Hot-tempered Ty Cobb charges into the stands during a game in New York and beats up a physically disabled heckler. AL President Ban Johnson suspends Cobb indefinitely, and his teammates rally to support the sometimes unpopular player, vowing that they will not take the field until the suspension is lifted. Neither side will budge, forcing Detroit Tigers Manager Hughie Jennings to field a team of sandlot players, collegians, and over-the-hill coaches for Detroit's May 18 game; the Athletics win 23–2. Philadelphia Manager Connie Mack agrees to postpone the next game, scheduled for May 20, and the Tigers return for the next game. The Georgia Peach is reinstated five days later, but his return hardly sparks the Tigers to a stellar season; they stumble to a sixth-place finish.

July 8, 1912: The Cubs beat the Giants with a score of 7–2 at the Polo Grounds, snapping Rube Marquard's record 19-game winning streak.

A New Players Union Is Formed
October 1912: In the closing days of the season a new players union, called the Players Fraternity, is organized by attorney David Fultz, a former Major League Baseball player. Although the threat of the Federal League will soon put the owners in a conciliatory mood, the union on the whole faces an uphill battle and wins few concessions from management.

1913: The face of New York baseball changes as the Brooklyn Dodgers move from Washington Park into newly built Ebbets Field, and the New York Yankees, formerly the Highlanders, move from Hilltop Park to share the Polo Grounds with the Giants.

1913: Former Pennsylvania governor John K. Tener becomes the eighth president of the National League.

1913: Washington's Walter Johnson posts the best season of his career. "The Big Train" rolls over the opposition with AL bests in wins (36, against just 7 losses), complete games (30), innings pitched (346), strikeouts (243), and ERA (1.14).

February 25, 1913: *The Sixteenth Amendment to the Constitution, which authorizes an income tax, is adopted. It was proposed by Congress in 1909.*

New Competition from the Federal League

1914: James A. Gilmore, president of the minor Federal League (formerly the United States League), declares his circuit a major league and throws down the gauntlet in front of the two established leagues. The FL sets up direct-competition franchises in four cities: Chicago (Chifeds, or Whales), Brooklyn (Tip-Tops, or Brookfeds), Pittsburgh (Rebels), and St. Louis (Terriers), as well as well-funded clubs in Indianapolis (Federals, or Hoosiers), Baltimore (Terrapins), Kansas City (Packers), and Buffalo (Buffeds). The NL is hit hardest as the FL's higher salaries lure numerous stars, including Joe Tinker, Three Finger Brown, Hal Chase, and Tom Seaton. The following year Chief Bender, Eddie Plank, and Ed Konetchy are among the stars to move to the FL, while Ty Cobb refuses the FL's offer and remains with the Detroit Tigers.

1914: William "Spittin' Bill" Doak, a pitcher with the St. Louis Cardinals, designs a new baseball glove that features a webbed pocket. The Doak model soon becomes the top-selling baseball glove.

1914: Dutch Leonard of the Red Sox wins a career-high 19 games and posts a 1.01 ERA for the season, still the lowest in major league history.

April 1914: Chicago's Weeghman Park, home of the Federal League's Whales, opens. The park is named for team owner Charles H. Weeghman, who, after the FL folds, purchases the NL's Cubs from the Taft Family of Cincinnati and moves them into the park in 1916. The park will later be renamed Wrigley Field in honor of William Wrigley, Jr., who becomes the majority stockholder in 1921.

June 28, 1914: *Archduke Francis Ferdinand, the crown prince of Austria, is assassinated by a Bosnian Serb in Sarajevo. Five days later Austria-Hungary declares war on Serbia, and World War I begins. In August, Germany will declare*

Rube Marquard won a major league record 19 straight games from April to July of 1912, slipped to 7–11 thereafter, but then rebounded with 2 wins against Boston in the Series.

Joe Tinker put in 11 solid seasons with the Cubs and was traded to Cincinnati for the 1913 season, but then jumped to the Federal League's Chicago Whales for a $2,000 salary increase.

war on Russia and France, and Great Britain will declare war on Germany. Austria-Hungary declares war on Russia, and Japan declares war on Germany.

July 1914: The Red Sox purchase from Providence of the International League the contract of a nineteen-year-old lefty named Babe Ruth. His first big-league contract pays him one hundred dollars a month. He appears in 5 games for the Red Sox, 4 as a pitcher, and posts a 2–1 record.

Braves Complete Miracle

October 13, 1914: The miracle Boston Braves, who came from 15 games back in July to win the NL pennant by 10½ games, cap their championship season with a 4-game sweep of the Athletics in the World Series. Dick Rudolph, who wins the clincher and Bill James are the pitching stars—each wins 2 games and they allow just 1 earned run between them in 29 innings—and catcher Hank Gowdy, with a .545 average and 5 extra-base hits in 11 at bats, is the offensive standout.

May 7, 1915: *The Lusitania is sunk without warning, claiming the lives of 1,198 of its 1,924 passengers.*

August 18, 1915: Boston's Braves Field opens.

September 9, 1915: Albert Spalding dies at age sixty-five in Point Loma, California.

A Costly Peace: The End of the Federal League

December 21, 1915: With the bottom line looking worse and worse, the Federal League is forced to sign a peace treaty with the National League and American League. Player salaries and legal fees are spiraling, and the FL had moved its defending champion Indianapolis franchise to Newark, New Jersey, for the 1915 season, but the club did not draw well in the nation's number one market. Under the terms of the peace settlement, the FL will disband immediately; all players, with the exception of those on the Chicago and St. Louis rosters, are to be sold to the highest bidder; and FL owners must assume responsibility for all existing contracts. In addition, two FL owners—Chicago's Charles Weeghman and St. Louis' Phil Ball—are permitted to purchase one of the major league teams in their respective cities; Weeghman buys the Cubs and Ball the St. Louis Browns. The settlement itself cost the NL and AL an estimated $300,000. One key footnote results from an antitrust suit filed by the Baltimore Terrapins owners, who feel they have been unfairly shoved out of the major league picture. This leads to Justice Oliver Wendell Holmes' 1922 ruling that baseball is exempt from antitrust laws.

1916: Pete Alexander of the Philadelphia Phillies throws a record 16 shutouts. He had 12 the previous year. He leads the

Tris Speaker made the Boston Red Sox regret trading him in 1916; in his first season with the Cleveland Indians he hit .386 with 211 hits and 41 doubles, all American League highs.

league with a 33–12 record, 38 complete games, 167 strikeouts, and a 1.55 ERA.

February 15, 1916: Four-time AL home run champ Frank "Home Run" Baker, the hero of the 1911 World Series who sat out the entire 1915 season when the Athletics refused to renegotiate his three-year contract, is sold to the Yankees for $37,500.

April 1916: Fans at Chicago's Weeghman Park are allowed to keep baseballs hit into the stands. Around the majors, other teams will soon adopt this policy, which is popular with the fans.

April 12, 1916: The Red Sox trade their star center fielder, Tris Speaker, to the Cleveland Indians for pitcher Sad Sam Jones, third baseman Fred Thomas, and $55,000.

September 7–30, 1916: In the same season in which the Athletics tie a ten-year-old record by losing 20 straight games, the Giants set a modern-day record by winning 26 in a row. The streak ends in the second game of a September 30 doubleheader.

October 1916: For the first time in ten years, Ty Cobb fails to win the AL batting title. Cleveland's Tris Speaker, acquired from the Red Sox just before the season opens, wins it with a .386 average; Cobb, who will win the next three batting crowns, hits .371.

1917: Rules change: earned runs now include runs scored with the aid of stolen bases.

January 31, 1917: *Germany announces that it will resume unrestricted submarine warfare on any ships, armed or unarmed, that sail into German war zones. As a result, on February 3, Wilson breaks off diplomatic relations with Germany.*

February–April 1917: The Giants and Tigers eschew the Florida tradition and conduct spring training in Texas.

April 2, 1917: *Wilson asks Congress to declare war on Germany. Congress votes overwhelmingly for war, which is declared on April 6.*

June 23, 1917: Reliever Ernie Shore of the Red Sox throws a perfect game to beat Washington 4–0.

December 7, 1917: *The United States declares war on Austria-Hungary.*

The War Effort Takes Its Toll on Baseball

June 1918: With the U.S. war effort growing, Provost Marshall Gen. Enoch H. Crowder issues a "work or fight" order to force all draft-eligible men into either military service or an essential industry. Baseball is ruled "nonessential," and the season is shortened to September 2—no team plays even 130 games—although Secretary of War Newton D. Baker permits the World Series to be played starting September 5. Many players are drafted or enlisted into the armed forces; many others go to work in war-related industries.

NL President Tener Resigns

June 1918: A dispute between the Athletics and Braves over the rights to pitcher Scott Perry heightens dissension on the National Commission and leads to the resignation of NL President John K. Tener. John A. Heydler, who had held the office in 1909, assumes the presidency and is officially elected to the post following the season.

August 28, 1918: Cleveland's Tris Speaker assaults umpire Tom Connelly. Speaker is suspended for the balance of the season; the Indians finish 2½ games behind first-place Boston.

September 9, 1918: Red Sox left-hander Babe Ruth, who would stun the baseball world with 29 homers in 1919, extends his streak of consecutive scoreless innings in World Series play to 29⅔, a record that will stand for forty-three years.

October 9, 1918: *The kaiser abdicates and Germany's new parliamentary government makes peace overtures to the United States based on Wilson's Fourteen Points.*

November 11, 1918: *Germany signs the armistice treaty and hostilities cease.*

1919: Uncertain of baseball's popularity in the wake of World War I, the National Commission limits the season to 140 games. But postwar attendance rises to impressive levels and the majors go back to a 154-game schedule for the 1920 season. The commission also votes to extend the World Series to a best-of-nine format, which is maintained through 1921.

1919: New York legalizes Sunday baseball.

January 1919: The National Association of Professional Baseball Leagues, the minor leagues' umbrella organization, secedes from the National Agreement, refusing to allow major league teams to draft its players.

January 29, 1919: *The Eighteenth Amendment to the Constitution is ratified when Nebraska agrees to the Prohibition measure. The Volstead Act will be passed on October 28 to prohibit the sale of alcoholic beverages.*

July 13, 1919: After finishing the second inning of a game in Chicago, Red Sox pitcher Carl Mays storms off the mound, heads for the clubhouse, dresses, and takes the next train back to Boston. The volatile Mays offers no reason for his departure, but the rumor is that he is trying to provoke a trade to the Yankees, who will pay him more than the tight-fisted Red Sox. Although AL President Ban Johnson rules that Mays cannot be traded until he has been restored to the Red Sox in good standing, Boston owner Harry Frazee deals Mays to the Yankees for pitchers Allan Russell and Bob McGraw and forty thousand dollars. Irate, Johnson cancels the deal and suspends Mays, but the Yankees gain a New York court injunction and the court ultimately rules against Johnson.

Reds Upset White Sox in Series

October 9, 1919: Something seems fishy about Cincinnati's 5-games-to-3 upset of heavily favored Chicago in the World Series. There are rumors of a fix—the White Sox hit just .224, scored just 20 runs in 8 games, and committed 12 errors—but most observers figure that Chicago was merely worn down a bit from a tough pennant race with Cleveland, while the Reds had clinched early. Not until next September will the truth emerge: eight White Sox players had indeed conspired with gamblers to throw the Series.

The powerful 1919 White Sox should have won the World Series handily, most experts thought.

Man of the Decade: Frank "Home Run" Baker

Ty Cobb might be a more fitting choice, not only because he had great numbers but also because he displayed greed and a penchant for controversy in a decade that was marked by both. But Baker was baseball's original Mr. October, a player who came through in the spotlight: He hit .378 with 7 doubles, 3 home runs, and 18 RBI in four World Series with the Athletics, three of which Philadelphia won. He also led the league in homers four times and was baseball's premier power source until Babe Ruth came along and started tearing the cover off the ball.

Most Memorable Games

1. May 2, 1917, at Weeghman Park; Cincinnati Reds 1, Cubs 0. Chicago's Jim "Hippo" Vaughn and Cincinnati's Fred Toney each pitch no-hit ball for 9 innings—the only double no-hitter in baseball history. Only Toney will finish without allowing a hit, though. The Reds break through in the tenth when shortstop Larry Kopf, a career .249 hitter, lines a single to right for the game's first hit. After center fielder Cy Williams drops Hal Chase's fly ball, football great and 1912 Olympic decathlon gold medalist Jim Thorpe drives in the game's only run.

2. 1912 World Series, Game Eight, October 16 at Fenway Park; Boston Red Sox 3, New York Giants 2. Because Game Two had ended in a 6–6 tie and each team had recorded three victories, the Series goes to a decisive eighth game. The Giants break a 1–1 tie with a run in the top of the tenth, and Christy Mathewson is poised to close out Boston in the bottom of the frame. But thanks to a dropped fly ball by Fred Snodgrass, an RBI single by Tris Speaker, and Larry Gardner's sacrifice fly, the Red Sox rally to win. Snodgrass' blunder is dubbed the "$30,000 muff," because that was the difference between the winning and losing clubs' shares.

3. 1917 World Series, Game Six, October 15 at the Polo Grounds; Chicago White Sox 4, New York Giants 2. In a game in which the White Sox score all their runs on New York errors, the winning run appropriately scores when Giants third baseman Heinie Zimmerman chases Chicago's Eddie Collins across the plate in a botched rundown play.

4. 1911 World Series, Game Three, October 17 at the Polo Grounds; Athletics 3, Giants 2. Philadelphia trails Christy Mathewson and the Giants 1–0 in the ninth, but Frank "Home Run" Baker's solo shot ties the game. The Athletics score twice in the eleventh, and Harry Davis' RBI

Although his numbers were hardly Ruthian (in four league-leading seasons he hit a total of 42 homers, a number the Babe would later surpass in a single year), Frank "Home Run" Baker led the Philadelphia Athletics to four American League pennants and three world championships.

single proves decisive as New York answers with a run in the bottom of the eleventh off Jack Coombs, who goes the distance for the win.

5. 1918 World Series, Game Four, September 9 at Fenway Park; Boston Red Sox 3, Chicago Cubs 2. Chicago ties the game 2–2 in the eighth and ends Babe Ruth's record string of 29⅔ scoreless Series innings, but Boston's Wally Schang scores the go-ahead run in the bottom of the inning on Bill Killefer's passed ball and a wild pitch by Phil Douglas.

Best Pennant Races

1. 1914 National League: Boston Braves–New York Giants. Trailing by 15 games on July 4 and still mired in last place on the morning of July 19, Boston catches fire. The miracle Braves cap a 34–10 run by taking over sole possession of first place on September 8. They win the pennant by 10½ games, denying New York its fourth straight NL championship and pulling off the greatest comeback in major league history.

2. 1915 Federal League: Chicago Whales–St. Louis Terriers–Pittsburgh Rebels. The three top teams are separated by 1 game heading into the season's final day. Chicago and Pittsburgh split a doubleheader and St. Louis wins, leaving the Whales in first place by .001 over St. Louis, with Pittsburgh a half-game and .004 back (Chicago had played 2 fewer games than St. Louis because of rainouts but did not have to make those games up under league rules).

3. 1914 Federal League: Indianapolis Hoosiers–Chicago Whales. Almost every team flirts with the top spot at one time or another during the season, but by the final week of the season the race is down to Indianapolis and Chicago. The Whales drop a key October 6 doubleheader to the Kansas City Packers, allowing the Hoosiers to move into first place for good.

The Boston Braves' starting outfield for Game Two of the 1914 World Series (from left): *left fielder Ted Cather, center fielder Possum Whitted, and right fielder Les Mann. A .247 hitter, Mann drove in the only run of the day in Game Two and the Miracle Braves went on to sweep the Series over the heavily favored Philadelphia Athletics.*

Best Teams

1. 1915 Boston Red Sox, 101–50; player-manager: Bill Carrigan. Tris Speaker (.322), Duffy Lewis (.291), and Dick Hoblitzell (.283) paced the offense, and Rube Foster (20–8, 2.12 ERA), Ernie Shore (19–8, 1.64), and a twenty-year-old left-hander named Babe Ruth (18–6, 2.44) led the league's deepest pitching staff, which also featured a pair of 14-game winners in Smoky Joe Wood and Dutch Leonard. Working mainly out of the bullpen, Carl Mays won 4 games and saved a league-high 6. Ruth led the eventual World Series winners in home runs with 4 in 92 at bats. Foster, Shore, and Leonard pitched every inning of the 5-game Series against the Phillies and were 4–1 with a 1.84 ERA.

Chippewa Indian great Chief Bender, a mainstay in the rotation of five pennant winners with the Philadelphia Athletics, spent his adult life in baseball. He pitched in the minors until 1927 (when, at age forty-three, he went 7–3 with a 1.33 ERA for Johnstown) and worked as a minor league manager and a major league coach and scout until his death in 1954.

2. 1914 Boston Braves, 94–59; manager: George Stallings. As the Braves made their miracle run at first place and a World Series victory, Stallings called upon his top three pitchers to shoulder the load, and they answered the call: the NL victory leader, Dick Rudolph (27–10, 2.36 ERA), along with Bill James (26–7, 1.90) and Lefty Tyler (16–14, 2.69), started 107 of Boston's 153 games. Shortstop Rabbit Maranville (78 RBI) and second baseman Johnny Evers (.279, 81 runs) made the Braves solid up the middle, and Joe Connolly (.306, 9 homers) and Butch Schmidt (.285, 71 RBI) provided some offensive punch, although Connolly was the club's only .300 hitter.

3. 1910 Philadelphia Athletics, 102–48; manager: Connie Mack. Philadelphia had a couple of .300 hitters in the outfield in Danny Murphy and Rube Oldring, and the makings of what would later be dubbed the "$100,000 infield" in Eddie Collins (81 RBI, 81 runs, and a league-high 81 stolen bases), Jack Barry (.259, 60 RBI, 64 runs), and Frank Baker (.283, 64 RBI, 83 runs). But their pitching staff led the Athletics to the pennant and then on to a Series victory. The staff featured Jack Coombs (31–9, AL-best 13 shutouts), Chief Bender (23–5), Cy Morgan (18–12), and Eddie Plank (16–10); Plank had the highest ERA of the four at 2.02. The staff ERA was an American League–low 1.78.

"Gettysburg Eddie" Plank, who won 284 games in fourteen seasons with the Athletics, was one of several stars who jumped to the Federal League.

John McGraw, the fiery manager of the New York Giants, took his club to the World Series four times in the decade. Although all were exciting Series, the Giants lost all four, including three straight from 1911 to 1913; New York suffered 2 defeats at the hands of the powerful Philadelphia Athletics, lost a thrilling 7-gamer to the Boston Red Sox, and fell in 6 games in 1917 to the Chicago White Sox, who haven't won the Series since.

DECADE PITCHING LEADERS

	National League			American League		
YEAR	PLAYER	TEAM	ERA	PLAYER	TEAM	ERA
1910	George McQuillan	Philadelphia	1.60	Ed Walsh	Chicago	1.27
1911	Christy Mathewson	New York	1.99	Vean Gregg	Cleveland	1.81
1912	Jeff Tesreau	New York	1.96	Walter Johnson	Washington	1.39
1913	Christy Mathewson	New York	2.06	Walter Johnson	Washington	1.09
1914	Bill Doak	St. Louis	1.72	Dutch Leonard	Boston	1.01
1915	Grover Alexander	Philadelphia	1.22	Smoky Joe Wood	Boston	1.49
1916	Grover Alexander	Philadelphia	1.55	Babe Ruth	Boston	1.75
1917	Fred Anderson	New York	1.44	Eddie Cicotte	Chicago	1.53
1918	Hippo Vaughn	Chicago	1.74	Walter Johnson	Washington	1.27
1919	Grover Alexander	Chicago	1.72	Walter Johnson	Washington	1.49

1914	**Federal League**	Adam Johnson	Chicago	1.58
1915	**Federal League**	Earl Moseley	Newark	1.91

Best World Series

1. 1912, Boston Red Sox over New York Giants, 4 games to 3. Two heavyweights lock horns in what will go down as a classic Series, the first ever to be decided on the final pitch. The Red Sox win the opener, the second game ends in a tie, and the Giants win Game Three. Boston wins the next 2 to take a commanding 3–1 lead. Buck O'Brien and Smoky Joe Wood are lined up for the next two days to deliver the knockout blow. But New York jumps on both early, scoring 5 runs in the first inning off O'Brien to win Game Six, and 6 in the first inning off Wood in Game Seven to tie the Series at 3 games apiece. In the climactic eighth game, Boston wins a 3–2, 10-inning thriller on Larry Gardner's sacrifice fly after a costly error by Giants center fielder Fred Snodgrass.

2. 1911, Philadelphia Athletics over New York Giants, 4 games to 2. In a matchup of two managerial legends, Connie Mack and John McGraw, New York's Frank Baker takes center stage. Baker becomes "Home Run" Baker, thanks to his 2-run homer that wins Game Two and his solo shot that ties Game Three, which Philadelphia eventually wins in extra innings. Baker doubles twice in the Athletics' Game Four win and Chief Bender goes the distance in Game Six, allowing just 4 hits in a 13–2 laugher.

3. 1917, Chicago White Sox over New York Giants, 4 games to 2. John McGraw advances to the Series for the fifth time and comes away a loser for the fourth time, thanks in large part to Chicago's Red Faber, who wins 3 games and the Most Valuable Player Award in what will be his only Series appearance in a twenty-year, Hall-of-Fame career, and the Giants defense, which commits 3 costly errors in the decisive sixth game.

Worth Remembering

Philly's Fire Sale. Because of spiraling player salaries brought on by the Federal League's open checkbook policy, the two-time defending AL champion Athletics were forced to become the 1915 version of the 1993 San Diego Padres—they couldn't afford to keep their talent. Pitchers Chief Bender and Eddie Plank jumped to the Federal League; Eddie Collins and Ed Murphy went to the White Sox; Jack Coombs was released and signed with the Dodgers; and Home Run Baker sat out the season in a contract dispute (he was sold to the Yankees in 1916). Philadelphia's youth movement fell flat: the 1915 Athletics lost 109 games and became the first team in history to go from first to worst in successive years. The next year they lost a franchise-worst 117 games.

Rookie Mistake. In his *Historical Baseball Abstract*, historian Bill James recounts a ploy used by Cardinals player-manager Miller Huggins in 1915 to get a runner home from third base with 2 outs in the seventh inning of a tie game. Huggins, coaching at third, shouted to Brooklyn rookie pitcher Ed Appleton, "Let me see that ball." Appleton, apparently one to respect his elders, tossed the ball Huggins' way—and looked on in shock as Huggins stepped aside while the ball flew past him and the go-ahead run scored. The Dodgers protested, but the umpire reminded them that because time had not been called, the ball was still in play and Appleton was throwing it at his own risk.

Fast Friends. The defending champion Red Sox could not come to terms with Tris Speaker before the 1916 season, so they sold him to Cleveland. Speaker's friend and roommate, Smoky Joe Wood, held out for the entire season, until Boston dealt *him* to Cleveland. The Red Sox nonetheless won their second straight Series, while Wood came down with a sore arm and

Frank Baker sat out the 1915 season, playing semipro ball in Upland, Pennsylvania, and forced the Athletics to sell him to the Yankees.

WHAT'S IN/WHAT'S OUT IN THE 1910s

In	Out
Greed	The good of the game
The National League and American League vs. the Federal League	The National League and American League vs. each other
Large concrete-and-steel stadiums	Quickly built, intimate wooden ballparks
Saves	Complete games
Sunday baseball	Sunday bans
An ethnic mix of players	Irish dominance
Pinstripes	Plain white uniforms
Relief pitching	400-inning, 40-complete game men
Set pitching rotations	Iron men going when ready
Platooning	The same lineup every day
Nicknames on home uniforms	City names or initials
The American League winning the World Series	Series wins for the senior circuit
Player-owner lawsuits	Player-owner tranquility

DECADE BATTING LEADERS

YEAR	National League PLAYER	TEAM	AVG.	American League PLAYER	TEAM	AVG.
1910	Sherry Magee	Philadelphia	.331	Ty Cobb	Detroit	.385
1911	Honus Wagner	Pittsburgh	.334	Ty Cobb	Detroit	.420
1912	Heinie Zimmerman	Chicago	.372	Ty Cobb	Detroit	.410
1913	Jake Daubert	Brooklyn	.350	Ty Cobb	Detroit	.390
1914	Jake Daubert	Brooklyn	.329	Ty Cobb	Detroit	.368
1915	Larry Doyle	New York	.320	Ty Cobb	Detroit	.369
1916	Hal Chase	Cincinnati	.339	Tris Speaker	Cleveland	.386
1917	Edd Roush	Cincinnati	.341	Ty Cobb	Detroit	.383
1918	Zack Wheat	Brooklyn	.335	Ty Cobb	Detroit	.382
1919	Edd Roush	Cincinnati	.321	Ty Cobb	Detroit	.384.

1914	**Federal League**		Benny Kauff	Indianapolis	.370	
1915	**Federal League**		Benny Kauff	Brooklyn	.342	

Detroit's Ty Cobb waits for the pitch in a 1912 game. That season Cobb hit .410 to break the .400 mark for the second straight year and win the sixth of his nine consecutive American League batting crowns.

never won another game in the majors.

Federal League Flop. The Federal League helped several young stars make a jump to the major leagues, where they went on to successful careers. Such was not the case for Dutch Zwilling, who hit .300 in two years for the FL's Chicago Whales, leading the league in home runs one year and RBI the next. Other than earning the distinction of being the last player listed in *The Baseball Encyclopedia*, Zwilling didn't amount to much once the FL folded; he lasted just one year with the Cubs, hitting .113 in 35 games.

What Was the Name Again? There were two Pfeffer brothers pitching in the major leagues in the early 1900s: Francis Xavier Pfeffer (31–40 record from 1905 to 1911) and his younger brother Edward Joseph Pfeffer (158–112 from 1911 to 1924). The younger Pfeffer was known as Jeff and the older brother was called Big Jeff—even though he was shorter and lighter than his little brother. Fortunately, confusion was kept to a minimum because their major league careers overlapped by only one season and they never played for the same team.

DECADE SPOTLIGHT

Benny Kauff: The Ty Cobb of the Federal League

Under different circumstances, the story of Benny Kauff might well have been the archetypal tale of the American Dream realized. All the elements were there: Kauff, the son of an Ohio coal miner, joined his father in the mines at age eleven, working for three dollars a week. But unlike his father, a promising baseball prospect himself, the short, spunky Kauff pursued his goal of a pro career. By age twenty-two he was in the bigs, and three years later he was making seven thousand dollars a year with the Federal League's Indianapolis Hoosiers.

Although there's no guarantee Kauff would have gone on to the Hall of Fame, the fact is he never got the chance.

Kauff was victimized by bad judgment and questionable associations at the wrong time—an era of extreme paranoia over threats to baseball's integrity.

For most of his career it appeared that fate would smile on Benjamin Michael Kauff. Primarily used as a pitcher in his first pro season, he eventually was converted to an outfielder and despite his size—just 5 foot 8 inches (154 cm) and 157 pounds (71.2kg)—he proved he had power to go with his speed and keen batting eye. After a couple of solid seasons in the minors he got a chance with the Highlanders in 1912, but he appeared in only 5 games before he was sent down to Rochester of the International League for more seasoning. After he hit .345 in the Eastern Association, Kauff was ticketed for the American Association's Indianapolis Indians for the 1914 season when he got his big break. The newly formed Federal League was trying to attain major league status, and signing rising stars such as Kauff was a key part of the success strategy. When the FL's Indianapolis club offered to double Kauff's salary if he came aboard for the maiden season, the twenty-four-year-old jumped at the chance.

In his first year Kauff led the league in batting average, hits, runs, total bases, doubles, and stolen bases. After that season, comparisons between Kauff and Ty Cobb, the Detroit Tigers' star, became commonplace. But besides developing a reputation as a great player, Kauff was also becoming known as a brash bon vivant who relished the nightlife and spent his money on flashy clothes, expensive jewelry, and fast cars.

Despite winning the Federal League championship in 1914, the Indianapolis club lost money and was transferred to Newark, New Jersey, for the 1915 season. Kauff, meanwhile, ended up with the FL's Tip-Tops because his contract had been used as collateral for a loan that Brooklyn owner Robert Ward had extended to the Hoosiers. In what turned out to be a tumultuous season, Kauff put up more stellar numbers—and nearly touched off full-scale warfare between the FL and the established major leagues. Kauff tried to jump to the NL's New York Giants in late April, and actually took his position in center field in the Polo Grounds before NL President John Tener, not wishing to upset the delicate relationship with the FL, ordered Kauff off the field and ruled him ineligible. It was a good thing, too, according to Brooklyn business manager Dick Carroll, who promised that the FL would have quickly retaliated by stealing NL players in return.

Kauff ended up back with Brooklyn and led the Federal League in batting and stolen bases, becoming the first major league player since Honus Wagner in 1907 and 1908 to lead his league in those two categories in consecutive seasons. "Kauff is the premier slugger, premier fielder, premier base stealer, and best all-around player in the league," declared *Sporting Life*. "He is being called the second Ty Cobb, yet there are many followers of the Federal clubs who say that within the next season Kauff will play rings around the Georgia Peach."

Kauff got his chance to perform on the same stage as Cobb in 1916, when the Federal League folded and Kauff was sold to the Giants for a record thirty-five thousand dollars. Saying "I attained the ambition of my life," Kauff, with his tailored suits, silk shirts, and diamond rings—"a sort of Diamond Jim Brady reduced down to a baseball salary size," wrote sports columnist Damon Runyon—was finally in the National League. But batting titles and championships were not in Kauff's future.

Despite great expectations—some of which were the result of his predictions for his own success—Kauff hit just .264 in his first year with New York and .160 in his first and only World Series. He appeared "anxious," according to one report. A humbler Kauff—"He no longer blusters; he no longer struts," wrote sportswriter Thomas S. Rice—lifted his average to .308 in 1917.

A stint in the military cut short Kauff's 1918 season, in which he batted .315 in 67 games, and he slumped badly in the second half the following year and fell off to .277. Still, Kauff was only twenty-nine and there was reason to believe he would put together a solid season in 1920. But instead of stardom, the end of the line loomed before him.

Kauff opened an automobile parts business after the 1919 season, and in February of 1920 he was arrested and indicted for selling stolen cars. Troubled by the specter of an impending trial, he struggled in the 1920 season, and the Giants sent him to the International League in early July. Kauff would never play in the majors again.

Because Kauff was still under indictment, Commissioner Kenesaw Mountain Landis declared him ineligible in early April 1921. Kauff's case was not helped by the fact that exiled ballplayer Heinie Zimmerman claimed Kauff had accepted money to throw games and had been involved in the Black Sox scandal. Kauff was tried—and acquitted—on the car theft charges a month later, but Landis ultimately banned him from baseball for life anyway. Landis wrote to Kauff: "…your mere presence in the lineup would inevitably burden patrons of the game with grave apprehension as to its integrity." So it was that Kauff's career became the American Dream without the happy ending.

Sporting Life *called Federal League star Benny Kauff "the best all-around player in the league," and many baseball enthusiasts, professional sports writers and fans alike, believed that Kauff, given time, would surpass even Ty Cobb's superior performance. But Kauff never fulfilled that bold promise.*

The 1920s
The Babe and the Big Boom

For baseball, the task at hand at the beginning of the 1920s was a daunting one: rebuilding the game's integrity in the wake of the Black Sox scandal. The revelation that the World Series had been fixed shook baseball to the core and frightened club owners, who were willing to take drastic measures to repair the damage. Thus the stage was set for two men to dominate the decade, one off the field and one on it.

Judge Kenesaw Mountain Landis, a devoted Chicago Cubs fan who had called baseball "a national institution," demanded a broad power base before he agreed to accept the commissioner's job in 1921, claiming he needed absolute authority to clean up the game. The owners agreed. Armed with this power and with the antitrust exemption that baseball received through the courts in 1922, Landis dealt harshly with those who threatened the game's image, even by merely associating with gamblers or criminals. And although the "Eight Men Out" of the Black Sox

scandal were the most well known, there were plenty of other such offenders. According to historian Bill James, at least thirty-eight players were implicated—that is, either banned or confronted with serious charges—in various gambling and game-fixing scandals between 1917 and 1927, and eleven active players were banned from baseball for life for gambling connections or conspiring to throw games.

Although baseball had suffered its share of turmoil, on and off the field, this series of gambling scandals was something quite different. It was for many the moment in time when innocence in sport was lost and disillusionment was found. Perhaps the field of dreams had been just that: a lovely illusion that was never matched by reality.

It was Arnold Rothstein, a shadowy figure, who fixed the 1919 World Series. Former boxer Abe Attell was his go-between with the Chicago White Sox players. The image of the scandal was so deeply impressed in the American

mind that F. Scott Fitzgerald worked it into *The Great Gatsby* (1925). The character Meyer Wolfsheim was modeled on Rothstein, and after meeting him Nick Carraway observes, "The idea staggered me. It never occurred to me that one man could start to play with the faith of fifty million people—with the single-mindedness of a burglar blowing a safe."

In another passage, Fitzgerald comments on the decadence of the day, with poignant parallels to the destruction of America's faith in fair play in the wake of the Black Sox scandal: "They were careless people, Tom and Daisy. They smashed up things and creatures and then retreated back into their money or their vast carelessness, or whatever it was that kept them together, and let other people clean up the mess they had made."

While Landis was cleaning up matters outside the lines, Babe Ruth was almost single-handedly bringing an exciting atmosphere to the game. With Ruth's .376 batting average and record 54 home runs leading the way, the American League batted .283 in 1920, 10 points better than the century's previous best mark in 1911. Total home runs in the AL jumped 53 percent to a record 369. The National League jumped to a .270 average and 261 homers in 1920, then to .289 and 460—an eye-popping 115 percent power increase—the following season. There had not been a .400 hitter in the major leagues since Ty Cobb in 1912; from

Below: *A field-level view of action from the 1924 World Series, a thrilling seven-gamer won by the Washington Senators over the New York Giants.* Right: *Cut loose by the Indians after the 1926 season, Tris Speaker played the next year in Washington, where at age thirty-nine he hit .327.*

Major League Teams in the 1920s

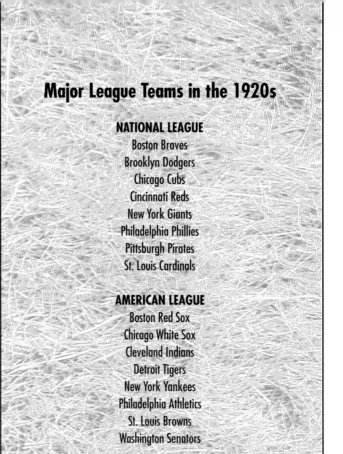

NATIONAL LEAGUE
Boston Braves
Brooklyn Dodgers
Chicago Cubs
Cincinnati Reds
New York Giants
Philadelphia Phillies
Pittsburgh Pirates
St. Louis Cardinals

AMERICAN LEAGUE
Boston Red Sox
Chicago White Sox
Cleveland Indians
Detroit Tigers
New York Yankees
Philadelphia Athletics
St. Louis Browns
Washington Senators

1920 to 1930 there were 8—more than half the total of the 13 who have done it this century.

St. Louis Cardinals second baseman Rogers Hornsby cleared the .400 plateau three times; .401 in 1922, .424 in 1924 (the fifth-highest average of all time), and .403 in 1925. George Sisler, who played for the St. Louis Browns of the American League, managed it twice, hitting .407 in 1920 and .420 (seventh on the all-time list) in 1922.

In many ways, 1920 was the window to an explosive decade. The Cleveland Indians became the first team in the century to produce three players with 100 runs batted in: Larry Gardner knocked in 118, followed by Tris Speaker (107) and Elmer Smith (103). The usually anemic Browns actually hit .308 as a team, a major-league high that was 5 points better than the Indians. When Philadelphia's Cy Williams led the National League with 15 home runs, it was the last season a league home run leader would hit fewer than 20. In 1920, the National League's four leading home-run hitters totaled 50 round-trippers. By 1929, the National League home run kings— Philadelphia's Chuck Klein (43, to set a new record), New York's Mel Ott (42, a close second), Chicago's Rogers Hornsby (39), and Chicago's Hack Wilson (39)—were all posting Ruthian numbers.

There were varying theories for the hitting explosion, the most revolutionary boom in offense the game has ever seen. Some attributed it to a livelier baseball, others to the increased use of clean baseballs during a game and the demise of such trick pitches as the spitball, others to smaller ballparks, and still others to the swing-for-the-fences style of hitting popularized by Ruth. The latter was a major factor, but whatever the cause, the owners had no interest in reining in the offense. Attendance was booming, reaching record totals almost every year, and like the

Top: The infield of the greatest team in baseball history, the 1927 Yankees (from left): first baseman Lou Gehrig, second baseman Tony Lazzeri, shortstop Mark Koenig, and third baseman Joe Dugan. Above: "the House that Ruth Built." Right: Babe Ruth, who hit 659 homers in fifteen years in a Yankee uniform.

country itself, baseball was enjoying the Roaring Twenties. Ruth, who made as much as eighty thousand dollars a year, was the icon of baseball's new era—the right man at the right time who became baseball's biggest star on the game's greatest team.

It was the Golden Age of Sports, and no one towered over the proceedings like Ruth. He stood tall over football player Red Grange, boxers Jack Dempsey and Gene Tunney, golfers Bobby Jones and Walter Hagan, and tennis star Bill Tilden. To those who watched him on the diamond, Ruth was the epitome of the all-around player, hitting, throwing, pitching, running, and fielding with enviable skill. In an era when newspaper and magazine coverage of baseball was growing, Ruth became a national hero, the most recognized American of the twenties. As Yankees pitcher Waite Hoyt

liked to say, "Wives of ball players, when they teach their children their prayers, should instruct them to say: 'God bless mommy, God bless daddy, God bless Babe Ruth! Babe has upped daddy's paycheck by 15 to 40 percent!'"

There were other hurdles ahead, but baseball's leaders could look back on the threats and obstacles of the recent past—insurrection by the players, the competition of the Federal League, the war, and the Black Sox scandal, as well as their own infighting—and accurately say that baseball had proved its staying power. Even in one of its darkest hours, the game had received the endorsement of the grand jury that investigated the 1919 Series fix. "Baseball is more than a national game," the grand jury's statement said: "it is an American institution." The future for that American institution was looking bright.

1920: Rules change: if a batter hits a home run in the bottom of the ninth or in a subsequent inning with the winning run on base, all runners, including the batter, will score (not just the winning run), and the batter is credited with a home run instead of just the necessary number of bases to score the winning run. A runner is not credited with a stolen base if no effort is made to throw him out. A position player must appear in at least 100 games to qualify for the league lead in batting average or fielding average (minimum for catchers' fielding average is 90 games).

1920: The major league schedule is restored to 154 games a team.

The Birth of the Negro National League
1920: All efforts to integrate Major League Baseball have failed. Most all-black clubs do not even have a league in which to play, and a 1919 proposal by Chicago American Giants Manager Rube Foster to place two all-black teams in the major leagues was rejected. So Foster brings together black club owners from across the country for a meeting at the Paseo YMCA in Kansas City to form the Negro National League. Original teams are the Chicago American Giants, Chicago Giants, Cuban Stars (based in Cincinnati), Detroit Stars, Kansas City Monarchs, St. Louis Giants, Dayton Marcos, and Indianapolis ABCs. The Atlantic City Bacharachs and a Hilldale club, based in the Philadelphia suburb of Darby, are added as associate members.

1920: With recent acquisitions Babe Ruth (54 home runs, .376 batting average) and Carl Mays (26 wins) helping the team to within 3 games of a pennant race, the New York Yankees become the first team in baseball history to draw a million fans in a season, attracting 1,289,422 spectators to the Polo Grounds.

1920: George Sisler of the St. Louis Browns strokes 257 hits, the highest single-season total in the twentieth century. Babe Ruth's .847 slugging percentage is the best of all time.

Whale of a Sale: Ruth to Yankees
January 3, 1920: The Boston Red Sox, world champs in 1918, have fallen to sixth place one season later. Strapped for funds, owner Harry Frazee decides to sell his biggest star, pitcher-turned-outfielder Babe Ruth, to the New York Yankees for $125,000 and a $300,000 loan. It is a trade that will haunt the Red Sox for decades as Ruth puts up unprecedented numbers—including a record-shattering 54

George Sisler (above) *didn't have Lou Gehrig's power (or Gehrig's strong supporting cast), but Sisler was the better defensive first baseman.*

homers—the following season and quickly becomes the game's biggest drawing card.

January 16, 1920: *Prohibition goes into effect.*

The Beginning of the End for the Spitter
February 10, 1920: Baseball's attempts to clean up its act extend to on-field rules as well: the spitball and other unorthodox deliveries are abolished. A special transitional provision allows each team to designate two pitchers who will be permitted to use the spitter for the 1920 season only, but the pitch will be completely outlawed thereafter.

Baseball's First On-Field Fatality
August 16, 1920: Yankees right-hander Carl Mays has a reputation for throwing inside, but on this afternoon at the Polo Grounds in New York City a fastball gets away from him and the results are tragic.

A team photo of the Chicago American Giants, including Rube Foster (back row, in suit), the legendary Negro Leagues pitcher, manager, and executive. Foster was elected to the Hall of Fame in 1981.

Mays' pitch strikes Cleveland shortstop Ray Chapman in the head and knocks him out. Chapman, twenty-nine, dies the next day without ever regaining consciousness. He remains the game's only on-field fatality.

August 26, 1920: *The Nineteenth Amendment is enacted, giving women the right to vote.*

Grand Jury Convenes; Black Sox Confess

September 7, 1920: Rumors of a 1919 World Series fix fade to the background during an exciting 1920 season, but the respite is short-lived. On September 4 a story breaks, alleging a fixed game between the Cubs and the Philadelphia Phillies. Three days later a Cook County, Illinois, grand jury convenes to investigate the Cubs-Phillies allegations, as well as baseball's gambling problems in general. Billy Maharg, a small-time gambler, boxer, and former baseball player from Philadelphia with an ax to grind because he did not receive his share from the fixed 1919 Series, testifies that eight Chicago White Sox players were promised $100,000 to throw the Series. The next day, "Black Sox" players Ed Cicotte and Joe Jackson confess that they, along with five other White Sox players, had indeed conspired with gamblers to lose the Series, that they had received only twenty thousand dollars of the promised fee, and that teammate Buck Weaver had been aware of the fix. The grand jury investigation also reveals that although there had been no public disclosure, three NL players—Hal Chase (a go-between in the Black Sox scandal), Heinie Zimmerman, and Lee Magee—were banned from baseball after the 1919 season for throwing games. Chicago owner Charles Comiskey immediately suspends his eight Black Sox, which costs his club the 1920 pennant.

October 1920: As a deterrent to gamblers, Cleveland Indians player-manager Tris Speaker does not name his World Series starting pitchers until game time.

October 10, 1920: Game Five of the World Series provides three memorable moments. Cleveland second baseman Bill Wambsganss turns the only unassisted triple play in Series history; with runners on first and second breaking on the pitch, Wambsganss makes a leaping catch on Clarence Mitchell's line drive, steps on

In eleven seasons with the Cleveland Indians Tris Speaker hit .354 , led the league in doubles six times, and managed the Tribe to the pennant and a World Series victory over the Brooklyn Dodgers in 1920.

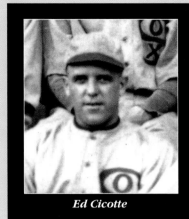
Ed Cicotte

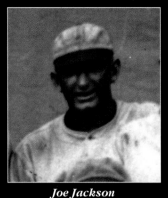
Joe Jackson

Lefty Williams

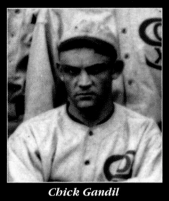
Chick Gandil

Eight men out: Commissioner Kenesaw Mountain Landis deals harshly with the White Sox players (above) accused of throwing the 1919 Series, despite their acquittal in an earlier Illinois trial. Landis bans them from baseball for life; despite numerous appeals, none of the eight ever plays in the major leagues again.

second to double up Pete Kilduff, and tags out Otto Miller near second base. Elmer Smith hits the first Series grand slam, and Jim Bagby becomes the first pitcher to hit a homer in the Series as Cleveland wins the game 8–1.

Landis Named Baseball's First Commissioner

November 12, 1920: Reeling from the damage of the Black Sox scandal and desperate to restore the game's faltering public image, baseball owners consider a radical solution: the Lasker Plan—named for originator Albert D. Lasker, a Chicago advertising executive and a Cubs stockholder—which proposes that baseball be governed by a three-man commission consisting of individuals outside the game. Among those considered to head the commission are former U.S. President William Howard Taft, Senator Hiram Johnson, General John J. Pershing, Major General Leonard Wood, and Judge Kenesaw Mountain Landis. The choice is Landis, but his terms for accepting the job are steep: a fifty-thousand-dollar annual salary and complete authority—that is, no three-man commission. The owners relent and give Landis total control under the new National Agreement of 1921.

1921: Seventeen pitchers—eight National Leaguers and nine American Leaguers—are designated as spitball pitchers and permitted to throw the pitch for the remainder of their careers. The last of these, future Hall of Famer Burleigh Grimes, retires after the 1934 season.

May 19, 1921: *Congress enacts the Emergency Quota Act, which restricts the*

Kenesaw Mountain Landis ardently defended the rights of the players, but he was just as quick to penalize them for serious transgressions.

number of immigrants allowed into the United States. It is the first seriously restrictive immigration bill enacted by Congress.

Landis Bans Black Sox

August 3, 1921: One of Landis' first moves is to ban for life the eight Black Sox involved in the scandal, even though the players had been acquitted in their August 1921 trial in Illinois. "Regardless of the verdict of juries," Landis announces, "no player that throws a ball game, no player that sits in conference with a bunch of crooked players and gamblers where the ways and means of throwing games are discussed, and does not promptly tell his club about it, will ever play professional ball." The action is regarded as harsh but

receives general public support. Despite numerous appeals, Ed Cicotte, Joe Jackson, Lefty Williams, Chick Gandil, Swede Risberg, Fred McMullin, Happy Felsch, and Buck Weaver never play another game in the major leagues.

Baseball Comes to Radio

August 5, 1921: The first radio broadcast of a baseball game hits the airwaves, with Harold Arlin of Pittsburgh's KDKA at the microphone. Owners are skeptical of radio's effect on attendance, making the medium slow to catch on. The Chicago Cubs are the only team to allow broadcasts of all their games in the 1920s, and owners give serious consideration to, but ultimately decide against, a complete ban on radio broadcasts.

December 1921: Commissioner Landis proves that he will take on even the game's biggest star when he suspends Babe Ruth and teammate Bob Meusel and withholds their Series checks for barnstorming after the 1921 season. Ruth and Meusel are permitted to return on May 20, 1922. After the season, with some major league teams losing exhibition games to powerful minor league clubs, Landis issues a complete ban on barnstorming to preserve the major leagues' credibility. He does, however, approve plans for an all-star team to play a series of exhibition games in the Far East.

Baseball Gains Antitrust Exemption

1922: In the long-running suit filed by the Baltimore Terrapins of the Federal League, the U.S. Supreme Court decides in favor of Major League Baseball, ruling that the sport is exempt from the statutes of the

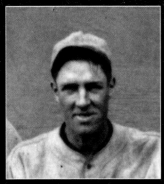
Swede Risberg

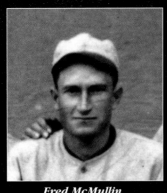
Fred McMullin

Happy Felsch

Buck Weaver

A familiar autumn sight: the voice of NBC's World Series broadcasts, Graham McNamee, interviews the game's most celebrated player and perennial Series participant, Babe Ruth, between innings.

Sherman Antitrust Act and that the contracts that hold players to their teams are legal and binding. Justice Oliver Wendell Holmes declares that the court does not consider baseball games to be a "trade or commerce in the commonly accepted use of the words" and that "baseball is exempt from antitrust regulations due to its peculiar nature."

April 30, 1922: Charlie Robertson of the White Sox pitches a perfect game to beat Detroit 2–0.

August 16, 1922: New York Giants ace Phil Douglas is confronted in his Pittsburgh hotel room by Manager John McGraw and Commissioner Landis in regard to a letter written by Douglas to Cardinals outfielder and former teammate Les Mann, in which Douglas offered to desert his team in exchange for a reward from the St. Louis players. Douglas, angry at McGraw for chewing him out, wrote: "I don't want to see this guy [McGraw] win the pennant. You know I can pitch and I am afraid if I stay I will win the pennant for him." Douglas, 11–4 at the time, admits to writing the letter and is banned for life.

October 1922: Rogers Hornsby of the Cardinals wins the Triple Crown with a .401 average, 42 homers, and 152 runs batted in. He also leads the league in slugging percentage (.559), hits (250), doubles (46), total bases (450), and runs (141), and hits in 33 straight games. George Sisler of the Browns tops the majors with a .420 average—second highest in the modern era—and ties for the major league lead with 51 stolen bases. He also hits in 41 straight games.

October 1922: The World Series, in its first broadcast on radio, is restored to a best-of-seven format.

1923: The Eastern Colored League, which will stay in business until 1928, is formed.

1923: The Philadelphia Athletics tie a major league record by dropping 20 games in a row.

April 18, 1923: After he is asked by the Giants to move his club out of the Polo Grounds, Yankees owner Colonel Jacob Ruppert undertakes the construction of baseball's most magnificent park, Yankee Stadium, located just a quarter mile (0.4 km) from the Giants' home on Coogan's Bluff. Completed in just 185 working days, the two-million-dollar stadium boasts a seating capacity of 62,000, about 10,000 more than the next-largest park, the Polo Grounds. Sportswriter Fred Lieb dubs it "the House that Ruth Built." In the stadium's inaugural contest, played on April 18 in front of a reported crowd of 74,000, with an estimated 25,000 turned away, Babe Ruth hits 2 home runs in a 4–1 win.

September 15, 1923: *J.C. Walton, governor of Oklahoma, places his state under martial law to stop the rising terrorism of the Ku Klux Klan.*

October 10, 1923: Graham McNamee debuts behind the World Series radio microphone, replacing Grantland Rice.

1924: Rogers Hornsby of the Cardinals wins his fifth consecutive batting title with a .424 average, the highest mark of the century.

1924: Giants outfielder Jimmy O'Connell and coach Cozy Dolan are banned from baseball for life for attempting to fix a game earlier in the season. O'Connell reportedly told Phillies shortstop Heinie Sand before the game, "It will be worth five hundred dollars to you if you don't bear down too hard against us today."

September 16, 1924: St. Louis first baseman Jim Bottomley goes 6-for-6 and drives in a major league record 12 runs to help the Cardinals beat the Brooklyn Dodgers 17–3 at Ebbets Field.

October 1924: The Kansas City Monarchs defeat the Philadelphia-area Hilldale team 5 games to 4 in Kansas City to win the first Colored World Series.

Above right: *Young Henry Louis Gehrig from Columbia University became a Yankee regular in 1925 and went on to a Hall of Fame career.* **Right:** *In his one season in New York, Rogers Hornsby hit .361 with 26 home runs and 125 runs batted in, and led the league in runs scored with 133.* **Below:** *The Kansas City Monarchs at the first Colored World Series.*

1925: A new, livelier, "cushioned cork center" baseball is introduced.

1925: St. Louis' Rogers Hornsby, who takes over as Cardinals manager late in the season, wins his second Triple Crown. His numbers: a .403 batting average for his sixth consecutive crown, 39 home runs, 143 RBI, and an NL-record .756 slugging percentage.

Ruth Felled by "Bellyache"

April 8, 1925: As the Yankees are heading north after spring training, Babe Ruth collapses from what one writer calls "the stomachache that was heard around the world." The Bambino returns to New York for surgery to remove an intestinal abscess. He will not play again until June, but even then he is not himself—his batting average falls below .300 for the first time since he became a regular outfielder—and the Yankees slide to seventh place. Ruth does, however, return to his life of excess off the field, which finally prompts Manager Miller Huggins to fine him a record five thousand dollars in September and suspend him for the rest of the season for insubordination and constant violation of team training rules.

June 2, 1925: Yankees first baseman Wally Pipp, a career .283 hitter who had batted .295 with a league-high 19 triples the year before, begs out of the day's lineup with a headache (he had been hit in the head by a pitch). Manager Miller Huggins replaces him with twenty-one-year-old Lou Gehrig from Columbia University. Gehrig hits .295 with 20 homers in 126 games for the season. He will go on to play in a record 2,130 con-

secutive games and post a career batting average of .340. Pipp is sold to the Cincinnati Reds after the season.

1926: Rules change: a ball hit in fair territory over a fence that is less than 250 feet (76.2m) from home plate is a ground rule double. A batter is credited with a sacrifice fly and not charged with a time at bat if he hits a fly ball that is caught but any runner advances on the catch. A pitcher is not credited with a strikeout if the hitter reaches first base on a third-strike wild pitch.

November 2, 1926: The Detroit Tigers release player-manager Ty Cobb, who had managed the club for the last six years and had batted .367 over the past twenty-two seasons. Cobb signs a playing contract with the Athletics in February, but he will never manage again.

December 20, 1926: Cardinals player-manager Rogers Hornsby, who had hit .317 and helped St. Louis win the World Series earlier in the year but had been feuding with team owner Sam Breadon, is traded to the Giants for second baseman Frankie Frisch and pitcher Jimmy Ring.

1927: *Sport* magazine begins publication.

1927: The Chicago Cubs become the first NL team to break the one-million mark in season attendance, drawing 1,163,347 fans to Wrigley Field.

1927: The end of the season also marks the end of the line for three significant baseball men. Washington's Walter Johnson retires after twenty-one seasons with 417 wins, 3,509 strikeouts, and a 2.17 earned-run average. AL President Ban Johnson, the only chief executive the American League has ever had, and Cincinnati Reds President August Herrmann, the former chairman of the National Commission, both step down. Ernest S. Barnard of Cleveland becomes the new AL president.

April 7, 1927: *The first public demonstration of television is set up by the American Telephone & Telegraph Company president, enabling bankers and investors in New York City to watch Secretary of Commerce Herbert Hoover give a speech in Washington, D.C.*

1928: Picking up on an idea that had been bandied about for the last twenty years, NL President John Heydler proposes that a designated hitter take the pitcher's place at the plate to "make baseball a better and livelier game." Fans across the country voice their opposition, and the recommendation goes nowhere. The American League outlaws the "quick pitch," which wily pitchers have used to sneak a strike past unsuspecting hitters. The National League still permits it.

1928: Two legendary players wrap up their careers as members of the Philadelphia Athletics. Ty Cobb (all-time best .367 career batting average and a record 4,191 hits in twenty-four years) bats .323 in 95 games, and Tris Speaker

Frankie Frisch, known as the Fordham Flash, was a take-charge player on the field who, after the Giants traded him in 1926, went on to manage the Cardinals, Pirates, and Cubs.

(.344 and a record 793 doubles in twenty-two seasons) hits .267 in 64 games.

August 27, 1928: *The Kellogg-Briand Pact is signed by the United States and fifteen other nations. The pact outlaws war as a means of settling disputes in favor of world opinion and the skills of diplomats.*

1929: Looking to make history, Des Moines of the Class A Western Association announces that it will play night games under the lights during the 1930 season.

1929: The Giants become the first team in the major leagues to use an electronic public address system, replacing the megaphone.

1929: Lefty O'Doul of the Phillies scores an NL-record 254 hits.

April 18, 1929: The defending world champion Yankees, repeating an experiment tried by the Cleveland Indians thirteen years earlier and the Cincinnati Red Stockings thirty-three years before that, make their first appearance with numbers on the back of their jerseys. This time the idea catches on.

October 12, 1929: Leading 8–0 in the seventh inning and poised to even the World Series at 2 games apiece, the Cubs are jolted by the Philadelphia Athletics' record 10-run inning.

October 23, 1929: *A steady decline in stock market prices since their peak in September causes panic on the New York Stock Exchange. On October 24, later known as "Black Thursday," the stock market collapses, despite the efforts of wealthy investors to bolster it. Five days after the collapse, on what becomes known as "Black Tuesday," some sixteen million shares of stock are sold at declining prices. It is the worst day in the history of the market and is the forerunner of the Great Depression.*

Man of the Decade: Babe Ruth

He was baseball's Sultan of Swat, but Babe Ruth's legendary persona went far beyond his prowess as the game's most prolific power hitter. At a time when baseball sorely needed a shot in the arm, Ruth was just what the doctor ordered. The epitome of the American Dream, a man who rose from a childhood in the St. Mary's Industrial Home for Boys to become the game's most popular and highest-paid player, Ruth carried the sport on his broad shoulders, promising a good time for all who came along for the ride and leaving the problems of the past in his considerable wake.

Babe Ruth's average season in the 1920s: a .355 batting average, 47 home runs, and 133 runs batted in; he also led the Yankees to six pennants and three world championships in the twenties. Ruth's average salary for the decade: fifty-two thousand dollars. How much would he be worth today?

Most Memorable Games

1. May 1, 1920, at Braves Field; Boston Braves 1, Brooklyn Dodgers 1. Boston's Joe Oeschger and Brooklyn's Leon Cadore engage in their own version of the Boston Marathon. In a record-setting performance that will never be equaled in this era of pitch counts and long relievers, each man throws 26 innings and allows just 1 run. Major League Baseball's longest game—which lasted just three hours and fifty minutes, not much longer than it takes to play 9 innings nowadays—was finally called because of darkness.

2. 1929 World Series, Game Four, October 12 at Shibe Park; Philadelphia Athletics 10, Chicago Cubs 8. Chicago trails in the Series 2 games to 1 but Cubs starter Charlie Root has an 8–0 lead in the middle of the seventh inning and is sailing along. Disaster strikes the Cubs in the bottom of the seventh as Philadelphia sends fifteen men to the plate in a Series-record 10-run inning. The big blow is a 3-run inside-the-park homer by Mule Haas, a ball that Cubs center fielder Hack Wilson—wearing a new pair of sunglasses because he had broken his regular pair a few days before—loses in the sun. The Athletics go on to win the game and the Series.

3. 1926 World Series, Game Seven, October 10 at Yankee Stadium; St. Louis Cardinals 3, New York Yankees 2. St. Louis starter Jesse Haines has an early 3–1 lead, but New York gets a run in the sixth and loads the bases with 2 out in the seventh. Cards Manager Rogers Hornsby summons thirty-nine-year-old Grover Cleveland "Pete" Alexander—who had pitched his second complete-game Series victory the day before and, as legend has it,

DECADE PITCHING LEADERS

	National League				American League		
YEAR	PLAYER	TEAM	ERA		PLAYER	TEAM	ERA
1920	Grover Alexander	Chicago	1.91		Bob Shawkey	New York	2.45
1921	Bill Doak	St. Louis	2.59		Red Faber	Chicago	2.48
1922	Phil Douglas	New York	2.63		Red Faber	Chicago	2.80
1923	Dolf Luque	Cincinnati	1.93		Stan Coveleski	Cleveland	2.76
1924	Dazzy Vance	Brooklyn	2.16		Walter Johnson	Washington	2.72
1925	Dolf Luque	Cincinnati	2.63		Stan Coveleski	Washington	2.84
1926	Ray Kremer	Pittsburgh	2.61		Lefty Grove	Philadelphia	2.51
1927	Ray Kremer	Pittsburgh	2.47		Wilcy Moore	New York	2.28
1928	Dazzy Vance	Brooklyn	2.09		Garland Braxton	Washington	2.51
1929	Bill Walker	New York	3.09		Lefty Grove	Philadelphia	2.81

was in the bullpen sleeping off the effects of the previous night's celebration—to face twenty-two-year-old Tony Lazzeri. After just 3 warmup pitches, Alexander fans Lazzeri to end the threat and doesn't allow another base runner until walking Babe Ruth with 2 out in the ninth. With Bob Meusel batting and Lou Gehrig on deck, Ruth inexplicably tries to steal second. Bob O'Farrell guns him down to end the Series.

4. 1924 World Series, Game Seven, October 10 at Griffith Stadium; Washington Senators 4, New York Giants 3. Washington trails 3–1 but loads the bases with 2 out in the eighth. Bucky Harris' grounder to third takes a bad hop over Fred Lindstrom's head for a 2-run single. Washington's thirty-six-year-old Walter Johnson comes on in the ninth and the game remains tied until the twelfth, when bad luck strikes the Giants again. Washington's Muddy Ruel pops up in foul territory between third and home, but catcher Hank Gowdy trips over his mask and fails to make the catch. Given new life, Ruel doubles to left. After Johnson reaches first on shortstop Travis Jackson's fielding error, Earl McNeely hits a hard grounder to third that, like Harris' hit, takes a crazy bounce over Lindstrom's head. Ruel scores to give the Senators the victory and Johnson his first Series win.

5. 1928 World Series, Game Four, October 9 at Sportsman's Park; New York Yankees 7, St. Louis Cardinals 3. New York puts the exclamation point on its second consecutive Series sweep and avenges its loss to the Cardinals in the 1926 Fall Classic as Babe Ruth hits a record 3 homers and Lou Gehrig clubs his fourth round-tripper in 4 games. Ruth bats a record .625 for the Series.

Right: *Grover Cleveland Alexander began his major league career with the Phillies, for whom he won 190 games.*

In the 1924 World Series, the first of his career, Walter Johnson (above) was a winner in Game Seven; the following year he suffered the opposite outcome.

Best Pennant Races

1. 1920 American League: Cleveland Indians–Chicago White Sox–New York Yankees. A dramatic story unfolds for each team: in Cleveland, player-manager Tris Speaker struggles to revive his team's morale after shortstop Ray Chapman is hit and killed by a pitch. In Chicago, the schism between the "straight" and "crooked" players from the previous year's World Series fix widens, until the conspirators are suspended with two weeks left in the season. In New York, Babe Ruth's epic feats, including 54 homers,

The New York Yankees' dynamic duo, Lou Gehrig (left) and Babe Ruth, share a moment of levity during batting practice. The two played together on four American League pennant winners and three world champions.

are the stuff of legends. In the end the Indians, with Speaker's .388 average, Jim Bagby's 31 wins, and key late-season help from two rookies—pitcher Duster Mails and Chapman's replacement, Joe Sewell—finish 2 games ahead of the White Sox and 3 in front of the Yankees.

2. 1928 American League: New York Yankees–Philadelphia Athletics. New York, a pennant winner by 19 games the year before, starts to pull away again. But Connie Mack's rebuilt club reels off a 25–8 record in July to pull close, stays hot in August, and finally grabs the lead with a win on September 8. A doubleheader between the two clubs the next day draws a record crowd of 85,264 to Yankee Stadium and produces a pair of New York wins, 3–0 and 7–3. The Yankees, who have the league's top three RBI men in Babe Ruth, Lou Gehrig, and Bob Meusel, and two of the three winningest pitchers in George Pipgras and Waite Hoyt, never relinquish the lead.

3. 1927 National League: Pittsburgh Pirates–St. Louis Cardinals–New York Giants–Chicago Cubs. Pittsburgh trails Chicago for much of the season before the Cubs pull a summer swoon and the Pirates beat them 4–3 at Pittsburgh's Forbes Field on September 1 to take the lead. Chicago continues to fade while St. Louis and New York

come on, but Pittsburgh, which has four hitters at .325 or better (Paul Waner, Lloyd Waner, Pie Traynor, and Joe Harris) and three pitchers with 19 or more wins (Carmen Hill, Ray Kremer, and Lee Meadows), takes the pennant by 1½ games over the Cards, 2 over the Giants, and 8½ over the once-promising Cubs.

Best Teams

1. 1927 New York Yankees, 110–44; manager: Miller Huggins. Widely regarded as the greatest baseball team of all time, New York's 1927 edition—the fifth of six pennant winners and the second of three World Series champs under Huggins—led wire to wire, topped the American League by an unprecedented 19 games, and swept the Pirates in the Series. Offense was the team's trademark: Babe Ruth hit .356 with 164 RBI and a record 60 home runs, more than any *team* in the league, and Lou Gehrig (.373, 47 homers, and a league-record 175 RBI), Bob Meusel (.337, 103 RBI), Tony Lazzeri (.309, 18 homers, 102 RBI), and Earle Combs (.356) provided additional firepower as the Yankees led the AL in every major offensive category except doubles and stolen bases. There was plenty of pitching, too: Waite Hoyt (22–7), Wilcy Moore (19–7, 13 saves), Herb Pennock (19–8), and Urban

DECADE BATTING LEADERS

	National League			American League		
YEAR	PLAYER	TEAM	AVG.	PLAYER	TEAM	AVG.
1920	Rogers Hornsby	St. Louis	.370	George Sisler	St. Louis	.407
1921	Rogers Hornsby	St. Louis	.397	Harry Heilmann	Detroit	.394
1922	Rogers Hornsby	St. Louis	.401	George Sisler	St. Louis	.420
1923	Rogers Hornsby	St. Louis	.384	Harry Heilmann	Detroit	.403
1924	Rogers Hornsby	St. Louis	.424	Babe Ruth	New York	.378
1925	Rogers Hornsby	St. Louis	.403	Harry Heilmann	Detroit	.393
1926	Bubbles Hargrave	Cincinnati	.353	Heinie Manush	Detroit	.378
1927	Paul Waner	Pittsburgh	.380	Harry Heilmann	Detroit	.398
1928	Rogers Hornsby	Boston	.387	Goose Goslin	Washington	.379
1929	Lefty O'Doul	Philadelphia	.398	Lew Fonseca	Cleveland	.369

Below left: *The American League's top four home run hitters in 1929* (left to right): *Jimmie Foxx (33), Babe Ruth (46), Lou Gehrig (35), and Al Simmons (34).* Bottom: *The pitching staff of the 1927 Yankees* (left to right): *Bob Shawkey, Joe Giard, Myles Thomas, Urban Shocker, Waite Hoyt, Herb Pennock, Wilcy Moore, Walter Beall, Dutch Ruether, and George Pipgras.*

Shocker (18–6) were the leaders of a staff that had the lowest ERA (3.20) in the majors.

2. 1929 Philadelphia Athletics, 104–46; manager: Connie Mack. The rebuilt Philadelphia club had broken the 90-win mark in each of the previous two seasons but couldn't get past the front-running Yankees. The breakthrough came in 1929, thanks to Al Simmons (.365, 34 homers, an AL-best 157 RBI) and Jimmie Foxx (.354, 33, 117), who led a group of six .300 hitters, and George Earnshaw (24–8), Lefty Grove (20–6), and Rube Walberg (18–11) on the mound.

3. 1922 New York Giants, 93–61; manager: John McGraw. The second of John McGraw's four consecutive pennant winners controlled the NL race all year and dom-

inated the Yankees in the World Series. All but one of New York's eight regulars hit better than .320, led by Irish Meusel (.331, 16 homers, 132 RBI), George Kelly (.328, 17, 107), Ross Youngs (.331), and Casey Stengel, who hit .368 after taking over in center field in midseason. The pitching staff overcame the loss of Phil Douglas (banned for life for offering to take a bribe to leave the team) because of the steady performance of Art Nehf (19–13) and league ERA champ Rosy Ryan (17–12, 3.00).

Best World Series

1. 1924, Washington Senators over New York Giants, 4 games to 3. A matchup between a veteran manager—John McGraw, in his ninth Series—and a rookie field general—twenty-seven-year-old Bucky Harris has Washington in its first—turns into a classic. After New York wins a 12-inning thriller in Game One, the teams trade victories in the next 5 games, setting the stage for a winner-take-all Game Seven. Walter Johnson, a loser in Games One and Five, pitches 4 scoreless innings of relief and earns the decisive win when Earl McNeely's grounder in the twelfth inning takes a bad hop over third baseman Fred Lindstrom's head and allows the winning run to score.

2. 1925, Pittsburgh Pirates over Washington Senators, 4 games to 3. Washington wins 3 of the first 4 contests, including 2 complete-game victories by Walter Johnson, and is poised to claim its second straight championship. Although Pittsburgh wins the next 2, the Senators

Above: *The opposing second basemen, field captain Frankie Frisch of the New York Giants (left) and player-manager Bucky Harris of the Washington Senators, shake hands before Game One of the 1924 World Series in Washington.* Below: *A view from the upper deck of Washington's Griffith Stadium during the sixth game of the 1924 Series, won by the Senators 2–1.*

have Johnson back on the hill for Game Seven. The Big Train is staked to a 6–3 lead after 4½ innings and a 7–6 advantage heading into the bottom of the eighth, but he can't hold either lead. The Pirates rally for a 9–7 win and become the first team to rebound from a 3-games-to-1 deficit in the Series.

3. 1926, St. Louis Cardinals over New York Yankees, 4 games to 3. St. Louis and New York split the first 6 games with Grover Cleveland "Pete" Alexander (complete-game victories in Games Two and Six) and Babe Ruth (3 homers to win Game Four) emerging as the heroes. In the climactic Game Seven, Alexander continues his mastery with a key, bases-loaded strikeout of Tony Lazzeri to end the seventh inning and preserve St. Louis's 3–2 lead. Ruth wears the goat horns when, with 2 outs, Bob Meusel at the plate, and Lou Gehrig on deck, he is thrown out trying to steal second and the game and the Series end.

Worth Remembering

Trading Places. May 30, 1922, was a memorable Memorial Day for Max Flack and Cliff Heathcote. That day Flack, a thirty-two-year-old outfielder for the Chicago Cubs, was traded for Heathcote, a twenty-four-year-old outfielder for the St. Louis Cardinals, between games of a morning-afternoon doubleheader between the two clubs. Each had played in the first game, and by playing in the nightcap for their new clubs they became the first players in major league history to play for 2 teams in one day. The change of scenery helped both men: Flack hit 70 points higher with the Cards and Heathcote 35 points better for the Cubs.

Better (Late) Than Ever. Pitcher Clarence Arthur "Dazzy" Vance didn't make the major leagues for good until 1922, at the age of thirty-one. He went 18–12 that year with Brooklyn—his third major league club—led the National League in strikeouts for the first of what would be eight straight seasons, and won 18 more games the next year. In 1924 he led the NL in wins (28–6), ERA (2.16), and complete games (30), and he topped the league in victories again in 1925 (22–9). He won 2 more ERA crowns in 1928 and 1930 and finished his career in 1935—at age forty-four—with 197 wins in sixteen seasons. He earned a spot in the Hall of Fame in 1955.

Last of the Iron Men. In the 1920s the use of relief pitching was becoming more popular while extraordinary feats of endurance by starters were growing rarer. In 1924, twenty-six-year-old rookie Hi Bell of the Cardinals became the last NL pitcher to start and win both games of a doubleheader. (Ironically, he won only 1 more game the rest of the year.) On August 28, 1926, twenty-five-year-old Dutch Levsen of the Cleveland Indians was the last pitcher in the majors to throw 2 complete-game victories in one day, beating Boston 6–1 and 5–1.

Above: *Dazzy Vance's major league record before his thirty-first birthday was 0–4. After that it was 197–140.* Right: *Grover Cleveland Alexander set a rookie record for victories in 1911 with 28, but that was only the beginning. He went on to win 345 more games in his career, breaking the 30-victory mark three times, and he pitched for three pennant winners.*

Great Names—and They Can Hit. In 1926 Cincinnati's Bubbles Hargrave (aka Eugene Franklin Hargrave), whose brother Pinky played for the Browns, hit .353 and became the first catcher to win a batting title. Teammate Walter Neils "Cuckoo" Christensen, a rookie left fielder, who was also nicknamed Seacap, hit .350 and finished second. Hargrave wrapped up a twelve-year career in 1930 but Christensen only played one more season.

Something Odd About This. Detroit's Harry Heilmann hit .398 in 1927 and won the batting title for the fourth consecutive odd-numbered year. There were suggestions that Heilmann's successive two-year contracts, each ending in those odd years, were the cause. After he slipped to .344 and failed to win the crown in 1929, the Tigers sold Heilmann to Cincinnati.

DECADE SPOTLIGHT

Joe Sewell: The Eyes Have It

Although he was elected to the Hall of Fame in 1977—by the veterans committee, not the writers—and he has one of the most distinctive resumes in major league history, Joe Sewell has not become a household name in baseball lore. He should be. Consider the following statistics and facts regarding Sewell:

Joe Sewell (above and below) *is remembered as a hitter who rarely struck out, but he also had a .312 career batting average, drove in 90 or more runs five times, and was one of the best defensive shortstops of his time.*

• He was, hands down, the toughest hitter in major league history to strike out. In his fourteen seasons in the majors, eleven in Cleveland, and the last three with the Yankees, the left-handed-hitting Sewell fanned only 114 times—about once every 16 games—by far the fewest of any hitter who played that long. In 1929 he went a record 115 games (437 at bats) without striking out. In his last nine seasons (1925 to 1933), Sewell went down swinging just 48 times in 1,267 games (4,785 at bats), approximately once every 27 games. During that span he had two seasons in which he struck out just three times (1930 and 1932) and three years with just 4 Ks

WHAT'S IN/WHAT'S OUT IN THE 1920s

In

The long ball and high batting averages
Babe Ruth and Rogers Hornsby
Commissioner Kenesaw Mountain Landis
Exposing and punishing gambling scandals
Clean, white baseballs
Getting players from the minor leagues
Landis's heavy-handed rule
The Yankees
The Negro Leagues
Best-of-seven World Series
Baseball's antitrust exemption
Lou Gehrig
The Philadelphia Athletics' rebuilding

Out

The stolen base, the sacrifice, and strategy
Ty Cobb and Tris Speaker
The National Commission
Keeping a lid on gambling scandals
Dirty baseballs and spitballs
Getting players from the colleges
Threats to baseball's integrity
The Red Sox
Black players in the majors under Landis
Best-of-nine World Series
Challenging the reserve clause
Wally Pipp
The Philadelphia Athletics' fire sale

(1925, 1929, and 1933); his highest single-season strikeout total in that period was 9, in 1928.

Those numbers look like misprints when compared with contemporary players' totals. In 1970 Bobby Bonds set the single-season record of 189 whiffs—75 more than Sewell's *career* total—and nowadays many players break the 100-strikeout mark each year. But even when compared with early twentieth-century players noted for great batting eyes, such as Ty Cobb and Tris Speaker, Sewell's numbers are superior. Those two players almost always had double-figure strikeout totals for a season.

• Sewell was almost certainly the best contact hitter the game has ever seen. He developed his stroke as a boy in rural Alabama by throwing rocks and lumps of coal into the air and hitting them with a broomstick. When he made contact it was always on the sweet spot of the bat; he was seldom fooled by pitchers. That's how he earned another unprecedented distinction: for his entire major league career he used the same bat—a 35-inch (88.9cm), 40-ounce (1.1kg), Cobb-model Louisville Slugger. He would season it with chewing tobacco and stroke it with a Coke bottle to keep it in condition. These days you might see a hitter break two or three bats in one game.

• His batting eye was one of the best and most widely respected in baseball. He claimed he could see the ball so well that he could make out the seams as it was nearing home plate. It was said that Sewell earned such a reputation for knowing the strike zone that he even influenced the judgment of some umpires, who figured that if Sewell took a pitch, it must not have been over the plate. That batting eye enabled Sewell to record 2,226 hits and a .312 career average. His best season came in 1923 when he hit .353 and drove in 109 runs. Although the 5-foot-7 (170.1cm), 155-pound (70.3kg) Sewell wasn't a power hitter, in 1932, his second year with the Yankees, he batted in front of Babe Ruth and hit 11 home runs.

• Sewell, who died in 1990 at age ninety-one, also had the rare distinction of playing on three championship baseball teams in one year. A star football and baseball player at the University of Alabama, where he played with his brother Luke and Riggs Stephenson, both future Indians teammates, Sewell led the Crimson Tide to four Southern Intercollegiate Athletic Association baseball championships and a 58–17 record in four seasons. After playing on Alabama's fourth title-winning team in 1920, Sewell joined the New Orleans Pelicans, who went on to win the Southern Association championship. Before the summer was over Sewell found himself starting at shortstop for the Indians, who went on to win their first-ever World Series that fall. Sewell later roomed with Lou Gehrig and played third base for a Series winner in New York in 1932.

• Sewell's major league career began under the most tragic circumstances in the game's history. He joined the Indians on September 7, 1920, in the heat of the pennant race, to replace shortstop Ray Chapman, who had been hit and killed by a pitch thrown by New York's Carl Mays. The rookie filled in brilliantly under the circumstances, hitting .329 in the final 22 games to help Cleveland finish in first place. Sewell did not miss a game for the Indians between his debut and May 2, 1930, which gave him a streak of 1,103 consecutive games played, a major league record at the time for a player with a single team.

Known as the man who never struck out, Sewell remains one of baseball's unsung stars. A 1928 newspaper article claimed that while Sewell's numbers "may not get the headlines, there is no more remarkable record than that of Joe Sewell in outguessing the pitchers." The test of time has proved that statement to be quite accurate.

The 1930s
Fighting Through the Great Depression

Baseball began the 1930s on such a high that it was hard to imagine the game struggling again. The boom in offense that had started in the 1920s grew to unprecedented proportions in 1930, particularly in the National League, where a juiced-up baseball led to some gaudy statistics—a .303 batting average for the league and an 18 percent increase in home runs. As is usually the case in baseball history, the increased offense was accompanied by a jump in attendance: total attendance broke the ten-million mark for the first time in the game's history.

A single player, Chuck Klein of the Philadelphia Phillies, illustrated the ludicrous turn of events after the National League livened the baseball and reduced the height of its stitching. In only his second full season, the right fielder hit .386 and produced 170 runs batted in, 40 home runs, 250 hits, and a slugging percentage of .687. Incredibly, Klein did not lead the league in any of those important hitting categories. As a team, the Phillies boasted five .300 hitters, but their collective batting average of .315 was still 4 points off the prodigious pace set by the New York Giants. Nine clubs in all averaged .300 or better. For perspective, consider that only one team after 1937 ever achieved the .300 mark.

The Giants' Bill Terry banged out 254 hits and posted an average of .401, marking him as the last National Leaguer to achieve a .400 average. The Chicago Cubs' Hack Wilson became the first to threaten Babe Ruth's single-season home run record. Wilson finished 4 behind, with 56, but drove in a major league record 190 runs—in 155 games. Only a single team, the Washington Senators, managed to record an earned-run average less than 4.00.

But the offensive numbers, the attendance figures, and the game itself came crashing back to reality pretty quickly, partly because the life was taken out of the baseball and partly because of the Great Depression—prosperous times were over for the nation as well. By 1932 the

An early finisher and a late bloomer: Hack Wilson (left), whose drinking cut short his career at age thirty-four, and Dazzy Vance, who didn't stick in the majors until age thirty-one, meet before a 1933 game at Ebbets Field. The two had been teammates with the Dodgers the year before.

number of organized baseball leagues in the United States had been halved, from thirty-two to sixteen, and support even for the remainder was diminishing. "Whereas in July 1930, it was a case of scaring up four bits for a bleacher seat at the stadium, [now] it is a matter of getting enough for a cheap meal," said a *Literary Digest* article in 1932.

Statistics returned quickly to earth as well. Klein's totals in Philadelphia fell from 40 home runs to 31 and 170

RBI to 121, but he led the National League in both categories in 1931. Babe Ruth's home run totals slipped from 49 in 1930, to 46 in 1931, to 41 in 1932. In Ruth's case it was more of a decline in skills than a deadened ball; he was thirty-six in 1931, his last season atop the American League in home runs. Like Ruth, many of the stars who had made the game the national pastime in the roar of the 1920s began to fade.

By 1933, runs per game were down from 5.5 in 1930 to 4.4, and total attendance had plummeted to 6.1 million. Prohibition, which banned beer sales at games, did nothing to help attendance, either. Outside the lines, the gross national product was half of the total from four years earlier, and unemployment had risen to more than 25 percent. That year Commissioner Kenesaw Mountain Landis took a 50 percent pay cut, and major league rosters were reduced from twenty-five to twenty-three players per team. Most clubs, save for the St. Louis Cardinals and other consistently successful teams in the larger markets such as the New York Yankees and New York Giants, found themselves wallowing in red ink.

Below: *Hard-throwing right-hander Bob Feller of the Cleveland Indians led the American League in strikeouts seven times and in victories six times, en route to winning 266 games.* **Right:** *Frank Demaree played on three World Series teams with the Chicago Cubs and was a starting outfielder for the National League in the 1936 and 1937 All-Star Games.*

Major League Teams in the 1930s

NATIONAL LEAGUE
Boston Braves
Brooklyn Dodgers
Chicago Cubs
Cincinnati Reds
New York Giants
Philadelphia Phillies
Pittsburgh Pirates
St. Louis Cardinals

AMERICAN LEAGUE
Boston Red Sox
Chicago White Sox
Cleveland Indians
Detroit Tigers
New York Yankees
Philadelphia Athletics
St. Louis Browns
Washington Senators

With so many Americans out of work, baseball play-ers were happy to have jobs, a decided change of heart after the labor skirmishes early in the century. Salaries, which had peaked in 1929 at around seventy-five hundred dollars, dropped closer to six thousand dollars. After hit-ting .329 and producing 30 home runs and 119 RBI in 1935, Yankees slugger Lou Gehrig was forced to take a pay cut.

Much like the nation, baseball needed bold thinking and innovation to get things moving, but as in the past, club owners proved that they are most resistant to change during tough times. Fortunately for baseball there were a few forward-thinkers. One new wrinkle that helped raise the game's national profile was the All-Star Game, first staged in 1933 because of the tireless efforts of *Chicago Tribune* sports editor Arch Ward, who organized the inau-gural game as part of Chicago's Century of Progress

Two of the greatest first basemen of the 1930s—and of all time—were Lou Gehrig of the New York Yankees and Hank Greenberg of the Detroit Tigers, pictured here in 1935; that year Gehrig led the American League in runs scored (125) and Greenberg was tops in home runs (36) and RBI (170).

Exposition. Another was night baseball, which Cincinnati Reds General Manager Larry MacPhail had pioneered in the American Association and brought to the major leagues in 1935. Radio broadcasts also helped foster fan interest. All these changes were regarded with skepticism and, in many cases, open opposition by some owners, al-though they all eventually helped the game recover.

It was, however, a painstakingly slow recovery. The birth of the National Baseball Hall of Fame helped increase interest in the game, and attendance creeped upward in the latter half of the decade, but it did not reach the high levels of the late 1920s again. The next big boom did not come until the post–World War II era.

Baseball's Big Boom

1930: Worried that attendance will fall because of the Depression, the National League livens things up by wrapping the baseball tighter and lowering the height of the stitching. The results are some unprecedented offensive numbers: the Giants hit a record .319 as a team; nine other clubs, including the last-place Philadelphia Phillies (.315), break the .300 mark; and the league earned-run average jumps to 4.97. Major league attendance, meanwhile, jumps to 10.1 million, the highest total of the pre–World War II era. Hack Wilson of the Chicago Cubs hits .356 with an NL record 56 homers and a major league record 190 runs batted in. Bill Terry of the Giants wins his only batting title with a .401 average and 254 hits—the second-highest total in history. Chuck Klein of the Phillies explodes in his second full season with a .386 batting average, 250 hits, 40 homers, 59 doubles, an NL-record 445 total bases, 170 RBI, and 44 assists.

April 28, 1930: Kansas of the Western Association hosts the first professional night baseball game. The same night in Oklahoma City, the Negro Leagues' Kansas City Monarchs play a night game under portable lights.

September 9, 1930: *Because of mounting unemployment, the State Department issues an order prohibiting almost all immigration. By December 21 unemployment in the nation is estimated at 4.5 million.*

December 11, 1930: *The Bank of the United States, a major private New York bank, closes, bringing the tally of bank closings since the crash of 1929 to approximately thirteen hundred.*

1931: Polished metal and glass buttons are prohibited on game uniforms.

1931: Earl Webb of the Boston Red Sox hits 67 doubles, a modern-era record. Lou Gehrig of the Yankees drives in an AL-record 184 runs.

1931: Rules change: a fair ball that bounces over or through the fence is a

ground-rule double instead of a home run. When a batter drives in the winning run in the bottom of the final inning, he is credited with the number of bases that the official scorer judges he would have made. When a runner is hit with a batted ball in fair territory, the putout is credited to the fielder nearest the runner. The pitcher is not credited with an assist when a runner is thrown out trying to steal home on the pitch. A batter is no longer credited with a sacrifice fly.

March 3, 1931: *"The Star Spangled Banner," written by Francis Scott Key in 1814, is designated the national anthem by the U.S. Congress and President Hoover.*

May 27, 1931: Sportswriter William Harridge becomes the AL president, replacing acting President Frank Navin, who served for two months following the death of Ernest Barnard.

The BBWAA Names Its First Most Valuable Players

October 1931: The idea of honoring the best player each season is not new; the Chalmers Award, similar to the modern MVP Award, was instituted twenty years earlier, and in the 1920s each league instituted a similar procedure for naming its best player, although all of these awards eventually died out. *The Sporting News* issued its own MVP Awards starting in 1929, but the Baseball Writers

Above left: *Hack Wilson played on World Series teams with the Giants (1924) and Cubs (1929) and set NL records for home runs (56) and RBIs (190) in 1930.* **Below:** *The Negro National League's legendary Pittsburgh Crawfords in 1932. Over the years owner Gus Greenlee's roster included stars such as Satchel Paige, Josh Gibson, Cool Papa Bell, Judy Johnson, Sam Bankhead, and Jimmie Crutchfield.*

CRAWFORDS of 1932
3-18-32.

Association of America MVP Awards, first issued in 1931, eventually become baseball's sole MVP Awards. The AL winner is Philadelphia's Lefty Grove, who leads the league in victories with 31 (against just 4 defeats), winning percentage (.886), strikeouts (175), ERA (2.05), complete games (27), and shutouts (4) and reels off 16 straight wins. Cardinals second baseman Frankie Frisch takes NL honors with a .311 average and a league-leading 28 stolen bases.

1932: The Negro National League goes out of business. The league is reorganized in 1933 with six teams—the Pittsburgh Crawfords, Chicago American Giants, Baltimore Black Sox, Nashville Elite Giants, Detroit Stars, and Columbus Blue Birds (a seventh, the Homestead Grays, joins in 1935)—and remains in operation until 1949.

June 3, 1932: Giants Manager John McGraw, age fifty-nine, announces his retirement after thirty years on the job. On the same day, Lou Gehrig of the Yankees, perennially upstaged by Babe Ruth, hits 4 home runs in a game but loses the headlines again.

June 22, 1932: The National League mandates that all players wear uniform numbers on both home and road jerseys.

July 2, 1932: *Franklin Delano Roosevelt wins the Democratic nomination for president and pledges a "new deal for the American people." Roosevelt goes on to win the election in November by a landslide and the Democrats take control of the House and the Senate.*

July 31, 1932: A crowd of 76,979 turns out to see the Cleveland Indians play their first game at Municipal Stadium. The Indians play all their games at the new park the following season, but starting with the 1934 season, they split time between Municipal Stadium and their old home, League Park, playing only Sunday and holiday games in the new stadium. They move all their games into Municipal Stadium in 1947.

August 2, 1932: With his club in first place at 53–44, Cubs owner William Veeck fires player-manager Rogers Hornsby, with whom he has clashed over policy matters. First baseman Charlie Grimm succeeds

The 1931—and first—Baseball Writers' Association MVPs: AL winner Lefty Grove (top) of the Philadelphia Athletics won 31 games and pitched his team to a third straight pennant; NL honoree Frankie Frisch (above) of the St. Louis Cardinals hit .311 and helped his club win a thrilling 7-game Series.

Hornsby and successfully guides Chicago to the pennant.

October 1, 1932: Babe Ruth's "called shot" home run helps the Yankees to a 7–5 win in Game Three of the World Series. It is Ruth's final Series homer.

1933: Eighteen-year-old Joe DiMaggio hits in 61 straight games for San Francisco of the Pacific Coast League.

February 20, 1933: *The Twenty-first Amendment, which would repeal the Eighteenth Amendment and end*

Prohibition, is submitted to the states for ratification; it goes into effect on December 5.

April 19, 1933: *President Roosevelt takes U.S. currency off the gold standard. As a result, money becomes more available to Americans, stimulating the economy.*

Baseball's First All-Star Game
July 6, 1933: With attendance falling because of the Depression, baseball executives decide to act on *Chicago Tribune* sports editor Arch Ward's proposal, based on the idea of sportswriter Grantland Rice, to stage a midseason All-Star Game between the NL and AL. The fans choose the players, and the game, initially staged as a fund-raiser for the National Association of Professional Baseball Players, is an instant success; forty-nine thousand fans pack Chicago's Comiskey Park to see sixty-one-year-old Connie Mack guide his AL charges to a 4–2 victory. The NL squad is led by former Giants Manager John McGraw, who comes out of retirement for the game. A 2-run homer by thirty-eight-year-old Babe Ruth proves to be the difference.

October 1933: Chuck Klein of the Phillies wins the NL Triple Crown with a .368 average, 28 homers, and 120 RBI. Jimmie Foxx of the Athletics turns the trick in the American League with a .356 average, 48 homers, and 163 RBI. It marks the only time in history that both leagues have a Triple Crown winner in the same season, and both winners play in Philadelphia.

1934: Fearful that fans will stay at home and listen to games on radio rather than coming to the park, the three New York teams, the Yankees, Giants, and Dodgers, sign an agreement calling for a complete ban of radio broadcasts. The pact remains in effect until 1939, when new Brooklyn General Manager Larry MacPhail refuses to renew it.

January 5, 1934: The NL and AL agree for the first time to use a uniform baseball.

February 6, 1934: Former sportswriter Ford Frick is named president of the National League, succeeding John Heydler.

October 1934: With a .363 batting average, 49 home runs, and 165 RBI, Lou Gehrig of the New York Yankees wins the only Triple Crown of his career—an honor that his more celebrated teammate, Babe Ruth, never won. Making just sixty-five hundred dollars because of the Depression, Dizzy Dean of the Cardinals proves quite a bargain; he goes 30–7 with a 2.65 ERA and remains the last 30-game winner in NL history.

February 26, 1935: The Yankees release forty-year-old Babe Ruth, who hit 708 home runs over the past twenty-one years, to the Boston Braves.

May 6, 1935: *The most extensive public works program yet under Roosevelt's New Deal begins. The Works Progress Administration will eventually put to work one-third of the nation's eleven million unemployed.*

Baseball Sees the Light
May 24, 1935: Picking up on an idea that their general manager, Larry MacPhail, tried in the minor leagues, the Cincinnati Reds play a night game against the Phillies under the lights. A crowd of 20,422 turns out on a chilly evening, and President Franklin D. Roosevelt pushes a button in the White House that illuminates Crosley Field for the contest. Cincinnati wins 2–1 on Paul Derringer's 6-hitter in what is the first of the Reds' 7 home night games in 1935, all sellouts.

The Babe Calls It Quits
June 1935: Babe Ruth, who homered off New York's Carl Hubbell in his first at bat in the National League but struggled thereafter, removes himself from the Braves lineup for good. The Bambino is hitting just .181 but has added 6 home runs to raise his career total to 714. Boston goes on to lose an NL-record 115 games.

August 14, 1935: *President Roosevelt signs into law the Social Security Act, one of the most important pieces of legislation in*

Below: *Few spectators were on hand at Boston's Braves Field on April 16, 1935, to see new Brave Babe Ruth cross home plate after hitting home run No. 709, his first in the National League.* **Bottom:** *The Pittsburgh Crawfords before a 1935 game in Yankee Stadium.*

American history. The Act provides a pension to all retired Americans sixty-five and older from employee and employer contributions.

December 10, 1935: The Athletics trade twenty-eight-year-old first baseman Jimmie Foxx, winner of three of the last four AL home run crowns, to the Boston Red Sox along with pitcher John Marcum for pitcher Gordon Rhodes, catcher George Savino, and $150,000. Foxx will hit 217 homers for Boston over the next six seasons.

1936: While on a West Coast scouting trip, Red Sox General Manager Eddie Collins purchases the rights to a slender, sweet-swinging slugger named Ted Williams.

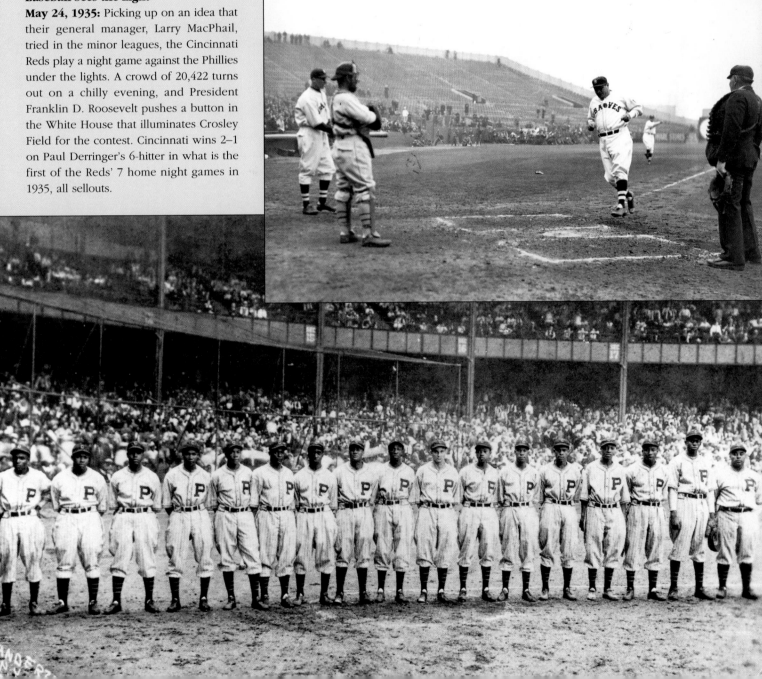

Umpire Steve Basil and Yankees catcher Bill Dickey come to the aid of Mickey Cochrane after the thirty-four-year-old Detroit Tigers catcher was hit in the head by a pitch from New York's Bump Hadley.

The First Hall of Famers

February 2, 1936: Commissioner Kenesaw Mountain Landis and NL President Ford Frick have long lobbied for a Hall of Fame to be built in Cooperstown, New York, baseball's birthplace. Though construction will not be completed for several years, the Baseball Writers Association of America votes in its first group of inductees: Ty Cobb (222 of 226 possible votes), Babe Ruth (215), Honus Wagner (215), Christy Mathewson (205), and Walter Johnson (189).

May 24, 1936: Yankees second baseman Tony Lazzeri becomes the first player in major league history to hit 2 grand slams in 1 game. He adds a solo homer and a 2-run triple for a record total of 11 RBI as New York pounds Philadelphia 25–2.

July 7, 1936: After 3 straight defeats, the National League records its first All-Star Game victory, going up 4–0 and then holding on for a 4–3 win at Boston's Braves Field.

August 23, 1936: Seventeen-year-old Bob Feller makes his major league debut for the Cleveland Indians, tossing a 6-hitter to beat the Browns 4–1. Feller strikes out 15, 1 shy of Rube Waddell's AL record and 2 below Dizzy Dean's major league mark. Three weeks later Feller fans 17 Athletics to tie Dean's record.

A New Negro League

1937: The glory days of the Negro Leagues are in full swing, leading to the formation of a second black league, the Negro American League. The inaugural teams are the Kansas City Monarchs, Chicago American Giants, Cincinnati Tigers, Memphis Red Sox, Detroit Stars, Birmingham Black Barons, Indianapolis Athletics, and St. Louis Stars. The league is an immediate success and stays in business until 1960.

January 19, 1937: In the second year of Hall of Fame balloting, three more players are elected: Nap Lajoie, Tris Speaker, and Cy Young. The Centennial Committee votes in five baseball pioneers: Ban Johnson; Connie Mack; John McGraw; former shortstop, manager, and umpire George Wright; and the National League's first president, Morgan Bulkeley.

May 25, 1937: The thirteen-year Hall of Fame playing career of Detroit Tigers catcher-manager Mickey Cochrane comes to a sudden end when he is hit by a pitch thrown by New York's Irving "Bump" Hadley and suffers a fractured skull. Cochrane returns as manager late in the season but never plays Major League Baseball again. Rookie Rudy York replaces him, and while he is far inferior defensively, York proves to be a slugger. He hits a record 18 homers in August and finishes with 35 for the year.

July 7, 1937: In the All-Star Game at Washington's Griffith Stadium, St. Louis' Dizzy Dean suffers a broken toe when he is hit on the foot by a line drive off the bat of Cleveland's Earl Averill. When he tries to come back too soon later in the season, Dean strains his arm and his brilliant career is effectively over, though he does not officially retire until 1941.

October 1937: Joe Medwick of the St. Louis Cardinals wins the Triple Crown with a .374 average, 31 homers, and 154 RBI.

1938: The Brooklyn Dodgers hire Babe Ruth to coach third base. He lasts one season in what will be his only coaching job in organized baseball.

April 16, 1938: The Cardinals trade Dizzy Dean to the Cubs for pitchers Curt Davis and Clyde Shoun, outfielder Tuck Stainback, and $185,000. Dean will go 16–8 for Chicago over the next three seasons before being released to become a coach for the Cubs.

June 1938: The Phillies announce their plans to leave Baker Bowl and play their home games at the Athletics' Shibe Park.

The Dutch Master Doubles His Pleasure

June 15, 1938: Cincinnati's Johnny Vander Meer, who had no-hit Boston 3–0 in his previous start on June 11, throws his second straight no-hitter to beat Brooklyn 6–0, becoming the first and only pitcher in major league history to throw back-to-back no-hitters. In his next outing four days later in Boston, Vander Meer extends his hitless streak into the fourth inning before Debs Garms snaps it in what will be a 14–1 Reds win.

October 2, 1938: Cleveland's Bob Feller strikes out 18 Tigers in the first game of a doubleheader to set a major league record.

November 28, 1938: White Sox pitching star Monty Stratton's career ends when he blows off his leg in an off-season hunting accident. The twenty-six-year-old right-hander had gone 30–14 over the previous two years.

1939: Rules change: a batter is once again credited with a sacrifice fly and not charged with a time at bat if he hits a fly ball that is caught but a runner scores on the catch. A batter is not credited with an RBI if he grounds into a double play and a runner scores.

Right: *A pair of aces: the Dean brothers, Dizzy (left) and Paul (Daffy), won 100 games for the St. Louis Cardinals from 1934 to 1935, including 4 in the 1934 World Series.* Below: *Lou Gehrig watches the field from an unfamiliar vantage point, the Yankees dugout, in 1939, his final season as a player.*

April 30, 1939: *The World's Fair opens in New York City, with President Roosevelt in attendance. The theme is "The World of Tomorrow."*

The Iron Horse Sits Down
May 2, 1939: Two days earlier Lou Gehrig played in his 2,130th consecutive—and final—game. Today the thirty-five-year-old first baseman asks Yankees Manager Joe McCarthy to take him out of the lineup because he feels his reflexes deteriorating. He retires with a .340 career batting average, 493 home runs, and 1,990 RBI. On June 21 the Mayo Clinic announces that

Gehrig is suffering from amyotrophic lateral sclerosis, a rare neuromuscular disease that will claim his life two years later. The condition later becomes known as Lou Gehrig's disease.

May 16, 1939: The Indians beat the Athletics 8–3 under the lights in Shibe Park in the AL's first night game.

May 17, 1939: W2XBS, an experimental NBC-TV station, televises the first sporting event, the second game of a baseball doubleheader between Princeton and Columbia at New York's Baker Field.

June 12, 1939: In the year that baseball celebrates its centennial, the National Baseball Hall of Fame opens its doors to the public. All eleven living members attend the ceremonies, and George Sisler, Eddie Collins, Willie Keeler, and Lou Gehrig (by special election) are voted in. The commission on old-timers adds Cap Anson, Charles Comiskey, Candy Cummings, Buck Ewing, Hoss Radbourne, and Albert Spalding.

July 4, 1939: Speaking before 61,808 fans at Yankee Stadium, Lou Gehrig says, "I consider myself the luckiest man on the face of the earth."

Lights, Camera, Action
August 26, 1939: It is a rudimentary beginning to be sure, with only two cameras in use, and it is slow to become widely popular, but the first televised Major League Baseball game, in which the Cincinnati Reds beat the Dodgers 5–2 at Ebbets Field in the first game of a doubleheader, is truly an intriguing event. Red Barber calls the action for station W2XBS in what is a unique telecast in another way: because the Saturday afternoon contest draws a crowd of 33,535, and considering that there are no more than four hundred television sets in New York City, more people view the game in person than watch it on television.

September 4, 1939: *Following Germany's aggressive and unprovoked invasion of Poland on September 1, Britain and France declare war on Germany. The United States maintains a policy of neutrality.*

Man of the Decade: Larry MacPhail

In an era when baseball sorely needed innovation but few with the power had the courage to take a chance, MacPhail was a most welcome figure. In 1935 he received grudging permission from club owners to pioneer night baseball, which proved to be immensely popular and profitable. MacPhail was also the first to sell season tickets, and he wisely consented to have all Reds games broadcast on radio at a time when other clubs were reducing or eliminating radio broadcast for fear it would hurt attendance. And when NBC-TV director Doc Morton wanted to try televising a Major League Baseball game in 1939, he knew which executive to ask: MacPhail, who by that time had moved on to become the Brooklyn Dodgers' executive vice president and general manager. Needless to say, the game was telecast.

Dodgers Executive Vice President/General Manager Larry MacPhail (left), along with Manager Leo Durocher, looks in on his players during a workout at Brooklyn's spring training camp in Clearwater, Florida.

Most Memorable Games

1. June 15, 1938, at Ebbets Field; Cincinnati Reds 6, Brooklyn Dodgers 0. As a rookie in 1937, Johnny Vander Meer did not show much promise: a 3–5 record and a 3.84 ERA. But for a 2-game stretch the following year, the Dutch Master is the best pitcher in baseball. First he no-hits the Braves on June 11. Then in his next start four days later—in the New York area's first night game—he turns the trick again, this time no-hitting Brooklyn. The unprecedented second no-hitter ends in dramatic fashion, with Vander Meer walking the bases loaded in the ninth before escaping unscathed. Vander Meer cannot sustain his mastery, however; he finishes his career in 1951 with a 119–121 record.

2. September 28, 1938, at Wrigley Field; Chicago Cubs 6, Pittsburgh Pirates 5. Chicago trails Pittsburgh by a half-game after winning the opener of a 3-game series the day before. The second game is tied 5–5 in the ninth and darkness is gathering—the contest will most certainly be called and declared a draw before it goes to extra innings. But with 2 outs in the bottom of the ninth and 2 strikes against him, Cubs catcher Gabby Hartnett hits his famed "homer in the gloamin'" into the left-field bleachers off Mace Brown to propel Chicago into first place—where they will stay for the rest of the season.

3. 1932 World Series, Game Three, October 1 at Wrigley Field; New York Yankees 7, Chicago Cubs 5. Did he or didn't he? The 1932 Series does not hold much drama—New York wins it in 4 games—save for the mystique surrounding Babe Ruth's fabled "called shot," his fifth-inning homer off Charlie Root that breaks a 4–4 tie in Game Three. Some observers claim that after taking 2 strikes, Ruth raises his arm and points with one finger. But whether he is telling the Cubs bench jockeys that he still has 1 strike left or is gesturing to the center-field bleachers—where he deposits Root's next pitch—is a question for the ages. The legend is disputed by many, including Cubs third base coach Woody English, who, along with Root, second baseman Billy Herman, and shortstop Billy Jurges, contends that Ruth was gesturing toward the Chicago dugout. "He held two fingers up above his head and said that's only two strikes," English told *Sport* magazine years later. "He didn't point." Many baseball historians hold that the called shot was created by sensationalistic New York baseball writers.

DECADE PITCHING LEADERS

	National League			American League		
YEAR	PLAYER	TEAM	ERA	PLAYER	TEAM	ERA
1930	Dazzy Vance	Brooklyn	2.61	Lefty Grove	Philadelphia	2.54
1931	Bill Walker	New York	2.26	Lefty Grove	Philadelphia	2.06
1932	Lon Warneke	Chicago	2.37	Lefty Grove	Philadelphia	2.84
1933	Carl Hubbell	New York	1.66	Monty Pearson	Cleveland	2.33
1934	Carl Hubbell	New York	2.30	Lefty Gomez	New York	2.33
1935	Cy Blanton	Pittsburgh	2.58	Lefty Grove	Boston	2.70
1936	Carl Hubbell	New York	2.31	Lefty Grove	Boston	2.81
1937	Jim Turner	Boston	2.38	Lefty Gomez	New York	2.33
1938	Bill Lee	Chicago	2.66	Lefty Grove	Boston	3.08
1939	Bucky Walters	Cincinnati	2.29	Lefty Grove	Boston	2.54

Below: Cincinnati's Johnny Vander Meer pitches to Dodgers left-fielder Buddy Hassett in the fifth inning of Vander Meer's second straight no-hitter; the runner at first base is Pete Coscarart, who had walked. Bottom: A young Giant named Carl Hubbell, who would go on to record one of the most spectacular feats in All-Star Game history.

4. 1934 All-Star Game, July 10 at the Polo Grounds; American League 9, National League 7. The American League rallies from a 4–0 deficit to win its second straight interleague clash of stars, but the enduring memory is of the man called the Meal Ticket, Carl Hubbell. King Carl provides one of the All-Star Games' greatest moments when he strikes out five consecutive future Hall of Famers: Babe Ruth, Lou Gehrig, Jimmie Foxx, Al Simmons, and Joe Cronin.

5. 1935 World Series, Game Three, October 4 at Wrigley Field; Detroit Tigers 6, Chicago Cubs 5. With the Series tied at 1 game apiece, Detroit rallies for 4 runs in the eighth inning to take a 5–3 lead in the pivotal third game. The Cubs stave off defeat with a 2-run rally of their own in the ninth, but the Tigers win it in the eleventh when Jo-Jo White's single drives in Marv Owen.

Best Pennant Races

1. 1938 National League: Chicago Cubs–Pittsburgh Pirates–New York Giants–Cincinnati Reds. Four teams are in the race until the final weeks, but by late September the battle is down to front-running Pittsburgh

and Chicago, who had caught fire after catcher Gabby Hartnett replaced Charlie Grimm as manager midway through the season. Trailing by 1½ games on September 27, the Cubs win the opener of a 3-game series with the Pirates at Wrigley Field, thanks to a strong outing by off-season acquisition Dizzy Dean. The next afternoon, Hartnett's "homer in the gloamin'" lifts Chicago to another win and sole possession of first place. A 10–1 victory in the series finale—their tenth straight win—all but wraps up the pennant for the Cubs, who win an astonishing 21 of their last 25 games.

2. 1934 National League: St. Louis Cardinals –New York Giants. New York leads for most of the year, but St. Louis gets hot at the right time: down the stretch. The Cardinals are 21–7 in September compared with the Giants' 14–13. The two teams are tied on September 28, but while the Dean brothers, Dizzy and Daffy, are pitching the Cards to 3 straight wins over the cellar-dwelling Reds by a combined score of 19–1, New York is suffering elimination at the hands of sixth-place Brooklyn.

3. 1930 National League: St. Louis Cardinals –Chicago Cubs –New York Giants–Brooklyn Dodgers. Defending NL-champion Chicago gets a monster year from Hack Wilson (.356, 56 homers, 190 RBI), but the pennant goes to the balanced St. Louis club, led by its new manager, Gabby Street, for whom all eight starters hit better than .300. Only 6 games separate the top four teams at the season's end.

Best Teams

1. 1936 New York Yankees, 102–51; manager: Joe McCarthy. New York returns to the top of the AL standings with a well-balanced club led by MVP Lou Gehrig's league-high 49 home runs. Bill Dickey hits .362 and is one of five Yankees to reach the 100-RBI plateau, and a twenty-two-year-old rookie left fielder named Joe DiMaggio hits .323 with 29 homers, 125 RBI, 15 triples,

Left: *The 1930 Chicago Cubs' version of a murderers' row* (from left): *Riggs Stephenson, Hack Wilson, Rogers Hornsby, and Kiki Cuyler.*
Above: *The Yankee Clipper, Joe DiMaggio, spears a line drive.*

132 runs, 367 total bases, and a league-best 22 assists. New York leads the league in runs (1,065), homers (182), slugging percentage (.483), ERA (4.17), strikeouts (624), and saves (21), and beats the New York Giants in 6 games in the World Series.

2. 1939 New York Yankees, 106–45; manager: Joe McCarthy. Not even the retirement of Lou Gehrig could slow the New York dynasty. Led by Joe DiMaggio (an AL-high .381 batting average, 30 homers, 126 RBI), Red Ruffing (21–7, 2.94 ERA), and Johnny Murphy (league-leading 19 saves), the balanced Yankees lead the American League in home runs (166), ERA (3.31), and fielding percentage (.978) and sweep the Cincinnati Reds to win their unprecedented fourth consecutive World Series. The ERA crown is the sixth in a row for the Yankee pitching staff, which had seven pitchers win at least 10 games each.

3 1934 St. Louis Cardinals, 95–58; player-manager: Frankie Frisch. The brothers Dean—Dizzy and Daffy—combine to win 49 games, led by Dizzy's NL-best 30–7 record and 2.65 ERA. On offense St. Louis sports six regulars with .300 averages, including Rip Collins, who hits .333 with 128 RBI and shares the league lead with 35

The 1934 St. Louis Cardinals, known as the Gashouse Gang, rode a high-octane offense and the pitching of the Dean brothers to claim their fifth pennant in nine years; they went on to capture a World Series victory over the Detroit Tigers.

home runs, and Joe Medwick, who hits .319 with 106 RBI and an NL-best 18 triples. The Cardinals offense leads the National League in batting average (.288), runs (799), hits (1,582), doubles (294), and stolen bases (69). The Dean brothers win 2 games apiece to lead the Cards to victory in a wild 7-game Series against the Tigers.

Best World Series

1. 1931, St. Louis Cardinals over Philadelphia Athletics, 4 games to 3. In what will be the final World Series for legendary Philadelphia Manager Connie Mack, St. Louis' rookie center fielder, Pepper Martin, steals the spotlight with 12 hits in 24 at bats. Martin collects 2 hits and 2 stolen bases as the Cards tie the Series with a win in Game Two, contributes 2 more hits in a Game Three win, spoils George Earnshaw's no-hitter by recording St. Louis' only 2 hits in Game Four, drives in 4 runs with 3 hits in the Cards' Game Five win, and snuffs Philadelphia's rally in the ninth inning of the finale by catching Max Bishop's scalded line drive with 2 out and 2 on to preserve a 4–2 victory.

2. 1934, St. Louis Cardinals over Detroit Tigers, 4 games to 3. Before the Series, Dizzy Dean proclaims that he and his brother Paul, a.k.a. Daffy, will single-handedly beat Detroit. The words ring true as each wins 2 games for the Gashouse Gang. The biggest story of the Series,

though, is the Game Seven rhubarb between St. Louis' Joe Medwick and Detroit's Marv Owen. With his club ahead 7–0 in the sixth inning, the Cards' left fielder hits a triple and, after a hard slide into the bag, gets into a row with Tigers third baseman Owen. Umpires manage to control the angry players but are ultimately powerless to restrain the volatile Detroit fans, who pelt Medwick with assorted debris when he tries to take his position on the field in the bottom of the inning. After consulting with Commissioner Kenesaw Mountain Landis, Medwick agrees for his own safety to leave the game, which St. Louis goes on to win 11–0.

3. 1935, Detroit Tigers over Chicago Cubs, 4 games to 2. Chicago wins the opener 3–0 and after Detroit slugger Hank Greenberg goes down with a broken wrist in Game Two, Cubs fans are tasting victory. But Detroit wins the second game and 3 of the next 4—including a classic 11-inning thriller in Game Three—to take the Series.

Worth Remembering

An Unexpected Surprise. The Washington Senators and St. Louis Browns hooked up on June 13, 1930, in a rare trade of future Hall of Fame outfielders. The Senators sent thirty-year-old Goose Goslin, who won the batting title with a .379 mark in 1928 but slipped to .288 the following year, to the Browns in exchange for twenty-eight-year-old Heinie Manush, who won the batting title in 1926 while with Detroit and hit .355 in 1929, and thirty-one-year-old pitcher General Crowder. The change of scenery agreed with both outfielders, although neither stayed in his new home for long: Goslin came back to Washington in a 1932 deal, and Manush was dealt to the Red Sox in 1935. Crowder, who started his big-league career with the Senators in 1926 before being traded to St. Louis, turned out to be the most pleasant surprise: he went 15–9 for Washington in the remainder of the 1930 season and 18–11 the next year, and topped the American League in victories for the next two seasons with records of 26–13 and 24–15.

Bucking the Trend. Judging by the incredible jump in NL offensive numbers across the board in 1930, Cincinnati's Hod Ford, a journeyman middle infielder who entered the 1930 season with a .268 career batting average, could have figured to be pushing the .300 mark. But the thirty-three-year-old Ford was left out in the cold by

Goose Goslin shows off his "camouflage bat," covered with black and white stripes running lengthwise, before an April 11, 1932, intercity exhibition game between Goslin's St. Louis Browns and the Cardinals.

the NL's offensive explosion of 1930. His batting average slipped from .276 the year before to a career-low .231, and he was the only player in the league with at least 400 at bats to hit below .250. Not surprisingly, Ford, who was playing for his fourth major league team in Cincinnati, was soon sent packing again; the Reds sold him to the Cardinals after the 1931 season.

He Gets Around. Not many players have been traded six times, and it's pretty unlikely that such a player would be elected into the Hall of Fame. But such was the case for spitballer Burleigh Grimes, who was traded twice in 1930 alone and was also involved in a memorable 1931 deal that sent him from the Cardinals to the Cubs for future Hall of Fame outfielder Hack Wilson and pitcher Bud Teachout. Besides the six trades, "Ol' Stubblebeard" was also released four times. He won 270 games and played for seven teams in his nineteen-year major league career, which ended after the 1934 season.

No Fool on the Hill. With the Yankees eliminated from the 1933 pennant race by the Senators, thirty-eight-year-old Babe Ruth, who had not pitched regularly since the 1919 season, returned to the mound for what would be the final pitching appearance of his career. The Sultan of Swat pitched the full 9 innings, hit 1 home run, and picked up a 6–5 victory. This was Ruth's fifth such mound cameo since he became a full-time outfielder; he earned the victory in all five.

The Curse of the Bambino? Energetic, young Tom Yawkey purchased the Red Sox in February of 1933, determined to bring a winner to Boston—whatever the cost. Yawkey soon proved he wasn't afraid to spend, but fate did not deal kindly with the club that sold Babe Ruth to the Yankees in 1920. Among the players Yawkey brought to Fenway Park in the mid-1930s—at a cost of more than half a million dollars—were Lefty Grove, Joe Cronin, Jimmie Foxx, Doc Cramer, Eric McNair, and John Marcum. The spending got Yawkey nowhere: the Red Sox finished no better than fourth and were an average of 25 games off the pace in Yawkey's first five seasons.

Acquired from the Philadelphia Athletics before the 1936 season, Jimmie "Double X" Foxx hit 198 home runs in his first five seasons in a Red Sox uniform. But that wasn't enough to push Boston past the powerful New York Yankees and into the World Series.

DECADE BATTING LEADERS

	National League			American League		
YEAR	PLAYER	TEAM	AVG.	PLAYER	TEAM	AVG.
1930	Bill Terry	New York	.401	Al Simmons	Philadelphia	.381
1931	Chick Hafey	St. Louis	.349	Al Simmons	Philadelphia	.390
1932	Lefty O'Doul	Brooklyn	.368	Dale Alexander	Det., Bos.	.367
1933	Chuck Klein	Philadelphia	.368	Jimmie Foxx	Philadelphia	.356
1934	Paul Waner	Pittsburgh	.362	Lou Gehrig	New York	.363
1935	Arky Vaughan	Pittsburgh	.385	Buddy Myer	Washington	.349
1936	Paul Waner	Pittsburgh	.373	Luke Appling	Chicago	.388
1937	Joe Medwick	St. Louis	.374	Charlie Gehringer	Detroit	.371
1938	Ernie Lombardi	Cincinnati	.342	Jimmie Foxx	Boston	.349
1939	Johnny Mize	St. Louis	.349	Joe DiMaggio	New York	.381

DECADE SPOTLIGHT
Moe Berg: Baseball's Renaissance Man

He was a ladies' man, who, according to one teammate, had "kissed the hands of more women than Valentino." His life has been the subject of two books, countless newspaper articles, and a feature piece in *Sports Illustrated.* After he matched wits with intellectuals on a radio quiz show, baseball Commissioner Kenesaw Mountain Landis told him, "You did more for the image of baseball in half an hour than I have since I became commissioner [eighteen years ago]." Sports columnist Frank Graham called him "without a doubt the most remarkable man baseball has ever known." This is not a description of Babe Ruth, Cy Young, Walter Johnson, or one of the game's other such well-known luminaries, but of Morris "Moe" Berg, who was, to say the least, much more than your typical ballplayer.

A catcher for most of his fifteen-year major league career (he broke in as a shortstop with Brooklyn in 1923), Berg was a .243 lifetime hitter who spent much of his time on the bench or warming up pitchers in the bullpen. His best season came in 1929 when he caught 106 games for the Chicago White Sox, hit .288, and allowed just 5 stolen bases. He caught 117 games for Cleveland and Washington from 1931 to 1934 without committing an error, an AL record that stood for twelve years, and earned the accurate label of a "good-field, no hit" player.

But on-field accomplishments are a small part of Berg's legacy. An honors graduate of Princeton, he earned a degree from New York's Columbia Law School and studied experimental phonetics at the Sorbonne in Paris. A charter member of the American Linguist Society, he spoke ten languages: Latin, Japanese, French, Spanish, Portuguese, Italian, Russian, Yiddish, Greek, and, of course, English; he also studied Sanskrit and Hebrew. To round out his résumé, Berg worked as a spy for the Office of Strategic Services (OSS), the predecessor of the CIA, before and during World War II. His major task was to evaluate and report on Germany's progress toward developing the atomic bomb.

Berg's espionage career began in 1934, during his second visit to Japan, as a member of a U.S. all-star team that included Babe Ruth, Lou Gehrig, and Jimmie Foxx. Berg saw little playing time on the tour, so his absence was hardly noticed one afternoon while the Americans were routing a team of Japanese collegians. Carrying a bouquet of flowers, Berg went instead to St. Luke's International

A baseball bat was not a dangerous weapon in the hands of war hero, linguist, and .243 career hitter Morris "Moe" Berg, who, according to one writer, "knew a dozen languages but couldn't hit in any of them."

Hospital, one of Tokyo's tallest buildings, ostensibly to visit the U.S. ambassador's daughter, who had just given birth. Berg was directed to the seventh floor and bowed politely to security officers before he boarded an elevator, but instead made his way to the roof. He removed from under his jacket a 16-millimeter movie camera and shot the surrounding industrial complexes, refineries, railroad lines, and shipyards, taking in images as distant as Mount Fuji, more than 50 miles (80 km) away. He left the flowers on the roof and departed with some valuable footage. Eight years later, after the Japanese bombing of Pearl Harbor, General Jimmy Doolittle's flyers raided Tokyo with an attack plan that had been mapped out using Berg's film.

Berg remained in baseball as a player and coach through the 1930s, playing his last game in 1939, but after war broke out in Europe he felt compelled to act on his patriotism and sense of duty. "Europe is in flames," he said, "withering in a fire set by Hitler. All over that continent men and women and children are dying. Soon we, too, will be involved. And what am I doing? I'm sitting in the bullpen, telling jokes to the relief pitchers."

Berg's first wartime post, obtained through his friend Nelson Rockefeller, the coordinator of the Office of Inter-American Affairs, was as a goodwill ambassador to Latin

WHAT'S IN/WHAT'S OUT IN THE 1930s

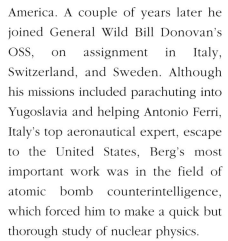

In	Out
The status quo on the field	Innovations such as major rule changes or interleague play
Lower attendance figures	Lower ticket prices
Rising home run totals	Stolen bases and sacrifices (still)
Jimmie Foxx	Babe Ruth
Banning radio broadcasts	Understanding the effects of radio
Player salary cuts	Rising—albeit slowly—player salaries
The BBWAA and *The Sporting News* MVP Awards	The AL and NL MVP Awards
The All-Star Game	The World Series as the only interleague lure for fans
Farm systems for major league teams	Major league caliber teams in the minors
Economic problems for small-market teams	A revenue-sharing plan
Sticking with a regular lineup	Platooning
Yankees Manager Joe McCarthy and Giants Manager Bill Terry	Yankees Manager Miller Huggins and Giants Manager John McGraw
Great NL pennant races	Great AL pennant races
Numbers on uniforms	Blank uniform backs
Baseball (one word)	Base ball (two words)

Moe Berg's love of baseball inspired a long, though undistinguished, career in the majors; his love of his country prompted a more memorable career as an American spy.

America. A couple of years later he joined General Wild Bill Donovan's OSS, on assignment in Italy, Switzerland, and Sweden. Although his missions included parachuting into Yugoslavia and helping Antonio Ferri, Italy's top aeronautical expert, escape to the United States, Berg's most important work was in the field of atomic bomb counterintelligence, which forced him to make a quick but thorough study of nuclear physics.

Berg, who was awarded—but refused—the Medal of Freedom, was issued a revolver and a cyanide capsule for one of his ensuing missions: to pose as a Swiss graduate student and attend a lecture by Werner Heisenberg, Germany's preeminent atomic scientist. Seated in the first row, Berg's orders were to kidnap or assassinate Heisenberg if he obtained sufficient evidence that Germany's atomic bomb experiments were proceeding successfully. But Heisenberg made no mention of atomic weapons production, so Berg left inconspicuously.

Long before he ever worked for the OSS, Berg established himself as an enigma—albeit a popular one—among his fellow baseball players. "Moe was really something in the bullpen," one teammate told *The Sporting News* in 1972. "We'd all sit around and listen to him discuss the Greeks, Romans, Japanese, anything. Hell, we didn't know what he was talking about, but it sure sounded good."

Joe Cascarella, another of Berg's teammates, echoed the sentiment of many regarding Berg, who obviously would have been more successful in pursuits other than baseball. "What was this man doing playing baseball?" wondered Cascarella. "Very puzzling."

According to Berg, who died in 1972 at age seventy, the answer was simple. "I love this game," he said. "It has given me a hobby, a profession, two trips around the world, and a lot of fun."

The 1940s

The Race Revolution and Another World War

Developments in the world of baseball almost always mirror those in the world around the game, and this was never more evident than in the 1940s. Besides the obvious ways in which both the United States and the game of baseball were affected by World War II (for example, depleted manpower, finances, and other resources), consider that during this period both the United States and baseball suffered the death of a leader who had navigated his constituency through some tough times; President Franklin D. Roosevelt and Commissioner Kenesaw Mountain Landis died within six months of each other in the mid-1940s. Both the country and the game saw women take a much larger role in positions that had been previously reserved for men, be it Rosie the Riveter on the assembly line or the women in the All-American Girls Professional Baseball League, which conducted play from 1943 to 1954. Consider, too, that both America and baseball enjoyed a postwar boom that was soon tempered by other problems; while the United States dealt with such postwar problems as labor unrest, racial tension, and fear of Communism, baseball had its own headaches, chief among them the defection of players to the rival Mexican League in 1946 and the Evangeline League gambling scandal of 1948.

One area where baseball set the pace for American society, however, was in racial desegregation. The Brooklyn Dodgers signed Jackie Robinson in 1945—ten years before the well-publicized Rosa Parks incident in Montgomery, Alabama, led to a federal court ruling that bus segregation was unconstitutional.

It would be nice to say that baseball's breaking down of the color barrier was a truly noble pursuit motivated by a desire to lead the way to racial equality in the United States, but that wasn't the case. Branch Rickey, the Brooklyn Dodgers general manager who signed Robinson, summed up his motive—and likely that of the other team officials who soon followed suit—in a 1945 letter to a sportswriter friend: "I don't mean to be a crusader," Rickey wrote. "My only purpose is to be fair to all people and my selfish objective is to win baseball games."

Jackie Robinson broke down racial barriers in the 1940s, but Moses Fleetwood Walker (back row, center), a college star at Oberlin, was the first African-American player in baseball's major leagues. Walker, pictured in 1884 with Toledo of the American Association, hit .263 in his only major league season before pressure from other players forced him out of the league.

What Rickey knew, the other owners soon figured out: by adding black baseball stars to their rosters, the owners could improve their teams on the field and help their clubs tap into the African-American fan base, which supported the Negro Leagues as an alternative to the whites-only majors. In both cases, the result was greater revenues—every team's obvious objective.

That African Americans could play the game of baseball with great skill was common knowledge among baseball men. In fact, Moses Fleetwood Walker was the first African American to play in the big leagues, in 1884 with Toledo of the American Association. A twenty-six-year-old center fielder, Walker hit .263, but after objections from Chicago manager and first baseman Cap Anson, among others, Walker was banned from the major leagues.

The only acceptable baseball venues of the time for African Americans were leagues of their own and barnstorming, exhibition teams, which were quite popular. The Homestead Grays, featuring Josh Gibson, and the Pittsburgh Crawfords, led by young pitcher Satchel Paige, were two such teams in the early 1930s. According to no less an authority than Washington Senators Manager Walter Johnson, Gibson could do everything. "He hits the ball a mile," Johnson said. "He catches so easy he might as well be in a rocking chair. Throws like a rifle." Celebrated St. Louis pitcher Dizzy Dean, who lost a 1934 exhibition game 1–0 in 17 innings to Paige, acknowledged, "He is the greatest pitcher in the world."

And while managers privately admitted they would readily sign talented African Americans, integration was still taboo as the sport entered the 1940s. In 1942, *The Sporting News* editorialized, "Clear minded men of tolerance of both races realize the tragic possibilities [of baseball integration] and have steered clear of such complications, because they realize it is to the benefit of each and also of the game."

Kenesaw Mountain Landis, baseball's first commissioner, enjoyed many successes, but integration was not one of them. He steadfastly resisted the idea to the end of his otherwise fruitful term, which ran from 1921 to 1944. His successor, Albert "Happy" Chandler, was more open-minded. When Branch Rickey broached the subject, Chandler encouraged him. "If a black man can make it in

Hall of Famer Josh Gibson, known as "the black Babe Ruth," starred for the Homestead Grays in the 1930s and 1940s, leading the team to nine straight Negro American League pennants. A power-hitting catcher, he led the Negro Leagues in home runs ten times and was credited with 84 homers one season. He also hit for average; his lifetime mark was .384.

Major League Teams in the 1940s

NATIONAL LEAGUE
Boston Braves
Brooklyn Dodgers
Chicago Cubs
Cincinnati Reds
New York Giants
Philadelphia Phillies
Pittsburgh Pirates
St. Louis Cardinals

AMERICAN LEAGUE
Boston Red Sox
Chicago White Sox
Cleveland Indians
Detroit Tigers
New York Yankees
Philadelphia Athletics
St. Louis Browns
Washington Senators

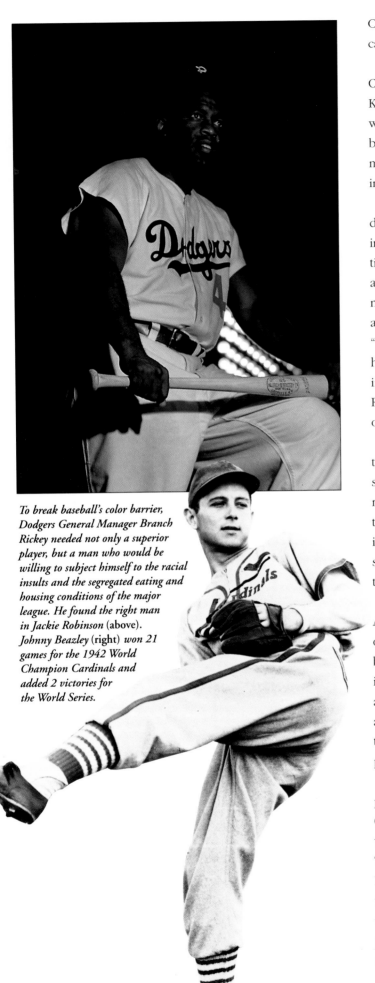

To break baseball's color barrier, Dodgers General Manager Branch Rickey needed not only a superior player, but a man who would be willing to subject himself to the racial insults and the segregated eating and housing conditions of the major league. He found the right man in Jackie Robinson (above). Johnny Beazley (right) won 21 games for the 1942 World Champion Cardinals and added 2 victories for the World Series.

Okinawa and go to Guadalcanal," Chandler observed, "he can make it in baseball."

In 1945, Rickey dispatched Brooklyn Dodgers scout Clyde Sukeforth to observe the young shortstop of the Kansas City Monarchs. After favorable reports, Robinson was summoned to Rickey's office. "Jack," Rickey said, "I've been looking for a great colored ballplayer, but I need more than a great player. I need a man who will accept insults, take abuse—in a word, carry the flag for his race."

Robinson, it turned out, was the perfect man for the difficult task of integration. Two seasons later, after leading Montreal to the 1946 Little World Series with a .349 batting average, Robinson played his first major league game at Ebbets Field on April 15, 1947. He was asked by naive newsmen if he had ever encountered a pitcher as tough as Johnny Sain, who was starting for the Atlanta Braves. "Well," said Robinson, "I hit against Bob Feller on the exhibition tour." Feller's fastball was the fastest ever recorded in major league history: 107.9 miles an hour (172.6kph). Robinson scored the winning run in his debut and went on to average .311 in ten seasons.

Baseball's race revolution made headlines in the forties, but the damaging effects World War II had on the sport looked to be of far greater proportions. With wartime restrictions on rubber forcing the use of a dead ball, the talent base depleted by the draft, and attendance slumping to levels even lower than those of the late 1930s, sportswriters were making dire forecasts for the future of the national pastime.

But baseball, like the country, came back after the war. Attendance boomed, thanks to an improved postwar economy, the return of star players, and the growth of night baseball, and radio broadcasts of games became increasingly popular. Baseball was catching on in other countries as well. Nowhere was that more true than in Japan where as a gesture of good will, postwar U.S. forces occupying that country eagerly helped the locals organize their own professional leagues.

On the diamonds at home, the New York Yankees (five pennants), St. Louis Cardinals (four), Brooklyn Dodgers (three), and Detroit Tigers (two) were the only teams to win more than one flag in the forties. The Cardinals and Tigers were shut out in the decade to come, while the two New York City clubs heightened their rivalry. But thanks to the postwar growth of television and air travel, baseball was spreading its wings and the Yankees-Dodgers competition was soon to have a new twist: it would be coast-to-coast instead of borough-to-borough.

1940: Rules change: a batter is no longer credited with a sacrifice fly, as had been done the previous season. (This rule will be changed back to its current form in 1954.) Runners are permitted to overslide the bases. A catcher is not permitted to interfere with a batter's swing. The distance from home plate down the left- and right-field foul lines must be at least 250 feet (76.2m). A curfew is instituted; no inning may start after 11:50 P.M. local time.

April 16, 1940: Cleveland's Bob Feller throws an Opening Day no-hitter to beat the Chicago White Sox 1–0 at Comiskey Park; it is still the only season-opening no-hitter in history.

August 3, 1940: Cincinnati Reds backup catcher Willard Hershberger, age thirty, commits suicide. After the starter, Ernie Lombardi, sprains an ankle in mid-September, forty-year-old coach Jimmie Wilson takes over and helps the Reds win the World Series.

September 24, 1940: Just short of his thirty-third birthday, Jimmie Foxx of the Boston Red Sox becomes the youngest player in history to reach the 500-homer plateau. But Foxx will hit just 34 more home runs before his career is over.

October 29, 1940: *Secretary of War Henry L. Stimson draws the first number, initiating a U.S. military service draft.*

DiMaggio and Williams Dominate
1941: All Ted Williams does in 1941 is hit—.406 with 37 homers and 120 runs batted in. The Splendid Splinter becomes the first player to hit .400 since Bill Terry in 1930; no one has done it since. The numbers are nearly good enough for a Triple Crown, but they don't even get Williams the AL Most Valuable Player award. That goes to Joe DiMaggio, who leads the Yankees to a pennant with a .357 average, 30 homers, 125 RBI, and, of course, baseball's longest hitting streak. Cleveland's Jeff Heath becomes the first player ever to collect at least 20 doubles, 20 triples, and 20 homers in a single season, hitting 32, 20, and 24, respectively.

1941: The Brooklyn Dodgers experiment with baseball's first batting helmet. The helmet is not adopted officially until the mid-1950s.

Some of Baseball's Best Are Off to War
1941: The United States' increasing war effort claims its first major league star baseball players in 1941, including Cleveland Indians ace Bob Feller and Tigers slugger Hank Greenberg. President Franklin Roosevelt later gives the green light to wartime baseball in his famous 1942 letter to Commissioner Kenesaw Mountain Landis. "I honestly feel that it would be best for the country to keep baseball going," Roosevelt wrote. "If 300 teams use 5,000 or 6,000 players, these players are a definite recreational asset to at least 20,000,000 of their fellow citizens—and that in my judgment is thoroughly worthwhile." So the game goes on, but suffers: the majors lose seventy-one players to military service in 1942; by

World War II meant uniform changes for many major league players, including Cleveland's Bob Feller (above), pictured here on duty in 1943. Feller joined the Navy as a physical education instructor, later applied for gunnery school, and was subsequently assigned to sea duty. Below: A 1945 reunion of American Leaguers at the Jacksonville Naval Air Station (from left): Ted Williams of the Red Sox, Charlie Gehringer of the Tigers, and Bob Kennedy of the White Sox. Williams and Kennedy were second lieutenants in the Marine Corps and Gehringer was in the physical training department.

1945 that number grows to 384. Baseball also endures travel restrictions, and a supposed rubber shortage forces use of a "bastard" ball that doesn't travel as far. The minor leagues are hit the hardest by far: only nine teams complete the 1943 season.

June 2, 1941: Hall of Famer Lou Gehrig, who played in a record 2,130 consecutive games, dies in Riverdale, New York, at age thirty-seven of amyotrophic lateral sclerosis, a disease that is later known by his name.

July 17, 1941: Joe DiMaggio's hitting streak, which began on May 15, is stopped at 56 games by Cleveland pitchers Al Smith and Jim Bagby, Jr., thanks largely to 2 great plays by third baseman Ken Keltner. The next day DiMaggio embarks on a 16-game hitting streak.

December 7, 1941: *Japan bombs Pearl Harbor, killing 2,403 and prompting a U.S. declaration of war on Japan and official entry into World War II the next day, as well as similar declarations on Germany and Italy two days after that.*

July 1942: *The Pride of the Yankees*, a movie based on the life of Lou Gehrig, opens. Gary Cooper portrays Gehrig, while Babe Ruth, Bill Dickey, Bob Meusel, Mark Koenig, and sportscaster Bill Stern play themselves.

August 1942: *Baseball Digest* publishes its first issue.

October 1942: Ted Williams of the Red Sox wins the Triple Crown with a .356 average, 36 homers, and 137 RBI. He again fails to win the MVP Award, which goes instead to Yankees second baseman Joe Gordon.

November 1, 1942: Branch Rickey resigns as general manager of the Cardinals to take the general manager post with the Brooklyn Dodgers.

1943: As part of a plan to restrict railroad travel because of the war, President Franklin D. Roosevelt mandates that Major League Baseball teams conduct spring training close to home, that is, in the North as opposed to the South.

1943: Spud Chandler of the New York Yankees leads the American League with

The 1946 Muskegon Lassies of the AAGPBL: (front row, from left) *Gladys (Terrie) Davis, Jo Lenard, Sara Reeser, Dorothy Montgomery, Margaret Wenzell, Donna Cook, Irene Applegren, Evelyn Warwyshyn;* (back row) *Dorothy Maguire, Erma Bergman, Dorothy Stolze, Norma Metrolis, Arlene Johnson, Nancy Warren, Alva Jo Fischer, Charlene Pryer, Eileen O'Brien, Manager Ralph Boyle.*

a 20–4 record and a 1.64 earned-run average, the lowest since Walter Johnson's 1.49 in 1919.

Women's Baseball League Opens Play

1943: Preparing for the possibility that Major League Baseball would cease operations during the war, Chicago Cubs owner and chewing gum kingpin Philip K. Wrigley plans to form a women's softball league that will play in major league stadiums around the country. When the majors stay in business, Wrigley goes with a scaled-down version of his plan: switching to baseball instead of softball and forming a four-team league with clubs in Kenosha, Wisconsin (Belles), Racine, Wisconsin (Belles), Rockford, Illinois (Peaches), and South Bend, Indiana (Blue Sox). The All-American Girls Professional Baseball League debuts with underhand pitching and a 12-inch (30.4cm) ball. Within a few years the league switches to overhand pitching and a smaller ball, and increases the distance between bases from 65 to 72 feet (19.8 to 21.9m). The league peaks in 1948 with ten teams and total attendance of close to a million; it folds in 1954.

February 24, 1943: With many of their players lost to military service, baseball

teams advertise for players in *The Sporting News.*

April 8, 1943: *In an effort to curb inflation, President Roosevelt freezes prices and wages.*

July 13, 1943: In Philadelphia, the American League prevails 5–4 in the first night All-Star Game. American soldiers stationed overseas hear the game on shortwave radio.

September 3, 1943: *Allied forces invade Italy and bring about an armistice.*

1944: Detroit's Hal Newhouser wins 29 games, the most by an American League pitcher since Lefty Grove's 31 in 1931.

February 29, 1944: *Over the past year a black market, serving Americans willing to pay extra for food, gasoline, and other items rationed or in short supply, has earned an estimated $1.2 billion.*

June 6, 1944: *U.S. and Allied troops invade Europe at Normandy as part of D-Day Operation Overlord.*

October 1944: The St. Louis Browns, who had finished over the .500 mark just once

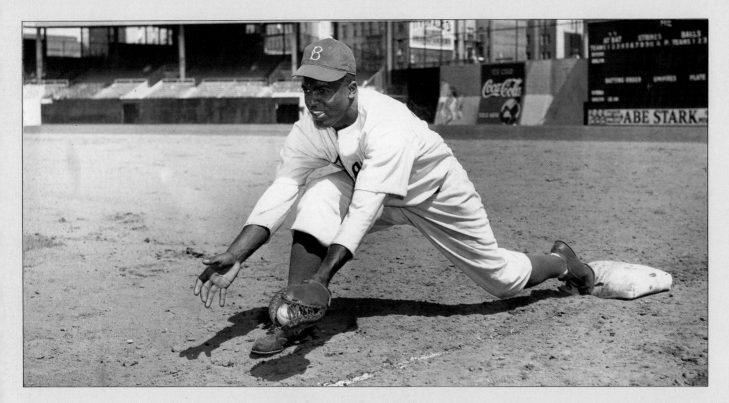

in the previous fourteen years, win their first AL pennant.

Jackie Robinson in 1947, his rookie year with the Dodgers. Robinson played first base that year, then moved to second base in 1948 after Brooklyn traded Eddie Stanky to the Boston Braves.

Landis Dies; Chandler Is New Commissioner

November 25, 1944: The end of an era comes when Kenesaw Mountain Landis, the only commissioner baseball has ever known, dies in Chicago at age seventy-eight. Albert B. "Happy" Chandler, a U.S. senator from Kentucky, is elected Landis' successor on April 24 of the following year and signs a seven-year contract for fifty thousand dollars a year. Chandler is not the domineering presence that Landis was. The owners show they don't want him to be when they increase the size of the game's advisory council, which Landis had dominated, to seven members. Chandler is at the opposite end of the spectrum from Landis on the issue of blacks in baseball, which means the stage is set for the color line to be broken. The new commissioner takes a pragmatic view, saying that if black men can make it in the military they can make it in baseball.

1945: Rules change: a player must have at least 400 at bats to qualify as the league leader in batting average or slugging percentage.

1945: War-induced travel restrictions force the cancellation of the 1945 All-Star Game, the first and only interruption in the series, which began in 1933.

1945: By the time World War II ends, it has become standard practice for "The Star Spangled Banner," which was declared the national anthem in 1931, to be sung or played before every baseball game.

February 4–11, 1945: *At the Yalta Conference in Crimea, President Roosevelt discusses with Churchill and Russian Premier Joseph Stalin plans for the final phase of the Allied assault on Germany. U.S. Marines land on Iwo Jima eight days after the conclusion of the conference.*

April 12, 1945: *President Roosevelt dies unexpectedly in Warm Springs, Georgia, at age sixty-three of a cerebral hemorrhage. Vice President Harry S. Truman assumes the presidency.*

May 7, 1945: *Germany surrenders to Allied forces at Rheims, France. Several days earlier Adolf Hitler, his mistress Eva Braun, and several of his followers had committed suicide in an underground bunker in Berlin.*

August 4, 1945: Bert Shepard, a one-legged former World War II fighter pilot and onetime minor league pitcher who had a successful tryout with the Washington Senators earlier in the year, makes the only major league appearance of his career. The twenty-five-year-old left-hander, who wears a prosthesis because his right leg was amputated below the knee after his plane was shot down in 1944, pitches 5⅔ innings and allows 1 run.

August 6, 1945: *The U.S. Air Force drops an atomic bomb on Hiroshima, Japan, ushering in the Atomic Age; after Japan's refusal to surrender, Nagasaki suffers a similar fate three days later. On September 2 Japan formally surrenders.*

October 1945: In the closest race in major league history, Snuffy Stirnweiss of the Yankees (.30854) wins the AL batting title over Tony Cuccinello of the White Sox (.30845) by .00009.

Robinson Breaks Baseball's Color Barrier

October 23, 1945: Branch Rickey lives up to his reputation as an innovator when he signs Jackie Robinson, a star shortstop with the Negro American League's Kansas City Monarchs, to a minor league contract. After leading the International League in hitting in 1946, Robinson makes his Brooklyn debut in 1947, becoming the first black player in the major leagues in the twentieth century. Playing at first base instead of his more customary position of shortstop or second base, Robinson hits .297, leads the league with 29 stolen bases, and wins the Rookie of the Year Award. He takes plenty of abuse both on and off the field, but proves Rickey correct in his estimation that Robinson has the strength of character to stand up to it. Rickey's bold move spurs other owners to follow suit; by 1949 there are four black players in the All-Star Game.

Players Make a Run for the Border
1946: It has been some time since the major leagues have had competition for their players, and though the defection to the new Mexican League, funded by millionaire Jorge Pasquel, is not on a grand scale, there are some notable players involved, including Dodgers catcher Mickey Owen, New York Giants pitcher Sal Maglie, and Cardinals pitcher Max Lanier. Commissioner Happy Chandler originally bans the defectors for five years but grants them amnesty after the Mexican League collapses in 1949.

The War Is Over; Attendance Booms
1946: With World War II ending, star players returning, and night baseball coming into vogue, attendance, which hit a record level of 10.8 million in 1945, jumps more than 70 percent to 18.5 million in 1946. The dire forecasts of just a few years before are a distant memory.

1946: Cleveland's Bob Feller wins 26 games and records 348 strikeouts, 1 short of Rube Waddell's forty-two-year-old major league record.

July 27, 1946: Rudy York of the Red Sox becomes only the third player in history to hit 2 grand slams in 1 game.

August 9, 1946: For the first time ever, all 8 major league games played are staged at night. Within two years the Chicago Cubs remain the only club that has not instituted night baseball.

The Fans Choose the Stars
1947: Since its inception in 1933 the All-Star Game has been immensely popular with the fans. In 1947 baseball affirms that this game is truly the property of the fans by turning over the selection of the starting lineup (save for pitchers) entirely to them. The fans had shared that duty

Only Babe Ruth was a more dominant power hitter in his prime than Ralph Kiner (above), who hit 306 home runs from 1947 to 1953.

with the managers for the first two All-Star Games, but the managers had held the privilege from 1935 to 1946.

Another Gambling Scandal
1947: Although the crisis isn't of the magnitude of the 1919 Black Sox debacle, the game suffers a blow to its image with the revelation in early 1947 that five players in the Evangeline League have been placed on organized baseball's ineligible list because of allegations that they conspired with gamblers to throw games in the 1946 playoffs.

Yankees-Dodgers Feud; Durocher Suspended
1947: A clash between Yankees owner Larry MacPhail and Brooklyn General Manager Branch Rickey and Manager Leo Durocher starts when MacPhail hires coach Charlie Dressen away from the Dodgers. It escalates into accusations of MacPhail consorting with gamblers, which leads to libel charges by MacPhail and finally to Commissioner Happy Chandler suspending Durocher for the season "as a

result of the accumulation of unpleasant incidents in which he has been involved." These include Durocher's reported friendships with reputed gamblers.

April 1, 1947: Major League Baseball adopts a retirement-insurance annuity plan for players.

April 15, 1947: Jackie Robinson, the first black player in modern major league history, makes his debut for the Dodgers, starting at first base in Brooklyn's 5–3 win over Boston at Ebbets Field. Robinson goes 0-for-3 with 1 run scored.

June 5, 1947: *The Marshall Plan, named for U.S. Secretary of State George Marshall, is introduced; under the plan the United States eventually allocates twelve billion dollars in relief funds for countries in Europe.*

July 5, 1947: Larry Doby becomes the first black player in the American League, striking out as a pinch hitter for the Indians in a 6–5 loss to the White Sox.

October 1947: Brooklyn's Jackie Robinson, who hits .297 with 12 home runs, 125 runs, and an NL-high 29 stolen bases, wins the first Rookie of the Year Award.

October 1947: Ted Williams of the Red Sox wins his second Triple Crown with a .343 average, 32 homers, and 114 RBI. Williams joins Rogers Hornsby as the only two-time Triple Crown winners.

October 18, 1947: *An probe into alleged Communist influence in the American movie industry is initiated by the House Un-American Activities Committee.*

1948: Denver's Mile High Stadium opens. In forty-five years, it will be the first home of the National League's expansion Colorado Rockies.

1948: Detroit's Tiger Stadium, the last AL venue without lights, is equipped for night baseball.

May 14, 1948: *Israel proclaims itself as an independent state, and the United States is the first to recognize the new nation.*

June 13, 1948: The Yankees retire Babe Ruth's uniform number 3 in a ceremony that marks the Babe's final appearance in Yankee Stadium.

June 20, 1948: Pittsburgh's Ralph Kiner homers in his eighth consecutive Sunday game.

August 16, 1948: Babe Ruth dies in New York of throat cancer at the age of fifty-three. *The Babe Ruth Story*, a movie starring William Bendix in the title role, debuts later in the year.

August 20, 1948: Forty-something Negro Leagues great Leroy "Satchel" Paige (his age was always a mystery), signed by the Indians on July 7, pitches a shutout in his first major league start.

October 1948: Led by Cleveland's record total of 2,620,627, Major League Baseball draws an all-time-high 20,920,842 fans for the season.

October 5, 1948: The Washington Homestead Grays defeat the Birmingham Black Barons in the final Colored World Series.

October 11, 1948: The Indians defeat the Boston Braves in 6 games to win their first World Series in twenty-eight years. They haven't won one since.

1949: Casey Stengel replaces Bucky Harris as manager of the Yankees.

April 4, 1949: *Twelve nations, including the United States, Canada, Great Britain, and France, sign the North Atlantic Treaty, a mutual defense agreement that lays the foundation for the establishment of NATO.*

June 15, 1949: Phillies first baseman Eddie Waitkus is shot in the chest by a female fan in her room at the Edgewater Beach Hotel in Chicago. He misses the rest of the season but returns to play six more years in the majors.

July 8, 1949: A black hitter, Hank Thompson of the Giants, faces a black pitcher, Brooklyn's Don Newcombe, for the first time in major league history.

October 1949: With 54 homers, Pittsburgh's Ralph Kiner is the first to crack the 50 mark since Hank Greenberg in 1938.

October 1949: After struggling through the war, Minor League Baseball sets an attendance record for the fourth straight year, this time with 41,982,335 fans. There are now a record fifty-nine minor leagues in operation.

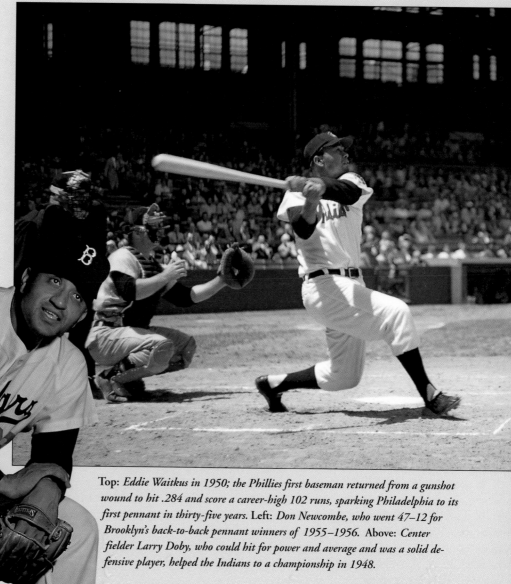

Top: *Eddie Waitkus in 1950; the Phillies first baseman returned from a gunshot wound to hit .284 and score a career-high 102 runs, sparking Philadelphia to its first pennant in thirty-five years.* Left: *Don Newcombe, who went 47–12 for Brooklyn's back-to-back pennant winners of 1955–1956.* Above: *Center fielder Larry Doby, who could hit for power and average and was a solid defensive player, helped the Indians to a championship in 1948.*

Man of the Decade: Jackie Robinson

He was the choice hands down. Robinson blazed a trail for other black stars to follow, and in the process changed the game forever. Dodgers General Manager Branch Rickey knew he needed a special player in order to pull off his "great experiment," and after studying and interviewing Robinson, he concluded that Jackie was the man for the job. It was a sound choice. Robinson handled himself with dignity and class at all times, even when those around him did not. By opening the door to Robinson and the other black players who soon followed him, baseball truly became "America's game."

Jackie Robinson quickly established himself as the spark plug of the Brooklyn Dodger offense; in his first three seasons he led the National League in stolen bases twice and scored more than 100 runs each year.

Most Memorable Games

1. 1947 World Series, Game Four, October 3 at Ebbets Field; Brooklyn Dodgers 3, New York Yankees 2. With a national television audience watching the World Series for the first time, New York's Bill Bevens comes within 1 out of the first no-hitter in Series history. But Bevens loses both the no-hitter and the game as Cookie Lavagetto's 2-run double ties the Series at 2 games apiece. What's worse for Bevens, the twenty-nine-year-old right-hander injures his arm during the game; his relief appearance in the Yankees' Game Seven victory will be his final major league appearance.

2. 1941 World Series, Game Four, October 5 at Ebbets Field; New York Yankees 7, Brooklyn Dodgers 4. Leading 4–3 with 2 outs in the ninth, the Dodgers are on the brink of evening out the series at 2 games apiece. Hugh Casey throws a third strike past Tommy Henrich that would have ended the game, except the ball gets past catcher Mickey Owen as well, allowing Henrich to reach first. The Yankees make the most of the opportunity as Charlie Keller double keys a 4-run, game-winning rally. New York wraps up the Series with a 3–1 win the next day.

3. 1946 World Series, Game Seven, October 15 at Sportsman's Park; St. Louis Cardinals 4, Boston Red Sox 3. Ignoring the stop sign from his third base coach, the Cardinals' "Old Warhorse," Enos Slaughter, dashes

delivers a 3-run homer to win the game. Pittsburgh's Arky Vaughan sets an All-Star Game record with 2 home runs in a losing cause.

5. October 1, 1944, at Sportsman's Park; St. Louis Browns 5, New York Yankees 2. Sig Jakucki, who had retired in 1938 with a lifetime 0–3 record, returns to win 13 games for the Browns, including the pennant-clincher on the final day of the season. It gives the Browns the first AL flag in their forty-four-year history.

Best Pennant Races

1. 1946 National League: St. Louis–Cardinals–Brooklyn Dodgers. The Cardinals lose some key pitchers to the Mexican League, but buoyed by the return of Enos Slaughter and Johnny Beazley from military service, St. Louis stays close to the top. Tied with 96–57 records entering the season's final day, the Cardinals and Dodgers both lose; a best-of-three playoff series is used to break the deadlock. Without star outfielder Pete Reiser, sidelined by injury, the Dodgers fall in 2 straight.

2. 1948 American League: Cleveland Indians–Boston Red Sox–New York Yankees. While the Yankees fall off the pace in the final few days, Boston wins its last 4 games to tie front-running Cleveland. The Indians and Red Sox both have 96 wins at season's end, just like the two top teams in the National League two years earlier. Unlike the NL's 3-game tiebreaker, however, the American League opts for a 1-game playoff, winner take all. The Indians rise to the occasion and win 8–3 behind player-manager Lou Boudreau's 2 home runs.

home all the way from first base to score the winning run on Harry Walker's hit in the eighth as shortstop Johnny Pesky hesitates on his relay throw to the plate. Slaughter plays the last 2 games of the Series despite a painful blood clot in his right elbow, the result of being hit by a Joe Dopson pitch in Game Five.

4. 1941 All-Star Game, July 8 at Tiger Stadium; American League 7, National League 5. The AL trails 5–4 with 2 outs in the ninth, but Boston's Ted Williams

The one that got away: (top) *Brooklyn leads 4–3 with 2 outs in the ninth inning of Game Four of the 1941 World Series. But a third strike gets past Dodger catcher Mickey Owen as Tommy Henrich runs for first (the umpire is Larry Goetz of the NL).* **Left:** *Moments later, Joe DiMaggio slides home with the go-ahead run on Charlie Keller's double. The Yankees go on to win 7–4 and wrap up the Series the next day.*

3. 1940 American League: Detroit Tigers–Cleveland Indians–New York Yankees. Detroit Manager Del Baker shifts first baseman Hank Greenberg to left field and inserts backup catcher Rudy York at first base to start the season. The two combine for a .328 average with 74 homers and 284 RBI as the Tigers finish a game ahead of Cleveland—whose players had unsuccessfully petitioned ownership for the ouster of Manager Ossie Vitt—and 2 games in front of New York.

Above: The 1942 St. Louis Cardinals were one of the best teams of all time and the first of three straight Cardinal pennant winners. Below: Hall of Fame shortstop Lou Boudreau led the American League in fielding percentage eight times, doubles three times, and had a career batting average of .295; his best season came in 1948, when he hit .355 with 18 homers and 106 RBI and managed the Cleveland Indians to the world championship.

Best Teams

1. 1942 St. Louis Cardinals, 106–48; manager: Billy Southworth. Talent may have been depleted in the 1940s, but this Cardinals club is nonetheless right up there with the best teams of all time. A twenty-one-year-old rookie named Stan Musial hit .315 and joined Enos Slaughter (.318) and Terry Moore (.288) in a formidable outfield, and the pitching staff was led by MVP Mort Cooper (22–7, league-leading 1.78 ERA) and rookie Johnny Beazley (21–6, 2.13). About the only thing the Cards didn't have was great power—they hit just 60 homers, third-worst in the National League—but that didn't stop them from leading the league in runs. They defeated a strong Yankees team in the World Series in 5 games.

2. 1948 Cleveland Indians, 97–58; manager: Lou Boudreau. Owner Bill Veeck's club brought Cleveland its first World Series championship since 1920. The Tribe led the league in hits (1,534), home runs (155), batting average (.283), shutouts (28), ERA (3.23), and saves (30). Rookie Gene Bearden (20–7, an AL-best 2.43 ERA), Bob Lemon (20–14, 2.82), and Bob Feller (19–15, 3.57) anchored the starting rotation, and Steve Gromek (9–3, 2.84), Russ Christopher (3–2, 2.90, a league-high 17 saves), Sam Zoldak (9–6, 2.80), and the ageless Satchel Paige (6–1, 2.47) gave Cleveland baseball's deepest pitching staff. Lou Boudreau, the AL MVP, hit .355 with 116 runs and 106 RBI. Joe Gordon (124) and Ken Keltner (119) also broke the 100-RBI mark, and Dale Mitchell hit .336.

3. 1940 Cincinnati Reds, 100–53; manager: Bill McKechnie.

The Reds displayed plenty of character in dealing with the August suicide of backup catcher Willard Hershberger and the season-ending ankle injury to starting catcher Ernie Lombardi in September. Cincinnati's knack for winning the close ones (they won 43 of their 100 victories by only 1 run) took them to the second-best season in Reds history and to an early finish in the pennant race. The pitching—Bucky Walters (22–10) and Paul Derringer (20–12) were the league's victory leaders—and an outstanding perform-ance by forty-year-old coach-turned-starting-catcher Jimmie Wilson—who hit .353 in the World Series—won it for the Reds.

Best World Series

1. 1947, New York Yankees over Brooklyn Dodgers, 4 games to 3.

A classic subway Series that features 3 1-run games, the first pinch-hit home run in World Series history (by Yankees rookie Yogi Berra in Game Three), a near no-hitter by New York's Bill Bevens in Game Four, Al Gionfriddo's phenomenal catch of Joe DiMaggio's 415-foot (126.4m) drive in Game Six, some great clutch hitting by New York's Tommy Henrich, and a 5-inning, shutout relief performance by Yankees reliever Joe Page in the clincher. New York's heroes include rookie Spec Shea, who wins 2 games, and Johnny Lindell, who goes 9-for-18 and drives in a Series-high 7 runs. An estimated 3.7 million viewers enjoy the first televised Fall Classic.

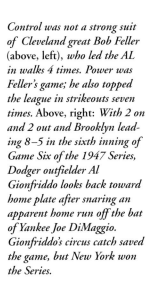

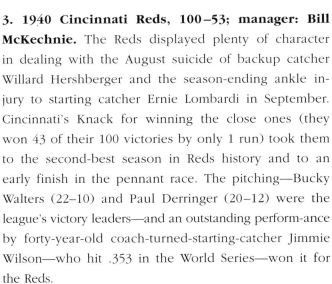

Control was not a strong suit of Cleveland great Bob Feller (above, left), who led the AL in walks 4 times. Power was Feller's game; he also topped the league in strikeouts seven times. Above, right: With 2 on and 2 out and Brooklyn leading 8–5 in the sixth inning of Game Six of the 1947 Series, Dodger outfielder Al Gionfriddo looks back toward home plate after snaring an apparent home run off the bat of Yankee Joe DiMaggio. Gionfriddo's circus catch saved the game, but New York won the Series.

DECADE PITCHING LEADERS

	National League			American League		
YEAR	PLAYER	TEAM	ERA	PLAYER	TEAM	ERA
1940	Bucky Walters	Cincinnati	2.48	Bob Feller	Cleveland	2.61
1941	Elmer Riddle	Cincinnati	2.24	Thornton Lee	Chicago	2.37
1942	Mort Cooper	St. Louis	1.78	Ted Lyons	Chicago	2.10
1943	Howie Pollet	St. Louis	1.75	Spud Chandler	New York	1.64
1944	Ed Heusser	Cincinnati	2.38	Dizzy Trout	Detroit	2.12
1945	Hank Borowy	Chicago	2.13	Hal Newhouser	Detroit	1.81
1946	Howie Pollet	St. Louis	2.10	Hal Newhouser	Detroit	1.94
1947	Warren Spahn	Boston	2.33	Joe Haynes	Chicago	2.42
1948	Harry Brecheen	St. Louis	2.24	Gene Bearden	Cleveland	2.43
1949	Dave Koslo	New York	2.50	Mike Garcia	Cleveland	2.36

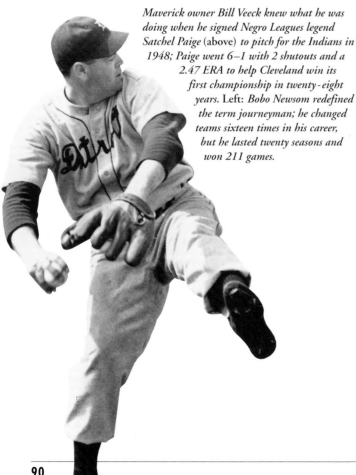

Maverick owner Bill Veeck knew what he was doing when he signed Negro Leagues legend Satchel Paige (above) to pitch for the Indians in 1948; Paige went 6–1 with 2 shutouts and a 2.47 ERA to help Cleveland win its first championship in twenty-eight years. Left: Bobo Newsom redefined the term journeyman; he changed teams sixteen times in his career, but he lasted twenty seasons and won 211 games.

2. 1946, St. Louis Cardinals over Boston Red Sox, 4 games to 3. This Series features two great hitters, Boston's Ted Williams and St. Louis's Stan Musial, as well as the National League's winningest pitcher, Howie Pollet (21–10). Stealing the spotlight, though, are Cardinals Harry Walker, who bats .412 and leads all players with 6 RBI, Enos Slaughter, who comes back after suffering a severe elbow injury in Game Five to score the decisive run in the final game, and Harry Brecheen, a .500 pitcher during the regular season who gives up just 1 earned run in 20 innings and wins 3 games in the Series.

3. 1940, Cincinnati Reds over Detroit Tigers, 4 games to 3. Detroit's Bobo Newsom wins his first 2 starts—tossing consecutive complete games and giving up just 2 runs in 18 innings—and comes back to pitch Game Seven on one day's rest. But he is outdueled by Cincinnati's Paul Derringer—whom he defeated in Game One—in a 2–1 thriller that gives the Reds their first World Series title since their tainted victory over the Black Sox in 1919.

Worth Remembering

More Than Your Typical Owner. Indians owner Bill Veeck added a lot of much-needed color to the game in the late 1940s with his zany promotions and innovative ideas. For example, he spent thirty thousand dollars to fly in orchids from Hawaii to give to the first twenty thousand women who attended an Indians game; he held a night for "Good Old Joe Earley," when gifts were presented to an average fan; he staged a nylon-stocking giveaway day for female fans; he conducted a burial ceremony for the 1948 pennant after the Indians had fallen out of the 1949 race; he opened a nursery in the stadium so parents could attend games together; he signed Negro Leagues legend Satchel Paige in 1948; and he allegedly played games with the fences in Municipal Stadium—putting the fences on wheels so they could be moved back when power-hitting teams such as the Yankees came to town. The 1948 season epitomized Veeck's success as a savvy baseball man, though: his club drew a record 2,260,627 fans and won its first World Series in twenty-eight years.

Winning with—and Without—the Lip. The controversial Leo Durocher managed the Dodgers for eight and a half years, winning a pennant in 1941, before he stunned the Brooklyn faithful by taking over as manager of the rival Giants in July 1948. New York finished fifth under

Durocher that season but went on to win two pennants and a World Series in seven seasons under the Lip. Meanwhile, Brooklyn, which won a pennant under Burt Shotton while Durocher was suspended in the 1947 season, finished first again under Shotton in 1949.

Gardella's Challenge. Danny Gardella, a former Giants outfielder who defected to the Mexican League in 1946, was one of eighteen former major leaguers granted amnesty and permitted to return to the majors in 1949. Gardella sued Major League Baseball for $300,000 in damages, challenging the validity of the reserve clause, which restricted a player to the team that owned his rights. Gardella won an out-of-court settlement when his case reached a federal circuit court; although no punitive action was taken against baseball, Gardella's challenge prompted a congressional investigation of Major League Baseball's monopoly practices and raised doubts about the future of the reserve clause, which would suffer its ultimate demise in the 1970s.

Poetry in Motion. Already famed in verse, the legendary trio of shortstop Joe Tinker, second baseman Johnny Evers, and first baseman Frank Chance, teammates with the Cubs from 1902 to 1912, were enshrined in the Hall of Fame—appropriately in the same year—when the Hall of Fame's Committee on Oldtimers selected them in 1946.

DiMaggio's Number Comes Up—Twice. On July 17, 1941, numbers were being drawn in New York City to determine which men would be drafted into the army. The second number drawn belonged to Joe DiMaggio—not

Nicknamed "Old Aches and Pains," Chicago White Sox shortstop Luke Appling hit .300 or better in nine straight seasons (1933–41) and sixteen times overall in his twenty-year career. He also set a major league record by leading the American League in assists seven straight years and played 2,218 games at shortstop to break Rabbit Maranville's record.

DECADE BATTING LEADERS

	National League			American League		
YEAR	PLAYER	TEAM	AVG.	PLAYER	TEAM	AVG.
1940	Debs Garms	Pittsburgh	.355	Joe DiMaggio	New York	.352
1941	Pete Reiser	Brooklyn	.343	Ted Williams	Boston	.406
1942	Ernie Lombardi	Boston	.330	Ted Williams	Boston	.356
1943	Stan Musial	St. Louis	.357	Luke Appling	Chicago	.328
1944	Dixie Walker	Brooklyn	.357	Lou Boudreau	Cleveland	.327
1945	Phil Cavarretta	Chicago	.355	Snuffy Stirnweiss	New York	.309
1946	Stan Musial	St. Louis	.365	Mickey Vernon	Washington	.353
1947	Harry Walker	St. Lo., Phil.	.363	Ted Williams	Boston	.343
1948	Stan Musial	St. Louis	.376	Ted Williams	Boston	.369
1949	Jackie Robinson	Brooklyn	.342	George Kell	Detroit	.343

the Joe DiMaggio, but a twenty-one-year-old with the same name. That night, Joltin' Joe's record 56-game hitting streak was snapped in Cleveland. The Yankee Clipper joined his namesake in the military for a three-year hitch after the 1942 season.

DECADE SPOTLIGHT

Pete Gray: Baseball's First One-Armed Wonder

Where does one begin to tell the story of Pete Gray, baseball's one-armed outfielder of 1945?

Do you start with Gray at the age of six, when he fell off the running board of a grocer's delivery truck near his home in Nanticoke, Pennsylvania, and caught and badly mangled his right arm in the spokes of the truck's wheel, which resulted in amputation of the arm just below the shoulder?

Do you start with Gray, who perfected his one-armed batting and fielding (he would catch the ball in his left-handed glove, let the ball roll across his chest as he stuck the glove under his stump, then catch the ball in his hand and throw it) well enough to get on semipro teams in Pine Grove and Scranton for one hundred dollars a week, washing out in his first pro tryout with the Cardinals?

A classic swing: Joe DiMaggio (top) *hit 30 or more home runs seven times and had a lifetime batting average of .325.* **Above:** *Pete Gray as a member of the Memphis Chicks on April 29, 1943; Gray made it to the major leagues two years later as a member of the St. Louis Browns.*

Do you start with Gray in 1942 at the age of twenty-seven, in his first season of organized baseball after finally convincing scouts that he could play, hitting .381 for the Three Rivers Club of the Canadian-American League before a broken collarbone and torn ligaments cut his season short after 42 games?

Do you start with Gray in the Southern Association in 1944, putting together the best season of his career—a .333 batting average, 5 home runs, 60 RBI, and a record-tying 68 stolen bases—and being named the "most courageous athlete of 1944" by the sportswriters of Philadelphia?

Or do you start in the spring of 1945, when the Browns, who had purchased Gray's contract for twenty thousand dollars, let the thirty-year-old finally realize his dream of playing in the major leagues? That year, Gray's only season in the bigs, is probably the best place to begin his story because his stint with the Browns is what made Gray, for better or worse, an icon of wartime baseball in the forties.

Gray, whose real last name was Wyshner—he changed it at that first tryout with the Cards—was not a bad player, one-armed or otherwise. He was fast on the base paths and in the field and adept with the drag bunt, but he was not a major league–caliber talent. Still, he managed to hit .218 with 6 doubles and 2 triples in 77 games with the Browns in his one major league season.

Gray's name resurfaced in news stories in the late 1980s when the California Angels drafted a one-handed pitcher from the University of Michigan named Jim Abbott, who continues to forge a successful major league career. Abbott's story is certainly a tale of triumph over adversity; Gray's is that and so much more. For although Gray was admired by fans for his talent and determination—his life was the subject of the 1986 made-for-TV movie *A Winner Never Quits* starring Keith Carradine—there are downsides to his legacy. He has gone down in history as the personification of baseball's depleted talent base during World War II—all too often the prevailing sentiment was: things were *so* bad during the war that the Browns actually had a guy with one arm playing the outfield.

WHAT'S IN/WHAT'S OUT IN THE 1940s

In	Out
Black players in the major leagues	Black players in the Negro Leagues
Low batting averages	Stolen bases
Inferior baseballs	Offensive production
Managerial strategy	Relying simply on talent
Power pitchers	Control pitchers
Fans choosing the All-Star team	Managers selecting the All-Star team
Commissioner Happy Chandler	Commissioner Kenesaw Mountain Landis
Yankees vs. Dodgers	Athletics vs. Cardinals
Baseball as a diversion from the war	Baseball as merely entertainment
Joe DiMaggio vs. Ted Williams	Babe Ruth vs. Jimmie Foxx
Women on the baseball diamond	Women in the kitchen
Baseball in Japan	Baseball as solely America's game
Night baseball	Day games only
Inferior players	Ted Williams, Joe DiMaggio, Bob Feller, and hundreds of other players—for three or four years, while they were off fighting World War II

And, while his presence helped boost attendance both at home and on the road at a time when the game sorely needed a draw, Gray's teammates hardly welcomed him enthusiastically. At least one St. Louis player, Mark Christman, believed Gray cost the defending AL-champion Browns a chance to return to the World Series in 1945. "Pete did great with what he had," Christman was quoted as saying in Bill Mead's *Even the Browns*. "But he cost us the pennant in '45. We finished third, only 6 games out. There were an awful lot of ground balls hit to him in center, and the hitters kept running right into second. That cost us 8 or 10 games." And many of the great black players of the day, who thought the wartime talent depletion might finally open the door for them to come to the majors, also resented Gray: "How do you think I felt when I saw a one-armed [white] outfielder?" pitcher Chet Brewer, a star with the Kansas City Monarchs of the Negro American League asked rhetorically.

These days, though, most of the bad memories of Gray's experience have faded, both for him and for the fans. Gray is still more than a historical footnote, however. "You'd think people would forget about me," Gray told a reporter from the *Baltimore Sun* a few years ago. "But I still get a lot of fan mail—three or four letters a day. I don't know where some people still find pictures of me."

The 1950s
Bad Times, Good Times

The 1950s are often referred to as "the golden age of baseball." But were things really that great? It depends on your perspective. If you were a New York Yankees fan you didn't want it to end; your club won eight pennants and six world championships in the decade. If you rooted for the Dodgers, Giants, or Braves you rode an emotional roller coaster; your teams perennially contended, won nine pennants between them, and—in the case of the Dodgers and Braves—even managed to beat the Yankees in the Series. But you also had to watch your club pick up and move west for greener—and more profitable—pastures. If you were a supporter of any other team, "wait till next year" was your motto.

But if you were the owner of a baseball team at the beginning of the decade, you weren't looking at a rosy picture. Baseball's antitrust exemption was jeopardized by several well-publicized congressional hearings. Total attendance in the major leagues, which had hit a postwar peak of nearly twenty-one million in 1948, dropped in each of the next five years and was down to 14.4 million by 1953. Down the ladder the outlook was even worse; total attendance in the minor leagues fell from a high of forty-two million in the previous decade to 15.5 million by 1957. Maverick Browns owner Bill Veeck correctly observed in 1958 that the days when baseball was "America's only game in town" were over.

Competition from other sources of leisure was indeed a big reason why baseball experienced financial problems during a period of great economic growth for the nation. The changing dynamics of the American city was another factor. Baseball had grown up and thrived in the major metropolises, but now the suburbs were becoming the center of family life. The neighborhoods around many urban stadiums—like the parks themselves—were decaying. And visitors from the suburbs needed parking, which was in short supply around stadiums such as Ebbets Field and the Polo Grounds. There were plenty of other forms

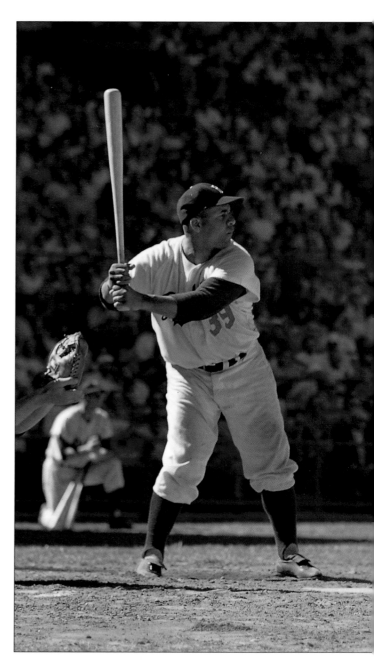

Hall of Famer Roy Campanella (above), *formerly of the Baltimore Elite Giants, was one of many Negro League stars who followed Jackie Robinson to the majors. Campy caught for the Brooklyn Dodgers for ten seasons and won three Most Valuable Player Awards. As the New York Yankee dynasty rolled on in the 1950s, into Joe DiMaggio's considerable shoes stepped Mickey Mantle* (opposite page), *another three-time MVP.*

of recreation besides attending a baseball game, and besides, one could always watch the game on TV. A *Sports Illustrated* reader from Abilene, Texas, summed up the prevalent attitude in a 1958 letter: "Why should a guy with a boat in the driveway, golf clubs in the car, bowling ball and tennis racket in the closet, a trunkful of camping equipment, two boys in Little League, and a body full of energy left over from shorter working hours pay to sit and do nothing but watch a mediocre game?"

The onus was clearly on the owners to do something, and—as is always the case when the bottom line is threatened—they did. If the fans wouldn't come to the game, they would take the game to the fans, or more accurately, they would take the team to a city where the fans *would* come out. So began the most tumultuous period of franchise movement in the game's history. Baseball's geographical setup had remained unchanged for half a century, but five teams relocated between 1953 and 1957. It started with the Boston Braves, who moved to Milwaukee and brand new County Stadium, unique and precedent-setting in that it was surrounded not by buildings but by spacious parking lots. It continued with the St. Louis Browns, who became the Baltimore Orioles and—in another portent of things to come—shared the game's first multipurpose stadium with the National Football League's Colts. The Athletics jumped to Kansas City, leaving New York and Chicago as the only cities with NL and AL teams, and even that would not be the case for long; the upheaval culminated with the moves that left New York City reeling: the Dodgers' and Giants' migrations to California.

The Giants, in particular, had suffered at the gate. Attendance at the shabby Polo Grounds had dropped 50 percent in three years. And while the Dodgers enjoyed a steady flow of customers at Ebbets Field, the creaking stadium seated only thirty-five thousand, restricting ticket receipts. The American League had attempted to place a team in Los Angeles in 1942, but World War II had postponed those plans. Dodgers owner Walter O'Malley, drawn by the promise of California's unlimited potential, decided to make the break after the 1957 season.

The burgeoning population on the West Coast was an attractive proposition for O'Malley, a cool visionary. He reasoned that improved air travel and the guarantee of large radio and television markets decreased the risk of a franchise move. To that point, the only baseball in Southern California was played by the Los Angeles Angels and the Hollywood Stars of the AAA Pacific Coast League. Arguing that there was strength in numbers, O'Malley con-

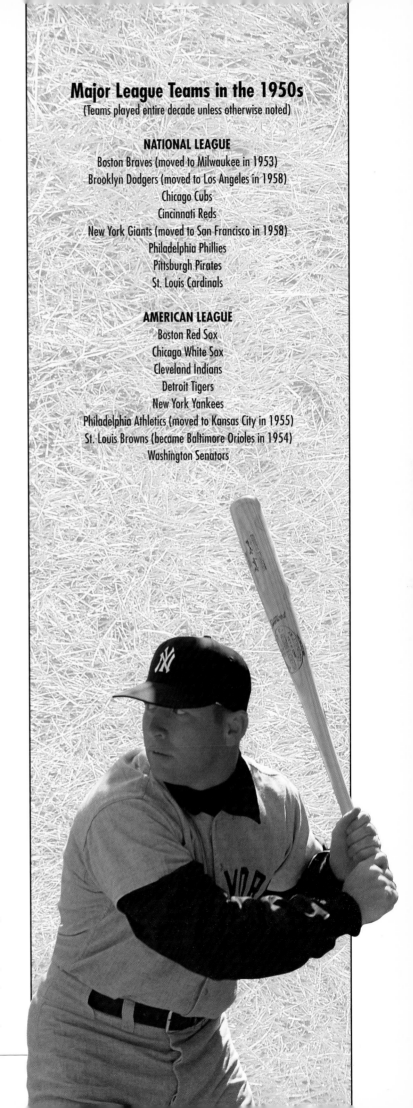

Major League Teams in the 1950s
(Teams played entire decade unless otherwise noted)

NATIONAL LEAGUE
Boston Braves (moved to Milwaukee in 1953)
Brooklyn Dodgers (moved to Los Angeles in 1958)
Chicago Cubs
Cincinnati Reds
New York Giants (moved to San Francisco in 1958)
Philadelphia Phillies
Pittsburgh Pirates
St. Louis Cardinals

AMERICAN LEAGUE
Boston Red Sox
Chicago White Sox
Cleveland Indians
Detroit Tigers
New York Yankees
Philadelphia Athletics (moved to Kansas City in 1955)
St. Louis Browns (became Baltimore Orioles in 1954)
Washington Senators

vinced Giants owner Horace Stoneham to move to San Francisco, another untapped market. According to Stoneham, it was a move based not on emotion but on fiscal reality. "We had to go now," Stoneham said, "because if we delayed, such a favorable opportunity might not present itself again. I am as sentimental a New Yorker as anyone else, but we simply didn't draw here."

And though that was only partly true, the decision was made. The response in New York was predictably hostile. Suddenly, two of the metropolitan area's three teams were headed three thousand miles away. This was a different, dislocated kind of feeling that fans experienced, one that future generations would come to know on a regular basis as teams played cities off one another for the best deal.

And so, the Dodgers—from Gil Hodges to Sandy Koufax to Duke Snider to Don Zimmer—all packed their bags for Los Angeles. Giants Manager Bill Rigney brought Willie Mays and Hank Sauer with him to San Francisco. The Dodgers played on a temporary field in the cavernous Los Angeles Memorial Coliseum, while the Giants made do in cramped Seals Stadium. By 1962, the Dodgers and Giants had their own state-of-the-art venues.

The moves jump-started attendance—the Braves set a single-season record of 1.8 million in 1953 and the two West Coast clubs drew very well—although the recovery would not happen overnight. Still, by planting teams in some of the major midwestern and western population centers, baseball was more aptly living up to its moniker of "the national game." There were more cities that wanted major league teams, however. In 1959 it appeared that the Continental League, a proposed third major league, might serve that purpose. But instead the threat of that competition, along with the prospect of congressional intervention, prompted baseball to make another radical change in the early sixties: expansion.

Reversal of fortune: in 1952 the Boston Braves finished in seventh place and drew just three hundred thousand fans. The next year they moved to Milwaukee, finished second, and saw attendance increase 500 percent. The following year they signed Hank Aaron (top). Three years later they won their first World Series since 1914. Willie Mays (above), who began his career in the Negro Leagues with the Birmingham Black Barons, later turned the Polo Grounds (below) into a field of dreams, helping the Giants to a pennant in 1951 and a world championship in 1954.

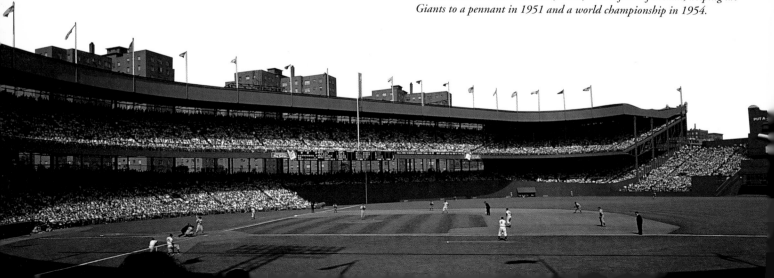

1950: Rules change: the strike zone is to include only the area from the batter's armpits to the top of his knees. A player must play in at least two-thirds of his team's scheduled games to qualify as the league leader in batting average or slugging percentage. A starting pitcher earns the win if he pitches at least 5 innings and his team is in the lead when the relief pitcher enters the game and never relinquishes the lead. If the starting pitcher does not pitch the required number of innings but relievers hold the lead, the official scorer credits the victory to the reliever he believes to be the most effective. Bats are limited to 42 inches (106.6cm) in length and no substance may be applied to the surface farther than 18 inches (45.7cm) from the base of the handle. Umpires may penalize a batter 1 strike for failing to get into the batter's box within a reasonable length of time.

1950: Ted Williams signs a contract with the Boston Red Sox for a record $125,000 for the 1950 season.

1950: Major League Baseball signs a six-million-dollar contract for television rights to the World Series, with all revenues to go to the players' pension fund.

February 1950: *Senator Joseph McCarthy announces that he possesses a list of people under suspicion of Communist connections, prompting a Senate subcommittee investigation.*

June 25, 1950: *Armed with Soviet-made weapons, North Korean troops invade South Korea. The next day President Truman authorizes U.S. forces to aid South Korean troops, and on June 27 the United Nations Security Council adopts a resolution calling for armed intervention in Korea.*

July 11, 1950: The National League wins an All-Star Game thriller—its first All-Star victory since 1944— on Red Schoendienst's fourteenth-inning home run. Red Sox slugger Ted Williams fractures his left elbow when, while making a catch in the first inning, he crashes into the left-field wall. He stays in the game until the ninth, but the injury will keep him out of the Boston

lineup until late in the year. Billy Goodman, Williams' replacement in the Red Sox outfield, who also plays all four infield positions during the season, hits .354 in 424 at bats to become the first utility player in major league history to win a batting title.

**The Tall Tactician Calls It a Career
October 18, 1950:** After fifty years as manager of the Philadelphia Athletics, Connie Mack retires from baseball. His fifty-three-year managerial career has produced 3,776 victories and 4,025 defeats in 7,878 games (all all-time highs), as well as eight pennants and five world championships. In 1953, Philadelphia's Shibe Park is renamed Connie Mack Stadium in his honor.

1951: The Topps Company introduces the first pack of baseball cards, packed with caramel candy, not chewing gum.

1951: Rules change: a pitcher must pitch a total of at least 1 inning for every scheduled game (rather than the 10 complete games and 100 innings previously required) to qualify as the league leader in earned-run average or fielding average. A player must have at least 400 times at bat to qualify as the league leader in batting average or slugging average.

July 10, 1951: The National League accounts for 4 of an All-Star Game—record 6 home runs to beat the American League 8–3 in Detroit's Tiger Stadium. The victory, which marks the first time that the NL wins back-to-back All-Star Games, is the second of the senior circuit's 4 straight wins.

The voice of experience: Philadelphia Athletics manager Connie Mack, a catcher for most of his playing career, shows his players that he knows a thing or two about pitching as well.

Standing 3-foot-7 (109.2cm) and wearing uniform number ⅛, Eddie Gaedel of the Browns watches a pitch land in the glove of Bob Swift for a ball. The umpire is Ed Hurley.

August 19, 1951: In what is St. Louis Browns owner Bill Veeck's most outrageous promotional stunt yet, twenty-six-year-old Eddie Gaedel, a 3-foot-7 (109.2cm), 65-pound (29.5kg) midget, comes to bat as a pinch hitter against Detroit. Tigers pitcher Bob Cain walks Gaedel on 4 pitches, but irate AL President Will Harridge sees to it that Gaedel never plays in the majors again.

Frick Replaces Chandler
September 20, 1951: Commissioner Happy Chandler, whose contract was not renewed at the major league meetings the previous December, steps down in midsummer. Ford Frick leaves his post as NL president to replace Chandler, who clashed with club owners on a variety of issues in the 1940s, including the integration of baseball, the Danny Gardella–reserve clause case, and the players' pension-fund movement. Cincinnati's Warren Giles takes over as NL president.

The Giants Win the Pennant
October 3, 1951: In the third and decisive NL playoff game, Bobby Thomson's "shot heard 'round the world," a 3-run homer off Brooklyn's Ralph Branca, lifts the New York Giants to a 5–4 win and the NL championship.

October 10, 1951: In the final game for Joe DiMaggio, who will retire after the

season, the Yankees beat the Giants 4–3 in Game Six to wrap up the World Series. DiMaggio's thirteen-year totals: a .325 batting average, 361 home runs, and a .579 slugging percentage. The Yankee Clipper's final season is also the first year in the majors for Mickey Mantle, who will take over in center field for the Yankees.

1952: By signing a contract with the Harrisburg Senators of the Interstate League, Mrs. Eleanor Engle becomes the first woman to sign a modern-day playing contract in organized baseball. But Minor Leagues Commissioner George Trautman, with Commissioner Ford Frick's approval, voids the contract.

1952: Ted Williams and Willie Mays are among the players who leave baseball for military service in the Korean War.

1952: Walt Dropo of the Detroit Tigers ties Pinky Higgins' 1938 record by recording 12 consecutive hits. Ron Necciai strikes out twenty-seven batters in a no-hitter for Bristol of the Appalachian League.

August 25, 1952: Detroit's Virgil Trucks, who will finish the year with a 5–19 record, pitches his second no-hitter of the season to beat the Yankees 1–0. Trucks' no-hitters are the only ones in the American League this year.

1953: The Major League Baseball Players Association is formed.

1953: As part of an agreement with several AL clubs, ABC-TV and the Falstaff Brewery introduce a televised Saturday afternoon baseball "game of the week." Dizzy Dean and Buddy Blattner provide the commentary for the telecasts, which move to CBS in 1955.

Big-League Ball in Milwaukee
April 1953: During a series of special Major League Baseball meetings to discuss franchise shifts, the American League vetoes St. Louis Browns owner Bill Veeck's proposal to move his club to Baltimore. A few days later, however, Lou Perini receives permission from his fellow NL owners to move his Braves to Milwaukee, giving Major League Baseball its first franchise movement since 1903. Playing in newly built County Stadium—the first stadium to be built with public funds—the Braves rise from seventh place to second and draw a league-record 1,826,397 fans, more than a 500 percent increase over the three hundred thousand they drew in Boston in 1952.

April 9, 1953: Strapped for funds, Browns owner Bill Veeck sells Sportsman's Park to Anheuser-Busch Brewery President August A. Busch, Jr., who renames the park Busch Stadium.

April 17, 1953: The Yankees' Mickey Mantle hits one of the longest home runs on record, a mammoth shot off Washington's Chuck Stobbs that sails out of Washington's Griffith Stadium and travels an estimated 565 feet (172.2m).

May 6, 1953: Bobo Holloman of the Browns becomes the first pitcher in the modern era to throw a no-hitter in his first major league start when he turns the trick against the Athletics. Holloman, however, drops seven of his next nine decisions and is back in the minors by July. He never pitches in the majors again.

June 18, 1953: The Red Sox score a record 17 runs in 1 inning against the Detroit Tigers.

July 27, 1953: *The Korean conflict ends as North Korean and U.N. officials meet in Panmunjom, Korea, to sign the armistice agreement.*

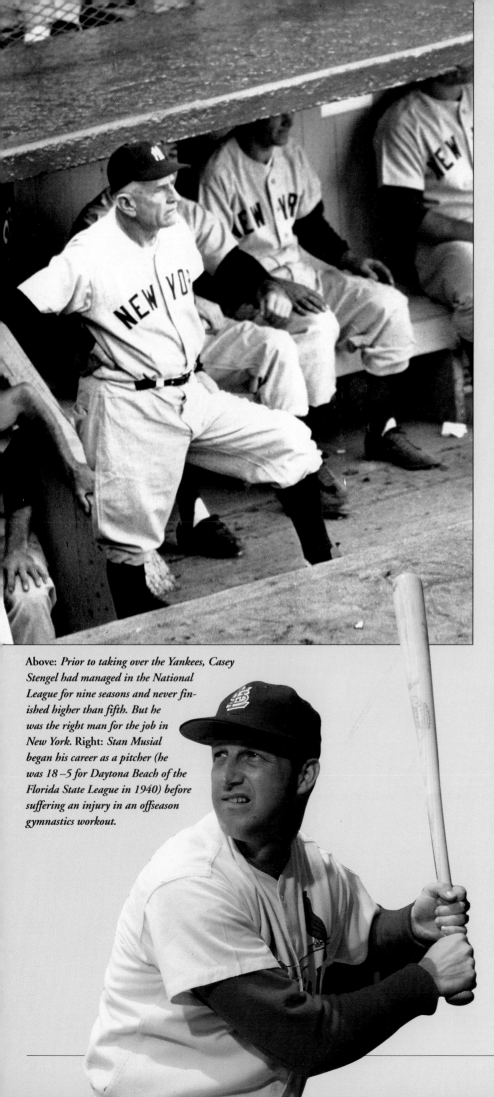

The Yankee Dynasty Rolls On

October 5, 1953: Manager Casey Stengel's Yankees beat the Brooklyn Dodgers 4–3 in Game Six of the World Series to wrap up their record fifth straight world championship.

November 9, 1953: In a case charging baseball with operating illegally in interstate commerce, the U.S. Supreme Court votes 7–2 to reaffirm Justice Oliver Wendell Holmes' 1922 decision that baseball is a sport rather than an interstate business as defined by the federal antitrust laws.

Baseball's Back in Baltimore

November 17, 1953: Browns owner Bill Veeck, whose antics are growing tiresome to his fellow owners, is pressured after the season to sell his financially strapped franchise to a syndicate headed by Clarence W. Miles. The new ownership gains approval to move the club to Baltimore—bringing Major League Baseball to that city for the first time since 1902—where they will take the nickname Orioles and play in Memorial Stadium, a multipurpose sports facility built in 1950.

1954: Cleveland Indians pitcher Bob Feller is elected president of the newly formed Major League Players Association.

1954: Rules change: the custom of players leaving their gloves on the field between innings is no longer permitted. A batter whose fair ball is hit by a thrown glove is awarded three bases. A batter is once again credited with a sacrifice fly if a runner scores on his fly out.

1954: Joe Baumann sets an organized baseball record by hitting 72 home runs for the Roswell club of the Class C Longhorn League. The 6-foot-5-inch (195.5cm), 235-pound (106.6kg) Baumann hits .400 with 188 runs and 224 RBI in just 138 games.

April 13, 1954: With newly acquired Bobby Thomson sidelined by a broken ankle, the Milwaukee Braves decide to try a rookie infielder named Hank Aaron in left field. Aaron hits .280 with 13 homers in 116 games.

May 2, 1954: Stan Musial of the St. Louis Cardinals hits a record 5 home runs in a doubleheader split with the Giants.

Above: *Prior to taking over the Yankees, Casey Stengel had managed in the National League for nine seasons and never finished higher than fifth. But he was the right man for the job in New York.* Right: *Stan Musial began his career as a pitcher (he was 18–5 for Daytona Beach of the Florida State League in 1940) before suffering an injury in an offseason gymnastics workout.*

May 17, 1954: *In* Brown *v.* Board of Education of Topeka, *the U.S. Supreme Court finds the long-standing "separate but equal" doctrine unconstitutional with respect to public education. Next year the court follows up its ruling by ordering that desegregation of public schools be accomplished with "all deliberate speed."*

July 13, 1954: Nellie Fox's 2-run single in the eighth inning lifts the American League to an 11–9 win in Cleveland in the highest-scoring All-Star Game in history. Washington's Dean Stone is the winning pitcher even though he does not retire a single hitter; he comes on with 2 down in the eighth and records his only out by catching Red Schoendienst on an attempted steal of home.

September 8, 1954: *The United States is one of the eight nations to join a defense alliance in Southeast Asia in an effort to contain and discourage Communism in that area of the world.*

September 12, 1954: The pennant-bound Indians draw a record crowd of 86,563 for a doubleheader against the Yankees.

The Athletics Are on the Move
November 1954: After the season, a group headed by Arnold Johnson of Chicago purchases the Athletics from the family of Connie Mack and moves the franchise to Kansas City, leaving New York and Chicago as the only two-team cities. Although the Athletics' new home field, Municipal Stadium (a rebuilt version of Blues Stadium, an existing Triple A facility), has just 30,611 seats, the club draws 1,393,054 in its first season in Kansas City.

1955: Dodgers owner Walter O'Malley makes arrangements for his Dodgers to play 7 home games in Jersey City's Roosevelt Stadium in 1956, and predicts that 1957 will be his team's last season at Ebbets Field.

1955: Rules change: umpires enforce a new rule to speed up games—a pitch that is not delivered within twenty seconds is called a ball.

1955: Batting helmets, introduced three years previously by Pittsburgh Pirates General Manager Branch Rickey, are required in the National League. The

American League follows suit in 1956, with a grandfather clause.

July 19, 1955: Detroit pitcher Babe Birrer records 6 runs batted in on a pair of 3-run homers in the Tigers' 12–4 win over the Baltimore Orioles. Those are the only runs Birrer will drive in during his three major league seasons.

1956: Pittsburgh's Dale Long sets a record by homering in 8 straight games. Mickey Mantle of the Yankees wins the Triple Crown with a .353 average, 52 homers, and 130 RBI.

Larsen's Perfection
October 8, 1956: Yankees pitcher Don Larsen makes history by throwing the only perfect game in World Series history, a 2–0 gem that beats the Dodgers and sets New York up for a 7-game Series victory. It is the major leagues' first perfect game since 1922.

Below: Yankees catcher Yogi Berra (8) jumps in the arms of Don Larsen and third baseman Andy Carey runs to join the celebration after Larsen struck out Dale Mitchell to wrap up his perfect game in the 1956 Series. Bottom: Cleveland's Herb Score, who won 36 games and led the league in strikeouts his first two seasons, was never the same after 1957.

October 1956: Brooklyn's Don Newcombe goes 27–7 with a 3.06 earned-run average to win the first Cy Young Award, given to honor the game's outstanding pitcher. Newcombe is also named the NL's MVP.

1957: The NBC television network debuts its own "game of the week" telecast, with Lindsay Nelson and veteran manager Leo Durocher at the mikes.

1957: Rules change: a player must have a total of at least 3.1 plate appearances for every scheduled game to qualify as the league leader in batting average or slugging percentage. An infielder or outfielder must play in at least two-thirds of the scheduled number of games at a position to qualify as the league leader in fielding average at that position; the minimum for catchers is one-half of the scheduled number of games. Any pitcher throwing an illegal pitch or a defaced ball is thrown out of the game and is subject to a ten-day suspension.

The Dodgers–Giants Rivalry Moves West

1957: NL owners approve two more franchise moves that dramatically alter the league's geographical setup. In August the Dodgers announce a move to Los Angeles, where they will play on a makeshift field at the Coliseum. In February of 1958 Giants owner Horace Stoneham, at the urging of Dodgers owner Walter O'Malley, moves his club to San Francisco, where they will play in tiny Seals Stadium, former home of the city's Pacific Coast League team. Both clubs draw well in 1958, however—the Dodgers attract a club-record 1,845,556 and the Giants draw 1,272,625—and by 1962 both teams will have large, new stadiums.

January 5, 1957: When the Dodgers trade him to the Giants, Brooklyn's Jackie Robinson opts to retire instead. He ends his spectacular ten-year career with a .311 batting average.

May 7, 1957: Cleveland's twenty-three-year-old sensation Herb Score, who had posted a 20–9 record in 1956 and led the league in strikeouts in each of his first two seasons, is struck in the eye by a line drive off the bat of the Yankees' Gil McDougald. Score returns, but he never regains his form; he goes 17–26 over the final five

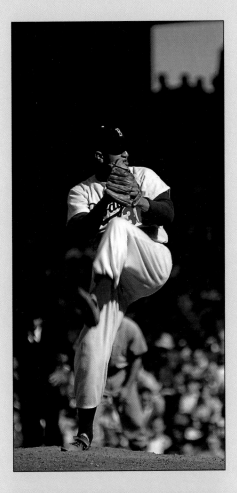

years of his career. The twenty-eight-year-old McDougald, likewise, is a different player after the incident; he enters the season with a .284 career average but falls off to .253 over his final three years.

Cincy Fans Stuff the Ballot Box

July 1957: Taking advantage of an All-Star voting system that has no safeguards against ballot-box stuffing, Cincinnati fans go wild and vote in Reds players at seven of the eight starting spots for the National League (St. Louis' Stan Musial is the only non-Reds player voted in). Commissioner Ford Frick intervenes and replaces Gus Bell and Wally Post in the starting outfield with Willie Mays and Hank Aaron. The all-star vote is subsequently taken from the fans and given to the players, managers, and coaches.

September 4, 1957: *By calling out the Arkansas National Guard to prevent black students from entering Central High School in Little Rock, Arkansas governor Orval Faubus violates the Supreme Court ruling in* Brown v. Board of Education of Topeka. *Sixteen days later, after conferring with President Eisenhower and receiving a federal injunction, Governor Faubus orders the state troops out of the high school. Three days later the black students withdraw from school because of rioting. But on September 25, U.S. Army troops arrive in Little Rock by order of President Eisenhower and escort the students to school.*

October 1957: The Braves set a single-season attendance record by drawing 2,215,104 fans.

October 4, 1957: *The Soviet Union sends the first satellite into space. The surprise launching of Sputnik prompts the United States to speed up its space program in an effort to establish preeminence in this expanding field.*

January 28, 1958: Dodgers all-star catcher Roy Campanella, age thirty-six, is paralyzed in an early-morning auto accident on Long Island. His career is over after ten years that produced a .276 batting average and 242 home runs.

Fueled by ex-Negro Leaguers such as Don Newcombe (top) *and Roy Campanella* (left), *the Dodgers won five pennants in the 1950s.*

Above: *The Splendid Splinter, Ted Williams, didn't tail off much at the end of his career; he won batting titles at age thirty-nine and forty and homered in his final at bat in 1960.* Below: *The Kitten, Harvey Haddix, pitched what might well be the greatest game ever on May 26, 1959 — and lost.*

October 1958: At age forty, Ted Williams hits .328 to win the sixth and final batting title of his career.

1959: Hall of Famer Joe Cronin, a successful player and manager who is the Red Sox general manager since 1948, replaces Will Harridge as AL president.

1959: Maverick owner Bill Veeck returns to baseball by purchasing controlling interest in the Chicago White Sox from the Comiskey family. The White Sox, who subsequently introduce the practice of uniforms with the players' names on the back, go on to win their first pennant in forty years.

1959: Rules change: professional fields built after June 1, 1958, must have a minimum of 325 feet (99m) down the first and third baselines and a minimum of 400 feet (121.9m) to the center-field fence.

1959: The Red Sox become the final major league club to break the color line when they add black infielder Pumpsie Green to the roster.

1959: The financial success of the All-Star Game prompts owners and players to add a second All-Star Game each summer to provide additional revenue for the players' pension fund. The new format is scrapped after four years in favor of the traditional single game.

1959: Branch Rickey announces plans for the formation of a third major league, to be called the Continental League, with franchises in New York, Houston, Toronto, Minneapolis, and Denver. In retrospect, the league, which includes Ford Frick, Warren Giles, and Joe Cronin among its backers, is regarded as an elaborate bluff to coerce the existing leagues into expansion.

1959: Pittsburgh's Roy Face posts an 18–1 record for a .947 winning percentage, the best mark in the modern era. All his decisions come in relief; he does not start a single game all season. The thirty-one-year-old righty also saves 10 games.

May 26, 1959: Pittsburgh's Harvey Haddix pitches an improbable 12 perfect innings against Milwaukee, but loses 1–0 on Joe Adcock's hit in the thirteenth.

October 6, 1959: Game Five of the World Series featuring the Dodgers and the White Sox draws a record crowd of 92,706 to the Los Angeles Coliseum.

Man of the Decade: Casey Stengel

He didn't look—or act—the part, but Stengel, who won ten pennants and seven World Series in his twelve seasons as manager of the Yankees, was a shrewd tactician and one of the game's most astute managers. Beneath his convoluted "Stengelese" was a wealth of innovative baseball knowledge. A student of the legendary John McGraw, Stengel furthered the science of platooning players, the use of relief pitching, and the concept of player versatility. Some say it was no great challenge to manage a team with the talent of the Yankees, but no manager in the game's history—no matter how much talent he had—has ever matched Stengel's run of five world championships in his first five seasons with the Yankees.

Most Memorable Games

1. October 3, 1951, at the Polo Grounds; New York Giants 5, Brooklyn Dodgers 4. In the third and decisive NL playoff game, Brooklyn's Don Newcombe has a 4–1 lead and needs just 3 outs to wrap up the pennant for the Dodgers. But singles by New York's Alvin Dark and Don Mueller and a double by Whitey Lockman cut the lead to 4–2. Ralph Branca—wearing uniform number 13—comes on to face Bobby Thomson, who makes history on the second pitch with a game-winning, 3-run homer to left.

2. 1956 World Series, Game Five, October 8 at Yankee Stadium; New York Yankees 2, Brooklyn Dodgers 0. With the Series tied at 2 games apiece, New York pins its hopes on Don Larsen, a twenty-seven-year-old right-hander with a 30–40 career record who was knocked out in the second inning of Game Two. On this day, however, Larsen is untouchable. He pitches the only perfect game in the history of the Fall Classic—requiring just 97 pitches—and puts the Yankees on the brink of another championship.

3. May 26, 1959, at County Stadium; Milwaukee Braves 1, Pittsburgh Pirates 0. Pittsburgh lefty Harvey Haddix throws 12 perfect innings, only to lose in the thirteenth when Felix Mantilla reaches base on third baseman Don Hoak's throwing error, Hank Aaron walks, and Joe Adcock doubles. Milwaukee's Lew Burdette allows 12 hits but no runs in 13 innings to earn the win.

The Old Professor, Casey Stengel, won ten pennants and seven World Series in twelve seasons as New York Yankee manager—including an unprecedented five championships in a row in his first 5 years, 1949–1953.

October 8, 1956: the Yankee Stadium scoreboard tells the story as Don Larsen delivers the ninety-seventh and final pitch of his World Series perfect game against the Brooklyn Dodgers. Billy Martin is the second baseman.

4. 1955 World Series, Game Seven, October 4 at Yankee Stadium; Brooklyn Dodgers 2, New York Yankees 0. Series Most Valuable Player Johnny Podres goes the distance to pick up his second win of the Series and give Brooklyn its first championship. With two on and none out in the sixth, Dodgers left fielder Sandy Amoros saves the day with a spectacular running, one-handed catch of Yogi Berra's drive just inside the foul line.

5. October 1, 1950, at Ebbets Field; Philadelphia Phillies 4, Brooklyn Dodgers 1. On the final day of the season, Brooklyn trails Philadelphia by 1 game and must win to force a playoff. With the score tied 1–1 in the ninth, Philly's Richie Ashburn throws out Cal Abrams at the plate, and Robin Roberts escapes a bases-loaded, 1-out jam by retiring Carl Furillo and Gil Hodges. Then in the top of the tenth, Dick Sisler deposits a Don Newcombe pitch into the left-field seats for a pennant-winning 3-run homer.

Roy Campanella won his third MVP award in five years in 1955, when he hit .318 with 32 homers and 107 RBI. He added 2 homers in the World Series as the Dodgers beat the Yankees for their first championship.

Best Pennant Races

1. 1951 National League: New York Giants–Brooklyn Dodgers. Brooklyn leads New York by 13½ games on August 12, but the Giants reel off 16 straight wins to narrow the gap and post an overall record of 39–8 down the stretch to finish in a dead heat with the Dodgers. After each team wins 1 game in the ensuing best-of-three play-off, the Giants stage another miracle comeback to take the flag with a dramatic 5–4 win in the third game; Bobby Thomson's 3-run homer caps New York's game-winning, 4-run rally in the ninth.

2. 1950 National League: Philadelphia Phillies– Brooklyn Dodgers. Brooklyn shaved the Whiz Kids' lead from 7 games to 1 in just nine days, and the Dodgers appear poised to repeat as NL champs. But the Phillies, needing to beat Brooklyn in the regular-season finale to avoid a pennant playoff, hold off the Dodgers 4–1 on Dick Sisler's 3-run homer in the tenth inning.

3. 1959 National League: Brooklyn Dodgers– Milwaukee Braves–New York Giants. New York leads Los Angeles and Milwaukee by 2 games with 8 to play, but the Dodgers beat the Giants three times in a row in late September and New York finishes with 7 losses in its last 8 games to fall out of the race. The Braves, meanwhile, keep pace with Brooklyn and force a playoff, the third in NL history. This time the Dodgers—who had lost the two previous playoffs in 1946 and 1951—make sure the third time is the charm by beating Milwaukee in 2 straight games.

DECADE PITCHING LEADERS

	National League			American League		
YEAR	PLAYER	TEAM	ERA	PLAYER	TEAM	ERA
1950	Jim Hearn	St. Lo./N.Y.	2.49	Early Wynn	Cleveland	3.20
1951	Chet Nichols	Boston	2.88	Saul Rogovin	Det./Chi.	2.78
1952	Hoyt Wilhelm	New York	2.43	Allie Reynolds	New York	2.06
1953	Warren Spahn	Milwaukee	2.10	Eddie Lopat	New York	2.42
1954	Johnny Antonelli	New York	2.30	Mike Garcia	Cleveland	2.64
1955	Bob Friend	Pittsburgh	2.83	Billy Pierce	Chicago	1.97
1956	Lew Burdette	Milwaukee	2.70	Whitey Ford	New York	2.47
1957	Johnny Podres	Brooklyn	2.66	Bobby Shantz	New York	2.45
1958	Stu Miller	San Francisco	2.47	Whitey Ford	New York	2.01
1959	Sam Jones	San Francisco	2.83	Hoyt Wilhelm	Baltimore	2.19

Best Teams

1. 1953 New York Yankees, 99–52; manager: Casey Stengel. On their way to an unprecedented fifth straight championship, the Yanks got out of the gate fast, winning 9 of their first 11 and posting an 18-game winning streak in May to pad a comfortable lead that they never relinquished. New York had baseball's best pitching (3.20 staff ERA), led by Whitey Ford (18–6), league ERA champ Eddie Lopat (16–4, 2.43), Johnny Sain (14–7), Vic Raschi (13–6), and Allie Reynolds (13–7, 13 saves). The Bronx Bombers also led the league in batting average (.273) and runs (801), with Yogi Berra (.296 batting average, 27 homers, 108 RBI) and Mickey Mantle (.295, 21, 92) leading the attack.

2. 1955 Brooklyn Dodgers, 98–55; manager: Walter Alston. Mighty Brooklyn had baseball's most powerful offense—clubbing a major league-high 201 homers—and won its first 10 games and 22 of its first 24 as it piled up a 12½-game lead by July 4. MVP Roy Campanella (.318, 32 homers, 107 RBI), league RBI champ Duke Snider (.309, 42, 136), Gil Hodges (.289, 27, 102), and Carl Furillo (.314, 26, 95) were the big bats, and Don Newcombe (20–5) and Clem Labine (13–5, 11 saves) were the top winners for the Dodgers, who wrapped up the pennant on September 8, the earliest clinching in NL history. Brooklyn, which had lost the World Series to the Yankees five times in the previous fourteen years, finally broke through with a thrilling 7-game triumph that brought the borough of Brooklyn its first—and only—world championship.

3. 1954 Cleveland Indians, 111–43; manager: Al Lopez. Cleveland set a league record for wins and snapped New York's pennant streak at five thanks to one of the game's greatest pitching staffs. The rotation featured AL-victory leaders Bob Lemon (23–7, 2.72 ERA) and Early Wynn (23–11, 2.72), league ERA champ Mike Garcia (19–8, 2.64), Art Houtteman (15–7, 3.35), and Bob Feller (13–3, 3.09), and in the bullpen were Ray Narleski (3–3, 2.22, 13 saves), Don Mossi (6–1, 1.94, 7 saves), and Hal Newhouser (7–2, 2.49, 7 saves). The offense was led by batting champ Bobby Avila (.341), home run and RBI

Two of the American League's better arms in the early 1950s: Steady Eddie Lopat (top, left) won 71 games in his first four seasons in Yankee pinstripes. From 1948 to 1956, Cleveland's Bob Lemon (left) averaged 20 wins per year and led the league in complete games five times.

leader Larry Doby (32, 126), and Al Rosen (.300, 24, 102). In the World Series, however, the Indians' pitching flopped and their attack fizzled; the Giants outscored them 21–9 in a 4-game sweep.

Best World Series

1. 1952, New York Yankees over Brooklyn Dodgers, 4 games to 3. In a thrilling Series in which only 1 game is decided by more than 2 runs, New York comes out on top—but it isn't easy. After Carl Erskine goes the distance and Duke Snider singles in the winning run in the eleventh inning of Game Five, the Dodgers return to Ebbets Field needing just 1 win to finish off the Yankees. But Vic Raschi beats the Bums 3–2 in Game Six; in Game Seven Mickey Mantle's sixth-inning homer gives New York the lead for good and Bob Kuzava retires the last eight Dodger hitters to give the Yanks their fourth straight world championship.

2. 1955, Brooklyn Dodgers over New York Yankees, 4 games to 3. The cry of "wait till next year" is wearing thin in Brooklyn, where the Dodgers have dropped four World Series to the Yankees in the past eight years. It looks like this subway series will deliver more of the same after the Bronx Bombers win the first 2 games at home, but Brooklyn wins the next 3 to put the Yanks on the brink. Whitey Ford's 4-hitter beats the Dodgers 5–1 to even the Series, but in Game Seven Johnny Podres pitches a shutout, Gil Hodges drives in the only 2 runs of the game, and Sandy Amoros makes a fantastic catch off Yogi Berra's fly down the left field line to bring Brooklyn its first, and only, championship flag.

Detroit's Al Kaline led the American League in hitting .340 in 1955 at the tender age of twenty, but even though he went on to a Hall of Fame career, he never again came within 13 points of that lofty mark and never won another batting title.

DECADE BATTING LEADERS

	National League			American League		
YEAR	PLAYER	TEAM	AVG.	PLAYER	TEAM	AVG.
1950	Stan Musial	St. Louis	.346	Billy Goodman	Boston	.354
1951	Stan Musial	St. Louis	.355	Ferris Fain	Philadelphia	.344
1952	Stan Musial	St. Louis	.336	Ferris Fain	Philadelphia	.327
1953	Carl Furillo	Brooklyn	.344	Mickey Vernon	Washington	.337
1954	Willie Mays	New York	.345	Bobby Avila	Cleveland	.341
1955	Richie Ashburn	Philadelphia	.338	Al Kaline	Detroit	.340
1956	Hank Aaron	Milwaukee	.328	Mickey Mantle	New York	.353
1957	Stan Musial	St. Louis	.351	Ted Williams	Boston	.388
1958	Richie Ashburn	Philadelphia	.350	Ted Williams	Boston	.328
1959	Hank Aaron	Milwaukee	.355	Harvey Kuenn	Detroit	.353

Above, left: *The Chairman of the Board, Whitey Ford, set World Series records for victories (10), strikeouts (94), and consecutive scoreless innings (33), while teammate Mickey Mantle* (above, right), *nicknamed the Commerce Comet, established Series marks for home runs (18), runs (42), and RBI (40).*

3. 1956, New York Yankees over Brooklyn Dodgers, 4 games to 3. With the Series tied at 2 wins apiece, Don Larsen turns the tide by throwing a perfect game to beat Brooklyn 2–0 in Game Five. The Dodgers win 1–0 the next day behind Clem Labine's 10-inning shutout pitching, but in Game Seven the Yankees' Johnny Kucks tosses a 3-hitter and Bill Skowron hits a grand slam as New York wins 9–0 and avenges the previous year's defeat.

Worth Remembering

The Kansas City Pipeline. The foundation of the Yankees' 1950s dynasty was built through the farm system, but General Manager George Weiss always displayed the knack for filling in the gaps with timely trades, many of which were executed at the expense of the Kansas City Athletics. The Athletics earned the reputation as an unofficial Yankees farm team in the fifties by fueling the New Yorkers' pennant drives with the likes of Enos Slaughter, Bobby Shantz, Art Ditmar, Clete Boyer, Ryne Duren, Ralph Terry, Hector Lopez, and Roger Maris. Some players, such as Slaughter, Terry, Ditmar, Bob Cerv, and Harry Simpson, rode the New York–Kansas City trade shuttle both ways during their careers.

Doing it with Mirrors? Of course, someone had to manage all that talent in the Bronx, and that man was Casey Stengel. Although he won eight pennants and six World Series in the decade, Stengel didn't simply sit back and fill out the same lineup card for ten years; rather, he always seemed to plug in the right player at the right time. In 1952, with Joe DiMaggio retired, infielders Bobby Brown and Jerry Coleman and pitcher Tom Morgan off to war, and 21-game winner Eddie Lopat plagued with a sore shoulder, Stengel kept the club on the pennant track by turning to Billy Martin, Gil McDougald, Mickey Mantle, and Johnny Sain. When Don Larsen, Bob Turley, Tommy Byrne, and Bob Grim all disappointed in 1956, Stengel came up with a pair of aces in Tom Sturdivant and Johnny Kucks. In all, twelve different Yankee regulars hit .300 or better in the decade and twelve different pitchers won 13 or more games.

The Dynasties That Never Were. Were it not for the Yankees, fans in Chicago and Cleveland might now look back on the fifties as the glory years for their teams. The Indians won at an impressive .588 clip for the decade, including an AL-record 111 victories in 1954, and broke the 90-win mark six times. The White Sox posted a .568 winning percentage from 1951 to 1959, and won 90 or more games four times. But each club won only one pennant in the decade (the only two flags not won by New York, which had a .621 decade winning percentage), and both clubs fell short in their lone World Series appearances. Cleveland finished second six times, and Chicago was second twice and third five times. The Yanks, Indians, and White Sox finished first, second, and third six times in the decade.

Rolling the Dice. Why don't today's managers try gambles like these? Having lost the ace of his staff, Curt Simmons, to military service, Phillies Manager Eddie Sawyer elected to go with bullpen closer and NL MVP Jim Konstanty—who hadn't started a game in four years—as his Game One starter. Konstanty gave up just 1 run, but the Yankees' Vic Raschi pitched a 2-hit shutout to beat him. Dodgers Manager Chuck Dressen tried a similar gamble in the 1952 Series, giving the ball to relief ace and Rookie of the Year Joe Black to start Game One. Black fared better, going the distance to become the first black pitcher to win a Series game.

Older and Wiser. With major league rosters depleted during World War II, fifteen-year-old Joe Nuxhall got a chance to pitch in the major leagues for the Cincinnati Reds. He walked 5 and gave up 5 hits in two-thirds of an inning—good for a 67.50 ERA. It would be eight years before Nuxhall would pitch in the majors again, but he pitched a lot better in his second tour of duty. He went 73–58 for the Reds from 1954 to 1959, and won 135 games in his sixteen-year career.

DECADE SPOTLIGHT

Bobo Holloman: He Left His Mark

One of the amazing features of the game of baseball is that on a given day, any starting pitcher—even a journeyman—can take the mound and make history by throwing a no-hitter. What's even more amazing is that the same pitcher who scales that mountain may never again reach such lofty heights. Bobo Holloman's story is vivid proof of that phenomenon.

On one magical evening, Holloman accomplished something that pitching legends Cy Young, Walter Johnson, and Christy Mathewson—along with every other Hall of Famer—never did. Yet Holloman won fewer games in the major leagues than Jess Dobernic, Bill Upham, Luther Roy, and hundreds of other pitchers who are not exactly household names. Because of what transpired on the evening of May 6, 1953, though, Holloman's name went down in baseball's annals while legions of other players have long since faded into obscurity.

Above, right: Joe Black, a former Baltimore Elite Giant and the NL Rookie of the Year in 1952, said that after his first year with the Dodgers he made a list of Negro League hitters who were better than the major leaguers he had pitched against. He had thirty-five names on his list. Right: Dubbed by teammates "a sure winner, but only in the conversational league," brash Bobo Holloman backed up his boasts on May 6, 1953.

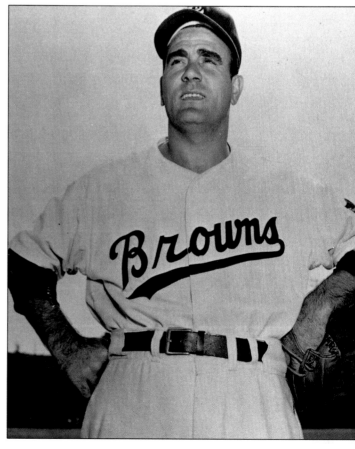

WHAT'S IN/WHAT'S OUT IN THE 1950s

In

Westward franchise shifts
Baseball on television
The golden years
Big, muscular, one-dimensional power hitters
The Yankees
Workhorse relief pitchers
Home runs
Pennants in New York City
Black-and-white photos in newspapers
Sports Illustrated
Flirting with Babe Ruth's 60-homer mark
All-Star Game ballot-box stuffing
The Athletics' managerial revolving door
Managers in uniform
George Weiss
Commissioner Ford Frick
Air travel

Out

Geographic stability
Understanding the effects of TV
The war era
Small, speedy, versatile singles hitters
The Cardinals
Workhorse starting pitchers
Doubles and triples
Pennants anywhere else
Cartoons and illustrations
Baseball magazine
Breaking the Babe's record
Fans voting for their All-Star favorite
Connie Mack
Managers in suits
Branch Rickey
Commissioner Happy Chandler
Train travel

On that cold, rainy night in St. Louis' Busch Stadium, the twenty-nine-year-old Holloman, who had pleaded with Browns Manager Marty Marion for a chance to get out of the bullpen and start a game, made the most of his opportunity. He became the first pitcher in modern major league history to throw a no-hitter in his first big-league start. Because of the inclement weather (Browns owner Bill Veeck had announced that rain checks would be honored even though the game would be played) and the downtrodden state of the two teams (they would finish as the bottom two clubs in the American League that year), only 2,473 fans were on hand to see the 6-foot-2 (187.9cm), dark-haired right-hander hold the Athletics hitless for 9 innings, walking 5 and striking out 3, while also driving in 3 runs with a pair of base hits.

Baseball players observe many superstitions during a no-hitter, such as not talking to the pitcher for fear of jinxing him. Holloman was a superstitious man himself—each time he took the mound he would draw the letters "N" (for his wife, Nan) and "G" (for his six-year-old son, Gary) in the dirt near the first or third baseline—but he wasn't worried about a hex that night. "I told [my teammates] I didn't care if they talked to me about it or not," Holloman, who died in 1987, told the *Akron Beacon Journal* in a 1975 interview. "I told them I knew I had the no-hitter and that

I was going to get it whether they talked to me or not, so they might as well talk to me." He did get it, thanks to outstanding defensive plays by left-fielder Jim Dyck and shortstop Billy Hunter.

Holloman's feat was not completely unprecedented. In 1892 a pitcher named Bumpus Jones also pitched a no-hitter in his first big-league start, leading Cincinnati to a 7–1 win over Pittsburgh. Like Holloman, Jones struggled after his no-hitter; he won only 1 more game in the majors.

As it did for Jones, though, the great start appeared to be the beginning of something big for Alva Lee Holloman, the brash, self-assured rookie from Thomaston, Georgia, who had nicknamed himself after Bobo Newsom, a major league pitcher for twenty years and one of the game's great characters. In his seven minor league seasons before making the Browns, Holloman compiled an impressive 103–58 record. He struggled as a reliever early in the 1953 season—his teammates dubbed him "a sure winner, but only in the conversational league"—and he even confided to one writer that he was thinking of quitting the game altogether. Those doubts were behind him, however—or so it seemed. He left his next start early because of a blister on his pitching hand, but in the following outing he took a no-hitter into the ninth inning before a single by Boston's Jimmy Piersall sent him to the showers.

But it all came unraveled for Holloman after that. He failed to go the distance in any of his next 7 starts (his no-hitter would be the only complete game he would ever throw in the majors), and when he was tagged for 6 runs in a 1⅓-inning relief stint on July 19, Veeck ran out of patience and shipped Holloman and his 3–7 record and 5.23 ERA to Toronto of the International League. Holloman came down with a sore arm the next spring and posted a combined 4–11 record with four minor league teams in 1954. He lasted two more years in the minors before calling it quits, leaving as his legacy the words Marion told reporters the night Holloman made history: "There's a guy who not only talks a great game but pitches one as well."

The 1960s
The Times They Are a-Changin'

Baseball marked its one hundredth anniversary in 1969, and it would have been a tall order to catalog the evolution of the game over the previous century. Charting the changes of the previous *decade* was difficult enough: the New York Mets—a team that didn't even exist in 1960—were the world champions in 1969. Minneapolis–St. Paul, Houston, Atlanta, Anaheim, Oakland, Montreal, San Diego, and Seattle, none of which had a major league team in 1960, all had them by 1969. By that same year the reserve clause, which at the beginning of the decade had appeared as unassailable as Babe Ruth's single-season home run record, was looking as vulnerable as Roger Maris proved Ruth's mark to be in 1961.

Although a few clubs had relocated in the fifties, the eight-team structure in each league had remained unchanged since 1901. Franchise movement remained popular in the sixties—the Twins (née the Senators), Braves, and Athletics all jumped to greener and more profitable pastures—but by 1960 it had become apparent that there simply were not enough major league clubs to go around. The nation and its interest in baseball was growing, and the sport could no longer satisfy fan interest by merely moving its existing teams to where the interest was. Besides, that practice was starting to get the sport into hot water with Congress, which listened to pleas from jilted fans in cities such as Brooklyn and Milwaukee and opened

the door for a proposed third major league, Branch Rickey's Continental League. The threat of congressional intervention and Continental competition, as well as the prospect for increased revenues, were enough to motivate baseball owners to charter new franchises: two in the American League in 1961 (Los Angeles and Washington, the latter to replace the original Senators), two in the

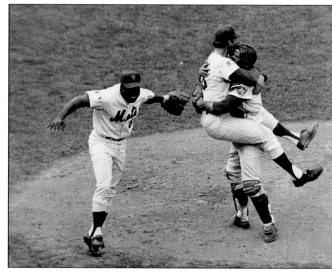

Above: *Jerry Koosman jumps into the arms of catcher Jerry Grote and third baseman Ed Charles joins the revelry as the Miracle Mets celebrate their Series-clinching victory in Game Five of the 1969 World Series against Baltimore.* Below: *The Houston Astrodome, "the eighth wonder of the world," attracted nationwide attention even during its construction. The facility occupies 9½ acres (3.8 ha).*

National League in 1962 (New York and Houston), and two in each league in 1969 (Kansas City and Seattle in the AL and San Diego and Montreal in the NL).

From the beginning, it was obvious the National League had been more astute in its site selection. Clearly, New York was prepared to support a second entry after the Dodgers and Giants had pulled up stakes. Houston was a growing city and quickly got behind the Colts and, later, the Astros. The Los Angeles Angels and second coming of the Washington Senators did not fare as well. The Senators, in fact, would eventually leave for Arlington, Texas. The second round of expansion was no better; the Seattle Pilots lasted one season before moving to Milwaukee. By comparison, San Diego and Montreal were well-conceived choices.

More teams meant more games, in both the regular season and the postseason. The American League and National League each went to a 162-game schedule, up from 154, when they increased to ten teams, and in 1969 each league changed to a two-division format with the division winners squaring off in a best-of-five playoff series for the pennant. More teams also meant more stadiums—and more different kinds of stadiums, such as the forty-five-million-dollar, fully enclosed Houston Astrodome, the most popular of the new breed of multipurpose stadiums that included such modern features as artificial turf, luxury boxes, and electronic video scoreboards. On the field, pitching made a comeback that reached fruition in 1968: that year the major league ERA was 2.99; there were 335 shutouts; and only six hitters broke the .300 mark.

There were a number of reasons for the resurgence of pitching. Umpires were more aggressive in calling the strike zone, which had been expanded in 1963 to include the area from the top of the shoulder to the bottom of the knee. When the talented pitchers of the time took to the 15-inch (38.1cm) mound, it was not a fair fight. And to make matters worse for hitters, relief pitchers began to come into vogue, which meant the end of late-game, tired-arm fastballs down the middle. As a result, major-league hitters hit a dismal .237 in 1968. Only four teams managed to score better than 4 runs a game.

The St. Louis Cardinals were particularly dominant that year. They led the major leagues with a team earned-run average of 2.49 and threw 30 shutouts. Cardinals right-hander Bob Gibson won 15 straight games at one point and finished with an earned-run average of 1.12—the lowest mark since 1914. The Dodgers' Don Drysdale pitched a searing 6 straight shutouts and a record 58⅔ scoreless

Major League Teams in the 1960s
(Teams played entire decade unless otherwise noted)

NATIONAL LEAGUE
Chicago Cubs
Cincinnati Reds
Houston Colt .45s/Astros (1962–1969)
Los Angeles Dodgers
Milwaukee Braves (moved to Atlanta in 1966)
Montreal Expos (1969)
New York Mets (1962–1969)
Philadelphia Phillies
Pittsburgh Pirates
St. Louis Cardinals
San Diego Padres (1969)
San Francisco Giants

AMERICAN LEAGUE
Baltimore Orioles
Boston Red Sox
Chicago White Sox
Cleveland Indians
Detroit Tigers
Kansas City Athletics (moved to Oakland in 1968)
Kansas City Royals (1969)
Los Angeles Angels (1961–1969) (became California Angels in 1965)
New York Yankees
Seattle Pilots (1969) (became Milwaukee Brewers in 1970)
(old) Washington Senators (became Minnesota Twins in 1961)
(new) Washington Senators (1961–1969)

Divisional alignment instituted in 1969
NATIONAL LEAGUE

East	West
Chicago Cubs	Atlanta Braves
Montreal Expos	Cincinnati Reds
New York Mets	Houston Astros
Philadelphia Phillies	Los Angeles Dodgers
Pittsburgh Pirates	San Diego Padres
St. Louis Cardinals	San Francisco Giants

AMERICAN LEAGUE

East	West
Baltimore Orioles	California Angels
Boston Red Sox	Chicago White Sox
Cleveland Indians	Kansas City Royals
Detroit Tigers	Minnesota Twins
New York Yankees	Oakland Athletics
Washington Senators	Seattle Pilots

St. Louis' Bob Gibson fires a pitch to Detroit's Norm Cash in the ninth inning of Game One of the 1968 World Series. Gibson fanned Cash for his Series-record sixteenth strikeout of the day. He struck out the next hitter, Willie Horton, to end the game and run his record total to 17.

innings. It was that kind of season. On April 15, the New York Mets and Houston Astros played a numbingly scoreless game that required six hours and six minutes before the Astros won 1–0 in the bottom of the twenty-fourth inning. The All-Star Game, the first ever played under the lights, was another sleep-inducing 1–0 affair, won by the National League. It was fitting when the San Francisco Giants and St. Louis Cardinals met in 2 September games and the hitters failed to produce any offense. Gaylord Perry threw a no-hitter at the Cardinals on September 17, and the next night St. Louis' Ray Washburn returned the favor and no-hit Perry's Giants.

Detroit's Denny McLain produced an astonishing record of 31–6, becoming the first pitcher to win 30 games since Dizzy Dean in 1934. And McLain wasn't even the American League leader in earned-run average; Cleveland's Luis Tiant (1.60) and Sam McDowell (1.81) and Baltimore's Dave McNally (1.95) all posted better marks than McLain's 1.96.

If not for Boston slugger Carl Yastrzemski, the American League would have gone an entire season without the benefit of a .300 hitter. As it was, the left fielder closed the season on a tear to finish with a .301 average. Oakland's Bert Campaneris led the American League with a relatively paltry 177 hits. The Detroit Tigers won the pennant with an infield that hit for a collective average of .210.

Concerned, as always, that the reduction in offense would lead to a similar decline in attendance, baseball made several immediate remedies. The strike zone was re-duced significantly before the 1969 season to include the area from the armpit to the top of the knee. The mound was lowered 5 inches (12.7cm), thus reducing some of the leverage pitchers enjoyed against hitters.

Although baseball had been ahead of society's curve when Jackie Robinson broke the color line in 1947, integration was a slow process, particularly in the American League. The National League more aggressively signed African-American and Latin players; between 1961 and 1978, only four National League batting championships, one slugging title, and five home run honors were won by white players.

In the United States, the decade of the 1960s was marked by the questioning of established authority, practices, and mores. Those same trends were evident in the world of baseball by the latter part of the decade—at least on the part of the players. When Marvin Miller, the newly appointed executive director of the Major League Baseball Players Association, toured spring training camps in 1966, he heard in no uncertain terms that the players wanted changes. They wanted their piece of the financial pie, as well as their freedom, that is, the elimination of the reserve clause, the provision of a player's contract that tied him to his team for life unless he retired or was traded, sold, or released. In his first four years on the job, Miller won the players a 43 percent increase in the minimum salary, a 33 percent increase in owner contributions to the players' pension fund, the right to agent representation in contract negotiations, and the adoption of a formal grievance procedure with the commissioner as the ultimate arbiter. It was just the beginning; in the next decade Miller would help win the players even more: free agency and an unprecedented salary windfall.

CHRONOLOGY

New Teams, New Turf

1960: The American League, which because of World War II had tabled its plans eighteen years earlier to move a franchise to California, succumbs to expansion pressures and plants a new team in Los Angeles for the 1961 season. A second expansion club is planted in Washington, D.C., to replace Calvin Griffith's Senators, who are granted approval to move to Minneapolis–St. Paul. The Los Angeles Angels, who will change their name to California Angels in 1965, play their first season in Wrigley Field, a longtime minor league park styled after the famous Chicago stadium, then become cotenants at Dodger Stadium for the next four years. The new Washington Senators take over Griffith Stadium for their first season, and the Minnesota Twins move into Metropolitan Stadium. The ten-team American League expands to a 162-game schedule for 1961.

1960: In his nineteenth and final major league season, forty-two-year-old Ted Williams hits .316 with 29 home runs and 72 RBI. In storybook fashion, Williams homers in his final plate appearance.

April 12, 1960: In front of a crowd of 42,269, the San Francisco Giants beat the St. Louis Cardinals 3–1 in the first game in Candlestick Park.

May 11, 1960: Six days after the Soviet Union shoots down a U.S. Air Force U-2 plane over Soviet territory, President Eisenhower publicly announces that the United States has been conducting reconnaissance missions over the Soviet Union for the past four years.

Mazeroski's Homer Makes Pittsburgh Pirates Champs

October 13, 1960: In the most dramatic finish in World Series history, Pittsburgh's Bill Mazeroski homers off the New York Yankees' Ralph Terry in the bottom of the ninth inning of Game Seven to give the Pirates a 10–9 win. It is Casey Stengel's final game as Yankees manager.

1961: En route to 107 losses and a last-place finish, the Philadelphia Phillies lose a record 23 straight games.

January 3, 1961: At President Eisenhower's direction, the United States breaks off diplomatic relations with Cuba. Three and a half months later, the Bay of Pigs invasion, attempted by Cuban exiles armed and trained by the United States, is defeated in its effort to overthrow Cuban President Fidel Castro.

July 31, 1961: The second All-Star Game of the year is the first ever to end in a tie, as rain falls in the ninth inning in Boston with the score 1–1.

Maris's 61 in '61

October 1, 1961: Facing Boston's Tracy Stallard in the fourth inning of the final game of the season, Yankees outfielder Roger Maris hits his sixty-first home run of the year—for the only run of the game—to eclipse Babe Ruth's single-season record of 60 set in 1927. Commissioner Ford Frick mandates that Maris' record go into the books with an asterisk, because Maris achieved the new standard in a 162-game schedule, as opposed to the 154-game slate that existed in Ruth's day. Maris and Mickey Mantle also set a record for home runs by two teammates (115), and the Yankees set a team mark with 240 round-trippers.

October 8, 1961: In New York's Game Four win over Cincinnati, Yankees left-hander Whitey Ford extends his World Series scoreless innings streak to 32, breaking Babe Ruth's record of 29⅔—a mark that Ruth once said he cherished more than his 60 homers.

The National League Returns To New York and Debuts in Houston

1962: The National League follows the American League's lead and adds two ex-

Hounded by reporters and fans for most of the season, Roger Maris overcame the pressures to club a record 61 homers in 1961.

pansion teams—the Mets and the Houston Colt .45s—for the 1962 season, and increases to a 162-game schedule. Managed by seventy-one-year-old Casey Stengel and playing in the Polo Grounds, the hapless Mets lose a record 120 games. The Colt .45s play in new Colt Stadium and finish in eighth place, 7 games ahead of the Chicago Cubs.

1962: Los Angeles' Dodger Stadium and Washington's District of Columbia Stadium (renamed Robert F. Kennedy Stadium in 1968) open.

1962: Dodgers shortstop Maury Wills steals 104 bases, breaking Ty Cobb's record of 96 set in 1915.

September 12, 1962: Senators right-hander Tom Cheney strikes out a single-game record 21 hitters in 16 innings as Washington beats the Baltimore Orioles 2–1. Cheney will finish his career in 1966 with a 19–29 record.

October 28, 1962: *The Cuban Missile Crisis ends when the Soviet Union agrees to remove its missiles and dismantle its bases in Cuba in exchange for a pledge from the United States not to invade Cuba.*

1963: Rules change: to combat rising offensive numbers, the strike zone is expanded slightly to include the area from the top of the hitter's shoulders to the bottom of his knees. Batting averages and home run totals in both leagues show noticeable declines in 1963.

1963: In his twenty-second and final season, forty-two-year-old Stan Musial hits .255 with 12 home runs and 58 RBI. In his first season, Cincinnati's Pete Rose bats .273 and scores 101 runs.

July 31, 1963: Paul Foytak of the Los Angeles Angels becomes the only pitcher in major league history to surrender 4 successive homers when Cleveland's Woodie Held, Pedro Ramos, Tito Francona, and Larry Brown take him deep in the Tribe's 9–5 win.

November 22, 1963: *While winding up his tour of eleven Western states, President Kennedy is assassinated in Dallas. Ninety-eight minutes after Kennedy's death, Vice President Lyndon Johnson takes the oath of office and assumes the presidency. Two*

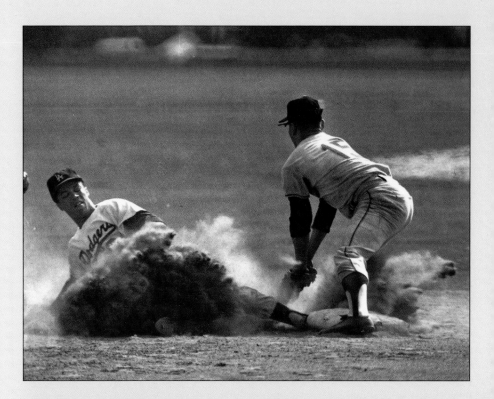

days later, Kennedy's alleged assassin, Lee Harvey Oswald, is killed by Dallas nightclub owner Jack Ruby.

1964: Rules change: colored bats are no longer permitted.

April 17, 1964: New York's Shea Stadium opens.

Top: *In the third game of the Dodgers' 1962 playoff series against the Giants, Los Angeles' Maury Wills slides under San Francisco third baseman Jim Davenport's glove for his record 104th stolen base of the season.* **Above:** *Jim Bunning of the Phillies strikes out Mets pinch hitter Johnny Stephenson for the final out of his June 21, 1964, perfect game in Shea Stadium.*

June 21, 1964: On Father's Day, Philadelphia's Jim Bunning, father of six, throws a perfect game—the first in the National League in the twentieth century—to beat the Mets 6–0.

August 7, 1964: *After North Vietnamese boats allegedly attack two U.S. destroyers, Congress passes the Tonkin Resolution, authorizing presidential action in Vietnam.*

September–October 1964: Leading the National League by 6½ games with two weeks left in the season, the Phillies, mismanaged by Gene Mauch, fall victim to one of the greatest collapses in history and drop 10 games in a row to hand the pennant to the Cardinals.

October 16, 1964: The day after the Cardinals defeat the Yankees in the World Series, St. Louis Manager Johnny Keane resigns, and Yankees skipper Yogi Berra is fired. Later that winter the Yankees hire Keane as their manager, and Berra joins Casey Stengel as a player-coach with the New York Mets.

**Atlanta: New Home of the Braves
1965:** The Milwaukee Braves petition the National League office for the right to relocate to Atlanta. The move gains approval, but citing the club's County Stadium lease (which still has one year remaining) and threatened litigation from the city, the NL requires that the Braves play out the 1965 season in Milwaukee before heading south. The club draws an embarrassing total of 555,584 fans in its lame-duck season, including several crowds under one thousand. When the Braves move the following year, they become the first major league team to uproot twice.

1965: A free-agent player draft is instituted to facilitate more even distribution of young talent and to reduce the lucrative bonus payments often given to untested players.

February 21, 1965: *As he is preparing to give a speech in New York City, Malcolm X, age thirty-nine, is shot and killed by members of the Black Muslims, the group from which he split in 1964.*

**Houston Unveils the "Eighth Wonder"
April 9, 1965:** The Houston Astrodome, home of the Astros (formerly the Colt .45s) and baseball's first enclosed, air-conditioned stadium, opens. Heralded as the Eighth Wonder of the World, the park features real grass grown under the lights. Two other new parks—Atlanta-Fulton County Stadium (into which the Braves will move in 1966) and Texas' Turnpike Stadium (which will be renamed Arlington Stadium and become the Rangers' home in 1972)—also open this year.

July 29, 1965: On the eve of his seventy-fifth birthday, Mets Manager Casey Stengel breaks his hip; the injury forces the Old Professor to retire and end his twenty-five-year managerial career.

August 22, 1965: Giants pitcher Juan Marichal hits Johnny Roseboro of the Los Angeles Dodgers on the head with his bat during an on-field argument; NL President Warren Giles fines Marichal $1,750 and suspends him for 9 days.

September 9, 1965: Sandy Koufax of the Dodgers throws a perfect game to beat the Cubs 1–0; it is his fourth no-hitter in four years. The final out is Harvey Kuenn, the same man Koufax retired to end his second no-hitter two years earlier.

September 25, 1965: At age fifty-nine (or thereabouts), Satchel Paige starts a game for the Kansas City Athletics and pitches 3 scoreless innings. Paige walks none and allows only 1 hit—a 2-out double in the first by Carl Yastrzemski—to become the oldest player ever to appear in a major league game.

Top: *Ageless Satchel Paige works to a Red Sox hitter during his 3-inning stint for the Athletics in 1965.* Above: *San Francisco's Juan Marichal swings his bat at Dodger catcher Johnny Roseboro as Sandy Koufax tries to come to Roseboro's aid. Marichal earned a costly 9-day suspension.*

November 17, 1965: General William Eckert replaces Ford Frick as baseball's commissioner.

December 9, 1965: The Cincinnati Reds trade Frank Robinson, the 1961 NL Most Valuable Player, to the Baltimore Orioles for outfielder Dick Simpson and pitchers Milt Pappas and Jack Baldschun. Robinson wins the AL MVP Award in 1966 with a Triple Crown performance (.316 batting average, 49 homers, and 122 RBI), becoming the first player to win an MVP Award in each league.

The Players Union Hires a Heavy Hitter

1966: Shortly before spring training, the Major League Baseball Players Association names Marvin Miller as its executive director. Miller, a longtime negotiator for the United Steelworkers Union, will ultimately help the players overthrow the reserve clause and achieve substantial increases in salaries, benefits, and licensing income.

1966: The Astrodome introduces an artificial grass playing surface developed by the Monsanto Company. In honor of the stadium and the home team, the Astros, the new surface is called AstroTurf.

1966: California's Anaheim Stadium, St. Louis' Busch Memorial Stadium, and the Oakland-Alameda County Coliseum—future home of the A's—open.

1966: Dodgers pitchers Sandy Koufax and Don Drysdale, who had combined for 49 wins in 1965, hire a Hollywood agent and stage a much-publicized spring training holdout, reportedly demanding a three-year, $1.05 million contract that the two would split evenly; their requested annual salary is $175,000, which would be a record. Koufax, who will retire after the season because of an arthritic elbow, eventually settles for $125,000; Drysdale takes $110,000. The two combine for 40 wins and help the Dodgers to a second straight pennant.

1966: General Manager Ralph Houk replaces Field Manager Johnny Keane in May, and the once-dominant Yankees sink to the AL basement for the first time in fifty-four years, finishing 26½ games behind the front-running Baltimore Orioles.

Top: *In 1968 MVP and Cy Young winner Denny McLain of the Tigers started 41 games and won 31 of them, to go with a 1.96 ERA. Above: Young Reggie Jackson in action in 1969, his second full season with the Oakland A's.*

January 31, 1966: *The United States resumes bombing raids in North Vietnam after attempted peace talks with the Communists fail.*

April 11, 1966: Emmett Ashford, fifty-one, umpires the Senators' home opener to become the first black umpire to work a major league game. Ashford will remain at the major league level through 1970.

July 3, 1966: Tony Cloninger of the Atlanta Braves becomes the first NL player—and the first pitcher in major league history—to hit 2 grand slams in 1 game. He drives in 9 runs and pitches a complete game 7-hitter to beat the Giants 17–3.

October 1966: Baltimore's Frank Robinson wins the Triple Crown with a .316 average, 49 homers, and 122 RBI.

October 1966: The Orioles sweep the Dodgers in the most stunning display of pitching mastery in World Series history. Los Angeles scores single runs in the second and third innings of Game One, but does not dent home plate again for the remainder of the Series. Jim Palmer, Wally Bunker, and Dave McNally throw shutouts in the final 3 games to cap Baltimore's amazing string of 33 consecutive scoreless innings. Dodgers center fielder Willie Davis commits a record 3 errors in 1 inning in L.A.'s Game Two loss.

1967: Rules change: managers and coaches are now required to remove a pitcher from the game upon making their second trip to the mound in 1 inning.

July 11, 1967: The longest All-Star Game in history ends when a fifteenth-inning home run by Cincinnati's Tony Perez gives the National League a 2–1 win.

August 30, 1967: San Diego Stadium (now known as Jack Murphy Stadium), home of the National Football League's Chargers and the Pacific Coast League's Padres—and the future home of the NL's expansion Padres—opens.

October 1967: Boston's Carl Yastrzemski wins the Triple Crown with a .326 batting average, 44 homers, and 121 RBI.

1968: Rules change: a pitcher is now forbidden to bring his hand to his mouth while on the pitching rubber.

1968: Their union strengthening, major league players threaten a strike over contract demands.

Finley: California, Here We Come

1968: Owner Charlie Finley moves his club from Kansas City to Oakland, making the Athletics the second team to pull up stakes twice. The A's play in the two-year-old Oakland-Alameda County Coliseum.

McLain Dominates the Year of the Pitcher

1968: Denny McLain, a twenty-four-year-old right-hander for the Detroit Tigers, posts a 31–6 record with a 1.96 ERA to win the AL MVP and Cy Young Awards.

McLain is the major leagues' first 30-game winner since Dizzy Dean in 1934.

1968: The Cubs are shut out four straight times amid a string of 48 consecutive scoreless innings.

April 4, 1968: *Martin Luther King, Jr., is assassinated in Memphis. Riots subsequently break out across the country. On June 8, James Earl Ray is arrested and charged with the murder.*

May 8, 1968: Jim "Catfish" Hunter pitches a perfect game as the Oakland A's beat Minnesota 4–0.

May 27, 1968: Future White Sox star Frank Thomas is born in Columbus, Georgia.

June 6, 1968: *While campaigning in Los Angeles, Robert Kennedy is assassinated by Jordanian immigrant Sirhan Sirhan.*

June 8, 1968: Los Angeles' Don Drysdale pitches 6 straight shutouts and fashions a streak of 58⅔ consecutive scoreless innings, breaking Walter Johnson's record of 56 set in 1913.

July 9, 1968: In a year of pitching dominance, the All-Star Game ends in a 1–0 score for the first time in history. Willie Mays scores the game's only run for the National League on a double play.

October 31, 1968: *To break a stalemate in the Paris peace talks, President Johnson announces an end to all U.S. bombing of North Vietnam.*

December 6, 1968: Commissioner William Eckert is fired by the owners at the conclusion of the season and replaced by Wall Street lawyer Bowie Kuhn.

More Teams, More Changes

1969: In baseball's centennial season, both leagues expand again, each adding two clubs to raise the total to twenty-four. The National League adds the Montreal Expos and San Diego Padres, and the American League adds the Kansas City Royals and Seattle Pilots. Each league also splits into two divisions, Eastern and Western, and sets up a playoff system whereby the division winners will play a best-of-five series to determine the pennant winner. The schedule is also changed so that instead of playing each team an equal number of times, each club will play 18 games against its division opponents and 12 games against teams from the other division. The Expos play in Jarry Park for their first eight seasons, the Padres in San Diego Stadium, the Royals in Municipal Stadium—the former home of the A's—for their first five seasons, and the Pilots in Sick's Stadium, where they draw just 677,944 in their only season in Seattle.

1969: Rules change: to reduce the pitchers' dominance, the pitching mound is lowered 5 inches (15.2cm) to a maximum height of 10 inches (25.4cm), and the strike zone is reduced to include only the area from the batter's armpits to the tops of his knees. Relief pitchers who enter the game after the start of an inning are credited with earned runs as if they pitched the entire inning.

June 8, 1969: Mickey Mantle, who hit just .237 in 1968, announces his retirement after eighteen often sensational—and often injury-plagued—seasons.

July 20, 1969: *The nation watches on television as Neil Armstrong becomes the first man to walk on the moon.*

October 7, 1969: The Cardinals trade outfielder Curt Flood to the Phillies as part of a seven-player swap. Flood, contending that he should be able to make a deal for himself and not be traded at the club's discretion, sits out the 1970 season and begins a long court battle against the reserve clause, which ties players to their teams for life unless they retire or are traded, sold, or released. Flood ultimately loses his case in the Supreme Court, but his suit nonetheless sets a precedent for other players and helps pave the way for free agency in the 1970s.

November 15, 1969: *In the largest anti-war rally in U.S. history, 250,000 people convene in Washington, D.C., to protest the Vietnam War.*

November 21, 1969: Ken Griffey, Jr., is born in Donora, Pennsylvania. He shares the same birthdate and home town with Hall of Famer Stan Musial and, like Musial, bats and throws left-handed and plays the outfield.

Tom Seaver delivers a pitch in the second inning of his near-perfect game against the Cubs on July 9, 1969. Chicago's Jimmy Qualls broke up Seaver's bid with a 1-out single in the ninth.

Man of the Decade: Sandy Koufax

Roger Maris broke one of the game's most revered records. Willie Mays, Hank Aaron, Frank Robinson, and Roberto Clemente established themselves as four of the game's greatest hitters. Bob Gibson and Juan Marichal won 352 games between them in the sixties. But in a decade in which power pitching made a comeback, Koufax's accomplishments made him the premier pitcher of his day. Between 1961 and 1966 the left-hander put together one of the most dominant six-year runs of any pitcher in the modern era: a 129–47 record, 35 shutouts, 1,713 strikeouts, and a 2.20 earned-run average. During that span he won three Cy Young Awards and one MVP, pitched 4 no-hitters, helped the Dodgers to three pennants and two world championships, and led the league in wins and shutouts three times, strikeouts four times, and ERA five times. Only an arthritic left elbow, which forced his retirement at age thirty, could stop Koufax.

Most Memorable Games

1. 1960 World Series, Game Seven, October 13 at Forbes Field; Pittsburgh Pirates 10, New York Yankees 9. A back-and-forth finale to a seesaw Series: Pittsburgh jumps out to an early 4–0 lead, watches New York go up 7–4 on homers by Bill Skowron and Yogi Berra, stages a 5-run rally in the eighth that is kept alive when an apparent double-play grounder takes a bad hop and hits Yankees shortstop Tony Kubek in the throat, then blows that lead when New York scores twice off Bob Friend in the ninth to tie the game 9–9. But Bill Mazeroski ends the suspense on Ralph Terry's second pitch in the bottom of the ninth by launching a Series-winning home run to left field. Mazeroski, incidentally, was soon to find out what creative opportunism was all about: he had his cap and glove stolen in the postgame melee, and as he walked from the clubhouse door to his car after the game, five different fans tried to sell him a baseball, each claiming that theirs was the game-winning homer ball.

2. October 1, 1961, at Yankee Stadium; New York Yankees 1, Boston Red Sox 0. With the Yankees coasting to their eleventh pennant in thirteen seasons and Mickey Mantle sidelined in September, the attention of fans and media is focused squarely on Roger Maris' run at Babe Ruth's record of 60 home runs in a season. Maris has

With a devastating combination of power and control, Sandy Koufax had a strikeout-to-walk ratio of about 3–1 in his twelve years in the majors, and he led the league in K's four times in his last six seasons.

DECADE PITCHING LEADERS

	National League				American League		
YEAR	PLAYER	TEAM	ERA		PLAYER	TEAM	ERA
1960	Mike McCormick	San Francisco	2.70		Frank Baumann	Chicago	2.67
1961	Warren Spahn	Milwaukee	3.02		Dick Donovan	Washington	2.40
1962	Sandy Koufax	Los Angeles	2.54		Hank Aguirre	Detroit	2.21
1963	Sandy Koufax	Los Angeles	1.88		Gary Peters	Chicago	2.33
1964	Sandy Koufax	Los Angeles	1.74		Dean Chance	Los Angeles	1.65
1965	Sandy Koufax	Los Angeles	2.04		Sam McDowell	Cleveland	2.18
1966	Sandy Koufax	Los Angeles	1.73		Gary Peters	Chicago	1.98
1967	Phil Niekro	Atlanta	1.87		Joe Horlen	Chicago	2.06
1968	Bob Gibson	St. Louis	1.12		Luis Tiant	Cleveland	1.60
1969	Juan Marichal	San Francisco	2.10		Dick Bosman	Washington	2.19

59 homers after 154 games, thus assuring that even if he is successful, his record will have an asterisk, because his season is 8 games longer than Ruth's. The asterisk is removed years later, but at the time the impact of the record is diminished, so a crowd of only 23,154—well short of capacity—is on hand to see Maris launch number 61 into the right-field seats off Boston's Tracy Stallard.

3. 1962 World Series, Game Seven, October 16 at Candlestick Park; New York Yankees 1, San Francisco Giants 0. The decisive game of the Series is also the third meeting and rubber match between New York's 23-game winner, Ralph Terry, and San Francisco's 24-game winner,

Left: Pittsburgh's Bill Mazeroski rounds third base after his ninth-inning homer beat the Yankees in Game Seven of the 1960 Series. The second baseman, who won seven Gold Gloves but never hit more than 19 homers in a season, prided himself more on defense than power. Below: Roger Maris hits home run number 61 on October 1, 1961, at Yankee Stadium.

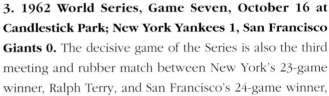

Jack Sanford. Terry goes the distance and scatters 4 hits for the win, which is saved when Yankee second baseman Bobby Richardson spears Willie McCovey's line drive with 2 on and 2 out in the ninth.

4. 1969 World Series, Game Four, October 15 at Shea Stadium; New York Mets 2, Baltimore Orioles 1. Tom Seaver is clinging to a 1–0 lead into the ninth when Baltimore mounts a threat on singles by Frank Robinson and Boog Powell. Brooks Robinson hits a drive to right-center that looks like a certain extra-base hit, but right fielder Ron Swoboda makes a brilliant, diving grab to short-circuit the rally. The tying run scores on Swoboda's catch, but the Miracle Mets win it in the tenth in typical bizarre fashion: J.C. Martin bunts and is hit on the wrist by pitcher Pete Richert's throw, allowing Rod Gaspar to score from second. Ironically, a newspaper photograph later shows Martin running in fair territory, for which he should have been called out.

5. 1961 All-Star Game (first of two), July 11 at Candlestick Park; National League 5, American League 4. In a wild game that features an All-Star record 7 errors and Giants reliever Stu Miller being blown off the mound by a strong Candlestick gale, the Nationals trail 4–3 in the tenth but tie the contest on Willie Mays' RBI double and win it on Roberto Clemente's base hit.

Best Pennant Races

1. 1967 American League: Boston Red Sox–Detroit Tigers–Minnesota Twins–Chicago White Sox. Each of the four teams has a compelling story: the Hitless Wonders from Chicago have no regulars who hit over .250 but hang in with pitching, defense, and guts; Minnesota catches fire after Cal Ermer replaces Sam Mele as manager in June; Detroit is the preseason favorite with a powerful lineup and a solid pitching rotation; Boston has Triple Crown winner and MVP Carl Yastrzemski and Cy Young winner Jim Lonborg leading its quest for the impossible dream. All four teams are in the hunt until the final week, but on the last day Lonborg beats the Twins and the Angels beat the Tigers to give the Red Sox their first pennant in twenty-one years.

2. 1962 National League: San Francisco Giants–Los Angeles Dodgers. Los Angeles is without the services of ace Sandy Koufax—sidelined in July by a circulatory

Above: *In Game Four of the 1969 Series, Baltimore pitcher Pete Richert throws to first in an attempt to retire Mets pinch hitter J. C. Martin, who had laid down a sacrifice bunt with runners on first and second. Richert's throw hit Martin on the wrist and ricocheted into right field, allowing Rod Gaspar to score the winning run. The O's argued to no avail that Martin was out of the baseline, which appears to be the case.* Below: *Gary Peters of the White Sox won 77 games and two ERA crowns from 1963 to 1967 but Chicago never finished better than second.*

ailment in his fingers—and the Dodgers miss him down the stretch, when they drop 10 of their last 13 games to allow San Francisco to climb into a first-place tie. The teams split the first 2 games of the ensuing best-of-three playoff series, and memories of 1951 ring all too true for the Dodgers, who blow a 4–2 lead in the ninth inning of the finale and lose 6–4.

3. 1964 National League: St. Louis Cardinals–Cincinnati Reds–Philadelphia Phillies–San Francisco Giants. Sitting on a 6½-game lead with two weeks left in the season, the Phillies are printing World Series tickets. But the anticipated celebration quickly turns into a wake as Manager Gene Mauch's experiment with a two-man pitching rotation sends the Phils spiraling into a 10-game losing streak that lets St. Louis, Cincinnati, and San Francisco back into the race. When the smoke clears, Philadelphia's pennant hopes are in ashes: the Cardinals are in front by one game over the Phils and the Reds, and by 3 games over the Giants.

Best Teams

1. 1961 New York Yankees, 109–53; manager: Ralph Houk. Generally regarded as the second-greatest team of all time (behind the 1927 edition), this club had the most powerful offense of its era; besides MVP Roger Maris, who eclipsed Babe Ruth's cherished mark by hitting 61 home runs, and Mickey Mantle, who hit a career-high 54 homers, New York's lineup—which belted a record 240 round-trippers—featured four other 20-homer men in Bill Skowron, Yogi Berra, Elston Howard, and Johnny Blanchard. Cy Young winner Whitey Ford (25–4), Ralph Terry (16–3),

DECADE BATTING LEADERS

	National League			American League		
YEAR	PLAYER	TEAM	AVG.	PLAYER	TEAM	AVG.
1960	Dick Groat	Pittsburgh	.325	Pete Runnels	Boston	.320
1961	Roberto Clemente	Pittsburgh	.351	Norm Cash	Detroit	.361
1962	Tommy Davis	Los Angeles	.346	Pete Runnels	Boston	.326
1963	Tommy Davis	Los Angeles	.326	Carl Yastrzemski	Boston	.321
1964	Roberto Clemente	Pittsburgh	.339	Tony Oliva	Minnesota	.323
1965	Roberto Clemente	Pittsburgh	.329	Tony Oliva	Minnesota	.321
1966	Matty Alou	Pittsburgh	.342	Frank Robinson	Baltimore	.316
1967	Roberto Clemente	Pittsburgh	.357	Carl Yastrzemski	Boston	.326
1968	Pete Rose	Cincinnati	.335	Carl Yastrzemski	Boston	.301
1969	Pete Rose	Cincinnati	.348	Rod Carew	Minnesota	.332

Top: Mickey Mantle connects for his forty-ninth home run of the year on September, 3, 1961, against the Detroit Tigers. Mantle kept pace with Yankees teammate Roger Maris for much of the season and finished with a career-high 54 round-trippers. Above: Two of the National League's most feared hitters of the 1960s: San Francisco's Willie McCovey and Pittsburgh's Roberto Clemente. In the decade McCovey led the NL in homers three times and Clemente won four batting titles.

Whitey Ford was the ace of the staff for the powerful 1961 Yankees, one of the greatest teams of all time. That year Ford notched career highs for wins (25), innings (283), and strikeouts (209) and was 2–0 in the Series.

Nicknamed the Baby Bull, Orlando Cepeda hit .297 and clubbed 379 home runs (including a league-leading 46 in 1961) in a seventeen-year major league career that saw him play for six different teams.

and Bill Stafford (14–9) were the big three of the pitching rotation, with Luis Arroyo (15–5, 29 saves) the bullpen ace. The Yankees made short work of the Reds in a 5-game World Series.

2. 1968 Detroit Tigers, 103–59; manager: Mayo Smith. In the year of the pitcher Detroit had two of baseball's best in right-hander Denny McLain (31–6, 1.96 ERA) and left-hander Mickey Lolich (17–9, 3.19). The offense lacked a .300 hitter or a 100-RBI man, but Willie Horton (36 homers), Bill Freehan (25), Norm Cash (25), and Jim Northrup (21) provided enough punch to help the eventual world champion Tigers lead the league in runs, home runs, and slugging percentage.

3. 1967 St. Louis Cardinals, 101–60; manager: Red Schoendienst. Orlando Cepeda (.325 batting average, 25 home runs, league-high 111 RBI), Lou Brock (.299, 21 homers, an NL-best 52 stolen bases), and Curt Flood (.335) led the offense, and the pitching staff got a boost from Dick Hughes (16–6, 2.68 ERA), Nelson Briles (14–5, 2.44), and Steve Carlton (14–9, 2.98) when Bob Gibson (13–7, 2.98) was sidelined by a broken leg in mid-July. Gibson returned to win 3 games in St. Louis' World Series victory over Boston. Both Gibson and Flood won Gold Glove Awards for their defensive play, and Cepeda earned the National League's Most Valuable Player Award.

Best World Series

1. 1960, Pittsburgh Pirates over New York Yankees, 4 games to 3. The Pirates are in their first Series since 1927, when the Yankees demolished them in a 4-game sweep. After a Pittsburgh win in Game One, this Series starts resembling a 1927 replay—New York wins the next 2 games 16–3 and 10–0. But the Pirates win the next 2 games, absorb another beating—12–0—in Game Six, and then win a wild 10–9 finale on Bill Mazeroski's ninth-inning homer. The Yankees fail to win what is Casey Stengel's final World Series despite outscoring Pittsburgh 55–27 and setting Series records for batting average (.338), hits (91), and runs. New York's Bobby Richardson drives in a Series-record 12 runs, including a single-game mark of 6 in Game Three.

2. 1968, Detroit Tigers over St. Louis Cardinals, 4 games to 3. The focus of the Series is on the battle between Detroit's Denny McLain and St. Louis' Bob Gibson, each of whom has won his league's Cy Young and MVP Awards. Gibson holds up his end, striking out a record 17 hitters in a Game One win and scattering 5 hits in Game Four to give St. Louis a 3–1 lead in the Series. McLain falters, losing 2 of his 3 starts, but Mickey Lolich picks him up by turning in 3 complete-game victories, including a 4–1 win over Gibson in Game Seven; Gibby's record

Right-hander Don Drysdale (above) *teamed with southpaw Sandy Koufax to give the Dodgers a deadly 1–2 punch in the starting pitching department. Drysdale's career ERA over fourteen seasons was just 2.95.*

Adding insult to injury: while the Cubs waded through a second consecutive pennantless decade in the 1960s, they watched Lou Brock, whom they traded in 1964, help the St. Louis Cardinals to three World Series.

7-game Series winning streak snaps as center fielder Curt Flood misplays Jim Northrup's seventh-inning drive into a 2-run triple that breaks up a scoreless game.

3. 1965, Los Angeles Dodgers over Minnesota Twins, 4 games to 3. Los Angeles is favored on the strength of its Sandy Koufax–Don Drysdale tandem, but Minnesota shocks the Dodgers by beating both aces in the first 2 games. Claude Osteen's Game Three shutout rights the ship for the Dodgers back in L.A., and Koufax and Drysdale return to form in the next 2 games to put the Dodgers up 3–2. Mudcat Grant beats Osteen in Game Six to tie the Series, but Koufax returns on two days' rest to pitch his second shutout in Game Seven.

Worth Remembering

They Still Talk About This One in Chicago. On June 15, 1964, the Cubs acquired pitchers Ernie Broglio and Bobby Shantz and outfielder Doug Clemens from the St. Louis Cardinals for pitchers Jack Spring and Paul Toth and an outfielder named Lou Brock three days shy of his twenty-fifth birthday. The other five players involved in the deal were all out of the big leagues by the end of the 1966 season—the same year that Brock won the first of what would be eight stolen-bases crowns in a career that took him to the Hall of Fame.

First Impressions Can Be Deceiving. Lew Krausse's career looked to be the stuff of which dreams are made: the son of a major league pitcher, he signed with the Kansas City Athletics right after his high school graduation, then came right to the majors and shut out the Angels on 3 hits in his pro debut. A's fans hoped he would be another Bob Feller. But it wasn't to be; Krausse dropped five of his remaining six decisions that year. He didn't make it back to the bigs until 1964, then went 2–6 over the next two seasons before having what appeared to be a break-through year in 1966, when he led the staff with a 14–9 record and a 2.98 ERA. But the next season he suffered through a suspension and a 7–17 record, and the A's dealt him to Milwaukee two years later. He bounced to three other clubs before calling it quits after the 1974 season with a career mark of 68–91.

He Couldn't Win for Losing. Roger Craig knew a few things about pitching—he had fashioned a 49–38 record in his first seven seasons with the Dodgers and would go on to a successful career as a pitching coach and manager, but not even Craig could figure out how to win with the dismal support he received as a starter for the 1962 and 1963 expansion Mets. Craig led the league with 24 losses in New York's maiden season, then lost 18 in a row in 1963 before he hit upon the idea of changing his uniform number to 13. That briefly changed Craig's luck—he immediately won his first game in three months—but he finished the year with 4 more losses to lead the league again, even though his ERA was a respectable 3.78. Craig's luck *really* changed after the season, though: the Mets traded him to St. Louis.

The Moose Bites Back. After the 1962 season the Yankees traded first baseman Bill "Moose" Skowron, a mainstay in pinstripes for the previous nine years, to the Dodgers to make room for twenty-two-year-old Joe Pepitone. It looked like a good move—Pepitone led the club with 27 homers—until the World Series, when the Yankees found themselves facing Skowron and the Dodgers. Pepitone hit just .154 and made a costly error in Game Four, while Skowron hit .385, drove in 2 runs in Game One, and homered in Game Two as L.A. swept the Series.

Four Heads Aren't Much Better Than One. After losing 94 games and enduring their fifteenth consecutive pennantless season in 1960, the Cubs tried an innovative idea in 1961: instead of appointing a manager, they went through the season with a rotating staff of four "head coaches": Vedie Himsl, Harry Craft, El Tappe, and Lou Klein. The results weren't encouraging: Chicago improved by just 4 games and finished in ninth place for the second year in a row.

DECADE SPOTLIGHT
Zoilo Versalles: Big Little Man

The list of men who won the American League's Most Valuable Player Award in the 1960s reads like a who's who of baseball stars. It includes Hall of Famers Mickey Mantle, Brooks Robinson, Frank Robinson, Carl Yastrzemski, and Harmon Killebrew, as well as New York Yankees legends Roger Maris—who won it twice—and Elston Howard, and 31-game winner Denny McLain.

The other player on the list is Minnesota Twins shortstop Zoilo Versalles, who, unlike the aforementioned luminaries, is a name that is all but forgotten three decades later. That's understandable considering that Versalles' major league career lasted a little more than nine full sea-

WHAT'S IN/WHAT'S OUT IN THE 1960s

In	Out
Expansion	Eight-team leagues
Swinging for the fences	Station-to-station baseball
The Dodgers as a pitching team	The Dodgers as a power team
Roger Maris' 61 (with an asterisk)	Babe Ruth's 60
Electronic scoreboards	Manual scoreboards
Dominant pitching	Dominant hitting
Clubs worrying about attendance	Clubs worrying about loyalty to their fans
Pitchers' parks	Hitters' parks
Sandy Koufax and Don Drysdale	Don Newcombe and Carl Erskine
The Mets as lovable losers	The Yankees as a dynasty
Leading the league with 30 saves	Leading the league with 15 saves
Marvin Miller taking on the owners	The MLBPA as powerless
Carl Yastrzemski and Roberto Clemente winning the batting title	Ted Williams and Stan Musial winning the batting title

A strange sight for Yankee fans: Moose Skowron, a Bronx Bomber for the previous nine years, poses in Dodger blue in 1963. Skowron, who had gained plenty of postseason experience in seven World Series with the Yankees, helped beat his former club in the 1963 Fall Classic.

Zoilo Versalles helped the Twins reach the Series with the best year of his career in 1965. Minnesota lost a thriller to the Dodgers, but Versalles hit safely in 6 of 7 games, including a 3-run homer in Game One.

sons and that he is the only one of the above-named players not to receive a single vote for Hall of Fame election, but it's also a bit ironic considering the long road that Versalles traveled to the summit of major league stardom.

When he came to the United States from Cuba at age seventeen, the 125-pound (56.7kg) Versalles looked more like a batboy than a future MVP candidate. "He was so skinny, I never thought he would be a hitter," Phil Howser, the general manager of the Twins' Charlotte, North Carolina, farm team, told *The Sporting News.* "You could tell he never had eaten well." Howser directed the scrawny shortstop to a restaurant for some fattening up, but there the language barrier proved to be a problem. "All I could get was soda and a piece of bread," Versalles recalled. "I didn't know how to ask. Boy, those days."

Papa Joe Cambria, a scout who signed many Cuban stars for Washington Senators–Minnesota Twins President Calvin Griffith, saw something special in Versalles, just as he had seen something special in Willie Miranda years before. Miranda was another Cuban shortstop signed by Cambria who went on to a successful major league career. When Cambria saw Versalles, he declared: "Someday this boy will be one of the greatest shortstops in the country. He will be greater than Willie Miranda."

Versalles would ultimately reward Cambria's confidence, but he encountered his share of problems—and critics—along the way. Griffith had several managers advise him to trade Versalles, insisting the Cuban product would never make it in the major leagues. Griffith held on to young Zoilo, however, even when a homesick Versalles left the Twins for a month in 1961—his first full season in the big leagues.

By 1962 Versalles had beefed up to 150 pounds (68.1kg) and was showing off a bigger bat, but he was also displaying a bigger mouth. He acquired a reputation as a hot dog and had earned the nickname "Zorro." Reporters quoted him as saying: "Someday I will be greater than Luis Aparicio," the future Hall of Fame short-stop with the White Sox. Versalles denied ever saying this, but the stigma of arrogance followed him.

His play nonetheless improved. In 1962 he played 160 games at shortstop for the Twins and hit 17 home runs. In 159 games in 1963 he hit .261 with 10 homers and a league-leading 13 triples, and won his first Gold Glove—beating out Aparicio, who had won the previous five. In 1964 he led the league in triples again and hit a career-high 20 homers.

Although he was silencing his critics, the cocky Cuban still had the problem of his own attitude to overcome. The turning point came in spring training in 1965. In an exhibition game a week before Opening Day, Twins Manager Sam Mele yanked Versalles after the shortstop made a half-hearted effort on a ground ball. When Versalles subsequently challenged Mele's authority, the manager held his ground and fined Zorro three hundred dollars. The incident gave Versalles the lesson in humility he needed. He responded with the best season of his career: 160 games played with a .273 average, 19 homers, 77 RBI, and 27 stolen bases, and AL-bests in runs (126), doubles (45), and triples (12) to go with his second Gold Glove. Killebrew, the Twins' big bat who had hit a league-high 49 homers the year before, missed two months with an elbow injury, but Versalles emerged as a team leader and sparked the franchise to its first pennant in thirty-two years. Zoilo was a near-unanimous MVP selection, the first AL shortstop to win the award since New York's Phil Rizzuto in 1950.

Versalles's quote to reporters after he learned he had won the award displayed his new maturity. "I couldn't believe I got so many votes," he said. "I thought anybody on our team could have got it and deserved it."

The 1970s
Liberty and the Pursuit of High Salaries

In the 1970s, the United States celebrated its bicentennial—the two hundredth anniversary of the nation's freedom from Mother England. In the same spirit during the seventies, Major League Baseball players staged a celebration of their own—for freedom from the reserve clause.

From baseball's beginnings, players belonged to the teams they signed contracts with. In 1970, Curtis Charles Flood began the movement that would change that oppressive dynamic. On October 7, 1969, the St. Louis Cardinals' center fielder had received a telephone call informing him that he had been traded to the Philadelphia Phillies. The call came as a shock, for Flood was coming off a fine .285 season in which he had led the National League with 362 putouts. The Cardinals had paid Flood ninety thousand dollars for his trouble and the Phillies offered him $100,000.

"I'm not going to let them do this to me," Flood told a friend. "They say if I don't go to Philadelphia, I don't play at all. Right there, they shoot down my rights. They shoot me down as a man. I won't stand for that."

As he wrote later in his autobiography, *The Way It Is*, "The lightning had struck. The dream lay shattered. It was a bad scene. To challenge the sanctity of organized baseball was to question one of the primary myths of American culture. To persist in the heresy required profound conviction, with endurance to match."

In a letter to Commissioner Bowie Kuhn, Flood challenged the premise of the reserve clause, terming it illegal and immoral. He believed his fourteen years of service in baseball entitled him to consider offers from other teams. Kuhn, trained as a lawyer, argued that a signed contract with St. Louis gave the Cardinals the legal right to reassign his contract to Philadelphia. Flood hired former Supreme Court Justice Arthur Goldberg to take his case through the legal system. On March 4, Judge Irving Ben Cooper denied Flood's requested injunction and recommended that the reserve clause be examined in a trial.

Curt Flood's pioneering challenge to the reserve clause left him out of the 1970 season. He played just one more year of Major League Baseball, for the Washington Senators.

George Steinbrenner's first free agent, Catfish Hunter, paid immediate dividends for the Yankees, winning 40 games in his first two seasons. Hunter's signing also paved the way for other big-money free agents.

"Baseball's status in the life of the nation is so pervasive that it would not strain credulity to say the Court can take judicial notice that baseball is everybody's business," Cooper wrote of *Flood* v. *Kuhn*. "To put it mildly and with restraint, it would be unfortunate indeed if a fine sport and profession, which brings surcease from daily travail and an escape from the ordinary to most inhabitants of this land, were to suffer in the least because of undue concentration by any one or any group on commercial and profit considerations. The game is on higher ground; it behooves everyone to keep it there."

For the sake of the case, Goldberg advised Flood to sit out the 1970 season. Flood watched in self-imposed exile in Denmark as the debate was joined. One of the interested parties was Jackie Robinson, the first African American to play modern major league baseball. "I think Curt is doing a service to all players in the leagues, especially for the younger players coming up who are not superstars," Robinson said. "All he is asking for is the right to negotiate."

Major League Teams in the 1970s
(Teams played entire decade unless otherwise noted)

NATIONAL LEAGUE
East
Chicago Cubs
Montreal Expos
New York Mets
Philadelphia Phillies
Pittsburgh Pirates
St. Louis Cardinals

West
Atlanta Braves
Cincinnati Reds
Houston Astros
Los Angeles Dodgers
San Diego Padres
San Francisco Giants

AMERICAN LEAGUE
East
Baltimore Orioles
Boston Red Sox
Cleveland Indians
Detroit Tigers
Milwaukee Brewers (in AL West 1970–1971; moved to AL East in 1972)
New York Yankees
Toronto Blue Jays (1977–1979)
Washington Senators

West
California Angels
Chicago White Sox
Kansas City Royals
Minnesota Twins
Oakland Athletics
Seattle Mariners (1977–1979)
Washington Senators (in AL East 1970–1971; became Texas Rangers and moved to AL West in 1972)

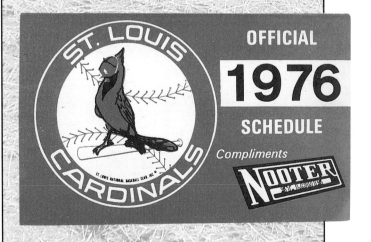

ST. LOUIS CARDINALS
ST. LOUIS NATIONAL BASEBALL CLUB, INC.

OFFICIAL
1976
SCHEDULE
Compliments
NOOTER
ST. LOUIS

That right was not upheld by the courts. Flood lost the battle but laid the foundation for a successful war.

Much like the real thing, the players' revolutionary war was not won overnight. The battle was waged for years, but it started to turn in the players' favor in the mid-1960s, when Marvin Miller was elected executive director of the Major League Baseball Players Association. Soon after he took over, Miller fired his first salvos on the owners by winning the players significant increases in the minimum salary and in the owners' contributions to the players' pension fund, as well as the right to agent representation in contract talks. The shooting grew heavier in 1972, when the first strike in baseball history won the players a key concession: salary arbitration. A player no longer had to simply take or leave the compensation his team offered. There were still more cannons to be fired, however. A big one went off after the 1974 season, when arbitrator Peter Seitz, a New York lawyer, declared Oakland's star pitcher Catfish Hunter a free agent because the A's had not honored all the terms of his contract. Of course, this status would not have worked to Hunter's advantage had the club owners remained unified in their agreed-upon "hands-off" posture; Hunter would have had no choice but to take Oakland's offer if it had been the only one on the table. But in a telling sign of the future, the owners—or at least one—could not hold back. Less than two weeks later, New York Yankees boss George Steinbrenner, bent on re-building his club at any cost, signed Hunter to a five-year, $3.75 million contract. While most of Steinbrenner's fellow owners covered their eyes, *The Sporting News* ominously—and accurately—forecasted that "baseball's establishment will live to regret the Catfish Hunter case, and baseball players will live to profit from it."

Having penetrated the owners' defenses, the players had only to find a way to get more of themselves on the open market; Hunter provided vivid proof that the money would undoubtedly be there. Again, it was Seitz who provided the solution. A year after the Hunter case, Seitz declared Los Angeles Dodgers pitcher Andy Messersmith and Montreal Expos pitcher Dave McNally free agents because, in the arbitrator's judgment, the reserve clause bound those players to their teams for only one year after completion of their contracts, not for life. Messersmith cashed in immediately—to the tune of one million dollars

The first free agent class produced mixed results. There were disappointments, such as Oakland's Joe Rudi (above, left), who signed with the Angels, hit .264 in his first year, and saw his average decline each of the next three seasons. Other free agents, such as Gary Matthews (left), who jumped from the Giants to the Braves, maintained their productivity.

for three years from the Atlanta Braves—and by July of 1976, after the dust of appeals, negotiations, and a spring-training lockout cleared, the owners had no choice but to agree to a free-agency system. Now the players had the opening they needed; into it stepped the twenty-four players who made up free agency's Class of 1976. The names included Oakland's Reggie Jackson, Sal Bando, Rollie Fingers, Joe Rudi, Gene Tenace, Don Baylor, Bert Campaneris, and Willie McCovey; Cincinnati's Don Gullett; Baltimore's Bobby Grich; the Yankees' Doyle Alexander; Minnesota's Bill Campbell; Pittsburgh's Richie Hebner; and San Francisco's Gary Matthews. Jackson (three million dollars for five years from the Yankees) and Rudi (two million dollars for five years from the California Angels) were among the twelve who signed million-dollar deals. By the end of the decade, seven-figure free agent deals were commonplace, even for mediocre players.

Besides its inflationary economics and its long hair and gaudy attire on the field, the baseball scene in the seventies mirrored life outside the lines in its revolutionary thinking. The climate in the seventies was right for a major change, and the American League made one with the institution of the designated hitter rule in 1973. The result was more offense—as well as a debate that still continues more than twenty years later, in large part because the National League has stuck to tradition and provided fans with a clear alternative.

Regardless of what fans were saying about free agency or the designated hitter rule, however, the game on the field captured the fans' attention; per-team attendance increased 48 percent from 1969 to 1979. At the center of that time span was the 1975 World Series, regarded as the moment when baseball captivated (or recaptivated, for those who may have strayed) a generation of fans. An estimated seventy million television viewers watched one of the most thrilling Series of all time, and witnessed the unforgettable image of Boston's Carlton Fisk waving his winning home run fair in the twelfth inning of Game Six. By 1977 there were two new expansion teams—the Toronto Blue Jays and Seattle Mariners—and total attendance soared to a record thirty-nine million. The bitter memories of players strikes and lockouts seemed light years away. Fans soon discovered, however, that such turmoil was in baseball's future as well as its past.

Above, right: *After three years with San Diego and Oakland, Willie McCovey returned to the Giants in 1977 via free agency. Here McCovey hits his 499th career home run on July 6, 1978.* **Right:** *Boston's Carlton Fisk is greeted by jubilant teammates after his twelfth-inning home run off Cincinnati's Pat Darcy in Game Six of the 1975 Series.*

1970: *Ball Four*, pitcher Jim Bouton's candid, colorful diary of the Seattle Pilots' 1969 season, interspersed with anecdotes about other players in both leagues, is published. It is a groundbreaking book, both humorous and revealing, and it brings the wrath of Commissioner Bowie Kuhn upon its author, who starts the season as a pitcher for the Houston Astros and ends up as a television commentator.

1970: Cincinnati's Riverfront Stadium and Pittsburgh's Three Rivers Stadium open.

1970: San Francisco's Bobby Bonds strikes out a record 189 times.

Bankrupt Pilots Fly to Milwaukee
March 30, 1970: With Opening Day just a few days off, AL club owners approve the move of the financially strapped Pilots to Milwaukee. The next day a Seattle bankruptcy court validates a $10.8 million offer for the club from Milwaukee Brewers Inc. The team draws 933,690 in its first season in Milwaukee.

April 22, 1970: Presented with his 1969 Cy Young Award before the game, New York Mets ace Tom Seaver celebrates by striking out a record 10 straight San Diego Padres on his way to a single-game record-tying total of 19 in 1 game.

April 30, 1970: *President Richard Nixon announces that the United States is sending troops into Cambodia to combat Communist forces. The president calls the action, which meets with criticism from many Americans, an extension of the Vietnam War, not an invasion.*

May 4, 1970: *A student antiwar demonstration at Kent State University ends in tragedy when National Guardsmen, called in to restore order, fire on the crowd, killing four and wounding nine.*

June 21, 1970: Cesar Gutierrez, a lifetime .235 hitter, ties a major league record with 7 hits in 7 at bats in a 12-inning Detroit win over Cleveland. Gutierrez's uniform number? Seven.

It's the Fans' Game Again
July 14, 1970: The fans elect the All-Star Game starters for the first time since 1957—a tradition that continues today. No matter who does the voting, however, the National League keeps winning; the senior circuit claims its eighth straight midsummer classic, 5–4, on Jim Hickman's twelfth-inning single.

October 1970: Commissioner Kuhn settles a one-day playoff strike by major league umpires by getting club owners to

Pittsburgh's Roberto Clemente triples off Baltimore's Jim Palmer in Game Six of the 1971 World Series. The Orioles won the game 3–2 in 10 innings to stay alive, but lost the Series the next day. The catcher is Ellie Hendricks and the umpire is John Kibler.

agree to recognize the newly formed Major League Umpires Association and to grant the umpires a minimum salary of twenty-two thousand dollars.

1971: Rules change: for the first time, all players are required to wear protective batting helmets. To qualify as a rookie, a player must not have more than 130 at bats or 50 innings pitched in the major leagues during the previous season or seasons, nor more than forty-five days of service on a major league roster between Opening Day and August 31.

1971: Philadelphia's Veterans Stadium opens.

April 20, 1971: *The Supreme Court rules that busing will remain the primary means of achieving school integration.*

July 13, 1971: The American League snaps an 8-game all-star losing streak as Reggie Jackson, Frank Robinson, and Harmon Killebrew hit home runs in a 6–4 win at Detroit's Tiger Stadium.

Washington's Loss Is Texas' Gain
September 20, 1971: At the conclusion of the season, the Washington Senators—the second incarnation of an AL team in the nation's capital—move to the Dallas–Fort Worth area and become the Texas Rangers. The club takes up residence in Arlington Stadium (which was formerly Turnpike Stadium).

Rod Carew, who won six batting titles from 1972 to 1978, moved from second base to first in 1976. His best year at the plate was 1978, when he hit .388 with 16 triples and 128 runs, all league highs.

October 13, 1971: The Pittsburgh Pirates beat the Baltimore Orioles 4–3 in Three Rivers Stadium in the first World Series night game. The experiment is judged a rousing success.

December 10, 1971: The New York Mets trade Nolan Ryan, Don Rose, Leroy Stanton, and Francisco Estrada to the California Angels for infielder Jim Fregosi in one of the worst deals of all time.

1972: California's Nolan Ryan allows an all-time-low 5.26 hits per 9 innings. Minnesota's Rod Carew hits .318 to become the first AL batting champ without a home run.

February 2, 1972: The Philadelphia Phillies acquire Steve Carlton from the St. Louis Cardinals for Rick Wise. Carlton proceeds to win 27 games and the first of his four Cy Young Awards in 1972.

Strike One, They're Out
April 1, 1972: A dispute over issues—mainly pension money—leads to the first general players strike in baseball history and delays the start of the season by ten days. Most teams lose several hundred thousand dollars and a total of 86 games are canceled before the two sides reach a settlement. The players association wins two key concessions: the right to seek the decision of an impartial arbitrator when management and player reach a salary impasse (the arbitrator must choose either the owner's proposed figure or that of the player) and "the ten and five rule," which allows a player with ten years of major league service, the last five with the same team, to veto a trade.

May 11, 1972: The San Francisco Giants trade Willie Mays to the Mets for pitcher Charlie Williams and fifty thousand dollars.

June 19, 1972: The Supreme Court rules against Curt Flood in the player's 1970 suit against the reserve clause.

December 31, 1972: The baseball world is shocked and saddened by the tragic death of Pirates star Roberto Clemente, killed in a plane crash while on a mercy mission for earthquake victims in Nicaragua. The thirty-eight-year-old Clemente recorded the three thousandth hit of his career just three months before. The five-year waiting period is waived and Clemente is voted into the Hall of Fame the next year.

Let the Controversy Begin
1973: Rules change: the American League gives birth to one of the greatest debates of the post–World War II era by instituting the designated hitter rule, which allows an additional hitter to bat in the pitcher's spot. Ron Blomberg of the Yankees becomes the first official designated hitter in what is initially adopted as a three-year experiment to put some more offense into the game. The National League, meanwhile, holds fast to tradition. A save is defined as follows: a relief pitcher is credited with a save when he enters a game with the potential tying or winning run either on base or at the plate or pitches at least 3 effective innings and, in either case, preserves the lead.

1973: Dick Allen signs a three-year contract with the Chicago White Sox that will pay him $250,000 a year and make him baseball's highest-paid player.

1973: Kansas City's Royals Stadium opens. It is renamed Ewing M. Kauffman Stadium twenty years later.

1973: In 326 innings, California's Nolan Ryan of the California Angels strikes out 383 hitters, breaking Sandy Koufax's single-season record of 382. Ryan nonetheless loses 16 of 37 decisions.

January 22, 1973: *In* Roe *v.* Wade, *the Supreme Court rules that all state laws that prohibit voluntary abortion before the third month are unconstitutional.*

January 27, 1973: *An immediate cease-fire begins in Vietnam upon the signing of the Paris peace agreement by North and South Vietnam, the Vietcong, and the United States. The agreement ends U.S. military involvement in Southeast Asia and prompts the secretary of defense to announce the end of the military draft. Henry Kissinger and Le Duc Tho win the Nobel Peace Prize for negotiating the agreement.*

February 7, 1973: *A committee is created by the Senate to investigate the Watergate conspiracy. The investigation leads to the*

Above: *A throwback to the iron men of old, Mike Marshall led the league in appearances, relief wins, and saves in both 1973 and 1974. His 208 innings in 1974 was a staggering total for a relief pitcher.* Right: *Cleveland's Frank Robinson hits a drive out of Fenway Park in 1974, his 574th career home run. The Indians named him their player-manager the next day.*

resignations of various presidential aides in the coming months. On July 16, the Senate Watergate committee learns that all conversations in the Oval Office are routinely taped. The committee issues a subpoena for all tapes in order to prove charges that Nixon was involved in the Watergate cover-up. On July 23, Nixon rejects the subpoena outright, calling the tapes privileged.

September 25, 1973: The Say Hey Kid, Willie Mays, calls it a career at age forty-two after twenty-two years in the major leagues. In 1979, in his first year of eligibility, Mays is elected to the Hall of Fame by a landslide, garnering the highest vote total in history.

October 8, 1973: During Game Three of the NL championship series, a fight between New York's Bud Harrelson and Cincinnati's Pete Rose ignites the Shea Stadium crowd into a frenzy, with fans hurling objects at Rose until the Reds left fielder and his teammates vacate the field. After Tom Seaver, Willie Mays, and a few other Mets players help settle the crowd and order is restored, New York goes on to a 9–2 win.

October 20, 1973: *The energy shortage in the United States is brought to a crisis level when Arab oil-producing countries place an embargo on oil exports to the United States that will last until March of next year.*

November–December 1973: Oakland A's stars Reggie Jackson, Sal Bando, Ken Holtzman, Rollie Fingers, and Darold Knowles are big winners while teammates Joe Rudi and Gene Tenace suffer defeat in the first round of salary arbitration. Third baseman Ron Santo of the Chicago Cubs becomes the first player to invoke "the ten and five rule" when he vetoes a trade to the California Angels.

1974: Three single-season records are set in the National League: St. Louis' Lou Brock steals 118 bases to break Maury Wills' mark; Los Angeles pitcher Mike Marshall—the first reliever ever to win the Cy Young Award—appears in 106 games; and Ed Kranepool of the Mets bats .486 as a pinch hitter.

January 1, 1974: Lee MacPhail replaces Joe Cronin as AL president.

Hammerin' Hank Passes the Babe
April 8, 1974: At 9:07 p.m. Eastern standard time, as a national television audience and a standing-room-only crowd of 53,775 looks on at Atlanta Stadium, the Braves' Hank Aaron clubs the 715th home run of his career—a shot over the left-field fence off Los Angeles' Al Downing—and breaks Babe Ruth's career home run record. Aaron finishes the year with a career total of 733 homers.

August 8, 1974: *President Nixon announces on national television that he is resigning, effective at noon the next day. His resignation, the first by a U.S. president, was urged by Republicans in Congress who warned that he would be convicted and impeached if he didn't resign. Gerald Ford is sworn in the next day; Nelson Rockefeller becomes vice president. On September 8, President Ford grants*

Lou Brock (top) *scored 100 or more runs seven times and was baseball's all-time stolen base king—until Rickey Henderson came along. Above: Sparky Lyle, the 1977 Cy Young Award winner and one of the game's most colorful players, in action in 1978, the year he wrote a tell-all book called* The Bronx Zoo *and saw the Yankees trade him to Texas.*

Nixon an unconditional pardon for any crimes he may have committed.

Robinson Breaks Managerial Color Line
October 3, 1974: The Cleveland Indians make history by naming Frank Robinson their player-manager, making the future Hall of Famer baseball's first black manager. The Indians finish in 1975 in fourth place with a 79–80 record in the first of Robinson's two-plus seasons at the helm.

October 17, 1974: The Oakland A's defeat the Dodgers in 5 games to win their third straight World Series, a feat accomplished by only the Yankees—and no other team since.

November 2, 1974: The Braves trade Hank Aaron to the Brewers for outfielder Dave May and pitcher Roger Alexander. Aaron will hit just 12 homers in his first year in Milwaukee while teammate George Scott leads the league in home runs (36) and runs batted in (109).

November 27, 1974: Commissioner Bowie Kuhn suspends George Steinbrenner after the volatile Yankees owner is convicted of illegal political campaign contributions.

Hunter Breaks the Bank
December 31, 1974: For baseball owners it is an ominous harbinger of things to come: Oakland's Jim "Catfish" Hunter, who less than two weeks earlier was declared a free agent by arbitrator Peter Seitz because A's owner Charlie Finley had failed to fulfill all the terms of the pitcher's contract, signs a five-year, $3.75 million contract with owner George Steinbrenner and the rebuilding Yankees.

1975: Rules change: the American League permanently adopts the designated hitter rule. The save rule is amended so that a pitcher is credited with a save when he is the finishing, but not the winning, pitcher, and when he qualifies under one of the following conditions: he enters the game with a lead of no more than 3 runs and pitches at least 1 inning; he enters the game with the potential tying run on base, at bat, or on deck; or he pitches effectively regardless of his team's lead. Umpires may now eject hitters and pitchers from a game for using doctored bats or balls.

April 30, 1975: *The Saigon government falls to the Communist Vietcong as all remaining Americans evacuate, marking the end of the war in Vietnam.*

June 1, 1975: California's Nolan Ryan pitches his his fourth no-hitter in three years to beat Baltimore by a score of 1–0 at Anaheim Stadium.

October 1975: Boston's Fred Lynn becomes the first player to be named Rookie of the Year and Most Valuable Player for the same season.

The Floodgates Are Open
December 23, 1975: Arbitrator Peter Seitz rules that Dodgers pitcher Andy Messersmith and Expos pitcher Dave McNally, who had played the 1975 season without contracts, are free agents because the reserve clause binds a player to his team for only one year after his contract expires; the clause is not automatically renewed in perpetuity as the owners contended. Seitz's ruling, which is seen as a way around the reserve clause, is upheld in the U.S. district courts. The ripple effects are felt immediately: McNally retires,

October 2, 1978: In a winner-take-all playoff game for the AL East title, Bucky Dent drives Red Sox right-hander Mike Torrez's pitch over Fenway Park's Green Monster for a 3-run homer that puts the Yankees ahead.

New York's Willie Randolph awaits the throw as Davey Lopes of the Dodgers tries to steal second in Game Four of the 1977 World Series. The Yankees won in 6 games to claim their first championship since 1962.

but Messersmith signs a three-year, one million dollar contract with Atlanta. The players find themselves locked out of spring training by the angry owners, but Commissioner Kuhn intervenes in time to get the season under way while negotiations and appeals continue and the owners try to stem the tide against a flood of big-money free agents.

1976: Rules change: an umpire may remove a bat from the game if any substance extends past the 18-inch (45.7cm) limit from the base of the handle.

April 1976: After a two-year stint in the Mets' Shea Stadium, the Yankees return to newly renovated Yankee Stadium for what will be their first pennant-winning season since 1964.

June 18, 1976: Citing "the best interests of baseball," Commissioner Kuhn voids Oakland A's owner Charlie Finley's $3.5 million sales of Vida Blue (to the Yankees) and Joe Rudi and Rollie Fingers (to the Red Sox). Finley's subsequent appeals are denied. Kuhn subsequently imposes a $400,000 limit on all such player-for-cash transactions.

July 1976: With the reserve clause essentially dead from the Messersmith-McNally case and all avenues of appeal exhausted, the owners consent to a new basic agreement that provides for a modified reserve system: a player will be eligible for free agency after six years in the majors, and a team that loses a free agent will receive only amateur draft picks as compensation. This winter twenty-four

players will test the market as free agents; half of them will sign seven-figure deals.

July 20, 1976: In what will be his final season, forty-two-year-old home run king Hank Aaron hits the 755th and final round-tripper of his twenty-three-year career off California's Dick Drago at Milwaukee's County Stadium.

October 21, 1976: The Cincinnati Reds, the National League's first repeat champs since 1922, sweep the Yankees to become the first NL team since 1954 to win back-to-back World Series. The designated hitter rule, which under a new plan will be used in the Series in alternating years, is employed for the first time.

Toronto's In, Seattle's Back
1977: The American League adds two new expansion franchises: the Toronto Blue Jays, who will play in Exhibition Stadium, and the Seattle Mariners, who move into the newly built Kingdome. The Blue Jays win only 54 games and finish in the AL East cellar; the Mariners win 64 and avoid last place by a half-game.

April 15, 1977: Montreal's Olympic Stadium opens.

May 11, 1977: Commissioner Kuhn suspends Braves owner Ted Turner for attempting to negotiate with San Francisco's Gary Matthews before the outfielder became a free agent.

August 29, 1977: St. Louis' thirty-eight-year-old Lou Brock steals the 893rd base of his career, breaking Ty Cobb's record.

October 1977: Sparky Lyle of the Yankees, 13–5 with 26 saves and a 2.17 earned-run average, becomes the first AL relief pitcher to win the Cy Young Award.

1978: Rules change: umpires now have the authority to warn pitchers against intentionally hitting batters; a second offense results in ejection. A victory will not be awarded to a relief pitcher who is ineffective in a brief appearance if a succeeding pitcher is effective in helping his team maintain the lead; in such cases the succeeding reliever will be credited with the victory. The game-winning RBI is added as an official statistic. Any games played to break a divisional tie will be included in the statistics for that regular season.

June 28, 1978: *The Supreme Court rules that fixed racial quotas in public educational institutions are unconstitutional.*

August 1, 1978: Recording his three thousandth career hit earlier in the season, Cincinnati slugger Pete Rose's hitting streak is stopped at 44 games in Atlanta. The streak ties Willie Keeler's NL record and is second only to Joe DiMaggio's mark of 56. After the season Rose signs a lucrative free agent deal with the Phillies.

September 23, 1978: California's twenty-seven-year-old outfielder Lyman Bostock, who had signed with the Angels as a free agent in the offseason, is murdered in Gary, Indiana.

October 2, 1978: The Yankees, who had trailed by 14 games in July, defeat the Boston Red Sox 5–4 in a 1-game playoff

at Fenway Park to win the AL East flag. It is the first AL East playoff since 1948—the year the Red Sox lost to the Cleveland Indians at Fenway.

1979: Pittsburgh's Dave Parker, the NL batting champ in 1978, becomes baseball's first million-dollar-a-year player. He proves his value by helping the Pirates win the World Series.

1979: Pointing to skyrocketing player salaries, major league umpires go on strike for all of spring training and into the regular season, seeking better wages and benefits. Finally, on May 18, after numerous complaints about the quality of the replacement umpires, the league presidents agree on a new contract.

March 26, 1979: *War between Egypt and Israel ends when Israeli Prime Minister Menachem Begin and Egyptian President Anwar Sadat sign a peace treaty in a ceremony at the White House.*

March 28, 1979: *The worst accident in history at a U.S. nuclear power plant occurs at Three Mile Island near Harrisburg, Pennsylvania, causing radioactive steam to be released into the atmosphere.*

May 17, 1979: With 2 outs in the tenth inning, Mike Schmidt's second homer of the day lifts the Phillies to a 23–22 win over the Cubs in windy Wrigley Field.

October 1979: Minnesota's Mike Marshall sets an AL record with 90 appearances. St. Louis shortstop Gary Templeton hits .314 and is the first switch-hitter to record 100 hits from each side of the plate in the same season.

November 4, 1979: *Iranian students storm the U.S. Embassy in Tehran, taking sixty-six Americans hostage and demanding that the ousted Shah be released from the United States. In the next few days, President Carter retaliates by freezing Iranian assets in U.S. banks and barring oil from Iran. He also sends mediators to Iran to negotiate the release of the hostages.*

Top left: *The Cobra, Dave Parker, landed a monster contract in 1979 and helped the Pirates wrap up a world championship with a .345 World Series batting average.* Left: *Pete Rose's 44-game hitting streak captured headlines in 1978. Here Rose, a.k.a. Charlie Hustle, lines a base hit on July 20 to extend the streak to 33 consecutive games.*

Man of the Decade: Nolan Ryan

Contemporaries such as Tom Seaver, Jim Palmer, Steve Carlton, and Catfish Hunter won more games in the seventies than Nolan Ryan, and each won at least one Cy Young Award and one World Series game in his career, neither of which Ryan ever achieved. But none mastered the art of the strikeout or the no-hitter as well as Ryan, who owns fifty-three major league records. Giving Ryan the nod here is as much a tribute to his impressive numbers in the decade—a 155–146 record, 2,678 strikeouts in 2,465 innings (he led the league seven times in the seventies), a 3.14 ERA, 164 complete games, 42 shutouts, and 4 no-hitters—as it is to his amazing longevity. He threw 2 no-hitters in the early nineties, long after the aforementioned foursome had hung 'em up.

Right: *Nolan Ryan wasn't much better than a .500 pitcher in the 1970s, but he stole the show with 4 no-hitters and 2,678 strikeouts.* **Below:** *Hammerin' Hank Aaron smacks a pitch from Los Angeles' Al Downing into the left-field bullpen at Fulton County Stadium for career home run number 715.*

Most Memorable Games

1. 1975 World Series, Game Six, October 21 at Fenway Park; Boston Red Sox 7, Cincinnati Reds 6. It is unlikely that anyone who saw it will ever forget the sight of Red Sox catcher Carlton Fisk waving his twelfth-inning, game-winning home run fair as 35,205 frantic Fenway fans hold their breath and a captivated audience watches on national television. The image is frozen in time as the definitive moment that baseball reaffirmed its position as the national pastime.

2. October 2, 1978, at Fenway Park; New York Yankees 5, Boston Red Sox 4. In a 1-game playoff for the AL East title, the Red Sox lead the Yankees and Cy Young shoo-in Ron Guidry 2–0 in the seventh when Bucky Dent, who has hit 4 home runs all season and just 22 in his six years in the majors, launches a 3-run homer over Fenway's vaunted Green Monster. The Yankees hold on to win the game and go on to take the pennant and the World Series.

3. April 8, 1974, at Atlanta-Fulton County Stadium; Atlanta Braves 7, Los Angeles Dodgers 4. Rarely has an April baseball game attracted such attention—a capacity crowd of 53,775 and a national TV audience. With the Dodgers leading 3–1 in the fourth inning, L.A. starter Al Downing tries to blow a 1–0 fastball by Braves cleanup hitter Hank Aaron. Hammerin' Hank swings and the rest is history: a home run to left field, the 715th of his career, pushes him past Babe Ruth into sole possession of the all-time home run crown. Braves reliever Tom House catches the ball in the bullpen and returns it to Aaron.

Few pitchers have been as dominant for a full season as Ron Guidry of the Yankees was in 1978. That year Guidry, whose home state and blazing fastball earned him the nickname Louisiana Lightning, led the league in wins (25, against just 3 defeats), ERA (1.74), and shutouts (9), en route to winning the Cy Young Award.

DECADE PITCHING LEADERS

	National League			American League		
YEAR	PLAYER	TEAM	ERA	PLAYER	TEAM	ERA
1970	Tom Seaver	New York	2.81	Diego Segui	Oakland	2.56
1971	Tom Seaver	New York	1.76	Vida Blue	Oakland	1.82
1972	Steve Carlton	Philadelphia	1.97	Luis Tiant	Boston	1.91
1973	Tom Seaver	New York	2.08	Jim Palmer	Baltimore	2.40
1974	Buzz Capra	Atlanta	2.28	Catfish Hunter	Oakland	2.49
1975	Randy Jones	San Diego	2.24	Jim Palmer	Baltimore	2.09
1976	John Denny	St. Louis	2.52	Mark Fidrych	Detroit	2.34
1977	John Candelaria	Pittsburgh	2.34	Frank Tanana	California	2.54
1978	Craig Swan	New York	2.43	Ron Guidry	New York	1.74
1979	J.R. Richard	Houston	2.71	Ron Guidry	New York	2.78

Dodger knuckleballer Charlie Hough surrenders Reggie Jackson's record-tying third home run in Game Six of the '77 Series. Los Angeles manager Tom Lasorda called it the "greatest performance I've ever seen."

4. 1977 World Series, Game Six, October 18 at Yankee Stadium; New York Yankees 8, Los Angeles Dodgers 4. He calls himself "the straw that stirs the drink." His fans call him "Mr. October." His critics call him a hot dog. But no one can deny that Reggie Jackson's performance on this night—3 homers on 3 consecutive swings in New York's Series-clinching win—is one of the greatest in baseball history. Jackson sets Series records for homers (5), runs (10), and total bases (25).

5. 1976 American League Championship Series, Game Five, October 14 at Yankee Stadium; New York Yankees 7, Kansas City Royals 6. The Royals rally from a 6–3 deficit in the eighth, but Chris Chambliss hits a dramatic ninth-inning home run, setting off pandemonium in the Bronx and lifting the Yankees to their first pennant since 1964.

Best Pennant Races

1. 1978 AL East: New York Yankees–Boston Red Sox. One of the most compelling and dramatic races in baseball history has the ebb and flow of a classic prize fight: first the Yankees, who are embroiled in controversy and trail by 14 games on July 17, come back to life after Bob Lemon replaces Billy Martin as manager. Then the Red Sox, who fell 3 games off the pace in mid-September, win their last 8 games and 12 of their last 14 to force a tie. New York finally delivers the knockout blow in a thrilling 1-game playoff.

Red Sox outfielder Fred Lynn turned in the finest season of his career in 1979, leading the American League with a .333 batting average, hitting 39 home runs, and driving in 122 runs. All three were career highs.

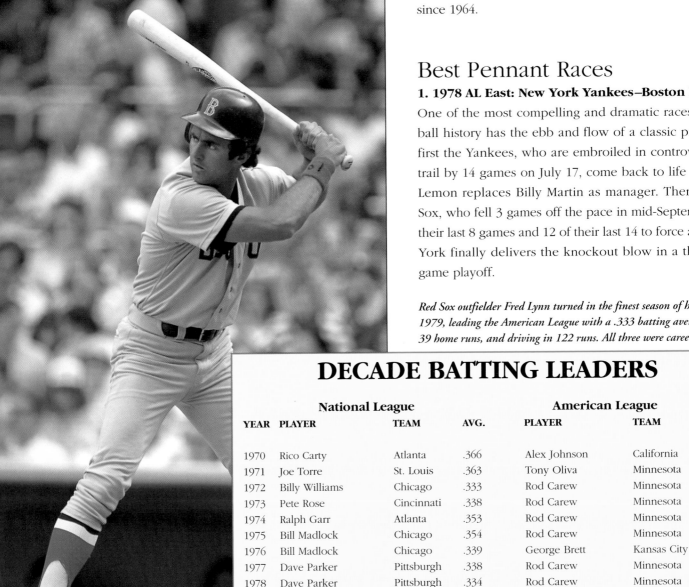

DECADE BATTING LEADERS

	National League			American League		
YEAR	PLAYER	TEAM	AVG.	PLAYER	TEAM	AVG.
1970	Rico Carty	Atlanta	.366	Alex Johnson	California	.329
1971	Joe Torre	St. Louis	.363	Tony Oliva	Minnesota	.337
1972	Billy Williams	Chicago	.333	Rod Carew	Minnesota	.318
1973	Pete Rose	Cincinnati	.338	Rod Carew	Minnesota	.350
1974	Ralph Garr	Atlanta	.353	Rod Carew	Minnesota	.364
1975	Bill Madlock	Chicago	.354	Rod Carew	Minnesota	.359
1976	Bill Madlock	Chicago	.339	George Brett	Kansas City	.333
1977	Dave Parker	Pittsburgh	.338	Rod Carew	Minnesota	.388
1978	Dave Parker	Pittsburgh	.334	Rod Carew	Minnesota	.333
1979	Keith Hernandez	St. Louis	.344	Fred Lynn	Boston	.333

2. 1973 NL East: New York Mets–St. Louis Cardinals–Pittsburgh Pirates–Montreal Expos–Chicago Cubs.
One of the wackiest and most wide-open races in the game's history goes down to the season's final weekend; Pittsburgh eliminates Montreal, and St. Louis, which suffered the loss of ace Bob Gibson down the stretch, stays alive while the Mets and Cubs do battle in Chicago. Rainouts extend the season an extra day and force New York and Chicago to play 4 games in the last two days. The Mets get a split in the first twin bill and Jon Matlack wins a 2-hit shutout in the first game on October 1 to give New York the flag. Despite posting the lowest winning percentage of any pennant winner in history (82–79, .509), the Mets—using reliever Tug McGraw's slogan of "You Gotta Believe" as a rallying cry—make Yogi Berra the only manager besides Joe McCarthy to win pennants in both the American and National Leagues.

3. 1972 AL East: Detroit Tigers–Boston Red Sox–Baltimore Orioles–New York Yankees. Four clubs are within striking distance of the top in the final month of a strike-shortened season, but Detroit and Boston are the only ones still alive as the season comes to a close. The two teams head into a season-ending series in a virtual deadlock, but the Tigers, led by Al Kaline, win 2 of the 3 games played before their home crowd to capture the division crown.

Best Teams

1. 1975 Cincinnati Reds, 108–54; manager: Sparky Anderson. The Big Red Machine cranked out a league-high 840 runs and rolled to the first of two world championships with offensive stars Joe Morgan (NL MVP with a .327 average, 17 homers, and 94 RBI), Johnny Bench (.283, 28, 110), George Foster (.300, 23, 78), Tony Perez (.282, 20, 109), Pete Rose (317, 7, 74), and Ken Griffey (305, 4, 46). Starters Don Gullet, Gary Nolan, and Jack Billingham each won 15 games, but the bullpen, led by Rawly Eastwick (22 saves) and Will McEnaney (15) was the league's most reliable, racking up an NL-best 50 saves—14 more than the league's next closest team, the St. Louis Cardinals.

2. 1973 Oakland A's, 94–68; manager: Dick Williams. In the midst of winning three straight World Series, these free-spirited, crazy A's made it look easy. And it was—thanks to a starting rotation that featured three 20-game winners in Catfish Hunter (21–5), Ken Holtzman (21–13), and Vida Blue (20–9), a bullpen led by Rollie Fingers (22 saves, 1.91 ERA), and a lineup card with names such as AL MVP Reggie Jackson (.293, 32 homers, 117 RBI), Sal Bando (.287, 29, 98), Gene Tenace (.259, 24, 84), Joe Rudi (.270, 12, 66), and Bill North (.285, 53 stolen bases).

3. 1970 Baltimore Orioles, 108–54; manager: Earl Weaver. Upset victims in the 1969 Series at the hands of the Miracle Mets, the O's were on a mission to claim the championship they felt was rightfully theirs. The mission was accomplished on the arms of a trio of 20-game winners—Mike Cuellar (24–8), Dave McNally (24–9), and Jim

Palmer (20–10)—who alone turned in more complete games (54) than any other team in the league, and the bats of league MVP Boog Powell (.297, 35 homers, 114 RBI), Frank Robinson (.306, 25, 78), and defensive wizard Brooks Robinson (.276, 18, 94).

Best World Series

1. 1975, Cincinnati Reds over Boston Red Sox, 4 games to 3. At a time when baseball's popularity is said to be waning, the Reds and Red Sox stage a classic confrontation. Cincinnati emerges victorious in a Series that has it all: great performances by MVP Pete Rose (a Series-high 10 hits and a .370 average), Tony Perez (3 homers and 7 RBI), and Luis Tiant (2 complete-game victories); the controversy of Ed Armbrister's alleged interference that helps the Reds win Game Three; and the drama of Carlton Fisk's game-winning homer in the twelfth inning of Game Six and Joe Morgan's 2-out RBI single that brings home the winning run in the finale.

2. 1979, Pittsburgh Pirates over Baltimore Orioles, 4 games to 3. The Orioles win 3 of the first 4 games and have Mike Flanagan, Jim Palmer, and Scott McGregor lined up to close things out. But the Pirates have other ideas—they win the final 3 games behind the hot hitting of Bill Madlock, Phil Garner, and Series MVP Willie Stargell, the thirty-eight-year-old first basemen who hits .400 with 3 homers and 7 RBI.

3. 1973, Oakland A's over New York Mets, 4 games to 3. Oakland wins a 7-game thriller for the second consecutive year, this time outlasting the resilient Mets behind the efforts of MVP Reggie Jackson (9 hits, 6 RBI), Ken

Tom Terrific, a.k.a. Tom Seaver of the Mets, delivers a pitch in Game Three of the 1973 World Series. Seaver was a model of consistency during his years in New York, striking out 200 or more hitters nine straight years. He also started 32 or more games in every season from 1967 to 1979.

Born in Chihuahua, Mexico, Pittsburgh Pirates shortstop Mario Aizpuro Mendoza was a good glove man, but it was his work with the bat—or lack thereof—that earned him popularity in the baseball world.

In 1968 and 1969 Detroit's Denny McLain was 55–15. In the next three seasons—his final three in the major leagues—he was 17–34, and he was out of baseball at twenty-eight, an age at which most pitchers are in their prime.

Holtzman (2 wins), Rollie Fingers (2 saves in six appearances), and Darold Knowles (2 saves in seven appearances). The A's provide their customary theatrics when flamboyant owner Charlie Finley tries to coerce Mike Andrews to go on the disabled list after the second baseman commits 2 costly errors in Game Two, and Manager Dick Williams announces minutes after the final out that he is quitting.

Worth Remembering

Drawing the Line. The term "Mendoza line," a figurative boundary in batting average, came into vogue in the late seventies as a means of gauging whether a player was really struggling at the plate. Its namesake is Mario Mendoza, a good-field, no-hit shortstop who played in the majors from 1974 to 1982 with the Pirates, Mariners, and Rangers and compiled a .215 career average. Coining of the term is attributed to Kansas City's George Brett, who, according to the book *Rotisserie League Baseball*, said, "The first thing I look for in the Sunday papers is who is below the Mendoza line." When Mendoza was active in the majors, the line was simply whatever his batting average was; nowadays the Mendoza line usually refers to the .200 mark.

McLain's Mastery Ends. Detroit's Denny McLain, who won Cy Young Awards in 1968 and 1969 and compiled a 55–15 record over that span, did for baseball in the seventies what Richard Nixon did for politics. In February of 1970, Commissioner Bowie Kuhn suspended McLain for his involvement in a bookmaking operation and his connections with underworld gamblers. When McLain returned on July 1, it quickly became apparent that he had lost his stuff. He slipped to a 3–5 record and was suspended twice more—once for dousing two local sportswriters with ice water and later for violating the commissioner's probationary restrictions by carrying a pistol. The Tigers unloaded McLain at the end of the season to the Washington Senators, with whom he fell to 10–22 in 1971. He lasted just one more season in the majors.

Teed Off. The Red Sox traded Ken "Hawk" Harrelson, the 1968 AL RBI leader, to the Indians early in the 1969 season. Harrelson drove in 92 runs that year but was unhappy in Cleveland and jumped ship after the season to join the professional golfer's tour. It was no lark—the Hawk is a

Mark Fidrych performing his customary groundskeeping duties on the pitching mound (right) *and in action for the Tigers* (below, right).

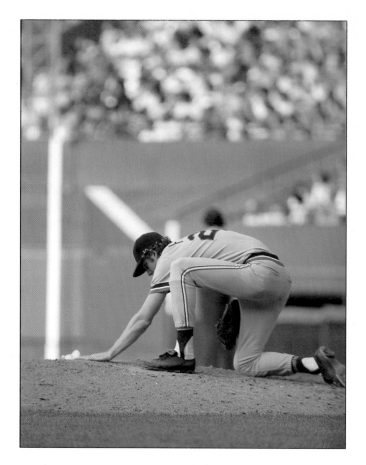

scratch golfer—but he eventually rejoined the Indians for 17 games in 1970. He finished his baseball career the following year with Cleveland.

Power, But No Pennant. The 1973 Braves led the National League with 206 home runs—45 more than runner-up San Francisco and the most of any NL team in the decade. Atlanta had three of the top four power men in the league: Dave Johnson, who had never hit more than 18 homers in a season, clubbed 43; Darrell Johnson hit a career-high 41; and Hank Aaron added 40. But where did the long ball take the Braves? A fifth-place finish, 22½ games behind front-running Cincinnati.

A Truly One-Dimensional Player. Baseball fans in the 1970s got their first look at the designated hitter. They also got the chance to see the first—and only—designated *runner*: Herb Washington of the Oakland A's. By order of innovative owner Charlie Finley, A's Manager Alvin Dark gave the twenty-fifth spot on his 1974 roster to Washington, a Lansing, Michigan, TV sports reporter who hadn't played organized ball since junior high but who had set world records in the 50- and 60-yard (45.7 and 54.8m) dashes at Michigan State a few years earlier. Washington was in the A's camp for one reason—to steal bases (Maury Wills was brought in to coach him)—and he swiped 29 in 45 attempts in 1974, including 17 of 21 during one stretch. He finished his career in 1975 having appeared in 105 games with 31 stolen bases and 33 runs scored, but without a single plate appearance.

DECADE SPOTLIGHT
Mark Fidrych: The Bird Was the Word in 1976

Throughout the history of baseball, some players have captured the fans' attention with fantastic displays of skill, while others have captivated the public with their colorful personalities. Few, however, have accomplished both with the same impact as Mark Fidrych.

The flamboyant Fidrych burst on the scene in 1976 as a twenty-one-year-old rookie pitcher with the Detroit Tigers. At a time when fans were being bombarded with news of baseball owners and players feuding about free agency, Fidrych was a welcome reminder of how much fun the game could be. His antics included talking to the baseball, performing his own groundskeeping chores with the pitcher's mound dirt, jubilantly hugging his infielders after great plays, and sprinting off the mound at the end of an inning. His long, curly, blond hair, along with his habit of flapping his arms on the mound, earned the gangly, 6-foot-3 (190.5cm) Fidrych the nickname "The Bird," after *Sesame Street*'s Big Bird.

The eccentric Fidrych could entertain a crowd, but more important than that, he could pitch. With a live arm and a nearly unhittable sinking fastball, the right-hander from Northboro, Massachusetts, took the American League by storm in 1976, winning nine of his first ten decisions and becoming the first rookie since Washington's Dave Stenhouse in 1962 to be named starting pitcher in the All-Star Game.

Fidrych went on to post a 19–9 record, but working for a fifth-place club that finished ninth out of twelve AL teams in runs scored, his mark easily could have been 23–5. Of his 9 losses, 2 were 1–0 scores, 1 was 2–0, and 1 was 2–1 in 12 innings. Had he accumulated those 23 victories to go with his AL-bests in ERA (2.34) and complete games (24), Fidrych might well have won the AL Cy Young Award. As it was, he was a near-unanimous choice for AL Rookie of the Year, garnering twenty-two of twenty-four votes to become the first pitcher to win the award since Stan Bahnsen of the Yankees in 1968. Fidrych finished second to Baltimore's Jim Palmer for the Cy Young, and it looked to be just a matter of time before his name was inscribed on that award as well.

The Bird, however, soon came back to earth. First Fidrych hurt his knee in spring training in 1977. Having apparently recovered from that injury, he opened the year

6–2 but then started having arm problems. He had a 2–0 lead with 2 outs in the sixth inning of a game against Baltimore when his arm began "feeling weird," as he later described it to a reporter; the Orioles pounded him for 6 runs. His arm still hurt the following day, and when it came time for his next scheduled start, the strange feeling persisted. "I tried it a third time," Fidrych said, "and my arm just petered out. I couldn't even pick my arm up. I knew something was wrong."

The Tigers had Fidrych examined by several doctors, including Dr. Frank Jobe, a noted orthopedist who had helped other major league pitchers return from arm troubles. The diagnoses varied, although all the experts agreed that Fidrych was too young for surgery. He therefore began a rehabilitation program that brought back some of his arm strength, but The Bird would never again pitch as he did in that spectacular rookie season of 1976. He spent most of the remainder of his career in the minor leagues, winning just 10 more games in the majors; after going 6–4 with Detroit in 1977, his major league marks for the next three years were 2–0, 0–3, and 2–3. He won his final major league game in 1980, the year he turned twenty-six.

Fidrych might just as easily have gone on to a long, successful career and a series of million-dollar contracts. Although his name now turns up under the heading of "Where Are They Now?" he quite possibly could have pitched into the early 1990s. He didn't turn forty until 1994; many pitchers older than him—including Nolan Ryan, Frank Tanana, Bert Blyleven, Terry Leach, Rich Gossage, Rick Honeycutt, and Larry Andersen—were effective in the early 1990s, when all were in their late thirties or older.

Fidrych has never been bitter, however—he prefers to look on the bright side. "I succeeded in ball where other guys wanted to and didn't," Fidrych, while languishing in the minors, told sportswriter Paul Meyer. "The only thing I haven't gotten is to play in the World Series. I've gotten everything else.

"You find an athlete that hasn't been hurt, and you've got a lucky guy. Of course, it bothers me maybe that I'm not in the major leagues. Sometimes I say, 'Dang it. I wish I was still there.' But then I say, 'This is life, Mark. Be happy you *were* there.'"

The 1980s
No Bed of Roses

If baseball in the 1980s were a player, it would be Pete Rose. "Charlie Hustle's" decade résumé included helping the Philadelphia Phillies win the World Series for the first time in their history and recording his 4,192nd career hit to pass Ty Cobb as the game's all-time leader. Rose was also suspended for shoving an umpire, and was ultimately banished from baseball for life for gambling. Clearly, this was a decade of high highs and lower lows.

While Reaganomics was helping the rich get richer, the same was happening in the world of baseball, where the poor didn't do too badly, either. Though slowed a bit in the mid-eighties when the owners colluded to lay off the free agent market, players' salaries were nonetheless on the rise, with new records being set almost every year. In 1979 a million-dollar-a-year player was rare. By 1982 there were four players making twice that much in a season. In 1979 the minimum player salary was twenty-one thousand dollars; the average was $113,558. By 1990 those figures were, respectively, $100,000 (a 476 percent increase) and $597,537 (a 526 percent jump).

All this opulence was not without a price, however. Baseball in the eighties tested the patience of its fans with two players' strikes, two umpires' strikes, and a trial in Pittsburgh in which a parade of players admitted to drug use. The 1981 walkout—the first work stoppage since the major leagues opened for business in 1876—lopped 713 games off the schedule and cost an estimated $100 million in players' salaries, ticket sales, concession revenues, and broadcast fees. The cost in negative public relations from all the squabbling and the tarnishing of the players' images was beyond measure. And the players had only themselves to blame when it came to a rash of cheating that was only too appropriate for the avarice of the times. While celebrated Wall Street brokers were making headlines for orchestrating sophisticated insider-trading schemes that violated the law, baseball players engaged in their own unethical behavior.

Above: *Mike Scott was 14–27 in four seasons with the Mets, but turned his career around after a 1982 trade to the Astros. Scott's improvement was so dramatic—in 1986 he was 18–10, led the league in strikeouts, shutouts, and ERA, and won the Cy Young Award—that opponents suspected him of scuffing the ball.* **Opposite page:** *Pete Rose's infectious enthusiasm helped turn the once-woeful Phillies into world champions.*

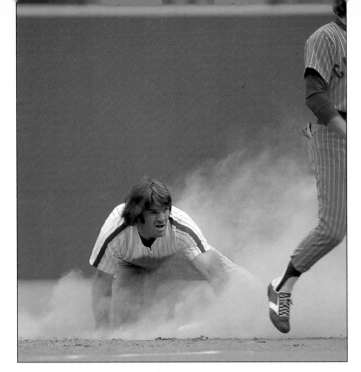

Players had cheated for years, applying saliva or petroleum jelly to baseballs to create elusive spitballs, but never was there a more concentrated series of disturbing incidents. When Houston Astros outfielder Billy Hatcher broke his bat, an illegal cork center was revealed. A cork center makes for a lighter bat head and, theoretically, a quicker swing through the strike zone. The result, players believe, is a higher bat speed and a hit with more distance. Hatcher, who claimed he borrowed the bat from a pitcher, was suspended. Philadelphia Phillies pitcher Kevin Gross was suspended when a tack was discovered in his glove. Major-league pitchers have the ability to turn even the slightest blemish on a baseball into an advantage, something that wasn't lost on knuckleballer Joe Niekro. The Minnesota Twins pitcher was also suspended when suspicious umpires discovered an emery board in Niekro's pocket during an on-mound search. Niekro said he liked to file his nails between innings. Houston pitcher Mike Scott spent much of the 1987 season denying the National League–wide charge that he was scuffing baseballs illegally to create more movement. Jay Howell of the Los Angeles Dodgers was ejected from the 1988 National League Championship Series for using sticky pine tar on his glove. The Dodgers' relief ace was suspended for three days when umpire chief Harry Wendelstedt discovered the foul substance on the mound in the eighth inning of Game Three. Howell claimed he was using the pitch to get a better grip on the ball in difficult weather conditions.

The Howell incident recalled George Brett's encounter with the rules regulating pine tar five years earlier. The Kansas City Royals star had just hit what appeared to be the dramatic, game-winning home run in the ninth inning against the New York Yankees when umpires ruled that

Major League Teams in the 1980s

NATIONAL LEAGUE
East
Chicago Cubs
Montreal Expos
New York Mets
Philadelphia Phillies
Pittsburgh Pirates
St. Louis Cardinals

West
Atlanta Braves
Cincinnati Reds
Houston Astros
Los Angeles Dodgers
San Diego Padres
San Francisco Giants

AMERICAN LEAGUE
East
Baltimore Orioles
Boston Red Sox
Cleveland Indians
Detroit Tigers
Milwaukee Brewers
New York Yankees
Toronto Blue Jays

West
California Angels
Chicago White Sox
Kansas City Royals
Minnesota Twins
Oakland Athletics
Seattle Mariners
Texas Rangers

Brett had more than the allowed 18 inches (45.7cm) of pine tar from the bat's handle. And though the pine tar did not affect the flight of the ball, the protest of combative Yankees Manager Billy Martin was upheld and New York was declared a 4–3 winner. Four days later, American League President Lee MacPhail reversed the umpires' decision and ordered the game resumed with the Royals' 5–4 lead intact.

Yet Brett's sticky adventure was almost mildly humorous compared to the calculated cheating of the later 1980s. In March 1988, Dr. Bobby Brown and A. Bartlett Giamatti, the presidents of the American and National Leagues, sent memos to each team, explaining that anti-cheating rules 1.10a-c and 6.06d would be vigorously enforced. The final sentence was dramatic, but earnest: "The integrity of the game of baseball is at issue here and we will continue to count on your cooperation and personal sense of responsibility to maintain that integrity."

The fans hung tough, though, which is proof of their resilience and evidence that the product on the field was pretty exciting. Besides raising salaries, free agency was affecting the game in other ways. It increased competitive balance; the days of the dynasty were over. For the first time since the 1940s, no team won consecutive World Series in the decade, and only one team—the Oakland A's—claimed back-to-back pennants, in 1988 and 1989. In the National League no team even managed two straight division titles. The New York Yankees had the decade's best cumulative record but never won the World Series. The Los Angeles Dodgers were the only team to win the Series twice in the decade (1981 and 1988), while three teams—the Philadelphia Phillies, the Kansas City Royals, and the Minnesota Twins—won their first championships ever. In the twelve seasons from 1979 to 1990, twenty-three of the twenty-six major league teams won a division title; only the Cleveland Indians, Texas Rangers, and Seattle Mariners came up dry.

The fans also responded because players in the eighties were posting big numbers in the box scores—in virtually every statistical category—as well as in their money

Below: *George Brett went ballistic in 1983 after umpires disallowed his game-winning homer against the Yankees because his bat had too much pine tar.* **Bottom:** *The (Nolan) Ryan Express came to Houston in 1980.*

market accounts. Outstanding individual seasons were turned in by Rickey Henderson, who stole a record 130 bases in 1982 and scored 146 runs in 1985, the most since 1949; George Brett, who hit .390 in 1980, the highest since 1941; Wade Boggs, who recorded 240 hits in 1985, the best in fifty-five years; Don Mattingly, who drove in 145 runs in 1985 and hit 53 doubles in 1986, each figure the most since 1977; Willie Wilson, whose 21 triples in 1985 were the most in thirty-six years; Mark McGwire and Andre Dawson, who each hit 49 homers in 1987, the most since 1977; David Cone, who in 1988 posted a 20–3 record for an .870 winning percentage, the highest in ten years; and John Tudor, who threw 10 shutouts in 1985, the most since 1975. The top three all-time strikeouts-per-9-innings figures also were posted in the eighties, by Nolan Ryan (11.50 in 1987), Dwight Gooden (11.38 in 1984), and Ryan, again (11.32 in 1989). The 40-save plateau, which had never been reached before 1983, was also attained or surpassed nine times—by seven different relievers—in the eighties.

Great performances such as these, along with some exciting pennant races, helped fans put the grim memories of the 1981 strike and the Pittsburgh drug trials of the mid-eighties out of their minds. Records for total attendance were set almost every year in the decade, including 1982, when all four division races were decided by 3 games or less, and 1987, when home run totals jumped to record levels. The decade ended on some low notes, however: the battle between Rose and Commissioner Bart Giamatti that ultimately resulted in Rose's lifetime suspension; the death of Giamatti, which cost the game a passionate and devoted leader and perpetuated a revolving door in the commissioner's office—four different men in five years; and the Bay Area earthquake of 1989, which cast a pall over the World Series.

Pro football had been gaining in popularity since the late sixties and pro basketball came on strong in the eighties with such stars as Magic Johnson and Larry Bird. Baseball held its own, though, both in the United States and abroad. According to the International Baseball Association, its membership doubled to sixty-eight countries in the decade. On the home front, fans were enjoying baseball not only by attending games; side industries such as trading cards and rotisserie leagues were gaining in popularity, and such movies as *The Natural*, *Eight Men Out*, *Field of Dreams*, and *Major League* drew wide audiences. In the nineties, however, baseball's propensity to cause problems for itself, plus growing competition for the fans' entertainment dollar, would make the going even tougher.

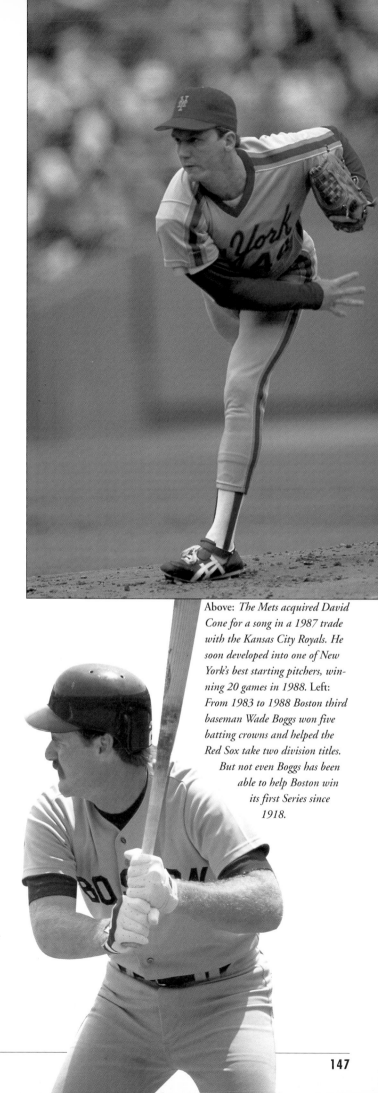

Above: *The Mets acquired David Cone for a song in a 1987 trade with the Kansas City Royals. He soon developed into one of New York's best starting pitchers, winning 20 games in 1988.* **Left:** *From 1983 to 1988 Boston third baseman Wade Boggs won five batting crowns and helped the Red Sox take two division titles. But not even Boggs has been able to help Boston win its first Series since 1918.*

September. He settles for .390, the highest average in the majors since Ted Williams' .406 in 1941.

October 21, 1980: Steve Carlton wins his second game of the Series and Most Valuable Player Mike Schmidt drives in 2 runs to lead the Phillies to a 4–1 win over the Royals in Game Six of the World Series. The win gives the Phillies their first championship since they joined the National League in 1883.

November–December 1980: After the season, free agent Dave Winfield jumps from the Padres to the Yankees for a record contract that pays him $1.5 million a year.

January 20, 1981: *The fifty-two Americans held hostage in Iran for 444 days are freed.*

1980: The 1979–1980 offseason brings a flurry of million-dollar free agent signings for both stars and journeymen. The big catch is Texas' signing of Nolan Ryan, who inks the first of his four seven-figure-per-year deals. Among the less-than-promising new millionaires are Dave Goltz (three million dollars for six years from the Dodgers), Don Stanhouse ($2.1 million for five years from the Dodgers), Rick Wise ($1.95 million for five years from the San Diego Padres), John Curtis ($1.8 million for five years from the Padres), and Rennie Stennett (three million dollars for five years, plus a one million dollar signing bonus, from the San Francisco Giants).

1980: A's owner Charlie Finley sells his club to Levi Strauss & Company for $13.7 million. Manager Jim Marshall is replaced by Billy Martin, who will take the A's to the league championship series in his second season.

July 30, 1980: Houston Astros ace J.R. Richard, who has posted an 84–55 record with 1,163 strikeouts and a 2.79 earned-run average over the past four and a half seasons, is felled by a major stroke caused by a blood clot in his neck, ending his career at age thirty.

September 1980: Kansas City's George Brett flirts with a .400 batting average all season and is still above the mark in early

Above: *George Brett, who won batting titles in three different decades, led the AL with a .390 mark in 1980.* Below: *Steve Carlton won 241 games in fifteen seasons in a Phillies uniform.* Below, right: *Steve Sax took over the Dodger second base job in 1982 and made the all-star team in each of his first two full seasons.*

March 30, 1981: *John W. Hinckley, Jr., opens fire on President Reagan, seriously wounding the president, his press secretary, James Brady, and two security guards. All four of the wounded recover.*

May 15, 1981: Len Barker of the Cleveland Indians throws a perfect game to beat Toronto 3–0.

The Hard Line
June 12, 1981: Major league players begin a strike that lasts seven weeks and a day—the first in-season strike baseball has ever seen and the longest work stoppage in major professional sports history. The players and owners are at odds over the issue of free agent compensation; the players are unwilling to grant the owners' proposal, in which a team that loses a free agent would receive as compensation a player from the middle of the roster (the sixteenth-best player) of the team that signed the free agent. The players hold their ground and reach a settlement once the owners' strike insurance from Lloyd's of London runs out. To salvage the season, the owners institute a split-season concept: the winners of the first half of the season will face the winners of the second half in an additional round of playoffs held before the league championship series. The big losers are the Cincinnati Reds, who post baseball's best overall record at 66–42 but are left out of the postseason picture.

October 1981: Milwaukee's Rollie Fingers (28 saves, 1.04 ERA) becomes the first reliever to win the Cy Young and MVP Awards in the same season. Los Angeles' Fernando Valenzuela (13–7, 2.48 ERA, 8 shutouts) is the first player to win both the Rookie of the Year and Cy Young Awards.

1982: Four players—Dave Winfield, Gary Carter, Mike Schmidt, and George Foster—earn two million dollars this season. The average major league player's salary is more than $241,497.

February 8, 1982: The Dodgers break up their Steve Garvey–Davey Lopes–Bill Russell–Ron Cey infield combination—which had been together for more than eight seasons, longer than any other in major league history—by trading Lopes to Oakland. Steve Sax replaces Lopes, hits .282, and is named NL Rookie of the Year.

Above: *Acquired from the St. Louis Cardinals before the 1981 season, Rollie Fingers paid immediate dividends, helping the Brewers reach the playoffs in each of his first two seasons in Milwaukee.* Below: *Ex-San Diego Padre Dave Winfield had a similar effect in New York, where he helped the Yankees reach the World Series in 1981 after signing as a free agent.*

April 1982: A freak snowstorm forces the cancellation of 19 games, including 6 home openers.

April 6, 1982: Minnesota's Hubert H. Humphrey Metrodome opens.

July 13, 1982: Dave Concepcion's 2-run homer lifts the National League to its eleventh straight All-Star Game victory. Played in Montreal's Olympic Stadium, it is the first All-Star Game held outside the United States.

October 1982: By season's end Oakland's Rickey Henderson steals a record 130 bases, breaking Lou Brock's single-season mark of 118.

October 1982: Philadelphia's Steve Carlton (23–11, 3.10 ERA, 286 strikeouts, 6 shutouts) wins his record fourth Cy Young Award.

Owners Can Kuhn
November 1, 1982: Unhappy with Commissioner Bowie Kuhn, baseball's chief executive for the past fourteen years, the owners effectively fire him and begin what will be a two-year search for a replacement. There are accusations that Kuhn's undoing is his tendency to put the good of the game—and not the good of the owners—first.

1983: Donald Fehr becomes the new executive director of the Major League Baseball Players Association.

Ryan Is the K King
April 27, 1983: Houston's Nolan Ryan strikes out the 3,509th batter of his career to break Walter Johnson's career record. Johnson took twenty-one years to set the standard, while Ryan needed a little more than fifteen full seasons to surpass it.

July 6, 1983: Led by Fred Lynn's grand slam, the American League snaps an 11-game All-Star skid and claims just its second win in the last 21 meetings with a 13–3 victory. The fiftieth anniversary game is played in Chicago's Comiskey Park, the site of the first contest.

July 24, 1983: George Brett and the Royals are in an uproar when Brett's 2-out, 2-run, game-winning homer in the ninth inning is disallowed after umpire Tim McClelland agrees with Yankees Manager Billy Martin's claim that the pine tar on Brett's bat extends beyond the 18-inch (45.7cm) limit from the end of the bat. Four days later, however, AL President Lee MacPhail overturns the umpire's decision and orders that the game be completed with the Royals leading 5–4. The teams meet on August 18 to play the final 4 outs, and Kansas City is the winner.

July 29, 1983: Steve Garvey of the San Diego Padres suffers a thumb injury that ends his NL-record streak of 1,207 consecutive games played.

October 1983: For the first time in a full season since 1931, the National League has no 20-game winner. Philadelphia's John Denny is closest with 19.

October 25, 1983: *U.S. troops invade the island of Grenada. President Reagan defends the attack as an effort to restore order and democracy after a military coup in Grenada on October 12 led by Marxists with strong Cuban and Soviet ties.*

April 13, 1984: Playing for the Montreal Expos, Pete Rose collects his four thousandth career hit.

April–May 1984: The powerful Detroit Tigers jump out to a record 35–5 start. They lead wire-to-wire on their way to winning the World Series.

Top: *Pete Rose acknowledges the hometown fans at Cincinnati's Riverfront Stadium after becoming baseball's all-time hit leader on September 11, 1985.* Above: *Former Dodger first baseman Steve Garvey signed with the Padres as a free agent before the 1983 season.*

September 3, 1984: California's Mike Witt pitches a perfect game to beat Texas 1–0.

Ueberroth Is New Commissioner
October 1, 1984: Peter Ueberroth, who earned praise as the president of the Los Angeles Olympic Organizing Committee, succeeds Bowie Kuhn as baseball commissioner, giving the game its first new chief executive since 1968. Dr. Bobby Brown replaces Lee MacPhail as AL president.

October 1984: Major league umpires stage a playoff strike that prompts Commissioner Ueberroth to sizably increase their postseason salaries.

1985: Rules change: no part of a uniform may bear an advertising patch.

1985: Curtis Strong, a former caterer in the Phillies clubhouse, is tried in Pittsburgh for selling cocaine to various ballplayers. More than twenty players take the stand and admit to cocaine use; all are subsequently disciplined by Commissioner Ueberroth. Strong gets four to twelve years and baseball gets a black eye.

April 1, 1985: As an April Fools' Day prank, George Plimpton writes an article for *Sports Illustrated* about Sidd Finch, a fictional pitcher in the New York Mets spring training camp who practices yoga, wears a hiking boot on the mound, and throws a 120-mph (192kph) fastball.

August 6, 1985: Lacking a basic labor agreement, major league players walk off the job. But mindful of the public relations damage done by the 1981 walkout, both the owners and players are unwilling to test the fans' patience any further. The two sides compromise on a five-year agreement two days later.

Rose Spins a Hit Record
September 11, 1985: In a season of milestones that help produce record attendance, Reds player-manager Pete Rose strokes a slider from San Diego's Eric Show into left field for the 4,192nd hit of his career, breaking Ty Cobb's all-time record. Other memorable moments include Nolan Ryan notching his four thousandth strikeout, Tom Seaver and Phil Neikro each winning their three hundredth game, and Rod Carew stroking his three thousandth hit.

October 1985: Twenty-year-old Dwight Gooden (24–4, 1.53 ERA, 268 strikeouts, 8 shutouts), the youngest pitcher ever to lead the majors in victories and ERA, wins the NL Cy Young Award. Boston's Wade Boggs strokes 240 hits, the most since 1930. Kansas City's Willie Wilson's 21 triples are the most since 1949.

October 1985: The league championship series in both leagues is increased to a best-of-seven format. The change proves costly to the Toronto Blue Jays, who win 3 of the first 4 but drop the final 3 games of the AL championship series to Kansas City. The Royals go on to win their first World Series defeating the St. Louis Cardinals. Arbitrator Richard M. Nixon awards the umpires a pay increase for working the extra playoff games.

1986: The Kansas City Royals sign Auburn running back Bo Jackson, the 1985 Heisman-Trophy winner, to a seven-million-dollar baseball contract.

1986: Rules change: the designated hitter will be used in all World Series games played in the AL city, as opposed to the alternating-years format used for the past ten years.

Collusion Charges Confirmed

1986: After two successive off-seasons in which even the big-name free agents garner little attention, the players union successfully convinces arbitrators that the owners have colluded for the past two seasons to keep player salaries down. The owners are therefore found to be in violation of the basic labor agreement and are hit with sanctions.

1986: Strikeout totals rise dramatically; Texas' Pete Incaviglia fans a record 185 times and the Seattle Mariners' hitters set a league record with 1,148 whiffs.

January 28, 1986: *The space shuttle Challenger explodes one minute after take-off, killing all seven crew members. New Hampshire schoolteacher Christa McAuliffe, one of the crew, was to be the first teacher in space.*

April 30, 1986: Roger Clemens of the Boston Red Sox strikes out twenty Seattle Mariners at Fenway Park in Boston to set a single-game record.

June 10, 1986: Former Yale University President A. Bartlett Giamatti is named NL president.

October 1986: In the most thrilling post-season of baseball's divisional era, the Red Sox rally from a 3-games-to-1 deficit to beat the California Angels, while the Mets edge the Astros in 6 games, despite 2 dominant complete-game victories by Mike Scott. New York then defeats Boston in a wild 7-game Series.

October 2, 1986: *The Senate overrides President Reagan's veto and passes a bill imposing sanctions on South Africa in hopes of ending apartheid.*

Top: *In 1985 Bret Saberhagen won the Cy Young Award with a 20–6 record and a 2.87 ERA and added 2 more wins in the World Series to lead the Royals to their first championship.* **Above:** *The following year Kansas City fans got their first look at a trend-setting two-sport star named Bo Jackson.*

Frank Viola made sweet music for the Twins in 1987 and 1988; his record was 41–17 and he won a World Series and a Cy Young Award.

A dependable starter who posted double-digit win totals seven straight years (1985–1991), Tom Browning pitched a perfect game on September 16, 1988.

1987: Miami's Joe Robbie Stadium opens. In six years, it will become the home of the National League's expansion team, the Florida Marlins.

1987: A minor rash of illegal equipment tampering develops. Astros outfielder Billy Hatcher breaks his bat and a cork center is discovered. A tack is found in the glove of Philadelphia Phillies pitcher Kevin Gross. Twins pitcher Joe Neikro is caught on the mound with an emery board in his back pocket and is suspected of illegally scuffing the ball. All three are suspended.

1987: Despite baseball officials' claims to the contrary, the baseball appears to be "juiced up." Total home runs jump 17 percent, to a record 4,458. The Blue Jays hit 10 homers in 1 game against Baltimore. The fans love it, though; total attendance rises to a record fifty-two million, a 9 percent increase over the previous year.

1987: Houston's Nolan Ryan strikes out an all-time record 11.50 batters per 9 innings. Paul Molitor of the Milwaukee Brewers fashions a 39-game hitting streak.

July 18, 1987: Don Mattingly of the Yankees ties Dale Long's major league record by homering in his eighth straight game. Mattingly will also set a record with 6 grand slams this season.

October 19, 1987: *On what is later known as Black Monday, Wall Street faces the worst day in the history of the stock market when the Dow Jones industrial average drops more than five hundred points.*

October 25, 1987: Series MVP Frank Viola pitches the Twins to a 4–2 win over the St. Louis Cardinals to bring Minnesota its first world championship.

November 13, 1987: *President Reagan admits that his administration sent arms to Iran in an attempt to improve relations with that country, but denies the actions were wrong.*

December 8, 1987: *President Reagan and Soviet leader Mikhail Gorbachev sign a comprehensive arms control treaty calling for the elimination of both countries' intermediate-range missiles.*

1988: Commissioner Peter Ueberroth announces that he will step down after the season. NL President Bart Giamatti will succeed Ueberroth, assuming office on April 1, 1989. New York Yankees broadcaster and former player Bill White is named NL president. He is the first black man in sports history to hold such an important position.

1988: A stricter interpretation of the balk rule leads to a record number of balks called on pitchers: 924, as opposed to 356 the year before.

1988: Oakland's Jose Canseco becomes the first 40–40 player in major league history, collecting 40 home runs and 40 stolen bases in one year.

April 30, 1988: Pete Rose shoves an umpire during an argument, prompting Commissioner Giamatti to suspend him for thirty days.

Cubs Say: Let There Be Lights
August 8, 1988: Having ended their holdout as the last major league team without lights for night baseball, the Chicago Cubs face the Mets in the first night contest in Wrigley Field history. Rain ends the game before 5 innings have been played, so the park's first official night game is played the following night. The Cubs beat the Mets 6–4.

August 30, 1988: Orel Hershiser of the Dodgers begins a record streak of 59 scoreless innings, breaking former Dodger Don Drysdale's mark.

September 16, 1988: Cincinnati's Tom Browning throws a perfect game to beat Los Angeles 1–0.

Gimpy Gibson Lifts Dodgers
October 15, 1988: The mighty A's lead the Dodgers 4–3 in Game One of the World Series with 2 outs in the ninth. But Kirk Gibson, sidelined by hamstring and knee injuries, comes off the bench to deliver a game-winning, 2-run homer off closer Dennis Eckersley.

December 7, 1988: *Some predict the beginning of the end of the Cold War when Soviet leader Mikhail Gorbachev addresses the United Nations and announces his country's plan to make major troop and weapon reductions, allow political freedom, encourage individual rights, and follow capitalistic economic policies.*

May 29, 1989: Philadelphia Phillies third baseman Mike Schmidt retires. His total of 548 home runs ranks seventh on the all-time list.

June 3, 1989: The Astros beat the Dodgers 5–4 in the longest night game in NL history. The game lasts 22 innings and takes seven hours and fourteen minutes. The winning hit is Rafael Ramirez's single off Jeff Hamilton, normally a third baseman. By the end of the game, Dodgers pitcher Fernando Valenzuela is playing first and first baseman Eddie Murray is playing third.

June 5, 1989: Toronto's SkyDome opens. The stadium features a retractable roof that can be opened or closed depending on the weather. With this innovation the Blue Jays draw a major league record 3,375,573 fans for the season.

June 5, 1989: *The United States suspends all arms sales to China after the previous day's killing of more than twenty-five hundred prodemocracy students by Chinese Communist troops on Tiananmen Square in Beijing.*

July 11, 1989: The American League wins its second straight All-Star Game 5–3, posting back-to-back All-Star wins for the first time since 1957 and 1958.

Giamatti versus Rose
August 23, 1989: Commissioner Giamatti suspends Reds Manager Pete Rose for life for gambling. The suspension also prevents Rose from gaining admittance to the Hall of Fame, for which he is an otherwise obvious candidate. Tommy Helms replaces Rose as Reds manager. Nine days after handing down the suspension, Giamatti, fifty-one, dies of a heart attack. He is replaced by Deputy Commissioner Fay Vincent.

Tragedy Strikes the Series
October 17, 1989: At 5:04 p.m. local time, shortly before the start of Game Three of the World Series, a devastating earthquake rocks Candlestick Park and the surrounding area. Dozens of people die around the Bay Area, and Commissioner Vincent suspends the Series for twelve days. When play resumes, the A's make short work of the Giants, completing a 4-game sweep.

November 10, 1989: *After twenty-eight years of dividing East and West Germany, the Berlin Wall, a symbol of Communist oppression, is dismantled.*

From 1985 to 1989 Orel Hershiser won 87 games and a Cy Young Award, broke Don Drysdale's record for consecutive scoreless innings, made the National League All-Star team three times, helped the Los Angeles Dodgers win two division titles and one world championship, and was named Series MVP in 1988.

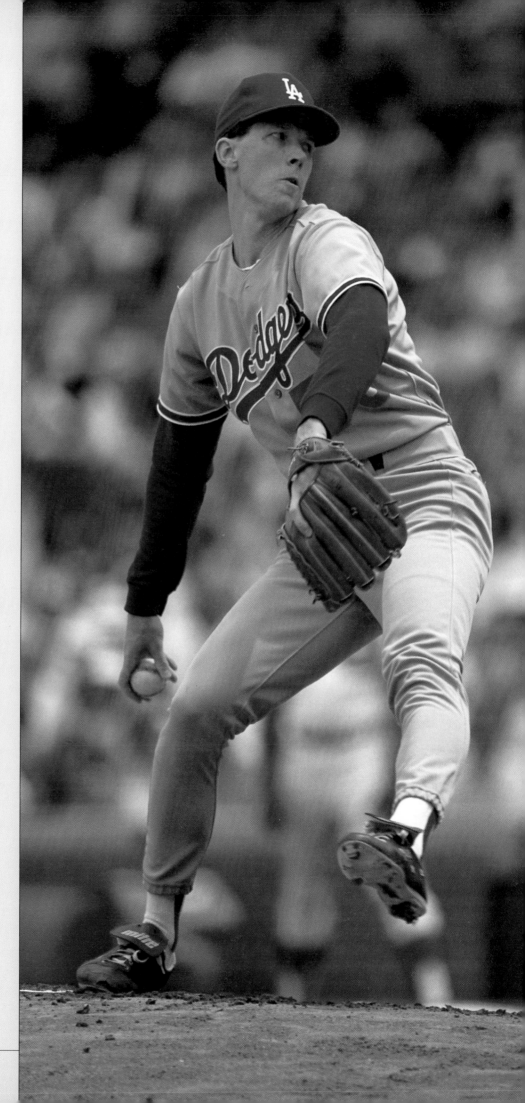

Man of the Decade: Mike Schmidt

The Phillies' star third baseman, who when he retired in 1989 recalled how he started his career "with two very bad knees and the dream to become a Major League Baseball player," went far beyond that lofty goal—all the way to the Hall of Fame. He hit 313 of his 548 home runs in the eighties—never fewer than 33 in a full season—and during the decade he led the league in round-trippers five times and runs batted in four times. He also had few peers on defense; he was a perennial Gold Glove winner who earned that honor ten times in his eighteen-year career, including six in the eighties.

No third baseman has been as consistent a power source as Philadelphia's Mike Schmidt, who from 1974 to 1987 hit more than 30 homers every year but one; Schmidt led the league in round-trippers eight times.

Most Memorable Games

1. 1986 World Series, Game Six, October 25 at Shea Stadium; New York Mets 6, Boston Red Sox 5. Leading 3–2 in the Series, the Red Sox are on the brink of victory after Dave Henderson's solo homer and an insurance run give them a 5–3 lead heading into the bottom of the tenth. Calvin Schiraldi retires the first two hitters but then yields consecutive singles to Gary Carter, Kevin Mitchell, and Ray Knight to cut the lead to 1. Bob Stanley enters and wild-pitches the tying run home, and Mookie Wilson follows with a slow roller through first baseman Bill Buckner's legs to give the Mets an unbelievable 6–5 win and hand the Red Sox another Series heartbreaker.

2. 1988 World Series, Game One, October 15 at Dodger Stadium; Los Angeles Dodgers 5, Oakland A's 4. The mighty A's, who won a major league high 104 games and swept the Red Sox in the AL playoffs, are heavy favorites over the upstart Dodgers. Oakland leads the Series opener 4–3 and has relief ace Dennis Eckersley, baseball's save leader with 45, on the mound for the ninth. Eckersley sets down the first two hitters but walks Mike Davis, and Dodgers Manager Tommy Lasorda tabs as a pinch hitter Kirk Gibson, who can't even run because of hamstring and knee injuries. In his only at bat of the Series, Gibson delivers a game-winning home run to right field and sets the tone for a Dodgers upset.

3. 1980 NL Championship Series, Game Five, October 12 at the Houston Astrodome; Philadelphia Phillies 8, Houston Astros 7. The Phillies capture their first pennant in thirty years by winning a seesaw game to cap a Series in which 4 of the 5 contests go to extra innings. Nolan Ryan and the Astros lead 5–2 and are just 6 outs away from victory before Philadelphia rallies for 5 runs and a 7–5 lead in the eighth. Houston answers with a pair of runs in the bottom of the eighth to tie the game, but the Phils push across a run in the tenth and reliever Dick Ruthven makes it stand up to put Philadelphia in the World Series.

4. 1981 NL Championship Series, Game Five, October 19 at Olympic Stadium; Los Angeles Dodgers 2, Montreal Expos 1. The Expos lead the series 2 games to 1 but cannot deliver the knockout blow. Steve Garvey's eighth-inning home run breaks a 1–1 tie in Game Four to spark the Dodgers to a 7–1 victory and set the stage for

Hollywood heroics: Gimpy Kirk Gibson, the NL's MVP, came off the bench to hit a game-winning homer in the opener of the 1988 World Series. It set the stage for a Dodger upset of the heavily favored Oakland A's.

the finale. Montreal's Ray Burris and L.A.'s Fernando Valenzuela lock horns for 8 innings before Steve Rogers (3–0 with a 0.67 ERA in the playoffs to that point) comes on in the ninth with the game tied 1–1 for his first relief appearance of the year. Rick Monday greets him with a pennant-winning solo homer.

5. 1986 AL Championship Series, Game Five, October 12 at Anaheim Stadium; Boston Red Sox 7, California Angels 6. California wins 3 of the first 4 games in the series and holds a 5–2 advantage in the top of the ninth of Game Five. Down to their last out, Boston gets a 2-run homer from Don Baylor off Mike Witt to cut the lead to a run. After reliever Gary Lucas hits Rich Gedman with a pitch, Angels Manager Gene Mauch calls on Donnie Moore to slam the door. He instead surrenders a 2-run homer to Dave Henderson that gives Boston the lead. The Angels score a run in the bottom of the ninth to tie it, but Boston wins it in the eleventh on a Henderson sacrifice fly. The Red Sox take the next 2 games by a combined score of 18–5.

DECADE PITCHING LEADERS

	National League			American League		
YEAR	PLAYER	TEAM	ERA	PLAYER	TEAM	ERA
1980	Don Sutton	Los Angeles	2.21	Rudy May	New York	2.47
1981	Nolan Ryan	Houston	1.69	Steve McCatty	Oakland	2.32
1982	Steve Rogers	Montreal	2.40	Rick Sutcliffe	Cleveland	2.96
1983	Atlee Hammaker	San Francisco	2.25	Rick Honeycutt	Texas	2.42
1984	Alejandro Pena	Los Angeles	2.48	Mike Boddicker	Baltimore	2.79
1985	Dwight Gooden	New York	1.53	Dave Stieb	Toronto	2.48
1986	Mike Scott	Houston	2.22	Roger Clemens	Boston	2.48
1987	Nolan Ryan	Houston	2.76	Jimmy Key	Toronto	2.76
1988	Joe Magrane	St. Louis	2.18	Allan Anderson	Minnesota	2.45
1989	Scott Garrelts	San Francisco	2.28	Bret Saberhagen	Kansas City	2.16

The premier power pitchers of the mid-to-late 1980s, Roger Clemens of the Red Sox (far left) and Dwight Gooden of the Mets (left) each debuted in the majors in 1984. Two years later the two squared off in a memorable World Series in which, ironically, neither won a game.

Best Pennant Races

1. 1980 NL West: Houston Astros–Los Angeles Dodgers. Houston loses ace J.R. Richard in late July when he suffers a severe stroke, but Joe Neikro, Vern Ruhle, Ken Forsch, Joaquin Andujar, and free agent signee Nolan Ryan solidify the rotation as the Astros build a 3-game lead with 3 to play. The problem is that those 3 final games are in Los Angeles, and the Dodgers win all three—each by a single run—to force a 1-game playoff. Neikro rights the ship and clinches the division title for Houston with a 6-hitter that earns him his twentieth win of the year.

2. 1982 AL East: Milwaukee Brewers–Baltimore Orioles. Milwaukee is buried in fifth place on June 2 when Harvey Kuenn replaces Bob Rodgers as manager. The move relaxes the club and "Harvey's Wallbangers," as the potent Brewer lineup is known, build a 6½-game lead by late August. A season-ending elbow injury to bullpen ace Rollie Fingers opens the door for Baltimore, however, and the O's—rallying to win a championship for retiring Manager Earl Weaver—cut the lead to 3 games heading into a season-ending 4-game series with the Brewers in Baltimore. The Orioles sweep a Friday doubleheader and win on Saturday afternoon to pull even with 1 game left. But Don Sutton outduels Jim Palmer, Robin Yount homers twice, and Milwaukee wins the division with a 10–2 victory.

3. 1987 AL East: Detroit Tigers–Toronto Blue Jays. On September 24 the Tigers open a 4-game series in Toronto, trailing the Blue Jays by a half-game. Detroit drops 3 of 4 to fall 2½ back, but manages a split of its next 4 games against Baltimore while Toronto drops 3 straight to Milwaukee. The Jays' lead is therefore down to 1 game as

Above: *From 1984 to 1991, San Diego's Tony Gwynn won four batting titles and five Gold Gloves.* Left: *Sidelined with a broken wrist for much of the 1989 season, Oakland's Jose Canseco returned to hit .357 in the World Series, including a three-run homer in Game Three.*

DECADE BATTING LEADERS

	National League			American League		
YEAR	PLAYER	TEAM	AVG.	PLAYER	TEAM	AVG.
1980	Bill Buckner	Chicago	.324	George Brett	Kansas City	.390
1981	Bill Madlock	Pittsburgh	.341	Carney Lansford	Boston	.336
1982	Al Oliver	Montreal	.331	Willie Wilson	Kansas City	.332
1983	Bill Madlock	Pittsburgh	.323	Wade Boggs	Boston	.361
1984	Tony Gwynn	San Diego	.351	Don Mattingly	New York	.343
1985	Willie McGee	St. Louis	.353	Wade Boggs	Boston	.368
1986	Tim Raines	Montreal	.334	Wade Boggs	Boston	.357
1987	Tony Gwynn	San Diego	.370	Wade Boggs	Boston	.363
1988	Tony Gwynn	San Diego	.313	Wade Boggs	Boston	.366
1989	Tony Gwynn	San Diego	.336	Kirby Puckett	Minnesota	.339

While many of the game's best players, including Darryl Strawberry (right), have opted for money over loyalty in recent years, changing teams via free agency, Kirby Puckett (above) has been an exception.

they journey to Detroit for a season-ending 3-game series. The Tigers win all 3 to claim their second division title in four years.

Best Teams

1. 1986 New York Mets, 108–54; manager: Dave Johnson. Second-place finishers in the NL East the previous two seasons, the self-assured Mets were determined to make this their year. They won a decade-high 108 games and captured a thrilling World Series behind the league's best pitching staff: starters Bob Ojeda (18–5, 2.57 ERA), Dwight Gooden (17–6, 2.84), Sid Fernandez (16–6, 3.52), Ron Darling (15–6, 2.81), and Rick Aguilera (10–7, 3.88), and relievers Jesse Orosco (8–6, 2.33, 21 saves) and Roger McDowell (14–9, 3.02, 22 saves). The potent lineup included Keith Hernandez (.310 batting average, 83 RBI), Darryl Strawberry (27 homers, 93 RBI), Gary Carter (25 homers, 105 RBI), Ray Knight (.298), Wally Backman, (.320), and Len Dykstra (.295).

2. 1989 Oakland A's, 99–63; manager: Tony LaRussa. Losers to the Dodgers in the 1988 World Series upset, the A's were a team on a mission, determined not to let anything—including injuries—get in their way. So even though both Bash Brothers, Jose Canseco (17 homers, 57 RBI in 65 games) and Mark McGwire (33 homers, 95 RBI),

A successful starter in the late 1970s and early 1980s, Dennis Eckersley became baseball's most effective relief pitcher in the late eighties. Eckersley won the Cy Young Award with 51 saves in 1992.

were sidelined for part of the year, along with closer Dennis Eckersley (4–0, 1.56 ERA, 33 saves) and shortstop Walt Weiss, Oakland rolled on to win the division by 7 games. The starting rotation, which featured Dave Stewart (21–9), Storm Davis (19–7), Mike Moore (19–11), and Bob Welch (17–8), was solid, and once everyone was healthy and June acquisition Rickey Henderson—the league leader in runs, walks, and stolen bases—was on board, Oakland rolled to the championship.

3. 1984 Detroit Tigers, 104–58; manager: Sparky Anderson. Lance Parrish (33 homers, 98 RBI), Kirk Gibson (27, 91), Chet Lemon (20, 76), and Alan Trammell (.314 batting average) led a powerful Tigers lineup that topped the league in runs. The AL's best pitching staff featured the big three of Jack Morris (19–11), Dan Petry (18–8), and Milt Wilcox (17–8); a top setup man in Aurelio Lopez (10–1, 14 saves); and the MVP and Cy Young winner in closer Willie Hernandez (9–3, 32 saves, 1.92 ERA), acquired during spring training from Philadelphia. Detroit jumped out to a 35–5 start and rolled right through the World Series.

Best World Series

1. 1986, New York Mets over Boston Red Sox, 4 games to 3. Boston shocks the favored Mets by winning the first 2 games in Shea Stadium, but the Mets answer with 2 straight victories in Boston. Bruce Hurst goes the distance in Game Five to win his second start of the Series, and the Red Sox have the Mets on the brink in Game Six before blowing a 5–3, tenth-inning lead in one of the wildest games in Series history. Buoyed by that improbable comeback, the Mets rally from a 3–0 deficit to win Game Seven, thanks to homers by Darryl Strawberry and Series MVP Ray Knight.

2. 1982, St. Louis Cardinals over Milwaukee Brewers, 4 games to 3. In a matchup of contrasting styles—the Brewers' power versus the Cardinals' speed and defense—Milwaukee sends a convincing message with a 10–0 win in Game One. St. Louis wins Games Two and Three but drops the next 2, blowing a 5–1 lead in Game Four and losing to Mike Caldwell for the second time in the Series in Game Five. The Brewers need 1 more win for the championship, but they don't get it; John Stuper's 4-hitter beats them in Game Six and Joaquin Andujar notches his second win of the Series in the finale.

Two of the Detroit Tigers' hitting stars, Kirk Gibson and Alan Trammell, exchange a high five during the 1984 World Series. In the Series Gibson and Trammell combined for a .395 average, 4 homers, and 13 RBI.

St. Louis second baseman Tommy Herr attempts to complete a double play in the 1987 Series, which the Cards lost to the Twins in 7 games.

3. 1987, Minnesota Twins over St. Louis Cardinals, 4 games to 3. During the regular season the Twins were baseball's best home team (56–25) and one of the worst road teams (29–52). They continue those trends in the Series, winning the first 2 games in the Metrodome (the first World Series games ever played indoors), losing the next 3 in St. Louis, and winning the final 2 games—both in come-from-behind fashion—on home turf. Frank Viola, the Series' Most Valuable Player, earns his second victory in the clincher.

Worth Remembering

Some Things Are Better Left Unsaid. Rich "Goose" Gossage, who learned all about inciting controversy while playing for George Steinbrenner's Yankees in the late seventies and early eighties, ruffled the wrong feathers in the summer of 1986. Then a pitcher for the Padres, the Goose alleged that team owner Joan Kroc, widow of McDonald's kingpin Ray Kroc, was poisoning the world with her hamburgers. The Padres suspended Gossage for his remarks.

Winners and Losers. Don Baylor was a player that winning teams wanted in the clubhouse; he played on seven division winners in his nineteen-year career, including three different AL teams in three straight years in the eighties: the Red Sox in 1986, the Twins in 1987, and the A's in 1988. Clint Hurdle was sort of an anti-Baylor; he was a reserve on the 1985 Mets (the year before New York won the World Series), the 1986 Cardinals (St. Louis won pennants in 1985 and 1987), and the 1987 Mets (New York won the division in 1988). As far as managers go, Gene Mauch had the hardest luck; he finished a twenty-six-year, pennantless career in 1987.

Richard Michael Gossage, better known as "Goose," in action in 1989 with the San Francisco Giants, the sixth of nine teams for which he has pitched in a twenty-two-year major league career.

A Rolling Stone. Prior to 1980 Steve Stone had pitched for four different teams and compiled a 78–79 record; his single-season high for victories was 15. But with the Orioles in 1980, Stone put it all together for one year, posting a 25–7 record—good for a league-best .781 winning percentage—with a 3.23 ERA to win the Cy Young Award. His success didn't last, though. The next year—the final season in the majors for the thirty-four-year-old right-hander—he was 4–7 with a 4.57 ERA.

Above: *An automatic tarp was about the only thing that could stop Cardinal outfielder Vince Coleman in the late 1980s. Coleman stole 549 bases from 1985 to 1990 and led the National League six straight years.* Right: *Kirk Gibson, who had helped the Tigers win a World Series in 1984 and a division title in 1987, brought his all-business style of play to Los Angeles in 1988. The Dodgers won a championship in his first year.*

A Bad Roll. St. Louis' Vince Coleman, the major leagues' stolen base leader in 1985 with 110, suffered one of the most bizarre injuries in baseball history before Game Four of the 1985 NL championship series. An automatic tarp at Busch Stadium rolled over Coleman's left leg, benching him for the rest of the playoffs. Even without Coleman, the Cards managed to beat the Dodgers in the playoffs, but they fell to Kansas City in the World Series in 7 games.

A No-Nonsense Leader. Kirk Gibson, a three-year, $4.5 million free agent signee by the Dodgers for the 1988 season, set the tone early in spring training. When Gibson took the field on March 3 for L.A.'s first preseason game, he discovered that a practical joker had covered the inside of his cap with shoe polish. Incensed by the childish antics, Gibson stormed off the field and left the park. When he returned one day later it was clear that his new teammates had gotten the message. The new attitude paid off: Gibson turned in an MVP season and the Dodgers won the World Series.

DECADE SPOTLIGHT
Larry Andersen: Humor in Uniform

Larry Andersen is a bit different from most ballplayers. His unique masks, penchant for practical jokes, and trademark thunderous belches are indicators. But all of that is just the beginning of Andersen's entertaining persona.

A favorite of players and media members alike for his sense of humor, Andersen parlayed a good slider and a decent fastball into a long and successful major league career as a relief pitcher. He broke in with the Cleveland

Indians in 1975; five teams and nearly two decades later, the forty-year-old right-hander was still pitching in the big leagues. On the field, Andersen was almost always the set-up man; only once, in 1990, did he save more than 6 games in a season. Off the field, though, he became known for delivering the punch line.

This is a man who once spray-painted his head, hemmed a teammate's pants up to midcalf, and filled the toilets in his manager's hotel suite with Jell-O. Although he poked fun at the athlete-sportswriter relationship by posting a list of baseball clichés (e.g., "We're taking it one game at a time") next to his locker and inviting reporters to use whatever they needed, most every writer who has covered Andersen has a notebook full of the pitcher's amusing observations. A sampling:

On long national anthems: "When you're playing a Canadian team and both [U.S. and Canadian] anthems are sung, it makes for a long pregame just waiting for them to get the songs over with," Andersen told Ralph Bernstein of the Associated Press. "Sometimes you get one of those opera-type singers and man, it gives you time to take a power nap before the game starts."

On "Take Me Out to the Ball Game": "In the seventh inning [the fans] get up and sing 'Take Me Out to the Ball Game,' and they're already there," Andersen told Bernstein. "It's a really stupid thing to say. The first person to do it must have been a moron. Then there's the line, 'We don't care if we never get back.' I don't believe that and I'm not going to. They have to convince me. I don't think they can."

WHAT'S IN/WHAT'S OUT IN THE 1980s

In

Parity
Twenty-six teams
Players strikes
Pete Rose's hit record
A revolving door in the commissioner's office
Fernando Valenzuela
Concern about player's alcohol and drug use
First-time World Series winners
Mike Scott
Dwight Gooden and Roger Clemens
Traditional-style uniforms
Wade Boggs winning the batting title

Out

Dynasties
Expansion
Fans' patience
Ty Cobb's hit record
Stability in the position
Mark Fidrych
Ignoring the problem
Back-to-back World Series winners
George Scott
Ferguson Jenkins and Catfish Hunter
The gaudy, multicolored look
Rod Carew winning the batting title

Larry Andersen (pictured with the Phillies in 1984) carefully cultivated his reputation for high jinks on the field: a good sense of humor, Andersen felt, was critical in relieving the high-stress atmosphere of Major League Baseball.

On his bad fastball: "If a guy is a good fastball hitter," Andersen asked Bernstein one spring, "shouldn't you throw him a bad fastball? Absolutely. I've been working on it all spring. I threw one yesterday."

On his many motions on the mound: "I'll go to my forehead, the back of my cap, my sleeve," Andersen told Frank Fitzpatrick of the *Philadelphia Inquirer*. "I'll rub the ball up a lot, so I make sure the hitter sees me."

On his longevity (he said that in the later years of his career he would check the team media guide each spring to see how many of his teammates weren't yet born when he began his pro career in Bend, Oregon, back in 1971): "That's so if someone says, 'Hey you're old enough to be my dad,' I'll know he's right," he told Bernstein.

On staying loose: "This is a high-pressure game," he told *Philadelphia Daily News* columnist Stan Hochman. "You've got to have some fun somewhere. If you can have it in the clubhouse, that's the best place to have it.'"

On handling crowd noise: "It's just instinctive," Andersen, who is deaf in his right ear, told *Philadelphia Daily News* columnist Rich Hofmann after a 1993 NL Championship Series game against the Atlanta Braves. "The adrenaline is pumping. I could hear half the stadium doing the Tomahawk Chop. I'm deaf in one ear, so I couldn't hear the other half." Were it not for that deafness, in fact, Andersen might never have played baseball. His first love has always been flying planes. He told one writer that he might try to have his hearing restored after his baseball career was over.

Did Andersen's shtick overshadow his competence as a pitcher? The thought has crossed his mind. "But that's all general-public stuff," he told Fitzpatrick. "I don't think my peers overlook what I can do on the field."

Baseball is, after all, a child's game, so you've got to be a bit of a child at heart to play it. And as Andersen told a *Philadelphia Daily News* writer, "Somebody's gotta do it."

The 1990s
Play Ball

So far in the 1990s, some of the most popular books on baseball have had titles such as *Coming Apart at the Seams* and *Play Ball: The Life and Troubled Times of Major League Baseball*. *Sports Illustrated* published an eight-page article that called today's baseball stars "antiheroes…players perceived as greedy and aloof." *TV Guide* ran a story that asked: "The National Pastime: Past Its Time?" Public television's *Frontline* aired a sixty-minute documentary titled "The Trouble with Baseball." And all this was before the August 1994 players strike that short-circuited the regular season and pulled the plug on the World Series.

The problems of the 1990s really began in the decade's first blighted season: that year began with a thirty-two-day spring training lockout of the players by the owners. At stake was a bigger piece of what had become a billion-dollar pie. The Grapefruit and Cactus Circuit schedules in Florida and Arizona were gutted as visitors from around the nation were greeted by padlocks at the ballparks. On March 18, a four-year agreement was struck and Opening Day was pushed back a week to April 9. "Neither side is particularly happy," allowed Chicago White Sox owner Jerry Reinsdorf, one of five owners involved in negotiations with the players. "But this kind of thing was inevitable."

The sticking point was the time at which players would become eligible for salary arbitration because, in this case, that time amounted to millions of dollars for the side that prevailed. Ultimately, it was agreed that some players with between two and three years of major league service would be eligible. Previously, only players with three years of service had been eligible. Both sides were aware that the 162 players who filed for salary arbitration in 1989 received raises that averaged more than 100 percent, or $430,000. But in reality, the new formula for eligibility expanded the potential arbitration pool by only a dozen or so players.

That same season Pete Rose, the man who collected more hits (4,256) than any man in baseball history, was convicted of tax evasion after he allegedly failed to report substantial winnings at the race track. Rose was sentenced to five months in federal prison and fined fifty thousand dollars. His 1992 election into the Hall of Fame at Cooperstown, New York, which had seemed such a certainty, was now very much in question.

Above: *Barry Bonds of the Giants hauls in a fly ball in the Candlestick Park outfield.* Opposite page: *Yankee first baseman Don Mattingly missed a chance at his first postseason appearance because of the 1994 strike.*

On July 30, Baseball Commissioner Fay Vincent ruled that George Steinbrenner must relinquish his controlling interest in the New York Yankees as punishment for his involvement with known gambler Howard Spira. Seven months earlier, Steinbrenner had paid Spira forty thousand dollars for damaging information concerning one of his Yankees stars, Dave Winfield. Based on evidence presented in a report by investigator John Dowd, Vincent concluded that "Mr. Steinbrenner's payment to Mr. Spira constitutes conduct not in the best interests of baseball."

And while many applauded the temporary departure of the bombastic "Boss," it was another strike against the grand game. Even a marvelous display of pitching—there were 9 no-hitters in 1990, one of them the sixth of Nolan Ryan's career—failed to refocus attention on the game itself.

If the opinions of the media in the early 1990s are any indication, baseball is in sorry shape. The problems chronicled by the media are numerous. Among them:

• Major League Baseball has a leadership vacuum; the commissioner's post was vacated in September 1992 and filled for too long by interim head Bud Selig, the owner of the Milwaukee Brewers, while the powers of the office were drastically reduced.

• Baseball players have low—or negative—public profiles. Much like their sport, they don't measure up in the eyes of the MTV generation, which favors the fast-

Major League Teams in the 1990s
(Teams played entire decade unless otherwise noted)

NATIONAL LEAGUE	AMERICAN LEAGUE
East	**East**
Chicago Cubs	Baltimore Orioles
Florida Marlins (1993–)	Boston Red Sox
Montreal Expos	Cleveland Indians
New York Mets	Detroit Tigers
Philadelphia Phillies	Milwaukee Brewers
Pittsburgh Pirates	New York Yankees
St. Louis Cardinals	Toronto Blue Jays
West	**West**
Atlanta Braves	California Angels
Cincinnati Reds	Chicago White Sox
Colorado Rockies (1993–)	Kansas City Royals
Houston Astros	Minnesota Twins
Los Angeles Dodgers	Oakland Athletics
San Diego Padres	Seattle Mariners
San Francisco Giants	Texas Rangers

Divisional realignment instituted in 1994

NATIONAL LEAGUE	AMERICAN LEAGUE
East	**East**
Atlanta Braves	Baltimore Orioles
Florida Marlins	Boston Red Sox
Montreal Expos	Detroit Tigers
New York Mets	New York Yankees
Philadelphia Phillies	Toronto Blue Jays
Central	**Central**
Chicago Cubs	Chicago White Sox
Cincinnati Reds	Cleveland Indians
Houston Astros	Kansas City Royals
Pittsburgh Pirates	Milwaukee Brewers
St. Louis Cardinals	Minnesota Twins
West	**West**
Colorado Rockies	California Angels
Los Angeles Dodgers	Oakland Athletics
San Diego Padres	Seattle Mariners
San Francisco Giants	Texas Rangers

once that first pitch is thrown each day of the spring, summer, and early autumn.

It used to be that other sports learned from baseball. Now it seems to be the other way around. While disregarding its own strengths, baseball has been in too big a hurry to take a page out of other sports leagues' books. The expanded playoffs are an example; it's something baseball didn't need. The importance of a 162-game season had always set the game apart from other sports that play shorter seasons and allow more teams in the postseason. Things can't be all that bad, considering that prior to the strike, 1994 attendance was running a little ahead of the record seventy-million pace of 1993.

There are, however, a few lessons that baseball's management could learn from other sports:

Kill the money complaints. There is so much carping by the owners when a free agent such as Barry Bonds signs a megabucks deal that it affects the fans' perceptions. Instead of arguing whether Bonds is better than Ken Griffey, Jr., fans are debating whether Bonds is worth the money he commands.

Besides, is money really that tight? The owners complained in the early 1990s that many teams lost money, but a study by *Chicago Tribune* baseball writer Jerome Holtzman indicated that the twenty-six major league teams made about $350 million in profits in 1991. If ownership of a major league team was such a poor investment, how come the ownership groups of the Florida Marlins and Colorado Rockies put up ninety-five million dollars apiece to have a crack at it? For that matter, would a new team in any other sport have inspired the massive fan support (a total attendance record of 4.5 million in 1993) of the Rockies?

paced game and well-publicized stars of the National Basketball Association.

• Both the players and owners are perceived as greedy, each trying to get more than their share of the profits, and each willing to sling mud at the other and resort to a strike or a lockout to get it.

• The three-division alignment and expanded playoffs have diluted the regular season, lessened baseball's competitive integrity, and robbed the game of its tradition.

• The new television contract with NBC and ABC provides for too few "free TV" national games, prohibits fans without cable television from seeing certain teams outside their cities, and denies all fans the opportunity to watch every playoff game.

• Player salaries and ticket prices are up. Attendance, television ratings, and revenues are down.

Can baseball survive?

It can and it will, because, as Shakespeare might have said, the game's the thing. Baseball's unique charm and appeal, its blend of simplicity and complexity, and its wonderful sense of tradition and continuity are always there

Play team ball. The owners and players in the NBA are partners, not adversaries, working together within a fair financial structure for the good of their sport, not separately for the detriment of one another. It makes sense—neither side could survive without the other, and the same is true for baseball. As far as management is concerned, this includes promoting the players. In 1993 only nine of the twenty-eight major league teams featured their players on the cover of their media guide; most opted for the team logo or some generic image. The game is full of stars, such as Bonds, Griffey, Frank Thomas, Tony Gwynn, and Jeff Bagwell, who are worthy of promotion and large-scale national recognition.

Add network telecasts earlier in the season. Besides being too regionalized—a fan without cable television in Detroit can't see Bonds' San Francisco Giants before the World Series—baseball's current national television deal is too limited. There were only 16 "games of the week" scheduled for 1994—down from 41 in 1987—and the first telecast wasn't until after the All-Star break. Don't the games in the first half of the season mean anything?

Schedule afternoon postseason games. Under the current television contract, only night playoff and World Series games will be telecast nationally. Management claims the games have to be played in the evening to bring better ratings, but the NBA and NFL appear to get by with some afternoon playoff telecasts. Baseball owes it to its next generation of fans to broadcast some of its showcase games at a time when those young fans aren't fast asleep.

Most of all, the people in the game have to keep in mind that they are not bigger than the game itself. Baseball was around long before any current player, owner, or executive was even born, and it will continue after they're gone, provided the game's caretakers remember that they are no more than that. Baseball has a glorious past, and it can have an even more glorious future.

Four players who had banner seasons cut short in 1994: Chicago White Sox first baseman Frank Thomas (opposite page), Houston Astros first baseman Jeff Bagwell (above), Seattle Mariners center fielder Ken Griffey, Jr., (below), and San Francisco Giants third baseman Matt Williams (below, right).

March 18, 1990: The owners' thirty-two-day spring training lockout of the players—caused by the lack of a new basic agreement—ends with the approval of a new four-year agreement. Spring training is reduced to three weeks; Opening Day is delayed until April 9; and the first week's games are postponed until later in the season.

April–October 1990: One concern about the lockout is that pitchers will not have enough spring training time to get ready for the season. The contrary is true—1990 becomes the year of the no-hitter. On the third day of the season, California's Mark Langston and Mike Witt throw a combined no-hitter; it is the first of 9 this season, including the sixth of Nolan Ryan's career on June 11 (at age forty-three Ryan becomes the oldest pitcher to throw a no-hit game), 2 on the same day on June 29, and New York Yankee Andy Hawkins' 4–0 no-hit loss to the Chicago White Sox two days later.

April 20, 1990: Pete Rose, baseball's all-time hit leader, is convicted of tax evasion, and receives a sentence of five months and a fine of fifty thousand dollars. He begins serving his sentence August 8 at the Marion (Illinois) Federal Prison Camp.

May 7, 1990: Boston reliever Rob Murphy comes on in the eighth inning to protect a 5–2 lead against Seattle, but he allows 2 runs on 2 hits and 2 walks. Hoping to change his luck between innings, he runs into the clubhouse and shaves off his four-day beard before returning to pitch the ninth. He then records the final 3 outs to earn his first save of the season.

July 30, 1990: George Steinbrenner agrees to "permanently" resign as general managing partner of the Yankees for his violation of "the best interests of baseball" rule. Commissioner Fay Vincent ordered an investigation of Steinbrenner's dealings with gambler Howard Spira, whom Steinbrenner admitted to hiring for the purpose of providing damaging information on Yankee Dave Winfield. The Yankees finish 67–95, their worst record in more than seventy years. But "the Boss" will be back—in less than three years.

Top: Ryne Sandberg gave the Chicago Cubs solid defense and surprising power from the second base position. Above: One of the biggest stories of the 1990s has been Cal Ripken's pursuit of Lou Gehrig's record for consecutive games played, a mark thought to be unassailable.

July 31, 1990: In Milwaukee, ageless Nolan Ryan wins his three hundredth game. He will lead the league in strikeouts for the ninth time in his career.

August 2, 1990: *Iraqi forces invade neighboring Kuwait. President Bush warns Iraqi leader Saddam Hussein that the invasion "will not stand." Six days later U.S. troops land in Dharan, Saudi Arabia, for Operation Desert Shield, to protect Saudi Arabia's oilfields.*

August 31, 1990: In Seattle, the Griffeys—Ken, Sr., and Ken, Jr.—are the first father and son ever to play together on the same major league team.

October 1990: It is a season of remarkable individual achievements. Detroit's Cecil Fielder, who played the previous year in Japan, hits 51 home runs to become the first major leaguer since 1977 and the first AL player since 1961 to break the 50 mark. Oakland's Bob Welch wins 27 games, the most in the majors since 1968. Bobby Thigpen of the White Sox saves a record 57 games. Kansas City's George Brett, thirty-seven, becomes the first player in history to win a batting title in three different decades. Ryne Sandberg of the Chicago Cubs is the first second baseman since Rogers Hornsby to lead the league in homers.

October 1990: Baltimore shortstop Cal Ripken extends his consecutive-games-played streak to 1,392, the second-longest in history. Ripken commits a record-low 3 errors and ends the season with a 104 straight errorless games.

April 18, 1991: The White Sox's new Comiskey Park opens.

May 1, 1991: Nolan Ryan, forty-four, pitches his seventh no-hitter, striking out 16 as Texas beats visiting Toronto 3–0. On the same night in Oakland, Rickey Henderson of the A's supplants Lou Brock as the all-time stolen base king by swiping number 939 of his career.

July 9, 1991: The American League wins its fourth straight All-Star Game for the first time since 1946–1949.

July 28, 1991: Montreal's Dennis Martinez throws a perfect game in Los Angeles to beat the Dodgers 2–0.

October 1991: The Toronto Blue Jays, playing in the SkyDome, draw a record four million fans for the season.

October 1991: The Minnesota Twins and Atlanta Braves, last-place teams the year before, win their respective divisions, something no team in major league history has ever done. The two clubs advance to the World Series, where the Twins prevail in a thriller. In another major league first, every AL West team finishes with a record of .500 or better.

October 6, 1991: David Cone of the New York Mets strikes out 19 Philadelphia Phillies to tie the NL single-game record.

December 25, 1991: *Soviet leader Mikhail Gorbachev resigns and the dissolution of the Soviet Union begins.*

1992: The big winners in the free agent market are Bobby Bonilla, whose new contract with the Mets will pay him $5.9 million this season, and Ryne Sandberg of the Cubs, whose new long-term deal will soon be worth seven million dollars a year.

April 6, 1992: Baltimore's Oriole Park at Camden Yards opens.

April 29, 1992: *Rioting and looting erupt in Los Angeles after a jury that included no blacks acquits four policemen charged with beating African-American motorist Rodney King. Violence will not subside until May 2, after the National Guard, Marines, and Army have been called in to keep the peace.*

June 11, 1992: Going against their long-standing policy of opposition to investors outside the United States and Canada, Major League Baseball owners approve the sale of the Seattle Mariners to a group headed by Nintendo Company Limited President

Above, left: *George Brett joins the exclusive 3,000-hit club with a base hit on September 30, 1992, in Anaheim Stadium.* **Left:** *Detroit's Cecil Fielder watches his fiftieth homer of the season fly into the left-field seats on October 3, 1990, in Yankee Stadium. Fielder became the eleventh player to reach the 50-homer mark.*

In 1987 San Diego's Benito Santiago hit .300 with 18 homers and 79 RBI and became the first catcher to be named Rookie of the Year in either league since Carlton Fisk of the Red Sox in 1972.

Hiroshi Yamauchi; his son-in-law, Nintendo of America President Minoru Arakawa; and Seattle investors.

September 7, 1992: Under pressure from angry baseball owners after he ordered the National League realigned "in the best interests of baseball," Commissioner Fay Vincent resigns. Vincent had upset the owners by trying to force the Cubs and St. Louis Cardinals to move to the NL West, and by his handling of the suspensions of Yankees owner George Steinbrenner and Yankees pitcher Steve Howe, as well as his refusal to take himself out of the upcoming negotiations with the players association. As chairman of the newly formed Executive Council, Milwaukee Brewers owner Bud Selig will act as interim commissioner while the owners organize a search committee for a replacement and set out to restructure the powers of the office.

October 1992: The season's highlights include Cecil Fielder becoming the first major leaguer since Babe Ruth to lead the league in runs batted in three straight years; Kansas City's George Brett and Milwaukee's Robin Yount each recording their three thousandth hit; Toronto's forty-year-old Dave Winfield becoming the

oldest player in history to drive in 100 runs; Boston's Jeff Reardon and St. Louis' Lee Smith each breaking Rollie Fingers' all-time save record; St. Louis' Bob Tewksbury; walking a mere 20 hitters in 233 innings, and San Diego's Gary Sheffield's pursuit of the Triple Crown (he finishes first in batting, third in homers, and fifth in RBI).

October 14, 1992: Francisco Cabrera's 2-out, 2-run single in the bottom of the ninth inning lifts the Atlanta Braves to a 3–2 win over the Pittsburgh Pirates in a dramatic Game Seven of the NL Championship Series.

October 24, 1992: The Blue Jays defeat the Braves in 6 games to become the first Canadian team to win the World Series.

1993: Randy Myers of the Cubs saves an NL-record 53 games.

1993: Former Pittsburgh Pirate Barry Bonds, signed by new Giants owner Peter McGowan to a six-year, $43.75 million free agent contract, responds with a Most Valuable Player season: a .336 average, 46 home runs, and 123 RBI. Cubs free agent Greg Maddux signs with Atlanta to give the NL West–champion Braves one of the

best pitching rotations of all time. The foursome of Maddux, Tom Glavine, Steve Avery, and John Smoltz wins 75 games; Maddux wins his second straight Cy Young Award.

January 1993: *President Clinton announces his compromise on the issue of gays in the military: new recruits are not to be asked their sexual orientation, and openly homosexual servicemen and women will be put on reserve status. In July the president will codify this policy as "don't ask, don't tell, don't pursue."*

February 3, 1993: Cincinnati Reds owner Marge Schott is suspended for one year for making racial and ethnic slurs.

February 26, 1993: *Five are killed and hundreds are injured when a bomb explodes in the underground parking garage between the twin towers of the World Trade Center in New York City.*

March 22, 1993: Cleveland Indians pitchers Steve Olin and Tim Crews are killed and teammate Bob Ojeda is severely injured in a boating accident during spring training in Clermont, Florida. Ojeda returns to the mound on August 7 and makes eight more appearances. Tragedy strikes the Indians again when reliever Cliff Young is killed in an auto accident in November.

April 1993: The National League's two new expansion teams, the Marlins and the Rockies, begin play. They are the first new major league teams since 1977 and the first additions to the NL since 1969.

April 9, 1993: Bo Jackson of the White Sox, the former baseball-football star who underwent hip replacement surgery and missed the entire 1992 season, hits a home run off Yankee Neal Heaton on his first swing of the season.

June 27, 1993: Anthony Young of the Mets loses his major league record–setting twenty-fourth consecutive game, snapping an eighty-two-year-old mark. Young goes on to lose 27 in a row before finally beating the Florida Marlins on July 28.

July 13, 1993: The American League extends its All-Star Game winning streak to 6 with a 9–3 victory. The AL had never won more than 4 All-Star Games in a row in the contest's sixty-year history.

July 28, 1993: Seattle's Ken Griffey, Jr., ties a major league record by hitting a home run in 8 consecutive games.

July–August 1993: In a disturbing sign of the times, San Diego Padres owner Tom Werner continues unloading high-priced veterans to reduce his payroll. In the past year the Padres have dumped pitchers Randy Myers, Craig Lefferts, Greg Harris, and Bruce Hurst, catcher Benito Santiago, shortstop Tony Fernandez, outfielder Darrin Jackson, third baseman Gary Sheffield, and first baseman Fred McGriff. The club offers refunds to dissatisfied season-ticket holders.

October 1993: Colorado's Andres Galarraga and Toronto's John Olerud each

Above, right: A 33–41 pitcher in his first four seasons in Atlanta, Tom Glavine broke through in 1991 with a starting assignment in the All-Star Game, a league-high 20 wins, and a Cy Young Award. Above: It took nineteen years and four teams, but Dave Winfield finally won a World Series with the Toronto Blue Jays in 1992. Winfield's 2-run double provided the margin of victory in the decisive sixth game. Right: San Francisco's Barry Bonds won his third MVP Award in four seasons in 1993.

flirt with a .400 batting average for much of the summer. Neither reaches the mark, but each wins his first batting title (Galarraga hits .370 and Olerud, .363).

October 1993: The Rockies draw a record 4.48 million fans in their first season. Both expansion teams are among the seven teams to break the three-million mark as attendance climbs to a record seventy million.

October 23, 1993: Joe Carter's 3-run, ninth-inning home run off Philadelphia's Mitch Williams wins Game Six and the World Series for the Blue Jays, who are baseball's first back-to-back champs since the 1977 and 1978 Yankees. The wildest contest of the Series is Game Four, in which the

Left: Atlanta's Greg Maddux, a valuable free agent acquisition from the Chicago Cubs, won his unprecedented third straight Cy Young Award and his fifth straight Gold Glove in 1994. Below, left: In nineteen major league seasons Dennis Martinez has thrown a perfect game and led his league for at least one year in wins, complete games, shutouts, and ERA. But a World Series championship still eludes him.

Phillies blew a 14–9 lead in the eighth inning and lost 15–14; that game is the longest in Series history and sets records for runs and hits.

1994: The major leagues realign into three divisions and add an extra round of play-offs, with an extra division winner and a wild-card team qualifying from each league. Major League Baseball also embarks on a new six-year network television contract with ABC and NBC; the deal was signed in the spring of 1993.

February 7, 1994: The White Sox announce that they have invited retired pro basketball legend Michael Jordan to spring training to try out for the team.

February 11, 1994: Baseball owners announce that the power of the commissioner's office—a post that has been vacant for more than seventeen months—will be significantly curtailed. Rather than having unlimited authority to act "in the best interests of baseball," as has always been the case, the commissioner's powers will no longer extend to matters concerning the World Series and postseason play, scheduling, interleague play, divisional alignment, expansion, the sale or relocation of teams, revenue sharing, or broadcast agreements.

April 1994: The Cleveland Indians' Gateway Complex and Texas Rangers'

new stadium, known simply as the Ballpark in Arlington, open.

August 12, 1994: Major league players go out on strike, baseball's eighth work stoppage since 1972. This one is by far the most severe: it ultimately wipes out the remainder of the regular season and forces the cancellation of the playoffs and the World Series—the first interruption in the continuity of the Fall Classic since 1904. Also lost are potential banner hitting seasons by Matt Williams, Ken Griffey, Jr., Frank Thomas, Albert Belle, Tony Gwynn, Barry Bonds, and Jeff Bagwell; pennant hopes for long-suffering fans of the Cleveland Indians, Texas Rangers, and Montreal Expos; and the revenue of an extra tier of playoffs. The major issue is a proposed salary cap, without which team owners claim they cannot survive and to which the players insist they will not agree under any circumstances.

October 16, 1994: *Jean-Bertrand Aristide, the duly elected president of Haiti, returns to the country after having been ousted by a military junta in September 1991. Aristide's restoration to power comes after an ultimatum, backed by the threat of military force, is delivered to Lieutenant General Raoul Cedras by U.S. negotiators.*

November 1, 1994: Its founders announce the formation of the United Baseball League, which features an innovative profit-sharing and equity plan for both its teams and its players. Created by Texas Congressman John Bryant, former Congressman Bob Mrazek, economist Andrew Zimbalist, and player agent Dick Moss, the new league hopes to attract as many current major league players, coaches, and managers as possible. Plans are to begin play in 1996 with ten teams.

DECADE PITCHING LEADERS

	National League			American League		
YEAR	PLAYER	TEAM	ERA	PLAYER	TEAM	ERA
1990	Danny Darwin	Houston	2.21	Roger Clemens	Boston	1.93
1991	Dennis Martinez	Montreal	2.39	Roger Clemens	Boston	2.62
1992	Bill Swift	San Francisco	2.08	Roger Clemens	Boston	2.41
1993	Greg Maddux	Atlanta	2.36	Kevin Appier	Kansas City	2.56
1994	Greg Maddux	Atlanta	1.56	Steve Ontiveros	Oakland	2.65

Epilogue

As this book was nearing completion, Major League Baseball was in the midst of a shutdown, the most serious work stoppage in the game's history. Yet many baseball fans—this writer included—held out hope that the major leagues would soon return. And we knew that when they did, so would we—to the ballparks, that is. Why? Are we hopelessly naive? Optimists blinded by nostalgia? Gluttons for punishment? Probably. But we are baseball fans, and, unfortunately, these days you have to be a little bit of each of these things if you want to watch the game played at the highest level. For our love of the game, we've been willing to put up with the problems although even our estimable patience is being severely tested. All we've really asked is that the owners and players running the show don't take us for granted, and it's hard to understand why that request often can't be honored. Without us, the games wouldn't really matter much, would they?

Over the years we've all enjoyed watching exciting moments unfold on the diamond. Some thrilled us. Some broke our hearts. Some are probably recounted in the pages of this book, which we hope, to paraphrase James Earl Jones in *Field of Dreams*, "reminds us of all that once was good, and can be good again." Yes, we remember. And we'll be back for more.

WHAT'S IN/WHAT'S OUT IN THE 1990s

In

Expansion, realignment, and wild-card teams
Serious challenges from other sports

Barry Bonds and Ken Griffey, Jr.
Retro-style, baseball-only ballparks
The best interests of the owners
Tom Glavine
Worrying about long games
Baseball on cable television
Owners complaining about player salaries
Deion Sanders' two-sport feats
Threatened franchise shifts
NBA and NFL stars topping the popularity polls
ESPN's "Baseball Tonight"
Rooting for your rotisserie players

Out

The status quo of the eighties
Baseball's unquestioned status as America's Game
Bobby Bonds and Ken Griffey, Sr.
Plain, symmetrical, multipurpose stadiums
The best interests of baseball
Tom Seaver
Simply enjoying the game
Baseball on network television
Owners positively promoting the game's stars
Bo Jackson's two-sport feats
Actual franchise shifts
Baseball stars dominating Madison Avenue
"This Week in Baseball"
Rooting for your home team

Above: Toronto's Joe Carter jumps for joy after his 3-run home run in the ninth inning lifted the Blue Jays to an 8–6 win over the Philadelphia Phillies in the decisive sixth game of the 1993 World Series. The Blue Jays became the first repeat Series champions since the 1977–1978 New York Yankees.

DECADE BATTING LEADERS

	National League			American League		
YEAR	PLAYER	TEAM	AVG.	PLAYER	TEAM	AVG.
1990	Willie McGee	St. Louis	.335	George Brett	Kansas City	.329
1991	Terry Pendleton	Atlanta	.319	Julio Franco	Texas	.341
1992	Gary Sheffield	San Diego	.330	Edgar Martinez	Seattle	.343
1993	Andres Galarraga	Colorado	.370	John Olerud	Toronto	.363
1994	Tony Gwynn	San Diego	.394	Paul O'Neill	New York	.359

Further Reading

Carter, Craig, and Joe Hoppel, eds. *Baseball: A Doubleheader Collection of Facts, Feats, and Firsts.* The Sporting News Publishing Company, 1993.

Chadwick, Bruce. *When the Game Was Black and White: The Illustrated History of Baseball's Negro Leagues.* Abbeville Press, 1992.

Cohen, Richard M., and David S. Neft. *The Sports Encyclopedia: Baseball.* St. Martin's Press, 1994.

——. *The World Series.* St. Martin's Press, 1990.

Dickson, Paul. *Baseball's Greatest Quotations.* HarperCollins Publishers, 1991.

Garber, Angus G. *The Baseball Companion.* Mallard Press, 1990.

James, Bill. *The Bill James Historical Baseball Abstract.* Villard Books, 1988.

Kirshon, John W., ed. *Chronicle of America.* JL International Publishing, 1993.

MacFarlane, Paul, ed. *The Sporting News Hall of Fame Fact Book.* The Sporting News Publishing Company, 1983.

Menke, Frank G. *The Encyclopedia of Sports.* A.S. Barnes and Company, Inc., 1978.

Nathan, David H., ed. *Baseball Quotations.* Ballantine Books, 1993.

Okkonen, Marc. *Baseball Memories 1900–1909.* Sterling Publishing Company, Inc., 1993.

——. *Baseball Memories 1950–1959.* Sterling Publishing Company, Inc., 1993.

Palmer, Pete, and John Thorn, eds. *Total Baseball.* HarperCollins Publishers, 1993.

Rader, Benjamin G. *Baseball: A History of America's Game.* University of Illinois Press, 1992.

Reichler, Joseph L., ed. *The Baseball Encyclopedia.* Macmillan Publishing Company, 1994.

Reidenbaugh, Lowell. *Baseball's 25 Greatest Games.* The Sporting News Publishing Company, 1986.

——. *Baseball's 25 Greatest Pennant Races.* The Sporting News Publishing Company, 1987.

——. *Baseball's 25 Greatest Teams.* The Sporting News Publishing Company, 1987.

——. *Take Me Out to the Ball Park.* The Sporting News Publishing Company, 1988.

Schlesinger, Arthur M., Jr., ed. *The Almanac of American History.* Barnes and Noble Books, 1993.

Schlossberg, Dan. *The Baseball Catalog.* Jonathan David Publishers, Inc., 1993.

Seymour, Harold. *Baseball: The Early Years.* Oxford University Press, 1989.

Snyder, John S. *Play Ball: Great Moments and Dubious Achievements in Baseball History.* Chronicle Books, 1991.

Photo Credits

© **Allsport USA:** Jim Commentucci: 169 left; J. Daniel: 153; Tim Defrisco: 170 bottom; Stephen Dunn: 2, 152 bottom, 167 top, 170 top; Steve Goldstein: 159 left; Stephen Green: 160 left; Otto Gruele: 162; William Hart: 150 top; Mike Powell: 154; Kirk Schlea: 156 top; Damian Strohmeyer: 155 bottom left

© **AP/Wide World Photos:** 18 top, 25 top, 31 top, 68, 69 top, 70, 71 top, 74, 75, 81 both, 83, 87 bottom, 92 both, 97, 110 top, 112, 113, 114 bottom, 115 bottom, 117, 119 both, 120 top, 121 top, 124, 130, 132 right, 134 left, 136 bottom, 138 top, 139 right, 140, 146 top, 155 top, 167 bottom, 171

Archive Photos: 86 bottom, 100 bottom

© **Bob Bartosz:** 128 bottom, 129 top, 132 left, 135 bottom, 142 bottom

© **Jeff Carlick/Sports Photo Masters, Inc.:** 6, 165 bottom right

Courtesy Dover Publications, Inc.: 19 left, 33 both, 38 both, 39, 41, 48 right, 59 top, 66 bottom

© **Focus on Sports:** 116 both, 123 both, 131, 133 left, 134 right, 137, 139 left, 141 top, 145 top, 148 top and center, 150 bottom, 152 top, 156 bottom, 158 bottom, 161, 165 center, 168; © Mickey Palmer: 138 bottom; © Jerry Wachter: 133 top, 135 top, 142 top

FPG International: 13 bottom, 15 top, 22, 28, 29 bottom, 32, 37, 51 bottom, 62, 63 right, 65 top, 67 top, 72 left, 88 bottom, 99 bottom, 105 top, 136 top; © Hy Pesken: 80 top, 85 center and bottom left, 94, 96 all, 101 both, 102 top, 103 top, 104, 105 bottom, 106, 107 both, 118, 122 both; Pittsburgh Black Heritage: 121 bottom; © Jack Zehrt: 95 bottom; © John Zimmerman: 127 top

National Baseball Library and Archive, Cooperstown, N.Y.: 6–7 background, 7 right, 9 both, 10 left, 10–11, 12, 14, 15 bottom, 16 both, 17 both, 18 bottom, 19 right, 20, 21, 23, 24, 25 bottom, 26, 27, 30 both, 31 bottom, 34, 35, 36, 40, 43, 44–45, 45 right, 46 both, 46–47, 48 left, 49, 50 all, 51 top left to right, 52 all, 53, 54, 55 both, 57 both, 58 both, 59 bottom, 60 both, 63 left, 64, 65 bottom, 66 top, 67 bottom, 71 bottom, 72 right, 73, 79, 80 bottom, 88 top, 89 both, 91, 99 top, 102 bottom, 108 bottom, 125, 126

Negro Leagues Baseball Museum, Inc.: 78

© **Bob Rosato:** 7 left, 163, 164, 166 top, 169 top and bottom right

© **Warren Schultz:** grass background throughout

© **Carl Seid:** 56

© **Sportschrome East/West:** 165 top left; © Robert Tringali, Jr.: 157 right

© **Dave Stock:** 1, 144, 145 bottom, 146 bottom, 147 both, 148 bottom right, 149 both, 151 both, 155 bottom right, 157 left, 158 top, 159 right, 160 right, 166 bottom

© **Dick Tripp/Detroit Free Press:** 141 bottom

© **UPI/Bettmann:** 69 bottom, 76, 77, 86 center left, 90 bottom, 98, 100 top, 103 bottom, 114 top, 115 top, 120 bottom, 128 top, 129 bottom

Index

ALEXANDRIA
the Site & the History

Essays by
Morsi Saad El-Din
Gamal Mokhtar
Mostafa El-Abbadi
Abdel/Azim Ramadan

Edited by
Gareth L. Steen

Photographs by
Araldo De Luca

New York University Press
New York and London

Published by New York University Press
New York and London

c 10 9 8 7 6 5 4 3 2 1

Editor: Gareth L. Steen
Consulting editor: Dr. Morsi Saad El-Din
Design: Franco Maria Ricci
Artistic director: Laura Casalis
Photography: Araldo De Luca
Printed in Hong Kong by Everbest Printing Co., Ltd.

Library of Congress Cataloging-in-Publication Data

Alexandria : the site & the history / essays by Morsi Saad El-Din . . .
[et al.] : photographs by Araldo De Luca.
p. cm.
Includes bibliographical references.
ISBN 0-8147-7986-7
1. Alexandria (Egypt)—History. I. Saad El-Din, Morsi.
II. De Luca, Araldo
DT154.A4A64 1993
962'.1—dc20
93-25746
CIP

Table of Contents

Foreword

Alexandria has always been a city celebrated in the collective memories of the ages. This "bride of the Mediterranean," as it is often called, is part of a select group of cities. Like Rome, Venice, Byzantium and Carthage, the mere mention of its name conjures up pictures from an exhilarating history.

Alexandria has always been a melting pot. It was a stepping stone between the civilizations of ancient Egypt and Greece, and the channel through which many of the ideas that inform our present age first passed.

These precepts not only passed through Alexandria, they were stored and disseminated for many centuries from its Great Library of antiquity. From its earliest days, the city was a clearinghouse for the most enlightened thoughts of its times.

The leaders of the Governorate of Alexandria have undertaken a number of large-scale projects to help the city regain its civic, touristic, cultural and academic face. One of the most challenging and exciting of these is the Bibliotheca Alexandrina, a major undertaking that will revive the

Great Library of Alexandria of old, and through an international effort, the project has gotten underway. It is our aim that the Bibliotheca Alexandrina will soon, once again, be a beacon the world over to students and academicians, tourists and laymen eager to be edified.

With similar diversity, this handsome book, Alexandria – the Site and the History, offers a fresh look at our city over centuries past through the eyes of four pre-eminent Egyptian academicians and writers: Dr. Morsi Saad El-Din, Dr. Gamal Mokhtar, Dr. Mostafa El-Abbadi and Dr. Abdel/Azim Ramadan; and an outstanding international creative team: editor Gareth L. Steen, consulting editor Dr. Saad El-Din, designer Franco Maria Ricci, art director Laura Casalis and photographer Araldo De Luca.

The book not only serves as an introduction to Alexandria, it also manages to capture the spirit of this renowned world metropolis, which is beloved by the Egyptian people. By sponsoring this book, Mobil Oil Egypt has once again made an important contribution to our city, country and culture, and that is greatly appreciated.

Chancellor / Alsayed Ismail Algawsaky
Governor of Alexandria

Introduction

by Dr. Morsi Saad El-Din

Why a new book about Alexandria when dozens already exist? The answer is a simple one. This is a book with a difference. It is a book about Alexandria, seen through the eyes of Egyptians who are experts in their fields.

Alexandria has had many faces and many phases. It developed from a mere anchorage – at times a hiding niche for pirates – to a city that came to be called "the bride of the Mediterranean."

The history of Alexandria is a record of ongoing civilization with all the cultural implications that word carries: politics, art, music, literature and science – all the humanities. Indeed, the world is indebted to Alexandria. As American classics professor John Rodenbeck writes:

"Whenever a pipe organ is played, Archimedes screw is used, an atlas or a Western calendar are consulted, grammar, geography, mechanics and geometry are taught, poems, novels, plays or operas are performed, examined by critics or cataloged by a scholar, we think of Alexandria."

It was in Alexandria that the Great Library of antiquity stood as a beacon for learning. Its thousands of volumes were administered by famous literati and critics like Zenodotus of Ephesus, Callimachus of Cyrene, Apollonius of Rhodes and Aristophanes of Byzantium.

All these men were leading figures in one form or another in science, art, and literature. Zenodotus was a collector of the works of Greek poets from Homer onwards. He not only collected the poems, he corrected and edited them. He was assisted by two poets, Lycophron of Chalcis and Alexander of Aetolia. Zenodotus was famous for his annotated and expurgated version of Homer's *Iliad* and the *Odyssey*.

Another famed librarian was the poet Callimachus of Cyrene. He is reputed to have produced the library's first catalog, covering its papyrus scrolls, listing the authors and classifying their works. "From these lists," writes Rodenbeck, "come our ideas of a literary 'canon,' and from the library's practice of publishing standard editions of works on its lists comes our own notion of standard or definitive editions."

The library contained 490,000 papyrus scrolls. The standard Greek version of the Old Testament, known as the *Septuagint* was translated by scholars from Alexandria's Jewish population. During the reign of Cleopatra, Antony presented the queen with 200,000 parchment volumes from the renowned Library of Pergamum.

The Great Library of Alexandria was also known for the acquisitions it managed to get from other libraries – and one could say this was the forerunner of the present system of interlibrary loans. The most famous of those acquisitions is Aristotle's library. It is recorded that this library was bought for the

Facing page:
Marble head of Alexander the Great [Alexander III of Macedon] (356-323 B.C.). Ptolemaic Period. Graeco-Roman Museum, Alexandria.

9

Alexandria library by Philadelphus, who commissioned the first translation of the first five books of the Old Testament from Hebrew to Greek.

Over the centuries, a variety of opinions were expressed from time to time about the burning of the Alexandria library. A number of theories evolved about who did it and the number of volumes destroyed. More details about the burning of the library and the books that were lost can be found in chapters two and three. But it is known that there were serious losses of books during Julius Caesar's invasion of Egypt in 48 B.C. He set fire to the ships of the Egyptian fleet, which spread, and in the words of Plutarch, the famous historian: "The fire destroyed the Great Library."

Seneca, the Roman philosopher wrote in 49 A.D. that 400,000 books were burned in Alexandria. Nearly a century later, Aulus Gellius reported that 700,000 volumes were destroyed. There are many theories about where and how the books were burned.

Another disaster came to the library in 391 A.D., when Christianity became the official religion of the Eastern Roman Empire, of which Egypt was part. The zealous Christians dismantled the temple and demolished it, burning many books of the famous library in the process.

But the question that concerns us here is whether the remains of the library were burned by Amr Ibn el As at the orders of Caliph Omar Ibn el Khattab, when Alexandria was taken over in 641 A.D. The story is based on two original accounts by Abdel Latif, a Moslem physician, writer and traveler who was born in Baghdad and Ibn el Qifti, a Moslem judge, historian and philosopher who was born in 1172 at Qift, between Qena and Luxor. The two statements are questionable since both writers lived five centuries after the event.

In Chapter 51 of Gibbon's *Decline and Fall of the Roman Empire*, the author sheds doubt over the authenticity of the two statements:

For my own part, I am strongly tempted to deny both the fact and the consequence. The solitary report of a stranger who wrote at the end of six hundred years on the confines of the Media is overbalanced by the silence of two analysts of a more early date, both Christian, both natives of Egypt and the most ancient of whom, Patriarch Eutychius, has amply described the conquest of Alexandria.

Historians and researchers later on marshaled more detailed explanations to prove that the Arabs did not burn the library.

Many books have appeared about Alexandria through the years. Some are guidebooks while others deal with its history. E. M. Forster called his famous book "History and Guide," but it is really more than this. It is a literary masterpiece. There is, however, another book that deserves mentioning and that is, perhaps, one of the best history books about Alexandria.

John Marlowe's *The Golden Age of Alexandria* is a comprehensive history that is written with a great deal of sympathy – almost love – of the city. The book begins with a quotation, which other writers have also used, from Amr Ibn el As, the commander of the Arab armies in September 642 A.D. Writing to Omar he says:

I have taken a city which I can but say that it contains 4,000 palaces, 4,000 baths, 400 cellars, 1,200 sellers of green vegetables.

One of the Arab soldiers accompanying Amr wrote:

The moonlight reflected from the white marble made the city so bright that a tailor could see to thread his needle without a lamp.

No one entered the city without having a covering on his eyes to veil him from the glare of the plaster and marble.

Up to the time of the Arab conquest in 642 A.D., Alexandria was probably the finest city in the world. From the time of its foundation by Alexander the Great in 331 B.C. to its capture by Octavius in 30 B.C., Alexandria had been the capital of a huge empire, the intellectual and social center of the Hellenic world. It was also a magnet that attracted both the material riches of Asia and Africa as well as the intellectual resources of the Greek world.

In his book Marlowe stresses that Alexandria had been the powerhouse that transmuted this wealth into a civilization and disseminated it throughout the Mediterranean. Even after the political center of gravity in the Mediterranean moved westward to Rome, Alexandria was still intellectually and culturally supreme and was still the principal avenue through which not only the material wealth but the spiritual ideas and lore of the East were channeled into what had become the Roman world of the Mediterranean.

Such is Marlowe's enthusiasm for Alexandria. To him Rome at its great heights was no more than a pale reflection of the venerable city on the opposite shore of the Mediterranean. In spite of competition from other cities, Alexandria remained intellectually supreme. In Ptolemaic times, Alexandria led the world in scientific discovery as well as in Hellenic culture generally, following the precept that "man was the measure of all things." And during the first six centuries of Christianity, Alexandria became the center of intense speculation about the nature of the universe, the relationship between God and man, the problem of evil and the nature of free will. It was in Alexandria that the literature of classical Greece was collected, edited, commented on and preserved for posterity. It was also in Roman Alexandria, as Marlowe calls her, that the writings, traditions and beliefs of primitive Christianity were refined and tempered into a "subtle intellectual and powerful political armory which served both to provide swords for attack and shields for defense against paganism and heresy."

In 451, following the Council of Chalcedon, outward and visible signs signaled the beginning of the end of the golden age of Alexandria. Hellenism was in retreat everywhere, not only in Alexandria, says Marlowe. Economically it had been despoiled over the centuries by the exactions of Roman tax collectors. Intellectually it had been debilitated by the sterility of a politically dominant Christianity. Externally it was threatened and finally overwhelmed by a convergence of Persians from the east, barbarians from the north and Arabs from the south.

Golden Alexandria lasted for almost a thousand years. In her heyday she had attracted and reflected the certainties of Hellenic culture and civilization; in her decline, she in turn, generated and disseminated all those qualities of obscurantism and intolerance that destroyed that civilization. Marlowe sadly says:

Nothing now remains of Ancient Alexandria above ground and in situ, except the tall column, known as Pompey's Pillar, on the site of what was once the Great Temple of Serapis. Almost everything else has disappeared, buried beneath the sea or the sand, dissolved in Nile mud, used as building material, or looted by foreign conquerors. Even the sites of the Museum [Mouseion] and Library are unknown for certain.

Marlowe continues in what sounds like a dirge, a lament. He gives us a feeling of nostalgia, of wanting to have been right there at the time when Alexandria was the lighthouse of learning, as one historian has described it. For more than a thousand years, says Marlowe, Alexandria was the most important city in the world. It was the world's greatest port and emporium of commerce.

Alexandria further declined when Cairo was made the capital city. And this is where most of the writers on Alexandria fell into the pit of accusations that Arabs ruined the city. Marlowe, for example, ends his book with the Arab conquest. Forster does the same thing, although he showers some praise on the Arabs and especially on Amr Ibn el As for his sense of humor. It is not a question of the Arabs destroying the glory of Alexandria; the Arabs were not seafarers and, in fact, they had no fleet whatever. Thus, as a capital, Alexandria would have been extremely vulnerable. So the Arabs moved their seat of government to Cairo, which could be defended by their land armies. It became a matter of replacing one capital with another.

When Mohammed Ali arrived, the value of Alexandria as a port was evident. He began a process of revival, acknowledged by all those who have written about the city. This is explained in chapter four.

Here it is useful to quote what some travelers and visitors to Alexandria have written. In his introduction to the latest edition of Forster's book, for example, Lawrence Durrell says:

The classical Alexandria is never in question save as an historical echo – how could it be? With the arrival of Amr and his Arab cavalry the famous, resplendent city nose-dived into oblivion; the sand dunes encroached and covered it. Between Amr and Napoleon stretch nearly a thousand years of silence and neglect. It had been something of an artifact, born of whim of the boy Alexander who had not stayed to see it actually built, but whose body had been brought back to be buried in the center of it, thus to become its tutelary god.

Jasper More offers further illumination in his book, *Land of Egypt*:

For a whole century, from the 1840s to the 1940s, it was the first Egyptian landfall, both for the traveler to Egypt and for the traveler to India. The curiously named 'Overland Route' came into fashion. Disembarking at Alexandria, the Indian traveler would proceed, in early days by canal, later by railway, to Cairo and would then drive a horse-drawn vehicle across the desert to Suez to take ship for Bombay. All this was made possible by the resurgence of Alexandria and indeed of Egypt by the extraordinary tyrantMehemet Ali. With the opening of the Suez Canal, Alexandria lost its monopoly. Port Said became a rival port and Indian travelers preferred to do the whole journey by sea. But it is the aeroplane that has almost wiped the city off the tourist map. Travelers to India no longer travel by sea at all and visitors to Egypt land at Cairo airport.

Sir Ronald Storrs writes in his book, *Orientations*:

Officially, as well as commercially, Alexandria was nearer to Europe than Cairo; and, remarkably for those old Islamic days, the repos hebdomadaire [weekly rest] was kept, both in the city and on the quays, not as elsewhere on Friday, but on the Christian Sunday.

He goes on to remark:

Alexandria is not an obvious city; she requires, before revealing herself, time, study and love. I liked her well, from the Sharia Sharif Pasha, which has something of the brilliant narrowness of Bond Street, to the sinister rowdiness of the Anastassi, the Gumruk Quarter and the Attarin Caracol.

There is no doubt that Alexandria today is different in many ways not only from the Alexandria of old, but even of the 1940s. It has not quite fallen from grace, but it has definitely declined. From a distance one can still see the glitter of the minarets and mosques and church steeples. The Corniche, with dozens of beaches along its length, looks attractive enough, especially in winter and autumn without the hordes of summer holidayers. But something has snapped that is not easy to put back.

A big factor in helping stabilize Alexandria's decline was the establishment of a secular university in the 1940s. Originally called Farouk University, it became the University of Alexandria after the 1952 Revolution. As it grew in size and respect, it attracted students not only from the city itself, but also from the rest of Egypt and the Middle East.

Efforts are continually being made to introduce better sewerage, to improve the city's streets, to clean its beaches, to make its facades and waterfront shine as they once did. One governor after another has tried, with some success, to revive the city, and to restore some of its old radiance. Once, the whole of the governorate – the king and all his men, including ministers and other high-ranking officials – moved to the city; then it was regarded as the summer capital of Egypt. Since the 1952 Revolution, this tradition has stopped, and the city has become simply a summer resort.

Lately, however, the national government has instructed that its official winter meetings and conferences should be convened in Alexandria. Furthermore, the city is having a revival on its cultural scene; there is a film festival in Alexandria and a book fair. Some foreign cultural centers are helping to bring back the city's old cultural vitality by organizing concerts, film shows, exhibitions and other events.

One project that is giving Alexandria a second wind is the planned rebuilding of the Alexandria Library, a reminder of the old, glorious seat of learning. With the assistance of UNESCO and the initiative of Alexandria University, the project is on its way to realization.

In October 1981, the director general of UNESCO appealed for support of the revival of the Great Library of Ancient Alexandria. It was, in fact, more than just a fund-raising appeal. It was also an historical exposition of the ancient world's greatest repository of knowledge.

After setting forth the purpose, the appeal went on to say:

The government of the Arab Republic of Egypt, in pursuance of its policy of safeguarding and protecting the country's outstanding historical heritage, and in order to contribute to the development of the Mediterranean basin as a whole, has now decided to revive the Library of Alexandria.

With those ringing words, efforts began that should result in the construction of a great library complex covering all fields of knowledge, welcoming researchers and specialists from the whole of the Mediterranean region and the world. This library should contain at least 200,000 volumes to start with, and have the space and requisite infrastructure to house 4 million, with the possibility of an extension to 8 million volumes. It will include vast reading rooms open to the general public, study rooms for researchers and accommodation facilities.

The executive board of

Following pages:
This red-granite sphinx, which takes the form of a recumbent lion with a human head, probably dates from the time of Ramses II. It is one of two such statues that seem to guard Pompey's Pillar (background), a 26.85 meter-high column of red granite erected around 292 A.D. in honor of the Emperor Diocletion. All three monuments stand amid ruins atop a hill that was once the "acropolis" of ancient Alexandria where the Serapeum and the Daughter Library are believed to have stood.

UNESCO invited its Director General to cooperate with the Egyptian Government in establishing the library. UNESCO sent several missions to Egypt in 1987 to prepare feasibility studies to be published in several languages by the University of Alexandria.

The Egyptian government has set the best possible conditions for the implementation of this project. A Higher National Council of the Library of Alexandria has been set up under the patronage of the president of the Arab Republic of Egypt, Hosni Mubarak. In addition, the Egyptian government hopes to involve the entire international community so that the project takes on a worldwide dimension. It has asked UNESCO to support its action through a universal appeal.

A call went out to governments worldwide, to public and private institutions, funding agencies and foundations, librarians and archivists and, last but not least, to the peoples of all countries to participate through contributions in cash, equipment, or services.

The Egyptian government's effort to reconstruct and equip a new Great Library of Alexandria, to reconstitute and preserve its collections and to train the requisite personnel, is an immense one.

By 1993, more than US$64 million had been raised toward the reconstruction from sources inside and outside Egypt, an impressive start, but not enough to complete the project. Nevertheless, activities surrounding the library project continued under the library's International Executive Committee chaired by Egypt's First Lady, Mrs. Susan Mubarak. Egyptian engineers and the project's Norwegian design group reconciled plan differences, and the committee is studying the plans, although funding remains a problem.

Meanwhile, restoration of rare manuscripts and editions found in the Library of Alexandria Governorate and from other organizations is underway. At the same time, the French National Library (Bibliotheque Nationale) and the General Organization of the Alexandria Library Committee are discussing other cooperative efforts. It appears that the 1990s might finally see the project, which will be called by its Latin name, *Bibliotheca Alexandrina*, take shape.

Another recent landmark added to the cultural and educational life of the country is the francophone institution, Senghor University. It is the first African university in which French is the teaching medium. The university was inaugurated in 1990 by President Mubarak, and a number of heads of governments attended the dedication ceremonies, including Presidents Mitterand of France and Senghor of Senegal.

Senghor is also a poet, an essayist and a philosopher, with many books to his name. He is the writer who propagated the "Negritude" movement, and is, at the same time, a great scholar in ancient Egyptian civilization. He is the driving force behind the establishment of this university. The choice of Alexandria as the seat of the university was not haphazard – it was made in light of the city's historical academic achievements. The Senghor University presents courses in the sciences, computers and modern technology that are badly needed in Africa.

There are many interesting, at times intriguing, stories associated with Alexandria. But perhaps the most intriguing of all is the search for the tomb of Alexander the Great. At first there were some doubts about its existence, but those doubts were exploded, and now it has been established that Alexander was indeed entombed in his namesake city.

Facing page:

Qayt Bay Fortress, built by the Sultan Ashraf Qayt Bay in 1495, faces the Mediterranean Sea and the Eastern Harbor on what was once Pharos Island. This was the site of the famous Lighthouse of Alexandria, one of the seven wonders of the ancient world, which rose nearly 400 feet above the sea. It is said that the fortress incorporates debris from the lighthouse, the remains of which were felled by an earthquake in 1100.

In his book on Alexandria, E. M. Forster discusses this issue. After giving details of Alexander's death in a foreign land, and how he was brought to Egypt, Forster writes:

But he [Alexander] was after all to return to her [Alexandria] eight years later. Having conquered Persia, he died and his body after some vicissitudes was brought to Memphis for burial.

Apparently, for some unknown reasons, the high priest refused to receive him there and ordered him to be buried in the city Alexander had built at the Pharaonic town of Rhakotis. So Alexander's body traveled on the Nile, wrapped in gold and, according to Forster and other historians, enclosed in a coffin of glass. He was buried in the center of Alexandria.

Where? That is the looming question.

Many people have tried to discover the site of the tomb, using methods that vary, as is said, from the sublime to the ridiculous. On the side of the absurd is the Greek waiter who claimed he discovered a book that contained the secret of Alexander's tomb. Nobody knows how, but the man got permission to dig in different areas of the city. He began to dig, left and right, but to no avail. Later, Dr. Gamal Mokhtar, a contributor to this volume, discovered that the man was a charlatan, that the book he had was a forgery, and the Greek waiter's digging was stopped.

The digging might have stopped, but not the search. Approaching the sublime end of the spectrum, a professor at Al-Azhar University recently theorized that Alexander's tomb lies under the floor of Nabi Daniel Mosque. Dr. Adel Abdel Azis even produced a book about the subject, and managed to get permission from the Egyptian Department of Antiquities to dig. But he was met with a tirade of opposition from academicians.

Special commissions were formed and a great deal of scientific bandying of words ensued; some academicians proposed other sites, based on historical deduction and rational logic, and as discussions continue, the problem remains unsolved.

Another interesting set of events was archaeologists' discovery of, and the subsequent efforts to salvage, French ships sunk at Abu Qir by the British Fleet. Some golden pieces and art objects were recovered and the question that arose was, "To whom do these discoveries belong – the French, since they were French ships, or to the Egyptians, since the salvage occurred in Egyptian waters?" The issue has not yet been resolved, and both sides are sticking to their claims.

This book is an effort to present Alexandria to the world at a time when she is elbowing her way, as it were, back to her former prominence. In it, our contributors have tried to pen a portrait of a living, throbbing city over the millennia. With the help of wonderful photographs by Araldo DeLuca, the story comes to life.

Alexandria is a city that lends itself to photographs. Its hues are beautifully summed up by Alexandre Dumas, the famous French writer, "It takes an artist to appreciate Alexandria's innumerable variety of colors."

Or, as the Italian poet Giuseppe Ungaretti expressed it:

And our drowsy Alexandria
in a flash,
started to glitter all along
its millennias, as I
had never seen anything glitter
before.

Facing page:
A carved bas-relief represents Arab-Andalusian art as seen on an exterior section of El-Morsi Abul Abbas Mosque. An earlier mosque of the same name also stood on this site. This building was completed in 1944.

Pre-Alexandria:
Keys to the Rise of an Immortal City

by Dr. Gamal Mokhtar

The civilizations of Pharaonic Egypt and of Greece blended for three centuries, starting from the time Alexander the Great conquered Egypt in 332 B.C. The Ptolemies, who ruled Egypt following the death of Alexander, followed policies that helped even closer relations develop between the Egyptians and the Greeks, mixing their civilizations in one melting pot.

Numerous scholars have felt compelled to trace the origin of relations between Egypt and Greece to their earliest stages up through the time that the city of Alexandria was built. Many scholars believe studying that era is significant to the development of civilization in general.

In fact, these early relationships provide the historical context for the rise of Alexandria, and are key to grasping the cultural, historical, political and economic circumstances from which this immortal city evolved.

Greek writers and historians wrote about the relationship between Egypt and Greece from their earliest recorded days until the rise of classical Greece in the 5th century B.C. They wove legends about Egypt, its people and cities, recognized the contribution Egyptians made to their civilization, and told about the fountains of thought that the pioneers of Greek philosophy drew on.

In the *Iliad* and *Odyssey*, Homer – more than 3,000 years ago – made passing references to Egypt that indicated his high esteem. In the *Odyssey*, for example, a passage refers to the abundance in Egypt of medical herbs widely used for their healing properties, and to the good reputation Egypt enjoyed in the ancient world of Asia, Africa and Europe. In other passages Homer relates the journey the Greek King Manelaus made to Egypt, his arrival at Pharos Island off the Mediterranean coast at the point where one of the branches of the Nile flows into the sea and about his 20-day sojourn in the country.

Another passage in the *Odyssey* tells of King Odysseus' journey to Egypt from Crete. He tells how the northerly wind helped his nine boats sail easily for five days until they reached the Nile. According to Homer, the Egyptians were extremely hospitable to the king and his entourage, and he greatly enjoyed his seven-year sojourn there.

The *Iliad* likewise alludes to Egypt. Homer recounts that Agamemnon infuriated Achilles by taking for himself the captive Lady Briseis. Achilles' withdrawal from the battlefield in anger resulted in many Greek losses, and Agamemnon tried to make amends and woo him back with offers of wealth. But Achilles rejected Agamemnon's offers, even if they included "all the riches of the Egyptian city of Thebes, a city whose treasuries overflowed with wealth, a city of a hundred gates with 200 warriors

Facing page:

Part of a statue of Ramses II in red granite. On the left and right shoulders are engraved the standard cartouches that contain the title and names of the king in hieroglyphs. It was found at Abu Qir (ancient Canopus), now part of the city. Graeco-Roman Museum, Alexandria.

on chariots proceeding from each."

Herodotus, the father of history, visited Egypt around 450 B.C. He devoted the second volume of his history to accounts about Egypt. Herodotus spoke highly about the country, and stressed Greece's indebtedness to it, so much so that some modern historians accuse him of partiality to Egypt at Greece's expense.

He says Egyptians were the first to hold public festivals and great processions, such as the Feast of Amon at Thebes and the Feast of the Nile Flood. Later Greek celebrations can be traced to festivals like these. He also mentions that Amasis, the fifth king of the 26th Pharaonic dynasty, mandated that Egyptians register their livelihoods with the ruler of their province. Whoever failed to do so, or could not prove that he earned his living honestly, was condemned to death. Herodotus says that Solon, the Athenian legislator, later laid out the same legal requirement for Athenian citizens. Herodotus even went so far as to say that the Egyptians culturally and scientifically surpassed all other societies of which he knew. Diodorus of Sicily, who visited Egypt around 59 B.C., subscribed to all of Herodotus' high opinions regarding Egyptian civilization.

The good relations that existed between the two civilizations were a main factor that facilitated Alexander the Great's conquest of Egypt. In previous eras the Egyptians thought of Greeks as friends and allies who often helped them regain their freedom following a defeat. This is why they saw in Alexander a savior from the much despised Persian imperialism.

Egypt's Contacts with the Ancient Greek World

The relationship between Egypt and Greece – besides that with nearby islands of which Crete is the most important – falls easily into three stages: The first comprises the period from the earliest days – including prehistoric times – until the beginning of the New Kingdom, about 1575 B.C.; the second stage comprises the New Kingdom and the Pharaonic Third Intermediate Period, to the beginning of the Saite era (the 26th Pharaonic dynasty) about 665 B.C.; the third stage starts with the Saite era and ends with Alexander the Great's conquest of Egypt in 332 B.C.

From its earliest days Egypt had, by virtue of its location, diverse communications with the eastern Mediterranean basin and southeastern Europe. During this first stage, the Minoan civilization rose in Crete, named after Minos, the legendary king. This was the region's oldest civilization, which eventually embraced Rhodes, the Aegean Sea islands and a large part of Asia Minor, until it included Greece itself. Remains of this civilization cover some 2,000 years and reach back as far as 3,000 years before Christ.

Trade and other cultural developments linked the Cretans with Egypt, and they adopted many aspects of Egyptian civilization. Many Egyptian-made relics have been uncovered in Crete, while, on the other hand, Cretan artifacts have been unearthed in some Egyptian archaeological sites.

In time, the Greeks spread into the Balkan peninsula and adopted many aspects of Cretan civilization that were influenced by Egypt. And the Phoenicians also carried to the lands they traded with, including Greece, facets of Egyptian civilization. Thus the Greeks were indirectly influenced by Egypt before they even came in direct contact with Egyptian civilization.

The second stage was the era of the New Kingdom, and it lasted more than a thousand years — from about 1500 to 500 B.C. It includes the last stages of Minoan civilization and the emergence of Hellenic civilization in Greece. The best source of information about this era is probably inscribed on the walls of the New Kingdom's tombs in the Necropolis of Thebes, now called Luxor. Other indications found in both Crete and Greece affirm that Egypt's contribution to these lands far exceeded their cultural influence on Egypt. All archaeological evidence indicates that the growth of peaceful relations between Egypt and Greece coincided with the decline of the Minoan state and the end of its trading activities.

Lack of archaeological evidence indicates that these strong Graeco-Egyptian relations were interrupted during the Third Intermediate Period, which began about 1085 B.C. and coincided with dwindling Greek trading. This is attributed on one hand to the disorderly state of Egypt's domestic and foreign affairs then. On the other hand, the political climate in the region discouraged trading as the Mediterranean peoples undertook great marine and military activities. Egypt remained isolated from the Greek world until the beginning of the 26th dynasty, when stronger and more direct relations than ever before were resumed.

The third stage spans the Saite era (named after Sais, the Greek name for Egypt's capital at the time). Beginning in 665 B.C. and ending in 525 B.C., it roughly corresponded with the Greek Archaic Period (750-500 B.C.). During this stage, Graeco-Egyptian relations reached their apex and assumed even more diverse aspects and directions.

The pharaohs, for example, hired great numbers of Greek mercenaries to serve in the Egyptian army and they played an important role. They helped Psammetichus I expel the Assyrians and establish the 26th dynasty, for instance, and helped him unify the country and subjugate the rulers of the provinces as well.

In the same period, Greek merchants flowed into Egypt in great numbers, trading Greek goods — mainly wines, oils and some other manufactured goods — for Egyptian commodities — such as wheat, flax and papyrus — which they exported.

Immense concessions were also granted to the Greek community in Egypt. Whole quarters were exclusively allotted to them in some Egyptian cities. The Greek city of Naukratis, which rose in the northeastern Delta, became the nucleus of the Greek trading community.

At that time, many Greek writers, scientists, scholars and other knowledge-seekers came to Egypt to absorb Egyptian culture. They benefited from and transferred to their country learning in science, astronomy, chemistry, mathematics, architecture, the arts, and all other areas that had been progressed in ancient Egypt.

Political relations in their modern sense started effectively and regularly only in the 6th century B.C., when Persia threatened both Egypt and Greece. King Psammetichus I, founder of the 26th dynasty, and after him King Amasis, concluded treaties of alliance with Greek city-states. The earlier absence of political relations might be because the Greek city-states were still in their formative years, and unable to set up binding political ties. Furthermore, the Greeks had not yet adopted their later settlement and colonization movement.

This state of affairs continued throughout the reign of Psammetichus I. Then, after the reign of King Amasis, the Persians occupied Egypt during the 27th dynasty. From the 28th dynasty through the 30th, the Greek presence gradually diminished. Then, when Alexander the Great conquered Egypt in 332 B.C., Graeco-Egyptian relations assumed totally new dimensions – Egypt became truly Hellenized.

Psammetichus I Intensifies Greek Presence in Egypt

Psammetichus I was the first Egyptian ruler to encourage the large-scale employment of Greek mercenaries in the Egyptian army. He was also the first to initiate Greek trading settlements in Egyptian cities and to set up a quarter for Greek mercenaries and another for their counterparts from the Greek state of Caria (now Turkey) in Asia Minor.

In his volume on Egypt, Herodotus makes no mention of the existence of Graeco-Egyptian relations before the 26th dynasty. But he speaks in detail about direct relations between the two countries during the reign of Psammetichus I. By all accounts, his rule was still alive in the minds of Egyptian people and priests 200 years later in Herodotus' time. And there is also no doubt that many of the people with whom the historian communicated were Greek residents.

The Greeks who flowed into Egypt during the Saite era formed part of the emigration movement that swept across Greece at that time. This influx took place when Egypt was wide open to Greeks, be they mercenaries, traders or knowledge-seekers. The pharaohs then felt a need for new blood, particularly in the army, and for a new policy based on contemporary realities. Modern archaeological studies confirm a good deal of Herodotus' writings about the Saite era in particular.

Herodotus gives us an account of how Psammetichus I ascended the throne, in which reality seemingly blends with mythology and the rich imagination of Greeks. He recounts that rulers of the *nomes* (Egyptian provinces), afraid that one of their own might attempt to seize the throne and claim sovereignty, together vowed not to undermine one another.

Herodotus then relates a long, almost mythological tale that lends credibility to the theory that Psammetichus I used priestly oracles to gain complete control of the country and ensure the princes' allegiance to him. He also enlisted experienced and well-equipped Greek mercenaries, and it was these soldiers who helped Psammetichus I expel the Assyrians, subjugate rulers of the provinces, and become the undisputed sovereign of all Egypt.

Psammetichus I gave these Greek soldiers the right to reside in three Egyptian cities: Elephantine in the south, Daphnae in the eastern Delta, and Mariya in the western Delta.

Elephantine:

Archaeological evidence points to the presence at that time of a Greek outpost on the island of Elephantine opposite the city of Aswan. On a statue of the ruler of Elephantine, for example, is inscribed an account of revolution by Greek and other mercenaries against Apries, the fourth king of the Saite era. On the other hand, there is no mention of the presence of Greek soldiers in Elephantine during the 5th century B.C. in the Aramaic papyrus rolls kept by Jewish dwellers of that city at that time. This implies that these soldiers, assuming they really existed, must have been transferred at some unknown time before or during the Persian invasion of Egypt.

Daphnae:

The city of Daphnae lay on the

eastern bank of the Nile's Pelusian branch (the easternmost and last-surviving of the Delta's ancient branches). Herodotus says that Psammetichus I granted the Greek and Carian soldiers who helped him the right to dwell in the Pelusian city of Daphnae to protect the country from dangers from the east. Archaeological research confirms the city's military nature. One ruined building, for example – most likely a stronghold – held spears, swords, shields and other military equipment. Other finds include a small silver box containing a statuette of Ra, ancient Egypt's sun god, and Greek pottery dating from the Saite era. This confirms that Greeks once lived side by side with Egyptians there. Daphnae's importance declined when Greeks were officially granted the city of Naukratis by Amasis.

Mariya:

The city of Mariya lies on the southern shore of Lake Mareotis, about 20 miles south of Alexandria. The village of Hawara in the Ameriya district now occupies the site. The name most probably comes from the ancient Egyptian word "Mereet," which means "port." The name of Lake Mareotis also probably dates to ancient Egypt. Psammetichus I chose this city to settle the Greek garrison entrusted with defense of the western Delta. The city prospered, particularly during the 27th dynasty.

When the mercenaries residing in Egypt returned to their native countries across the Mediterranean, they told exotic stories about Egypt's opulence, religious beliefs, language, arts and industries. Psammetichus I's fame thus spread throughout Greece – so much so, that the nephew of King Periandre of Corinth was named after him.

The successors of Psammetichus I apparently also used their friendship with Greek mercenaries to keep the Persians in check. According to Herodotus, Necho, the second pharaoh of the Saite era, brought in experienced sailors from the Greek Islands. He also used, in line with his military interests, three-tiered paddling ships known to Greeks as *triremes*. His fleet rivaled that of the seagoing Phoenicians.

Psammetichus II, third of the Saite era pharaohs, sent a military expedition of Greek soldiers to Nubia. There, they inscribed their names beside the graffiti of other mercenaries on the Ramses II colossus that stands in the pylon in front of the Great Temple of Abu Simbel.

Herodotus mentions that Apries, the fourth of the Saite era pharaohs, had a bodyguard comprised of Greeks and Carians, and that he was invited to conduct the Olympic games tournament in Greece. Apries also used the fleet created by Amasis to invade Phoenicia.

Amasis' Role in the Greek Presence in Egypt

Herodotus says that Amasis was nicknamed "he who loves Greeks." In fact, he donated many gifts to Greek cities and temples. He also contributed to the re-erection of the Temple of Delphi that had been destroyed. Moreover, he married a Greek woman named Ladika from Cyrenica, then a Greek province. However, Amasis' greatest service to the Greeks might well be his granting them a city on Egyptian soil – Naukratis – to call their own.

The city lay on the western bank of the Canopic branch of the Nile, the westernmost of the Nile's ancient branches. It was 50 kilometers from where the city of Alexandria would rise and just 17 kilometers from Sa El Hagar, Egypt's capital during the Saite era. Modern villages, like Kom

Gaef and Nokrashi, now stand on its site. Evidence exists that the city's south side had been inhabited earlier, during the days of Psammetichus I, by Greeks living side by side with the Egyptians. Later, as Greeks streamed in, the city's north side became likewise populated.

No Greek account about Naukratis can surpass the information given by Herodotus. He says that Amasis expressed his love and respect for the Greeks by donating Naukratis to Greeks immigrating to Egypt. To those coming for temporary residence and sightseeing, he granted parcels of land on which to erect temples and sanctuaries for their deities.

Herodotus also mentions that Egypt tried to monopolize trade with Greece through the city of Naukratis – it was the only Egyptian outlet for trade. If a ship arrived through any of the Nile's other mouths it was required to go back and return through the Canopic mouth. Herodotus also refers to the appointment of Greek consuls, counterparts of today's trade attaches and advisors, to oversee and protect Greek trade in Naukratis.

Herodotus' accounts of the city lead us to understand that the city was a Greek one that served as a trade center for commerce between Egypt and Greece, the eastern Mediterranean islands and Asia Minor. Consequently the city grew immensely in wealth, particularly in the days of Amasis.

Naukratis adopted the city-state system, and its inhabitants were totally free to hold their own religious beliefs, follow their own customs and traditions, and elect their local leaders. However, it should be noted that, despite its status, the city remained totally subject to the pharaoh's rule.

The city was famed for its belles, and a woman named Rodis was regarded as one of the most beautiful of all at the time. Cleomenes, the merchant who helped Alexander the Great establish Alexandria, also was a native of the city. Wealthy Greeks seeking entertainment also flocked there.

In the 6th century B.C., Naukratis attracted many Greek poets, artists and philosophers. Among those who visited the city were Solon, the famed Greek lawmaker; Thales, the philosopher; and Rhoikos, the architect believed to have designed the temple of the goddess Herapsamos.

This indicates that the Greeks commingled with the Egyptians, and that they grew acquainted with a civilization that they both appreciated and emulated. Naukratis can therefore be said to have served as a prelude to Alexandria economically, and socially.

However, when the last of the kings of the Saite era, Psammetichus III, was defeated by the Persians in 525 B.C., Egypt came under intransigent Persian rule. Naukratis lost many of the privileges granted it by the pharaohs, and the good fortune it had enjoyed dwindled as trade slumped. Conditions deteriorated even more sharply with the rise of Alexandria. By the 10th century A.D. the city virtually no longer existed, and on its site some insignificant villages grew over the centuries.

During the Saite era, Greeks were not uncommon outside the cities and quarters allotted to them either. Greek earthenware pots and other relics used exclusively by Greeks have been found at many archaeological sites that date from the Saite or earlier periods. These include Salhagar, Athrib (the present city of Banha), Tell Basta (the present city of Zakazik), Marsa Matrouh, Edfu, and Kom Frain, near Naukratis. Such large-scale distribution

indicates that Greeks freely moved and settled everywhere in Egypt, particularly during the reign of Amasis.

Ancient Egyptian Settlements within the Zone of Ptolemaic Alexandria (Rhakotis and Pharos)

Alexander the Great chose the site of his namesake city while on his way from Memphis to the oasis of Siwa to consult the oracle of Amun. He admired a village called Rhakotis that lay between the Mediterranean in the north and Lake Mareotis in the south and was near the Canopic branch of the Nile. The village was naturally protected from waves because it lay in front of Pharos Island, which was less than a mile away. No doubt its strategic location and its ability to serve both foreign and domestic trade encouraged Alexander to establish his new city in this remarkable spot.

Unfortunately, no monuments or texts have been found to help us outline the history of Pharaonic Rhakotis. Thus there are varying views. Some believe that, at that time, it was a major bastion in the northwest corner of the Nile Delta to repel invasions by Libyans and others coming from the west. These experts substantiate their assertion by the presence of statues of Ramses II and his successor kings of the New Kingdom and the Third Intermediate Period in scattered areas around Alexandria. This leads to the belief that Rhakotis flourished in the second half of the New Kingdom as an advanced military post in defense of the western Delta.

However, others believe that Rhakotis was an important city in the Pharaonic 30th dynasty and was not just a modest village. They cite as evidence the intention to bury King Nectanebo II, the last king of the 30th dynasty, in the royal necropolis there.

However, he fled from Egypt after the second Persian invasion, which occurred during his reign, and the sarcophagus prepared for him was not used. Interestingly, Alexander the Great was later buried near Rhakotis after Alexandria was built, but the exact site has never been proven.

According to Strabo, the Greek geographer, the pharaohs had a garrison in Rhakotis to stop the infiltration of foreign traders trying to bring in goods illegally through routes other than Naukratis. Shepherds in the area helped the garrison repel the intruders. Strabo believes that particular attention was paid to Rhakotis for economic rather than military reasons. According to Greek sources there were 16 villages in the area. Rhakotis was the most important and was the administrative center of them all. Twelve canals are said to have passed through the villages, but eventually all but two were filled in with mud. The main streets of Alexandria were built over these former canals. Rhakotis became part of Ptolemaic Alexandria. The present quarters of Mina el Bassal, Kom el-Shugafa and Kermous are built on its ruins.

The small, rocky island of Pharos, less than a mile long, is famous because of its mention in Homer's *Iliad*, and the renowned Lighthouse of Alexandria, one of the seven wonders of the ancient world, that was built on it later. In 1915, underwater excavations adjacent to Pharos Island revealed the remains of huge quays, a breakwater and a harbor extending from the north to the west of the island, where the Anfoushi and Ras el Tin quarters lie today. The stones used in the harbor were huge, weighing up to six tons, and are similar to the stones from the local Mex and Dekheila quarries on the other side of the the old harbor. The huge size of the quay indicates the

magnitude of maritime trade from Pharos Island. However, all the port facilities were later inundated when the land on which Alexandria was built at that time gradually sank below sea level.

Experts hold different views on the history of the submerged maritime installations. Some historians believe they belong to the reign of Ramses II, while others believe they are part of Crete's expansion after it managed to occupy part of the Egyptian coast. They also believe that Pharaonic Egypt did not object to the establishment of this big foreign port on a deserted island. However, yet another group believes that the Phoenicians, with their long naval experience, had a role in the construction itself. Perhaps underwater archaeological surveys will lead to useful information about this island's early history.

The Town of Canopus

Before Alexandria was established, the place now occupied by the Abu Qir suburb (which got its name in the Christian era from Saint Abe Cur) was originally a small town in the Greek age known as Canopus. It overlooked the Canopic branch of the Nile and took its name from it.

According to Greek mythology the city was named after a Greek navigator accompanying Manelaus, Agamemnon's younger son, on his return from the Trojan War. The story goes that his ship was wrecked in the place now occupied by Abu Qir. He and his men sought refuge in this place, but the navigator – Canopus – died after being bitten by a poisonous snake. He was buried in a great ceremony in the same place where the town was established.

Others hold the more plausible opinion that the town was named after Canup, an ancient deity represented as a pot whose cover is made in the shape of a man's head. This deity was one of the representations of Osiris, and two beautiful statues of it are now shown at the Graeco-Roman Museum in Alexandria. The same deity is also drawn on some pots on which the name Canup is inscribed.

The town was of particular importance before the advent of Alexander the Great since it lay beside the Nile's Canopic branch, the only one that foreign ships were allowed to sail through to Naukratis. The town thus could control trading activity along the entire branch.

Many Greek travelers referred to the Canopic branch as the most important of the Delta's ancient seven branches. It was the one Herodotus sailed through on his visit to Egypt. Ptolemy [the geographer] called it "the great river," to distinguish it from the Nile's other branches.

Relics from Pharaonic times have been unearthed in Canopus. These include a sphinx believed to belong to the epoch of Amenemhat IV, and statues of Ramses II from the 13th century B.C. They are on view at Alexandria's Graeco-Roman Museum.

It should be noted, however, that this was by no means a major town. During the Pharaonic days no town close to the sea had particular importance. Canopus became significant only when Alexandria was built nearby. From that time, its fortunes rose and fell with the vicissitudes of the new city.

The Shift from Memphis to Alexandria

Throughout the Pharaonic epoch the city of Memphis retained its paramount importance. It was the first capital of united Egypt and the oldest royal city. It was also the holy city of Ptah, the deity believed to be the creator of all life. Throughout the ages the city retained its administrative, strategic and military importance. Greeks hungry for knowledge also went to Memphis. And it was the Greeks who called the whole region "Egypt" after "Agyptos," one of the old names for Memphis. The capture of Memphis was always the target of Egypt's invaders during its late Pharaonic periods, including the Nubians, the Assyrians, the Persians and the Macedonians.

Although administrative rule from the time of Ptolemy I shifted to Alexandria, Memphis remained the country's second capital. There the Ptolemaic king was crowned king of Egypt, and Alexander the Great's body was brought from Babylon to be buried there before it was later permanently entombed in Alexandria.

Memphis and Alexandria stood for vastly different things to Egyptians. Memphis symbolized the hope that someday the king of Egypt would again take up residence and administer the country from there. On the other hand, Alexandria stood for foreign rule by the Ptolemies, who replaced the town's original Egyptian name of Rhakotis (Ra Kadit) with that of Alexander the Macedonian.

Memphis was strongly associated with Egyptian nationalistic feelings, and a religiously tinged folk literature that smacked of national aspirations originated there. One such tale is called "the potter's prophecy." It tells about a potter who once prophesied to King Amenhotep of the 18th Pharaonic dynasty that a time would come when the people of Egypt would suffer difficult rule by foreigners. However, an Egyptian from Ihnasia El Medineh (a city that the Greeks named Heracleopolis Magna) would rise against the foreigners, rid the country of their presence and make Memphis its capital.

The demotic history document is another example. This was passed down in demotic – the popular version of hieroglyphics – as well as in a Greek translation. It is attributed by its author to the days of King Takhos, the second in line of the 30th dynasty (4th century B.C.). It prophesied that the Persians and the Greeks would occupy the country, and that an Egyptian would then emerge to successfully shake off the foreign yoke. Both stories eventually came true, of course.

The old relationships between the Egyptians and Greeks encouraged Alexander the Great to establish a Greek city in Egypt, near the sites of Rhakotis and Pharos, and the understanding between the two peoples that began many hundreds of years earlier surely helped to develop Alexandria.

At the same time, the Egyptians kept Memphis as their spiritual capital, and the Ptolemies accepted this status. Thus it is understandable that Alexandria remained the capital of Egypt for nearly a millennium.

Following page:

A red-granite head of Alexander the Great. The choice of stone and style suggest that this is the work of an Egyptian sculptor. Inlaid eyes are typical, and on the head are traces of the uraeus, or sacred asp, symbol of Egyptian divinity and protection. Ptolemaic Period. Graeco-Roman Museum, Alexandria.

Alexandria: Thousand-Year Capital of Egypt

by Dr. Mostafa El-Abbadi

The Egypt of the pharaohs had one traditional capital – the city of Memphis, not far from the site of present-day Cairo on the west bank of the Nile. At times, for political or religious reasons, the royal residence of the pharaoh moved south to Thebes (Luxor), as it did during the New Kingdom, or north to Sais, in the middle of the Delta, as it did during the 26th dynasty. From the beginning of the 1st dynasty about 3100 B.C., Memphis continued to be the official administrative capital.

Thus, soon after Alexander's conquest in 332 B.C., it must have come as a surprise to the Egyptians to find their capital moved to the new city of Alexandria by the sea in the far north of the country. The decision had far-reaching consequences, not only for the history of Egypt during the millennium that followed, but even for the character of the country today.

How did Alexander and his Greek companions arrive at their historic decision? As with everything connected with Alexander, fact and fiction are often closely interwoven. According to one tradition, for example, when Alexander visited the shrine of Ammon, god of creation, in Siwa, he recalled that his mother, Olympias, had told him that he was the son of Ammon. He prayed to the god,

saying, "Father, if my mother spoke the truth in calling me your son, give me an oracle." In a dream, the god embraced his mother, and Alexander demanded to receive a further oracle from the god as to where he should found a city bearing his name. And he saw in his sleep the god who said to him: "King, to you I speak. Behold the god of the ram's horns.... Build an illustrious city above the island of Proteus (Pharos)."

According to another tradition, Alexander followed the guidance of Homer, who also appeared to him in a dream and recited the famous lines from the *Odyssey* where Menelaus takes refuge on the island of Pharos. In response, Plutarch recounts:

Alexander immediately left his bed and went to Pharos, which at that time was an island lying a little above the Canopic mouth of the Nile.... He no sooner cast his eyes upon the mouth of the place than he perceived the advantages of the site. It was a tongue of land, not unlike an isthmus, whose breadth was proportionable to its length. On one side it had a great lake and on the other the sea, which there formed a capacious harbor. This led him to declare [that] 'Homer, among his admirable qualifications, was also an excellent architect,' and he ordered a city to be planned, suitable to the ground and its appendant conveniences.

These two legends are not without significance. One was obviously addressed to the Egyptians and the other to the Greeks. Alexander was anxious to win Egyptian goodwill, and when he first entered Memphis, he went directly to the temple of the god Ptah and had himself crowned pharaoh in true Egyptian tradition as son of the god Ammon. And again, when he founded his new city, he declared that the choice of the site fulfilled the will of Ammon. But when he addressed the Greeks, he emphasized his association with the great bard of Greek heroic tradition.

Military genius and brilliant politician though he was, Alexander was no sailor. Choosing a site was no simple matter; it required a thorough knowledge of Egypt's seacoast, which he did not possess. So Alexander sought the advice of Greek experts familiar with navigating across the Mediterranean to Egypt, as well as with sailing and trading. He is said to have consulted a group of experts and architects in choosing the site for a new harbor in Egypt. Among his consultants were Cleomenes of Naukratis, Deinokratis of Rhodes, Krateros of Olynthos and Hero of Libya. Cleomenes was a citizen and well-known merchant of Naukratis, the Greek colony on the Canopic branch of the Nile, and he had firsthand knowledge of sailing and trading conditions in Egypt prior to the arrival of Alexander.

Contemporary and subsequent writers provide us with the lines of thought at these meetings. Hecataeus of Abdera – companion of Alexander in part of the campaign, and close associate of Ptolemy I in Egypt – describes the northern coast of Egypt as "practically harborless." Eratosthenes, the great geographer, makes the same remark and adds that even the harbor that Egypt did have, "the one at Pharos, gave no access." The harbor on the island of Pharos was mentioned in the *Odyssey* and was presumably well-known to the Greeks since the 8th century B.C., if not earlier. It served as their last port of call before entering Egypt through the Canopic mouth of the Nile about 30 kilometers from Pharos. According to Herodotus, who wrote a century earlier, all Greek vessels, at least since the 6th century B.C., had to enter Egypt through the Canopic branch, where customs dues were collected.

Thus Greek sailors and merchants were familiar with the whole coastal region around the island of Pharos and the village of Rhakotis on the mainland and were aware of its potential. They also knew that the anchorages at Canopus and Pelusium, at the mouths of the Nile's two branches to the extreme west and east of the Delta, were deficient as harbors by Greek standards. They were shallow, and every few years became unusable due to silting from the annual Nile flood. In addition, like the whole northern coast of Egypt, they were exposed to the north wind's blasts during winter, as well as to continuous west-to-east sea currents.

It was obvious that a site that avoided these disadvantages would have to be sought west of the Delta. And the suggestion to build a causeway connecting the island of Pharos with the coast near Rhakotis seemed to be the ideal solution. In this way, the new (eastern) harbor, or the "Great Harbor," as it was called, would be protected from the sea current, while the mass of the island would serve as a natural bulwark against the north wind. Construction of the causeway created a second harbor to the west called *Eunostus Haven* (Port of Happy Return), but this was used less in antiquity.

Facing page:

A colossal head in grey granite of Ptolemy VI Philometor (181-145 B.C.). On the forehead can be seen the diadem and the uraeus. It is a fine specimen of Graeco-Egyptian sculpture despite the missing nose. From Abu Qir (ancient Canopus). Graeco-Roman Museum, Alexandria.

Facing and following pages:
A black-granite sculpture of Apis the Bull is a virile and dignified representation of its incarnation as Serapis. The solar disk and uraeus between his horns are symbols of divinity and protection. It was dedicated by the Emperor Hadrian (117-138 A.D.) and discovered in 1895 at the entrance to the underground galleries beneath the area where the Serapeum stood in Alexandria.
Graeco-Roman Museum, Alexandria.

Other advantages were self-evident: Lake Mareotis, in the south, would provide direct access to the Nile, whereas a short canal from the Canopic branch would provide a permanent freshwater supply. Undoubtedly, this was the best place to establish a first-rate harbor on Egypt's Mediterranean coast.

Accordingly the architect Deinokratis of Rhodes was instructed to lay out plans for the new city. Alexander, meanwhile, continued his arduous trek westward on his pilgrimage to the Temple of Ammon in the Siwa Oasis. On his return journey that winter of 332-331 B.C., he stopped at the site of Alexandria to inspect and approve Deinokratis' plan. The architect had laid out the new city in an east-to-west oblong, with a great thoroughfare, 33 meters wide, running its length. It was intersected near its center by another major street running north to south, and the other streets ran parallel to these two arteries to form a grid pattern. At either end of the main avenue were two principal gates. The easternmost was later called the Gate of the Sun, and the westernmost, the Gate of the Moon. Colonnades ran the whole length of the street and offered protection from the sun. Alexander was pleased and authorized work on the site to begin. He commissioned his finance minister for Egypt, Cleomenes of Naukratis, to supervise and provide the necessary funds for the construction work. The foundation day is believed to have been April 7, 331 B.C. To this day, Alexandria remains the best harbor Egypt has ever had.

The City and its People
From its beginning, Alexandria developed rapidly into one of the world's greatest and most influential cities and remained so for a thousand years during three successive periods of history: Ptolemaic, Roman and Byzantine. In order to understand its dazzling career, it is necessary to know the city's intended functions, because these were the bases that influenced her general character and vitalized her historic role as world emporium and world cultural center.

It was clear from the site and from the causeway connecting Pharos with the mainland – known as the Heptastadium – that the architect was designing a first-class port. This aspect of the city was the earliest developed while Alexander was still alive. When Alexander died in 323 B.C., his successor in Egypt, Ptolemy I, embarked on the construction of the famous lighthouse at the entrance of the Great Harbor, on the eastern end of Pharos. It was considered one of the seven wonders of the ancient world and survived to the 13th century when it was destroyed by an earthquake. It was designed by Sostratus of Cnidus and was inaugurated early in the reign of Ptolemy II, Philadelphus, who dedicated it to Ptolemy I and his wife under the title "the Savior Gods." It rose to a height of some 120 meters – nearly 400 feet – in three setbacks. It had elevators in addition to a staircase, and its powerful light was visible some 55 kilometers at sea. Many historians believe it also had some kind of telescope, perhaps worked by refracting mirrors.

Another strong influence on Alexandria's development was the fact that it became Egypt's new capital. It is disputed, however, whether this was Alexander's original intention or a later decision made by Ptolemy I. But at least one ancient author, Justin, assumes that "on his return from Siwa, Alexander founded Alexandria, ordered it to be a

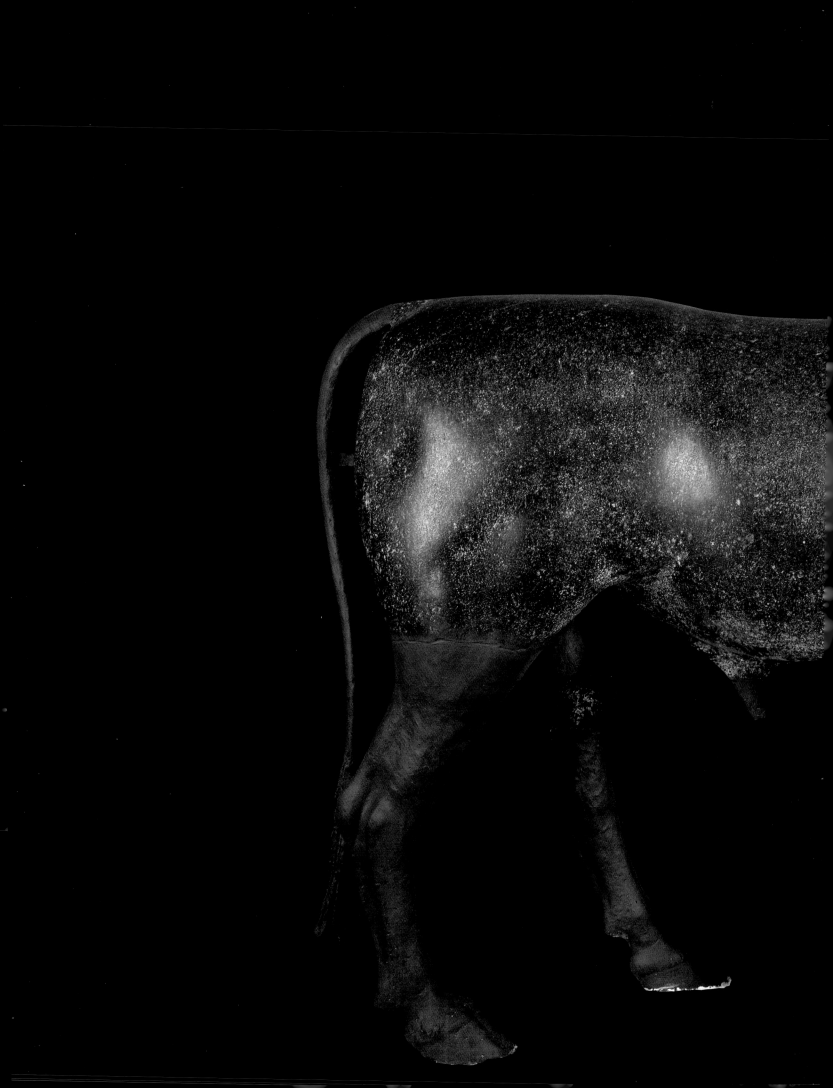

Alexandria: Capital of Egypt

A headless statue of a young woman. Her tunic of fine, almost transparent linen gracefully accentuates the lines of her body. The artist followed the canons of Egyptian art, positioning the arms downward and the left leg forward. Limestone.
Graeco-Roman Museum, Alexandria.

Macedonian colony and the capital of Egypt." The final steps of the transfer of the seat of government with its entire apparatus of administration was accomplished by Ptolemy I in 320 B.C., only three years after Alexander's death.

The third important characteristic of Alexandria was that it was a *polis*, the Greek word for a city-state. In fact, in Egypt it was considered the *polis* par excellence. Because the notion of self-government is fundamental to the concept of the *polis*, Alexandria had to have its own citizenship and constitution. On the other hand, the Ptolemies, who wielded an absolute monarchy, would not tolerate a fully autonomous constitution. Thus, when Alexandria became the official royal residence and seat of central government, it was permitted – in practical terms – only a restricted degree of autonomy, similar to that of a municipality.

Cosmopolitan Population

From the beginning, Alexandria was destined to grow into a cosmopolitan city. It was composed essentially of a Macedonian colony drawn from Alexander's forces, a Greek community from the older settlements of Naukratis and Memphis, and an Egyptian population from Rhakotis, Canopus and other neighboring villages. After Alexander's death in 323 B.C., the city's makeup grew more and more complex. The actual adoption of Alexandria as Egypt's capital city coincided with an ambitious plan of construction started by Ptolemy I and pursued by his successors throughout the 3rd century B.C.

Ptolemy I, with the fabulous wealth of ancient Egypt in his hands, constructed a series of important monuments. One was the previously mentioned wonder of the ancient world, the Lighthouse of Pharos. He also built fortification walls around the city and erected new temples for the two recently adopted cults – of Serapis as tutelary god of the dynasty, and of Alexander as guardian genius of the city. The latter cult was connected with the construction of Alexander's magnificent mausoleum, commonly called by the Greek term *Soma*. Ptolemy I also took the initial steps to establish Alexandria's Great Library with its renowned research center, known as the Mouseion. The *Soma*, the library and the Mouseion were in the area of the royal palaces, or *basileia*, that constituted one quarter or perhaps even one third of the city. Many of the undertakings of Ptolemy I were not completed during his life. They were finished by his son Philadelphus (285-246 B.C.), who was also a great builder and a lover of luxury and festivities. Numerous theaters, a zoological garden and, most beautiful of all, the gymnasium – which had porticos more than a stadium long, or about 200 yards – were largely the work of Philadelphus. Tradition, therefore, often accredits the embellishment of Alexandria to the son and gives less credit to the father.

Euergetes, the third Ptolemy (246-221 B.C.), also made an important addition to the monuments of Alexandria. He rebuilt the Serapeum in the Egyptian quarter (on the site of Rhakotis), and in it – in accordance with Egyptian tradition – he incorporated a branch of the Great Library. The new Serapeum and its so-called Daughter Library became an outstanding landmark of the city.

Thus, opportunities for work, wealth and fame attracted Egyptians and outsiders alike to immigrate. The Egyptian inhabitants more than doubled, and streams of Greeks and Hellenized people flowed into the city, where they were in great demand as mercenaries in the Ptolemaic army and as functionaries in the central administration. It was easy for young men from the Aegean, seeking employment and good pay, to enlist in the Ptolemaic army. The great poet Theocritus, when still at Cos in the Aegean and seeking the patronage of the "best paymaster a freeman could have, King Ptolemy" (Philadelphus), laughs at himself and jokes that if his poems do not meet with royal favor, he could always "clasp the warrior's cloak about him and legs astride to abide the onset of the hardy foeman, off to Egypt." Sure enough, Philadelphus granted him patronage as a poet and not as a mercenary. Once in Alexandria, Theocritus observed the numerous Greek dialects the immigrants spoke. He recorded this in the first poem he wrote in the city, commemorating the Festival of Adonis.

The persistent use of mercenaries in the army sometimes brought rather undesirable elements to Alexandria. Julius Caesar later observed that the Ptolemaic army also consisted of "...men collected from among the freebooters and brigands of Syria and the province of Cilicia and the neighboring regions; also many condemned criminals and exiles had joined them. All our own fugitive slaves had a sure place of refuge at Alexandria, and assurance of their lives as long as they registered themselves among the soldiers."

Another group who immigrated in large numbers were the Jews who followed in Alexander's wake and were encouraged by the Ptolemies to stay. Their high concentration in the fourth district, known as Delta (the whole city was divided into five districts named after the first five letters of the Greek alphabet), is well attested. Due to the Jews' special faith and religious practices, they were permitted to form their own social organization, technically termed *politeuma*. Despite having their own synagogues and enjoying religious freedom, they were greatly Hellenized before the end of the 3rd century B.C. In fact, a Greek translation of the Old Testament, called the *Septuagint*, was made by Jewish scholars for prayers in the synagogues.

Immigrants in lesser numbers came from Syria and Asia Minor as well as Italy, Syracuse, Libya, Carthagenia and Massillia in the western Mediterranean. There is also evidence that some individuals came from as far away as India, as happened when there was an exchange of embassies between King Asoka (264-230 B.C.) of India and Philadelphus. After his conversion, Asoka became an apostle for Buddhism, which he invited all nations to adopt. Among the kings he approached was Ptolemy Philadelphus. Not only were Buddhist monks with their flowing robes and austere simplicity seen in the crowded streets of Alexandria, but historians tell that in a grand procession, around 270 B.C., Alexandrians could view "Indian women, Indian dogs and 26 pure-white Indian cattle."

With the exception of the mass of Egyptians, this heterogeneous populace gradually went through a high degree of assimilation and Hellenization by the middle of the 2nd century B.C. The Ptolemies did not enforce any systematic policy of Hellenization, yet certain measures encouraged that process. The adoption of Greek as the official administrative language no doubt led to its

Following pages:
A cinerary urn of pottery used to preserve the ashes of the deceased. A gilded wreath surrounds its neck. Found at Chatby, Alexandria. 3rd century B.C. Graeco-Roman Museum, Alexandria.

Alexandria: Capital of Egypt

Below:

A painted funerary stele, or pillar, depicts Aristobius, "The Thinker." (The pose is very similar to the famous work of the same name by 19th century French sculptor Auguste Rodin.) Near the figure's left foot is a Greek-style tragic mask. Limestone. Ptolemaic Period. Found at Chatby, Alexandria.
Graeco-Roman Museum, Alexandria.

Facing page:

A painted funerary stele, or pillar, depicts an armed cavalry officer cantering on a superb, richly harnessed horse. The rider's chlamys, clasped at the breast, flows behind him. He is followed by an attendant. Limestone. 3rd century B.C. Found at Chatby, Alexandria.
Graeco-Roman Museum, Alexandria.

22108

becoming the *lingua franca* among the settlers. At the same time, in addition to the principle civic gymnasium, many other private gymnasia arose that provided the necessary primary schooling in the Greek educational tradition. It is no wonder, therefore, that Greek customs and the Greek language prevailed.

Alexandria's Egyptians formed the city's largest single community from the very beginning. They lived mainly in the southern district, around the precinct of the Serapeum, where the village of Rhakotis once stood. They usually wore their own garb, used their own language and lived their own way of life. Yet, a number of middle-class Egyptians who wished to improve their social status gradually adopted Greek names and costumes. Toward the end of the 3rd century B.C., the number of new mercenaries from the Aegean dwindled, and the Ptolemies had to depend on Egyptian recruits. The turning point for Egyptians in Alexandria, as well as in the country as a whole, was at the Battle of Raphia in 217 B.C. There, the Greek mercenaries were routed by Antiochus IV, king of Syria, but much to everyone's surprise, the newly recruited Egyptians stood their ground and won the day for Ptolemy IV. The consequences of their victory were far-reaching, for with a fresh feeling of self-assurance, the Egyptians started a protracted revolution against Ptolemaic rule. In the words of Polybius:

The Egyptians were so elated, that there was a revolt of the native population which continued for some years. When the revolt was finally suppressed, the Egyptian element in the country had established their power and could no longer be ignored.

A God for a Special Purpose

So many nationalities coexisting in the same city inevitably resulted in daily frictions – often in open strife. Aware of this situation, Ptolemy I adopted an enlightened policy that promoted mutual understanding and tolerance between the two main segments of the population, the Greeks and the Egyptians. His handling of competing religious factions at that time vividly illustrates this new policy: One of the fundamental problems that Ptolemy I had to deal with was to select a tutelary god for his new dynasty. This was no simple task since the choice had to be acceptable to both Egyptians and Greeks in order to help unify the kingdom's divergent components. Every possible religious sensitivity of both Greeks and Egyptians had to be taken into account.

Undoubtedly there were differences between the two pantheons, but there were also similarities that could be exploited, and Ptolemy sought the advice of Egyptian and Greek religious experts. His chief counselors were two priests: Manethon, the Egyptian, was knowledgeable in the lore of his country; Timotheus, the Athenian, came from a priestly family linked with the mystery rites of Demeter and Persephone, and he was also familiar with the Greek shrines at Eleusis and Delphi. Deliberations centered around the local cult of the Apis bull at Memphis which was connected with the cult of Osiris. In Egyptian theology, Osiris had a dual role: He was god of the dead and – not incompatibly – was also the observer of life on earth. As the latter, he was connected with the god Ptah and was represented as the all-seeing eye of the sun, reborn each day. As such, he was known in Memphis as Osiris-Ptah, lord of life. As for his connection with the Apis bull, it is best expressed in the words of

Herodotus who described the bull's immaculate conception:

This Apis is a young calf, born of a cow which is unable thereafter to conceive other offspring. And the Egyptians say that the fire descends upon the cow from heaven, and by this she conceives Apis.

Apis, thus miraculously conceived, was considered to be the incarnation of Osiris-Ptah. In other words, the living bull represented the natural and physical forces of life, and after his death he was unified with Osiris and was worshiped under the name of Osiris-Apis or Osorapis. Not only was he greatly venerated by the Egyptians, but at Memphis he had followers among non-Egyptians, especially the Greeks who had settled there since the 26th dynasty.

The new god who would represent the Ptolemaic dynasty had to be suitable in both name and shape; the Egyptians would continue to use the traditional name Osorapis, but the Greeks found that name heavy on the tongue and derived the name Serapis. The Greeks also found it natural for the god to take a human shape, whereas the Egyptians were familiar with both human and animal representations of their gods (although Osiris was the only deity always portrayed with human features). But Osiris-Apis or Osorapis was worshiped in both bull and human shape. Thus Ptolemy would not offend Egyptian religious feelings when he introduced to the Greek newcomers the god Osiris-Apis, alias Osorapis, alias Serapis in a human guise.

The next step was to fashion a suitable cult statue to place in the god's new sanctuary in Alexandria. Thus, the magnificent sculpture of Jupiter Dis (Pluton), attributed to the sculptor Bryaxis, was transferred from Sinope in Asia Minor to Alexandria. It showed the god as a majestic father figure.

Although originating from Osorapis at Memphis, the newly formed cult of Serapis took the new capital of Alexandria as its center and a fitting sanctuary was built for it there. According to religious tradition, Serapis formed a trinity with Isis as his consort (as she was of Osiris) and Horus as their son. Other temples were erected around the country, but although the most magnificent Serapeum was in Alexandria, the most venerated was still in Memphis.

The Serapeum was looked upon as an official cult center and did not appeal to the vast masses of Egyptians initially. It was only a century or two later that its popularity was fully established, and under the Romans, it became the greatest center of pagan worship in all Egypt.

A second official cult introduced by Ptolemy I was that of Alexander the Great. As founder of the city, and with his burial in the mausoleum, the *Soma*, in its center, Alexander was worshiped as the guardian genius of Alexandria. The priest in charge of his cult became the city's official head priest, by whose name documents were dated. The cult of Alexander also paved the way for the deification of the Ptolemies. Under Roman rule, the cult of the kings was replaced by the cult of the Caesars. At the same time, old pagan gods, both Egyptian and Greek, continued to be worshiped, and the most popular was Isis.

Alexandria Under Roman Rule

What became of Alexandria when Rome annexed Egypt in 30 B.C.? Rome's influence in Alexandria had been increasingly felt ever since the 2nd century B.C.; as the Ptolemies grew weaker their dependence on Rome grew stronger. Military intervention occurred more than once. In 58 B.C. a Roman force

Facing page:

A cinerary terra-cotta urn decorated with the mythological winged horse, Pegasus, galloping between two Doric columns. 3rd century B.C. Found at Hadara, Alexandria.
Graeco-Roman Museum, Alexandria.

Page 54:

A graceful, headless statue of the goddess Isis stands on a base, in the Egyptian attitude. She carries a cornucopia in her left hand and the Egyptian ankh, or sign of life, in her right. She wears the customary Isis garment. A good example of Graeco-Egyptian sculpture. Made of basalt and found in the Abu Qir district in 1989.
Graeco-Roman Museum, Alexandria.

Page 55:

Head of a beautiful woman, probably a princess or priestess. Locks of hair hang beneath the head veil in the Pharaonic style. 3rd-2nd century B.C.
Graeco-Roman Museum, Alexandria.

Pages 56-57:

Ptolemaic tomb cut out of rock in the necropolis of Anfushi. The front chamber is relatively well preserved and brightly decorated. The ceiling, slightly vaulted, is painted with yellow octagons connected by black squares. The walls are divided into two main panels: The bottom one is painted in imitation-alabaster facing; the upper left half is decorated with three rows of small black and white squares; between them are three imitation-alabaster strips. Two sphinxes lie atop two pedestals to the right and left of the door leading to the inner funerary chamber. In the curved tympanum above the door, the solar disk floats.

was permanently stationed in Alexandria to protect the king from the recurring disturbances of the population. Then in 48 B.C. Julius Caesar came to the city in pursuit of Pompey and fought on the side of Cleopatra VII against her brother Ptolemy XIII. Finally, in 30 B.C., after the defeat and death of Mark Antony and Cleopatra (the last of the Ptolemies), Augustus Caesar entered Alexandria at the head of a victorious army. The Alexandrians expected the worst, but although he abolished their senate, he granted one important privilege: He exempted them from a heavy new poll tax imposed on all other Egyptians.

Nevertheless, the abolition of the senate, the hallmark of a self-governing *polis*, left a scar the Alexandrians never forgot. Surviving papyri from the early Roman period indicate that the Alexandrians often appealed to the Roman emperor to restore their senate. But Alexandria remained 230 years without one until in 200 A.D. when Emperor Septimius Severus visited Egypt and introduced the first major reform since Augustus. He granted both Alexandria and the *metropoleis* of the country districts of Egypt the right to have their own town councils. These councils had no legislative or political functions, but performed local administrative duties such as nominating suitable men for town offices and collecting taxes. Thus, placing Alexandria on a par with the local *metropoleis* and restricting its administrative role aroused discontent among Alexandrians.

A further development in Roman Alexandria greatly jeopardized the city's large Jewish community. As stated earlier, this large segment of the populace was allowed under the Ptolemies to form an association called *politeuma*, to freely practice their faith and to manage their affairs in accordance with Jewish law. After the Roman conquest, Alexandria's Jews were favorably treated by the emperor because of the help and support Augustus had received from the king of Judea. He not only confirmed all the privileges they had enjoyed under the Ptolemies, but also granted them the right to form their own *gerousia*, a body or board of elders to manage the community's private affairs. Contrasted with the humiliating treatment of the Egyptians, who were not allowed to have their senate, it is not surprising that the latter deeply resented the situation. But after their first attempt at resistance was ruthlessly crushed by the Roman occupation army, the Alexandrians refrained from declaring open revolt against Roman domination. Instead they vented their anger against the Jews as the proteges of the Romans.

In spite of their political grievances, Roman Alexandria appears to have had a degree of material prosperity perhaps not inferior to that of its golden days under the Ptolemies. The Romans took care to continue its prosperity, and the Alexandrians were second only to the Romans at the head of the Egyptian class structure. Roman rule was represented by a magnificent new temple called the Caesareum. It was originally started by Cleopatra as a temple dedicated to Antony, but after the Roman conquest it was completed to honor Augustus.

Philo recorded the following description:

There is not in the whole world such a precinct as the so-called Caesareum, the temple of Caesar, patron of mariners, which rises conspicuous opposite the excellent harbors, very large and noticeable and unmatched for the wealth of its votive offerings, being surrounded with pictures, statues, silver and gold. In the

extensive precinct are porticoes, libraries, men's apartments, sacred groves, propylaea, pen spaces, halls open to the sky: In fact, it is embellished in the most sumptuous way and gives hope of safety alike to those who set out and to those who disembark.

International trade maintained the cosmopolitan character of the city. As Dion Chrysostom, a leading orator at the turn of the 2nd century, remarked when he spoke to the Alexandrians at the Great Theater, "There were not only Greeks and Italians, but also Syrians, Libyans, Cilicians (from Asia Minor) and still others from farther countries – Ethiopians, Arabs as well as Bactrians, Scythians, Persians and a few Indians." Most, if not all of these, would also have been found in Ptolemaic Alexandria, but it is very probable that Alexandria's population increased during the first two centuries of Roman rule. The most conspicuous increase, naturally, was in the Roman and Italian contingent, which comprised the bulk of the new occupation army, as well as government officials and some businessmen. At the beginning, the Roman soldiers in Egypt numbered slightly more than 27,000, but as peace and stability prevailed, their number was more than halved. Smaller units of this force were stationed at three other strategic points in Egypt, but most of the army remained at Alexandria. Here in the capital, at a new site east of the city, Augustus set up an enormous Roman camp called Nikepolis, or City of Victory. It is the site of present-day Mostafa Kamel.

Encouraged by the prolonged *Pax Romana* and the lack of military action, many soldiers got involved in the life of the city. Roman soldiers repeatedly were parties to business transactions. And because Roman law forbade its soldiers to marry during their active service, which could last up to 25 years, it was inevitable that many of them formulated secret alliances with local women. In one case, a marriage contract was disguised as a deposit contract; in lieu of a dowry, the soldier acknowledged receipt of female clothing, jewelry and money from a local woman as deposit to be returned on demand. Upon a soldier's discharge, his clandestine marriage and resulting offspring were usually officially recognized. The soldiers quite often stayed in Egypt and settled down. They were often granted remuneration, and in some cases, even a piece of land. Thus, this new class of Roman citizens was not totally isolated from the old class of Alexandrians. In fact, the commingling of these two groups was hastened by the imperial Roman custom of granting Roman citizenship on special occasions to members of the Alexandrian aristocracy. The economic significance of the combined class was soon recognized by the land surveyors who found it practical to tax Roman and Alexandrian landowners as one group.

This melding process continued in other areas as well. To attain Alexandrian citizenship, an individual needed two things: a birth certificate to prove one's descent from parents who were both Alexandrian citizens, and an *ephebeia*, or diploma from the civic gymnasium, obtained at age 14. Without Alexandrian parentage, no authority in Egypt, not even the prefect, could grant citizenship. This was solely the prerogative of the emperor, and occasionally can be traced. Pliny the Younger, for example, a Roman nobleman and close associate of the Emperor Trajan, was seriously ill. He was finally cured by a gifted Egyptian doctor named Arpocras. In recognition, Pliny appealed to the emperor to grant Arpocras citizenship. The

emperor explained that the doctor, being Egyptian, could not be granted Roman citizenship without first obtaining Alexandrian citizenship. But to gratify Pliny, he granted Arpocras both citizenships at once.

Ancient writers described Alexandrian social life as rich, opulent, merry, productive and frivolous. The moral sophist Dion Chrysostom, who visited the city about 100 A.D., was mainly struck by the people's passion for music. In his speech at the Great Theater, he said:

It is not easy for a stranger to endure the clamor of so great a multitude or to face these tens of thousands unless he comes provided with a lute and a song. For this is an antidote against your populace....and myself, if I were a musical man, should never have come hither without some song or air.

Almost a century later, the distinguished Christian teacher, Clement of Alexandria, depicts yet another aspect of Alexandrian social life that greatly offended austere moralists like himself – the extravagance and frivolity of women. Among their many vices are: "...their adornments and dyed wools and variegated colors and wrought stones and gold jewelry; their artificial hair and wreathed tresses, their paintings under the eyes; their plucking out of hair and rougings and cosmetics and dying hair and all such evil arts of deceit...their gold-wrought fabrics, their Indian silk and over-wrought silken stuffs...."

These are descriptions of the Hellenized upper and middle classes, examples of which can be seen in the Tanagra figurines in Alexandria's Graeco-Roman Museum. But the mass of the poorer Egyptian community continued to provide the necessary manual labor. It appears that the prolonged prosperity of the city encouraged more and more

Egyptians to move there from the country. Periodically, there were signs of economic crisis. When the Nile flood failed to irrigate the fields, for example, many peasants abandoned their leaseholds and ran from their villages for fear of torture at the hands of tax collectors. They often sought refuge in the large, crowded city of Alexandria where they were safely hidden and could hope to find employment. A papyrus letter, written in the 2nd century A.D. by a young Egyptian man from the Fayoum to a relative, illustrates this phenomenon. He says:

...it came to my knowledge that my father is planning to run away. I therefore write to you in order to inform him not to do so without my knowledge. If still he does not wish me to know his whereabouts, let him send me a hundred drachmae, so I can travel to Alexandria and remain there for some time; for I cannot stay here in Arsinoe (Fayoum) after his departure. The Strategus (local governor) and Artemidorus and all his men know me well, and will certainly take their vengeance on me. This is why, Sir, I write to you, so that you may show him my letter and inform him of my opinion. Please do so....

Papyri frequently reported such cases of flight from the villages. This resulted in overcrowding in the Egyptian quarter as well as in other parts of Alexandria. The Roman administration periodically issued declarations commanding Egyptians whose work was not in the city, to return to their villages. This mingling of various social elements was accelerated by the growth of a major crisis, and the administrative and legislative measures taken to stem it, early in the 3rd century A.D. As already mentioned, Emperor Severus' edict in 200 A.D. set up municipal

Facing page:

A round mosaic probably depicts a personification of Alexandria as mistress of the sea. Her headdress is in the shape of a ship's prow. 2nd century B.C. Found at Thmuis (Tmai el-Amdid), Delta. Graeco-Roman Museum, Alexandria.

Following pages:

A magnificent rectangular mosaic is probably another representation of Alexandria as mistress of the sea. (It was recently suggested that the face is that of Queen Berenice II, wife of Ptolemy III, 246-221 B.C.). She holds a mast and is crowned with a headdress in the form of a ship's prow. In the upper-left corner, the artist's name is written: "Sophilos made it." 3rd-2nd century B.C. Found at Thmuis (Tmai el-Amdid), Delta. Graeco-Roman Museum, Alexandria.

Alexandria: Capital of Egypt

councils in Alexandria and the local *metropoleis*. In practical terms, this downgraded Alexandria to the status of any local *polis*. And legislation enacted by Emperor Caracalla in 212 A.D. downgraded the city even more. This legislation – which "bestowed Roman citizenship on all free subjects of the Roman Empire..." – had implications that were both complicated and far-reaching. Basically, it eliminated most of the pre-existing distinctions and classifications. But when all inhabitants of free birth became Romans, Alexandrian citizenship became irrelevant and practically ceased to exist. The new law categorized people by their place of origin or permanent domicile and not by a specific hereditary legal status. Yet the legal assimilation implicit in the law had no relevance to social equality; on the contrary, private wealth became even more important. It became the only real mark of distinction and the only means of protection against increasing social injustice. The succeeding centuries would witness unprecedented class divisions.

"The Greatest Emporium in the Inhabited World"

As mentioned earlier, Alexandria was established primarily as a port. Indeed, the importance of the harbor to the city's economic life can not be exaggerated. Strabo best defines this aspect:

Among the happy advantages of the city, the greatest is the fact that this is the only place in all Egypt which is by nature well-situated with reference to a two-fold function – both to commerce by sea on account of the good harbors, and to commerce by land, because the river easily conveys and brings together everything into a place so situated – [making it] the greatest emporium in the inhabited world.

Even in its earliest years, during Alexander's lifetime when it was not yet a capital city, Cleomenes of Naukratis, the merchant mentioned earlier, conducted his international grain-trade monopoly from Alexandria's as yet unfinished harbors. When it became Egypt's capital under the Ptolemies, the city's economic life grew even faster. It soon became the center of many industries, notably textiles, papyrus paper, glass, oil, perfumes, wine, and ivory and ebony work. These were all age-old traditional Egyptian industries, and the availability of raw materials and of ready, cheap manual labor in the Egyptian community, combined with fresh Greek expertise, helped the city industrialize rapidly.

The situation was complicated, however, by the Ptolemies' monopolistic policies. Essentially, state or royal funds controlled most of the major industries, not only in Alexandria, but throughout Egypt. Industries like salt and oil and, to a lesser extent, linen textiles and papyrus paper were under royal monopoly. Lesser industries such as woolen textiles, glass, wine, perfumes and the like, though state controlled, were largely left in private hands. Foreign trade, such as grain and papyrus exports, was also a strict state monopoly. Yet with the passage of time and the weakening of the Ptolemaic dynasty in the 2nd century B.C., the tight grip of the state on the economy gradually loosened, especially in foreign trade.

In the 3rd century B.C., under the early Ptolemies, practically all navigation and trade in the Red Sea was the personal concern of the kings. Philadelphus and Euergetes I regularly sent organized expeditions to the east coast of Africa to hunt elephants and other exotic animals and to import much-prized frankincense,

myrrh, and the even more valuable gold and ebony. Capturing live elephants was important to the Ptolemaic army, as elephants had become strategic war equipment following Alexander's campaign in India. In addition, the intellectual stimulation of acquiring strange wild animals was one of Philadelphus' dominating passions. Diodorus tells us that he willingly "gave great rewards to those who succeeded in capturing against odds the most valiant of those beasts," expending large sums of money to satisfy his passion. He not only collected great herds of war elephants, but also brought to the Greeks knowledge of other kinds of animals which had never before been seen and were objects of amazement. New animals such as giraffes, wild cats, ostriches, rhinoceroses, hyenas, giant snakes, baboons and monkeys were imported and shown not only as curiosities, but Alexandrian scholars could also observe and study them in Philadelphus' zoological gardens.

The rise of Rome as a world power in the Mediterranean at that time greatly influenced the commercial market in Alexandria. Powerful Roman and Italian businessmen who had their headquarters at Delos began to invest their money in the Alexandrian trade. The stronger presence of Roman businessmen in the city and the invigorating infusion of Roman capital into the market directed Alexandria's southern trade further afield.

Then, during the 2nd century B.C., Rome's dominance in the Mediterranean grew and Roman investments in the Alexandria markets increased. Trade up and down the Red Sea oriented to Alexandria rose considerably. About that time, the discovery by Alexandrian seamen of the monsoon winds and their usefulness in crossing the Indian Ocean led to a revolution in navigation and trade with India. For the first time, Pliny tells us, the round-trip journey between Egypt and India could be accomplished in one year. As a result, the number of ships sailing to India doubled, and about 100 B.C. the state set up a new office called "Commander of the Red and Indian Seas." The creation of such an office implies that regular commercial traffic to India was well established and that there were valuable interests to protect. After the Roman conquest of Egypt, Alexandria-India trade flourished even more as a result of Augustus' inroads to Arabia in 24-23 B.C., and his subsequent sacking of the important Arabian harbor of Eudaemon (Aden).

Despite the political humiliation of the Roman occupation, Alexandria seems to have flourished economically during the first two centuries A.D. An important factor, no doubt, was Rome's economic policy that encouraged private enterprise. Alexandrian tradesmen and businessmen, who had dealt with Roman financiers before, now took full advantage of the new policy, and the city's industry and commerce probably prospered more than ever. The following passage, attributed to the Emperor Hadrian, describes the city's economic life:

The city is prosperous, rich and productive, and in it no one is idle. Some are blowers of glass, others makers of paper, all are at least weavers of linen or seem to belong to one craft or another; the lame have their occupations, the eunuchs have theirs, the blind have theirs, and not even those whose hands are crippled are idle. Their only god is money, and this the Christians, the Jews, and in fact, all nations adore.

This passage is of value as it touches upon the three important

Below:

A rare statue in sycamore wood of the god Serapis in his human form. Remains of the original paints coloring the clothes can be seen. From Fayoum. Roman Period.
Graeco-Roman Museum, Alexandria.

Facing page:

A *dignified marble bust of the god Serapis in his human form with the characteristic* calathos, *a basket symbolizing abundance and fertility, on his head. Roman Period.*
Graeco-Roman Museum, Alexandria.

Alexandrian industries – glass, papyrus and the weaving of linen – that were firmly established under Ptolemaic monopoly. These industries, incidentally, seem to have improved under Rome's free market economy. Alexandrian multicolored glass was very popular abroad, and it has been found in Greece, Italy, France and Germany.

As Egypt was the only producer and exporter of papyrus paper, demand in the vast worldwide market of the Roman Empire more than doubled Alexandria's trade in it. It is interesting to read Strabo's description of how some Alexandrian capitalists responded to the new, more favorable conditions:

Papyrus grows in large quantities in the lower parts of the Delta, one being inferior and the other superior, that is hieratica [i.e. sacred, of the temples]. And here too, certain of those who wished to increase their income adopted the shrewd practice of the Judeans, which the latter had invented in the case of the palm tree... and the balsam tree; for they do not allow the papyrus plant to grow in many places, and because of the scarcity they set a higher price on it and thus increase their income, though they injure the common use of the plant.

The practice which Strabo describes might well be confirmed by a lease contract dating to 5 B.C. in which an Alexandrian proprietor stipulates conditions to limit the production of papyrus from his land.

Finally, linen textiles – the material traditionally worn by Egyptians – were manufactured everywhere in Egypt. But surplus grain, once exported in exchange for imports, was now sent free to Rome as tribute. Thus, Alexandrian traders had to depend on exporting papyrus and linen instead. Pliny assumes that

Egyptian linen exports practically covered the cost of Red Sea trade in the 1st century. Late in the 3rd century, Alexandrian linens are mentioned in the document known as "Diocletian's price list," the standard for international trade, which proves the cloth continued to be exported to Mediterranean markets as well.

A smaller, lucrative trade also flourished in materials originally imported from India, southern Arabia and Africa. This included perfumes, aromatics, frankincense, myrrh, jewelry, engraved ivory and wrought ebony. These important materials were treated and prepared in Alexandria and re-exported to other Mediterranean countries. Pliny estimates the value of goods imported from India and Arabia to the Roman Empire, at 100 million *sesterces* or about $4.3 million by the pre-World War II gold standard – and much more on today's gold market. He adds, "So much we pay for the luxury of our women." There is no way to estimate the wealth accumulated by some Alexandrian merchants, but one indication may be the case of a businessman named Firmus who traded in papyrus and gum arabic: In the 3rd century A.D., he was able to raise, at his own expense, an army against Rome and temporarily declare himself emperor in support of Queen Zenobia of Palmyra.

Alexandria in a Changing World: from Pagan to Christian

In the Roman Empire at large, the 3rd century A.D. was a turbulent period of crisis and reform in almost every aspect of life – social, economic, administrative and religious. It must have seemed as if the whole empire would be shaken to its very foundations. Some institutional change had already begun with the reforms of the Emperors Severus and Caracalla, and the

A marble statue of Aphrodite stands with her left foot raised to take off her slippers. At her side the winged Eros (Cupid) stands on a vase and lifts his arms to hold the goddess. Found at Al-Muhammarah, near Alexandria. Roman Period. Graeco-Roman Museum, Alexandria.

cycle would be completed at the end of the century with Diocletian's reforms. But before looking at the impact this had on Alexandria, the city's crucial role in religious doctrine must be considered.

The birth and rise of Christianity during the 1st century passed almost unnoticed in Alexandria and Egypt. The story related rather cautiously by Eusebius, the 4th century church historian, is that St. Mark came from Rome to Alexandria about the middle of the 1st century. This is the only allusion to any Christian activity in the city at that time. The scene looked different in the 2nd century, however, when papyri provide us with a number of Christian documents: a text from St. John, the *Sayings of Jesus*, an epistle of Barnabas and fragments of uncanonical gospels. Although they were found outside Alexandria, it is believed that they originated from a Judeo-Christian group in the city. The obscurity of their origin denotes the secrecy early Christians had to preserve most of the time. Yet, during the second half of the 2nd century, Christianity appears to have secured a recognizable following in Alexandria complete with an active catechetical school to compete with other philosophical schools. One of the objectives of this Christian school was to draw students from all over the Mediterranean, attracted by Alexandria's reputation as a great center of learning. Against this background, early Christian teachers, usually well-grounded in Greek philosophy, had to adapt their methods to Hellenic education. Pantaenus, the first reported head of the school, was a converted Stoic, and his pupil and successor, Clement, illustrates how the catechetical school became a focus of learning and conversion in the latter half of the

2nd century. Clement came to Alexandria as a pagan student, probably from Athens, to study philosophy. But after attending the lectures of Pantaenus, he was converted to Christianity and became one of the school's great teachers. His pupil and successor, in turn, was Origen, the son of Christian parents. He joined the school around 200.

The success of the school reflects the success the Alexandrian church achieved elsewhere. Rome was annoyed by these developments, and in 202, a Christian persecution was launched by imperial edict of the Emperor Severus. The persecution was directed from Alexandria, and prisoners were brought there from all over Egypt to be tried and put to a martyr's death. The catechetical school was a target, and Clement and a group of teachers went into hiding and re-appeared in Palestine. Origen escaped martyrdom, but his father was beheaded. He was the only teacher left at the school, and Bishop Demetrius appointed him its head in 203 when Origen was still only 18 years old. When the persecution was over, church and school resumed their activities there for half a century, when another more systematic wave of persecution was launched by Emperor Decius. This time it aimed at eradicating all Christians throughout the empire. Official committees were set up in almost every village to test inhabitants. Those who joined in traditional pagan rites and sacrifices were given formal certificates by the committee; papyrus samples of these have been found. Those who resisted were beaten or arrested and often tortured to death.

In spite of this, Christianity actively continued and grew. There is a letter from this period that reveals Alexandria's role as a link between Egyptian Christian groups and those outside the

country. The letter was written by a Christian of obvious distinction in Rome who asked his "brethren" in the Fayoum to collect money and send it to Alexandria so that it would be there on his arrival. The letter also refers to the bishop of Alexandria as "Papa Maximus." This is notable because it shows that the bishop of Alexandria was already acknowledged as head of all the Christians in Egypt, long before the state recognized Christianity.

In the meantime, there was strife and contention among the Roman generals. Finally, in 284, one of them, Diocletian, suppressed all the others. He established his own rule throughout the empire and set himself the task of overcoming the causes of the crisis. His initial concern was administration and finance – he aimed basically for decentralization and conformity. In Egypt, he put the military force under one separate command, and divided the country into three provinces: Alexandria and the western Delta formed one; the eastern Delta and middle Egypt, the second; and Upper Egypt (Thebaid), the third. The province of Alexandria ranked higher than the other two, but in practice the division and decentralization further downgraded the city from its position as chief capital. Besides, the new, fully developed municipal system encouraged many Alexandrians who owned land elsewhere to leave and eventually settle down on their property. Thus, as a result of the 3rd century reforms, Alexandria lost much of its distinguished status, at least economically.

Before the administrative reform, a Roman general named Domitianus and a supporter called Achilleus revolted in Alexandria and usurped the title of emperor in 297. Faced with this provocation, Diocletian came the

following year and besieged the city for eight months and finally crushed the rebellion. Conditions in the city were so bad that Diocletian established a regular free distribution of grain. It is probable that to honor him the populace set up the great granite monolith commonly known as Pompey's Pillar in front of the Serapeum. Before his departure, Diocletian toured the country to assure that the new reforms were put into effect.

Diocletian was also concerned about religious upheaval in the empire. Guided by conservatism and conformity, he could not tolerate the religious division created by Christianity. He was a staunch believer in the old gods who had blessed and promoted the greatness of Rome. He believed that Christianity was an insidious movement, opposed not only to the ancient gods but also to the empire itself. But he proceeded cautiously, and finally after 20 years in which peaceful measures failed to check Christianity's spread, he acted decisively. In 303, he unleashed the most ferocious campaign yet of persecution against the Christians. Alexandria and Egypt always remembered it with such horror that in later years the Coptic Church called the period following Diocletian's accession in 284 "the Era of the Martyrs."

Faraway developments in the autumn of 312 turned events in a dramatic new direction, although the great Christian persecution continued unabated in Egypt. Alexandria's bishop, for instance, was beheaded with several other Egyptian bishops in November 312. Yet only a month earlier, in October 312, the stage of history began to change, as the forces of the Emperor Constantine suddenly appeared in battle in central Italy, their shields marked with the Christian cross. Constantine was victorious against his adversary, Maxentius, who suffered an ignoble defeat.

With the definitive victory of Constantine, Christianity became the official religion of the empire, although pagan cults were still tolerated. Yet freedom and state protection did not solve all the Christians' problems: There had long been grievances and dissensions in their own ranks that had to be contained. But now they could afford to openly declare their differences and even fight them out. The situation became acute in Alexandria where the very unity of the church was threatened.

First, there was the controversy that broke out between Alexander, bishop of Alexandria, and Arius, one of his priests, regarding the Incarnation – Jesus as both God and man. By 324, the Arian controversy had embroiled not only all of Egypt, but every province in the East from Libya to Asia Minor and Thrace. In his youth, Arius was a pupil of the great Christian philosopher at Antioch, Lucian, who had developed his theory in the tradition of the great Origen, whose Christian Platonism greatly appealed to intellectuals of the church. Lucian's theology was an extension of Origen's doctrine of the Trinity, stressing the subordination of Christ the Son to God the Father, and both to the Holy Spirit. Arius carried this to its extreme. He argued from purely philosophical premises, and by clever deductions reached neat theological conclusions. He taught that the Son of God was a created being of whom one could say: "There was a time when He was not." Bishop Alexander was shocked by these teachings and held two debates with Arius, but Arius remained arrogantly adamant. The exasperated bishop convened a council of 100 bishops from the provinces subject to Alexandria, and Arius and his

adherents were excommunicated.

Arius sought the support of other fellow-Lucianists who had risen to influential positions in the new era of Constantine. One of them was Eusebius, bishop of Nicomedia. As bishop of the city where the Emperor then resided, he was politically powerful. Arius' letter to Eusebius has survived, and it shows that he was anxious to emphasize that he was not alone in his creed for the Trinity:

The bishop is assaulting and persecuting us greatly.... so that he has expelled us from the city as atheists because we do not agree with him when he says publicly: 'Always God, always the Son; at the same time the Father, at the same time the Son...' We cannot endure to hear these impieties, if the heretics threaten us with a thousand deaths.

Eusebius' response was favorable and reassuring:

Your views are right; pray that all may believe as you do. It is plain to anyone that which is made does not exist before it comes into being: that which comes into being has a beginning of its being.

Thus heartened, Arius lost no time in going to Nicomedia himself.

The bishop of Alexandria had tried to contain the controversy in Egypt. Now he felt embarrassed and obliged to explain his actions to the other bishops of the East. He was particularly provoked by Eusebius' intervention, and he made no secret of it. He told them to "pay no attention if Eusebius writes to you."

The texts of the documents quoted above are of special interest, not only to the Arian controversy, or heresy as it is often termed, and to our understanding of the spirit of the age, but also because they reveal for the first time the rivalry and perhaps also the resentment felt by the church in Alexandria

A terra-cotta lantern modeled after the celebrated Lighthouse of Alexandria. Roman Period. Graeco-Roman Museum, Alexandria.

Following pages:
The Roman amphitheatre in downtown Alexandria was discovered in 1963 while foundation work for a new building was underway. The theatre was probably built in the 3rd century A.D. as an odeon to replace an older and larger structure. In Byzantine times it was used as a meeting hall. A Roman road runs through the foreground. An enormous adjacent area is now under excavation.

ORCHESTRA

towards the church in the city of imperial residence. The spirit of nationalism detectable in Alexander's circular and felt by the church in Alexandria would grow stronger. These letters were followed by an exchange of polemical pamphlets and regional councils supporting one party or the other. At this stage, Constantine intervened. He did not try to understand the theological and metaphysical subtleties of the two concepts, for his main purpose was to preserve the unity of the church. The letter he drafted to both Alexander and Arius shows his disappointment that the East was even more divided than the West by disputes over what he considered an extremely trifling matter, and he advised them simply to agree to differ.

The situation, however, was far more complicated than Constantine thought. There was another serious schism – of less moment, but equally intractable and of longer standing – rocking the church in Egypt. This was the so-called Meletian controversy that went back to the early years of the great persecution, about 305. At the height of the persecution, some Christians lost courage and agreed to sacrifice to the ancient gods and thus were set free. Others suffered torture without relenting and were taken as prisoners to Alexandria. These included bishops, priests, and ordinary individuals; prominent among them were Peter, bishop of Alexandria at the time, and Meletius, bishop of Lycopolis (Asyut).

While still in prison, they argued about how to deal with Christians who had lapsed. Peter advocated leniency, while Meletius said they should be dealt with rigorously, recommending that lapsed clergy should never again be permitted to resume their sacred functions. They reached

no agreement, so Peter hung a curtain to divide the cell and announced: "Let those who are of my opinion come over to me and those who agree with Meletius to him." The majority went over to Meletius, although a small group stayed with Peter.

Thus the Meletian schism began, and although of no serious doctrinal consequence, it was nevertheless a stubborn and vexing dilemma within the church in Egypt long after the persecution.

Such were the problems that troubled the important Alexandrian church, and these issues were put before Constantine for arbitration as soon as he took up residence at Nicomedia. The emperor realized that these were matters he could not cope with alone, and he decided to set a vital precedent in the relationship between church and state. In 325, he convened and presided over a universal council at Nicaea of all heads of the churches in the empire. More than 300 bishops and their delegations came from Egypt, Syria, Assyria, Asia Minor, Greece and the West. Alexandria was strongly represented by Bishop Alexander and his exceptionally able deacon, Athanasius. These two played a very influential role in the council's proceedings judging by the outcome. On the statement of faith, they were determined to reach a formula unacceptable to the Arian party and they were successful. After much deliberation, the council, probably at the instigation of Constantine himself, adopted a statement acceptable to a vast majority. In it, Jesus the Son was called *Homoousion* – of one essence with God the Father – a concept rejected by the Arians. On the Meletian schism, the council's decision was very mild: Meletius himself was to retain the title of bishop only in name; he

was forbidden to exercise any episcopal functions. The other Meletian bishops and clergy were to keep their functions, but they were ranked below Bishop Alexander and could not ordain new clergy without his permission.

The apparent unity manifested at Nicaea was only due to the personal authority of the emperor and not to a universal acceptance of the Nicene Creed. The employment of the term *Homoousion* was tolerated only as long as Constantine was alive. And Arianism continued to lurk among people in the East. Constantine was aware of that, and it remained his ambition to unify the church by bringing Arians – and Arius himself – into the fold.

Two years after the council, the emperor recalled Arius from exile and asked Bishop Alexander to re-admit him to the church.

But Alexander was adamant and refused. The situation was complicated by Alexander's death a year later and the appointment of Athanasius, the most powerful of all Alexandrian bishops, as his successor.

Athanasius was very much a national leader who consolidated Egyptian support under his episcopal authority. He stood firm in his opposition to Constantinople, the new capital in the East where Constantine and the church had moved on May 11, 330. Athanasius' episcopacy was both long (328-373) and eventful. For the purpose of this book, however, it suffices to say that his continuous involvement in politics and his adamant opposition to the emperor and the church in Constantinople led to his repeatedly being deposed and banished from Alexandria.

An important event in Alexandria's Christian history occurred towards the close of the century, when the Emperor Theodosius embarked on a new policy that affected the city. To enhance Constantinople's religious prestige, he declared in 391 that the church in Constantinople should also rank first in the East and second only to Rome in the whole empire, a position previously enjoyed by Alexandria. To accelerate matters the emperor convened a council at Constantinople, with Alexandria's participation, to confirm the superior position of his capital as the *Nova Roma* of the East. Thus Alexandria was outmaneuvered and could not react promptly enough. Besides, there were other pressing developments at hand, and it was not wise to openly confront the emperor.

Sentiment was brewing inside Alexandria for a final showdown with the pagans. The Emperor Theodosius had embroiled the churches of the provinces in an attempt to eradicate paganism from the empire. In Alexandria, events took a tragic turn. Theophilus, the fanatic bishop at the time, obtained the emperor's approval to transform the Temple of Dionysus into a church. His drastic measures frightened many pagan inhabitants who, with anguish and foreboding, sought refuge in the formidable compound of the Serapeum. It was like a stronghold, massively built on raised ground in the midst of the crowded Egyptian quarter south of the city. As mentioned earlier, a "daughter branch" of the old Great Library had survived on the premises, protected by the sanctity of the temple.

Authorized by imperial decree, Theophilus led his fanatic mob to the entrance of the Serapeum and read the emperor's words to a terrified crowd. Filled with alarm and panic, they took flight, while Theophilus strode up the temple steps and gave the first blow to the cult statue of Serapis. His frenzied Christian followers ran amok in the temple, destroying,

demolishing and plundering. When the devastation was complete, Theophilus ordered a church to be built in its place and named after Honorius, the emperor's youngest son.

The attack on the Serapeum put an end to the library as well as to the temple. The war on the ancient "pagan" books extended to other temples as well, such as the Caesareum which was converted into a church by Athanasius. The Christian historian Orosius, who visited Alexandria in 415, records with sorrow:

There are temples nowadays, which we have seen, whose book-cases have been emptied by our men. And this is a matter that admits no doubt.

It is very probable that the Mouseion, whose very name signified "Temple of the Muses," could not have long survived Theodosius' decree of 391. The last-known scholar from that famous institution was Theon, the distinguished mathematician active from about 365 to 380. Soon after the tragic events of the Serapeum, Theophilus' successor, Bishop Cyril, launched an attack on the still-popular philosophical schools of the city. One of the most distinguished victims of that campaign was Hypatia, the pagan philosopher, daughter of Theon, renowned for her knowledge and beauty and whose lectures were attended by both pagan and Christian students. She became the target of Cyril's campaign and, in 415, was ruthlessly attacked, mutilated and murdered by monks from the vicinity of Alexandria who were the bishop's followers.

The World Emporium in an Age of Faith

The Alexandria of the Byzantine age was still one of the world's great centers of trade and industry; free enterprise prevailed and, with the church, played a prominent role in the city's economic life. Glass, papyri and linen continued to be Alexandria's main industries, although their quality had deteriorated. Minor industries of ivory and ebony carvings, and the preparation of perfumes, aromatics and spices, which depended on imports, also flourished as Alexandrian merchants carried on much of their traditional international trade. A 4th century list of customs dues at the entrance of the canal to Alexandria mentions "sailors to India," and the accounts of the voyages of Cosmas, the Egyptian sailor-monk in the 6th century, bear witness to Alexandria's ongoing trade with Arabia, India and Ceylon. Alexandrian ships continued to sail to all the main Mediterranean ports with one significant change: Constantinople was gradually taking the place of Rome.

A 6th century papyrus document illustrates Constantinople's new prominence following the fall of Rome. It lists a loan of 20 *solidi* (a Byzantine gold coin weighing about 4.25 grams) to two Egyptians from Aphroditopolis (Kom Ishqao) in Upper Egypt, by Flavius Anastasius, the financier and head of the "Holy Bank" – the Imperial Bank in Constantinople. They borrowed the money at 8 percent interest and repaid it in Alexandria. This contract shows the close financial connection between Alexandria and Constantinople. Anastasius' office in Alexandria not only undertook commercial transactions, it also performed the duties of an international bank. The money that the two debtors paid at Alexandria was not forwarded to Constantinople, but remained in Alexandria to be employed in other commercial transactions. This also shows how big financiers and businessmen from Constantinople replaced those from Rome with their own offices and agents in Alexandria.

The church itself, like the temples of old, became an important economic concern. It owned large areas of land in many villages scattered around Alexandria and Lake Mareotis. It also invested in foreign trade. The biography of St. John the Almsgiver – perhaps the most humane and likable of Alexandrian bishops in the hard times of the early 7th century, not long before the Arab conquest – reveals the great wealth of the Alexandrian church. It owned its own commercial fleet in the Mediterranean that imported grains from Sicily in time of famine, and on another occasion was dispatched to Jerusalem with provisions when that city

was attacked by the Persians. Historians also record 13 ships of the Alexandrian church, each loaded with 10,000 *artabae* of wheat, linen, silver and other precious goods, sinking in a storm in the Adriatic Sea. One of the stories of miracles tells how John the Alsmgiver loaned a ship to a pious Alexandrian merchant whose own vessel had been wrecked. It was to sail to Britain with 20,000 *artabae* of wheat to be exchanged for tin. On the return voyage, the tin is said to have miraculously turned to silver.

The general impression on the eve of the Arab conquest is that the church in Alexandria grew stronger and richer as the central government in Constantinople grew weaker.

Left:

Head of Emperor Augustus (30 B.C.-14 A.D.) sculpted in marble. Graeco-Roman Museum, Alexandria.

81

The Great Library and Mouseion: Intellectual Center of the World

by Dr. Mostafa El-Abbadi

Alexander's conquests in Europe, Asia and Africa had far-reaching consequences. His ambition to set up a universal state was coupled with a serious desire to explore distant regions of the then little-known world, and he commissioned many expeditions. Though his dream of a world state did not materialize due to his early death, the reports from these expeditions survived and later motivated unprecedented scientific investigation of the earth. In fact, a renaissance of human culture had begun, and it was at this opportune moment in history that the Great Library and the Mouseion, its research center, were founded. A great light began to shine in Alexandria.

Soon after Alexander's death, his generals divided up his empire and eventually set up their own independent kingdoms. A feverish rivalry arose among them; each wanted his kingdom to be the greatest and most prestigious in learning and culture. Outstanding in this respect were the Ptolemies of Egypt, the Seleucids of Syria and the Attalids of Pergamum. Each, in an effort to achieve cultural supremacy, established libraries in their capitals.

In fact, libraries as an institution are very old. All ancient and medieval civilizations had their great libraries: Egypt, Mesopotamia, Syria, Greece, Rome and the Islamic world. And all of them perished in time. But the most famous among them all was undoubtedly the Great Library of Alexandria. Not only was it the largest in antiquity, but it induced remarkable momentum in scientific research that attracted scholars from all over the Mediterranean. Even after its disappearance with the decline of the ancient world, it survived in the memory of medieval authors. To this day, its fate continues to attract speculation and spark contention among scholars. This extraordinary interest in the Great Library and its research institute, the Mouseion, is understandable: They were the chief representations of the civilization of their time. They upheld the banner of international scholarship and learning for more than seven centuries throughout the then-known world.

Alexandria's Great Library and Mouseion were founded in about 295 B.C. when King Ptolemy I appointed Demetrius of Phaleron, a former pupil of Aristotle, to take charge of the twin institutions. The earliest reports assert that Demetrius had a large budget and a mandate from the king to collect "all books in the world." The goal was to collect a half-million manuscripts, and successive Ptolemaic kings were indomitable in their efforts to acquire them. Fabulous stories circulated about the lengths they would go to achieve this aim. One report says they confiscated any books not in stock in the library from passengers who sailed into Alexandria. Another tells how Ptolemy III deceived Athenian authorities when they let him borrow the original manuscripts of Aeschylus, Sophocles and Euripides against a large amount of silver as surety. He kept the originals, sent back carefully made copies and forfeited the silver. The usual procedure, however, was to purchase books from the famous marts of Athens, Rhodes and other Mediterranean cities. It is believed that before long the bulk of classical Greek works had been amassed in Alexandria.

But the universal library envisaged for the city "had to contain the writings of all nations" – that is, all those worth serious attention – according to the ancient writers Aristeas, Irenaeus, and Justinus. Foremost among non-Greek writings were the Egyptian "sacred records" that Manethon, the Egyptian priest who knew Greek, had compiled. Berossus, a Chaldean priest, wrote a history of Babylonia in Greek; Hermippus, a pupil of Callimachus – the great Alexandrian poet-scholar in the 3rd century B.C. – wrote a book "in two million lines" on Zoroastrianism that infers that records of the Perisan Mazdean faith were available in Alexandria. Buddhist writings could also be found as a result of the exchange of embassies between the Indian Prince Asoka and Ptolemy II. Finally, the rapid Hellenization of the large Jewish community in Alexandria and Egypt made the translation into Greek of the *Pentateuch* – the first five books of the Old Testament – a practical necessity. The result was the *Septuagint* version of the Old Testament that has survived as one of the most valuable

translations in history.

Within half a century, the Great Library proved too small for the wealth of books acquired, so Ptolemy III (246-221 B.C.) decided to attach to the newly rebuilt Serapeum, a branch known as the Daughter Library.

The Mouseion followed the basic pattern of the two famous Athenian philosophic schools, the Academy of Plato and the Lyceum of Aristotle. The name Mouseion means "Temple of the Muses," and indicates Greek roots since such shrines were customary features of the Athenian schools. Philosophic and artistic inspiration was commonly attributed to the Muses, and Vitruvius, the 1st century A.D. Roman architectural writer, included science in that category. He quotes the story of Pythagoras, who believed that he would not have made a certain mathematical discovery had it not been for the inspiration of the Muses to whom he sacrificed and gave thanks. The combination of the study of science and literature was first represented at the Lyceum in Athens, and later, at the Mouseion in Alexandria. Strabo describes the layout of the Mouseion:
It was part of the royal palaces, it had a walk, peripatos, *an arcade,* exedra, *and a large house in which was a refectory for the members. They formed a community who held property in common with a priest appointed by the kings (and under the Roman Empire, by Caesar) in charge of the Mouseion.*
Mention of the presiding priest underlines the religious character of the institution.

And under the Ptolemies' patronage and renowned generosity, the Mouseion rapidly attained international fame. It attracted the best minds of the age. Strato, the leading physicist from the Athens Lyceum, was received there in the 3rd century B.C. and tutored Ptolemy Soter's

Facing page:

A strong head in grey granite believed to be that of Mark Antony (d. 30 B.C.). Another identification as King Ptolemy VIII (d. 116 B.C.) has also been suggested. Graeco-Roman Museum, Alexandria.

son; two other distinguished men of letters and critics, Philitas of Cos and Zenodotus of Ephesus responded to Soter's invitation and took charge of the literary education of Philadelphus. But the name that outshone all others was Euclid, the father of mathematics, who is believed to have been an Alexandrian by birth. His famous *Elementa Mathematica* was presented to Soter.

Soter's successors were all well educated, and they continued to acquire the foremost scholars of the time in the various branches of knowledge. Scholars could reside either in the large facilities at the Mouseion mentioned by Strabo or in lodgings in town. Free board and lodging and exemption from taxation were not the only attractions of membership in the Mouseion, for high stipends were also paid.

Although Strabo called the Mouseion a *synodos*, or community that shared property and enjoyed a certain degree of autonomy in running its own affairs, it was, in fact, in no way a free association of scholars. The impression given is that it was a "royal society" in the strictest sense of these words – membership depended on the king's approval. Admittedly, scholars freely pursued their work, but they were fully aware that they were on "His Majesty's service." Their work and pension depended solely on the king's pleasure. In the 2nd century B.C., a civil war developed between Ptolemy VI and his younger brother Euergetes II. Euergetes persecuted several groups, including members of the Mouseion who were forced to flee the country. There must have been many who fled since Menecles of Barca, the historian, later stated that Alexandrian scholars in their diaspora educated Hellenes and barbarians alike in every branch of knowledge.

Under the Ptolemies, the Mouseion was basically a research center; no regular teaching is reported to have taken place there. Yet we frequently read in the scholars' biographies that they were teachers or pupils of an eminent member of the Mouseion. This could be explained by the practice of enlisting young men as research assistants. Thus Apollonius of Perga is said to have been "a pupil in Alexandria of the pupils of Euclid." In medicine, a form of apprenticeship seems to have developed within the clinics of the distinguished masters. Public teaching in the form of lectures and symposia, occasionally attended by the king, must have also taken place. It is generally believed, however, that teaching gradually increased with time. By the end of Ptolemaic rule in Egypt and the arrival of the Romans, scholarship was on the decline, but Alexandria still offered the best academic training available.

The Best Minds in the World

The supremacy of Alexandria in literature is indicated by the fact that the term "Alexandrian" has been applied to Greek poetry composed between about 300 to 30 B.C. In fact, Alexandria seemed to be the literary capital of the Greek world due to its Great Library and Mouseion. Given Alexandria's scholarly background, the new poets perceived that the great Athenian literature of the 5th century was so much the product of a particular time and place, that to imitate it would be futile. Thus, they consciously sought to be original and turned to earlier narrative and lyric verse that they evolved along new, unexplored lines. They created two new poetic forms that have become a part of the world's literary culture. One is the epigram, a short poem that

Facing page:

A fresco from a tomb at Wardian, a district in western Alexandria, depicts a vivid scene from Egyptian rural life: Two robust oxen draw a sakiyeh, *or water-wheel, while a boy in charge plays a set of pipes. Below them is a canal or pond with plants and water fowl. Roman Period. Graeco-Roman Museum, Alexandria.*

expresses one simple emotion – particularly love – in pointed, often ingenious ways; the other extended the elegiac couplet from mournful themes to narrative of any kind. With these forms as vehicles, poets indefatigably sought new subjects or old themes that could be treated from fresh angles in language that retained the flavor of antiquity, but showed some novelty of formation or new shade of meaning at every turn. The emphasis was on polished style, erudition and learning. From this period stem the most influential of the poets whose works have survived to this day – Callimachus of Cyrene, Theocritus of Syracuse and Apollonius of Rhodes (Rhodius).

These three masters highlight the Alexandrian school of poetry, but there were many others – their contemporaries as well as their successors, into the 1st century B.C. – who maintained with varying degrees of success the literary principles formulated by the great masters. The literary modes and forms of this school spanned the entire Mediterranean area, and its influence was particularly strong during the golden age of Latin literature. Alexandrianism became fashionable in Rome in the last century of the republic and in the early days of the empire when Alexandrian literary models were widely translated, adapted and imitated. This is reflected in the bucolics of Virgil, the love poems of Catullus, the epigrams of Propertius and in Ovid's *Amores* and *Metamorphosis*.

The founding of the Mouseion and the Great Library established the right approach to sound academic research in Alexandria. The time was ripe for new developments in the human intellectual experience. It is true that great heights had already been reached that would be difficult to surpass, especially

in epic poetry, drama and philosophy. But in other fields, such as linguistics and literary and scientific studies, the situation was different. These could not be effectively pursued without prolonged and sustained scholarship, and this was possible only under the patronage of the rival Hellenistic monarchies. Due to its overt consciousness of the importance of manuscripts and libraries, Hellenistic civilization has been disparagingly described as bookish. Fortunately, recent studies reveal the originality of much of the work accomplished by the pioneers of the 3rd and 2nd centuries B.C. Perhaps for the first time, the principles of scientific research were developed and applied with impressive results in disciplines as diverse as mathematics, physics, medicine, geography, astronomy and textual criticism. The wealth of books the Alexandrian scholars had at their disposal was a necessary tool, and what an unprecedented resource that was. It combined, for the first time, the experience of both classical Greece and the ancient Near East. But even more important was the critical attitude taken by the earlier Alexandrian scholars. No book, no written authority, however great, was accepted on trust alone; for their final judgement, these scholars accepted only experimentation, mathematical proof and arguments based on evidence.

Great research had already been done in civilizations in the ancient Near East and in classical Greece, of course, but there is little doubt that, as a result of Alexander's global adventure, the world stood on the threshold of a new intellectual experience, and Alexandria was leading the way. A few examples illustrate the nature of Alexandrian scholarship. First, in literary studies their approach was singular; their immediate concern was the preservation and

Facing page:
The head of a statue of a woman stands in a niche in the vestibule on the second sub-story of the Catacombs of Kom el-Shugafa. The style of the headdress is reminiscent of mummy portraits. Limestone. 2nd-3rd century B.C.

Following pages:
A funerary scene from the Catacombs of Kom el-Shugafa, the largest Roman funerary complex in Egypt and the most important in Alexandria. The scene portrays Osiris mummified and laid out on a funeral couch shaped like a lion. Anubis, god of embalming (with a dog's head), stands behind the couch. On the floor are three canopic jars to preserve the entrails of the deceased: One has a hawk's head as a cover, another a human head, and the third, a dog's head. The entire scene illustrates the dominance of Egyptian religious beliefs in Alexandria during the Roman Period.

understanding of works written in past ages. This new discipline came to be called textual criticism. Various copies of the same work in the Great Library presented scholars with both the problem and the opportunity to decide the correct reading of a text. The process required extensive investigation, not only into the language and diction of the author, but also into the age in which the text was written. This discipline is now pursued universally and is considered basic for literary studies.

Other fields in which Alexandria excelled were astronomy and geography. These appear to have been introduced under Philadelphus by Aristarchus of Samos, one of antiquity's most original minds. It is unfortunate that none of his writings have survived. His brilliant observation that the sun and not the earth is the center of the universe is known only because it is mentioned in passing byArchimides. The great Eratosthenes of Cyrene, one of the eminent scholars who occupied the post of chief librarian, is better known today. He is famed for his scholarship in a variety of fields. Indeed, his versatility and many facets call to mind the great humanists of the European Renaissance. His scholarship embraces poetry, philosophy, literary criticism, geography, astronomy, mathematics and scientific chronology. But Eratosthenes' greatest achievement was in geography. In his book, *On the Measurements of the Earth*, he not only made an unprecedented attempt to measure the circumference of the earth, he also tried to determine the distance of locales from each other, as well as their latitude and longitude. In his main work, the *Geographica*, he showed how familiar and critical he was regarding the entire earlier history of geography. As a result,

as Strabo observed, he found it necessary "to make a complete revision of the early geographical map." He was also a great humanist, which was rare if not unique in his time. He censured those who divided mankind into two groups, Greeks and non-Greeks, and he condemned those who advised Alexander the Great to treat the Greeks as friends and non-Greeks as enemies. Eratosthenes praised Alexander for disregarding this advice and advocated the Stoic moral principles of virtue and vice as the criteria for judging men.

Alexandria had an advantage over other centers of medical study and training: Ptolemaic patronage, which encouraged the development of academic research. In the Greek world before Alexandria, all medical practitioners belonged to the traditional discipline founded by Hippocrates. In the Hellenistic age, several new medical schools, or "houses," appeared as a result of new research developed at Alexandria and its rival capital Antioch-on-Orontes. One of the leading professors of the "new medicine," was Herophilus of Chalcedon, who had his school in Alexandria.

Herophilus and his "house" directed their greatest efforts toward "scientific" medicine. In contrast to the classified mass of physical observations and disease descriptions compiled by Hippocrates' school on the island of Cos, the Herophileans developed direct knowledge and precise terminology. To achieve this, Herophilus embarked on a new study of the human body based on anatomy and human vivisection. His pioneer work was later bitterly criticized by the inferior methodist school of medicine in Rome whose representative, Tertullian, described the great Alexandrian surgeon as: "Herophilus, the

Facing page and below:
The limestone statue of a man stands in a niche cut in the wall in the vestibule of the Catacombs of Kom el-Shugafa. The Catacombs are unique in that they are on three subterranean levels to a depth of about 150 feet, reached by a circular staircase. The lowest level is in danger of being submerged by rising ground water, as seen below. Besides the vestibule, there is a rotunda and a banquet hall. In this particular statue, the torso itself is Egyptian in style, whereas the head is of Greek design. It is a good example of the mixture of styles in Roman Egypt. 2nd-3rd century A.D.

Intellectual Center

A bas-relief represents a priest wearing two feathers on his head and clothed in a panther skin thrown over a long robe. He offers a lotus bud and a cup with an ewer to a deified woman who wears a wig and a diadem surmounted by the solar disk. In the middle stands an altar shaped like a sheaf of papyrus. 2nd-3rd century B.C. Catacombs of Kom el-Shugafa.

physician, that butcher who cut up hundreds of human beings so that he could study nature." But Galen, the distinguished 2nd century A.D. physician, was genuinely appreciative.

In connection with the ovarian arteries and veins observed by Herophilus in his anatomy of the womb, Galen admits:

I have not seen this myself in other animals except occasionally in monkeys. But I do not disbelieve that Herophilus observed them in women; for he was efficient in other aspects of his art, and his knowledge of facts acquired through anatomy was exceedingly precise and most of his observations were made, not as in the case with most of us, on brute beasts, but on human beings themselves.

A breakthrough was also achieved in neurology and brain function. Earlier, Aristotle had followed others and depended on mere intelligent observation. He gave ten excellent but mistaken reasons for locating the seat of thinking in the heart. Herophilus, however, through his anatomical studies of the nervous system, proved once and for all that the brain and not the heart was the seat of human intelligence.

To what extent was there an interchange between Greek and Egyptian medical experience? Details are still debated among specialists, but it can be shown that the two traditions were not isolated from each other. Since the 5th century B.C., the Greeks thought highly of the advances made by Egyptian doctors. Herodotus, more than 100 years before the founding of Alexandria, reports with admiration that medical specialization was highly developed in Pharaonic Egypt. He mentions specialized doctors for the eyes, the head, the teeth, the stomach and even for what he calls the "invisible diseases" –

probably meaning nervous disorders.

A papyrus fragment from the 2nd century B.C. refers to an Egyptian specialist in Alexandria. A woman writes:

I understand you studied the Egyptian language.
I congratulate you and myself, because now you will go to the city (Alexandria) and teach pupils at the teaching clinic of clyster [enema]-specialists of Phalu, and you will have provision for your old age.

This papyrus provides an interesting insight. Besides the "teaching houses" of Greek doctors, it also documents an Egyptian clyster-specialist, Phalu, who had his own training establishment in Alexandria. The city's bilingualism confronted him with Greek-speaking pupils, and to overcome the language barrier, he employed a Greek who also knew Egyptian to help him instruct those pupils.

Phalu's case seems to represent a high standard of medical practice among Egyptians in Graeco-Roman Egypt. By the end of the 1st century A.D., [as mentioned in chapter two], Pliny the Younger had been cured from a serious illness by a gifted Egyptian doctor from Memphis called Arpocras, who was a resident alien in Rome. At Pliny's request, the Emperor Trajan granted the doctor both Alexandrian and Roman citizenship in one stroke. Arpocras is another indication of the use of Graeco-Egyptian medical expertise.

In Roman times, the Mouseion functioned more and more as a teaching institution. Early in the Augustan Age (30 B.C.-14 A.D.), Strabo still admired it and compared it favorably with schools on the other side of the Mediterranean. The Roman emperors still protected its members by perpetuating their right to sustenance and exemption from taxation. One report tells that the Emperor Claudius made "an addition to the Old Mouseion of Alexandria," and that Hadrian, a philhellene, also showed interest in its welfare.

Alexandria maintained its scientific movement, and in the 1st century A.D., Hero, an ingenious engineer, described simple steam engine devices. Unfortunately his principles for steam power were put to use only for fanciful toys and mechanical tricks, but never for large-scale practical purposes. In the 2nd century, Claudius Ptolemaeus, who came from middle Egypt, was the last and perhaps the most influential of all the ancient geographers and astronomers. His work was translated into Arabic under the title of *Almagesti*. It was respected as the last word in geography throughout the Middle Ages and the early Renaissance. He followed the earth-as-center-of-the-universe theory rather than Aristarchus' heliocentric concept. In this error he was followed by all medieval geographers, both in the East and West, until 1543, when Copernicus dethroned the earth and put the sun at the center of all planetary orbits. In the 2nd century, Alexandria's reputation for medical studies attracted Galen, the last of the great physicians of the ancient world. The impact of this education on Galen was so great that he immortalized much of what we know of Alexandrian medicine in his writings.

The Rise of Spiritual Philosophy

Philosophy did not flourish under the Ptolemies, and the few Sceptic philosophers who briefly sojourned in the city during the 3rd century B.C. did not arouse genuine philosophical interest among Alexandrian scholars. In the 1st century B.C., however, there was definitely a growing interest in philosophy. This was

probably in response to certain tendencies that prevailed among intellectuals around the Mediterranean and grew as the Roman Empire expanded. For it had become customary among intellectuals and the upper classes to adhere to one of the more popular philosophies of the day, especially Stoicism and Epicurianism. Others belonged to schools such as the Academics, the Peripatetics, the Sceptics, the Cynics and the Neo-Pythagorians. This was true in practically all the centers of civilization around the Mediterranean, and seems to have taken root in Alexandria during the 1st century B.C. There, it was best represented by Antiochus of Ascalon, the philosopher whose views were distinguished by eclecticism, or a blending together of different systems of thought. Although a professed Academician, he emphasized the similarities between Plato and Aristotle; he also incorporated certain elements of Stoic morals, human partnership and pervasive reason. His blending of these three major philosophies was to have a far-reaching influence on the development of Neoplatonism and later, on the Arabs' understanding of Aristotle.

This fusion of various religious beliefs with philosophical eclecticism had a profound impact on many a conscientious and sensitive thinker during the Roman Empire. In Alexandria however, two main reactions are recognizable. One developed within the religious thought of the Jews, and of the Christians afterwards; the other was formulated by the pagan philosophers. The Jewish philosopher Philo is considered the precursor of the Judaeo-Christian school of thought, for he was both a staunch believer in the Holy Scriptures as well as a great admirer of Greek philosophy as it had developed in Alexandria. Yet

27031

he was also alarmed by the number of young, educated Jews attracted to the philosophic schools and abandoning Judaism. Thus he took a new approach to philosophically interpreting the Jewish faith. He achieved this by falling back on the prevailing eclectic method derived from the various schools, and by drawing on an Alexandrian blend of Platonism and Stocism already formulated a century earlier by Antiochus.

Yet Philo's main contribution was not to philosophy but to the study of Judaic and Christian theology. By the beginning of the 3rd century, Christianity had grown into a powerful movement, a threat already felt by the imperial government. It had its own teachers and school that openly challenged the pagan Mouseion and its affiliated philosophic schools. One of Christianity's great early scholars was Origen (185-252 A.D.), who was born in Alexandria of Christian parents and in 203 succeeded Clement as head of the Christian school. As a senior contemporary of Plotinus, the great Alexandrian philosopher, he was exposed equally to the influences of philosophic and Gnostic teachings prevailing in Alexandria at the time. In order to better understand pagan thought, he attended the Neoplatonic lectures of Ammonius Saccas and also visited Rome. As a biblical scholar, he followed the characteristic Alexandrian method of textual criticism. In his study of the Old Testament he compared the original Hebrew text with the four Greek translations, including the *Septuagint*. His study of the New Testament testifies to his vast knowledge and extensive reading of earlier works. He based his understanding on the belief that the Scriptures had three senses – the literal, the moral and the spiritual – which he compared to the body, the soul and the spirit, a method directly derived from Stoic philosophy.

The fundamental religious issues were not confined to Judaism and Christianity. They appear to have dominated the entire intellectual environment of the time. Under the influence of monotheistic trends, a new, independent and very active movement known as Gnosticism grew and, during the first three centuries of the empire, constituted a challenge to almost all other religions. Gnostics resented the traditional pagan religions and rejected the principle of revelation connected with the monotheistic religions. It was a religious philosophy that believed in the existence of a divine supreme being and was based on mystic knowledge of that being. The attainment of true knowledge – namely knowledge of God and the universe – was a gift from God that could be gained only by special spiritual exercises and prolonged meditation. In spite of its attraction for certain contemplative individuals, Gnosticism never became popular with the common people. For them it lacked the positive vigor that arouses the enthusiasm of the multitudes. On the other hand, it also failed to attract the more sophisticated minds because it lacked the rigor and precise thinking necessary to a coherent philosophic system. It is not surprising either that many Gnostics gradually turned into mystic Christians.

The full philosophic response to this challenging religio-intellectual situation can be found in Neoplatonism, the last phase in the history of ancient philosophy. This school of thought evolved out of the eclectic tendency that reached its zenith in the 3rd century in the hands of Plotinus, the greatest representative of the Alexandrian school of philosophy.

Facing page:

Fresco from the Tegran Tomb, Alexandria, depicts two women mourners facing each other as protectors of the mummified corpse laid on the bier. They are perhaps meant to represent the goddesses Isis and Nephtis. On the back wall above the bier is the winged sun-disk. On the ceiling is a head of Medusa encircled by garlands. 2nd century A.D.

Below:

Below:
A gilded silver goblet decorated with a vintage scene in high relief. The entire surface is covered with vines and bunches of grapes. Ptolemaic Period. Graeco-Roman Museum, Alexandria.

Plotinus was born in 204 A.D. at Lycopolis (Assiout) in Upper Egypt. He, like Origen, studied under Ammonius Saccas, the distinguished teacher of Platonic philosophy at Alexandria. Aware of and sensitive to the religious crosscurrents in the cosmopolitan city, he undertook the challenging task of working out a philosophic system that would encompass the entire complexity of religiophilosophic issues as they had developed in the 3rd century. In formulating his doctrines, he depended primarily on Plato and the Neo-Pythagorians. Yet multiple elements from the earlier philosophies were also incorporated into his coherent, but very intricate system. Much of his teaching has been preserved in six groups of nine books called the *Enneades.*

In its simplest terms, Plotinus' system is based on the concept of the dualism of – and, at the same time, the sharp contrast between – reason and matter, the intelligibles and sensibles, and the supersensual and phenomenal. In the supersensual, there is God: source of all being, the First, the Absolute One, unlimited and indivisible. From the First proceeds the thought and the soul, which have eternal timeless life. The sensual world, in contrast, is the realm of the divided and changeable; it is also the primary evil. Nevertheless, matter is necessary; mind must become matter, and the soul must bring forth the body as its abode. Since it is formed by the soul, however, the nature of things is as beautiful and perfect as a material world can be.

Finally, comes the mystic union, or *unio mystica.* Since the soul by nature belongs to a higher world, its highest aim can only be to free itself from inclination toward the sensual. Thus for Plotinus, happiness is the perfect life, which consists of thought. In other words, the soul's first condition is to liberate itself from the body and all that is connected with it in order to attain purification, or *katharsis.* The highest level is attained only when we are buried in ourselves. Then, when raised above thought in a state of unconsciousness, ecstasy and simplification, we are suddenly filled with divine light and become so completely one with the Primary Being that all differences between us and Him disappear. Plotinus is supposed to have attained that state of mystic union at least four times. But there are many problems in Plotinus' philosophy that we fail to understand. His strong belief in the Absolute One and his claim of divine union often lead us to forget that he belonged to the pagan world and that he accepted the existence of lesser gods.

The Church and Culture

Christianity became the official religion of the empire in the 4th century, and it gradually dominated many aspects of life. In Alexandria, however, long a great center of learning, multiple elements formulated the city's intellectual life.

In the 3rd and 4th centuries, a noteworthy development affected the Egyptian language. The vast majority of Egyptians, even in Alexandria, continued to speak and write their own language in its demotic form, which was a simplified modification of hieroglyphic script. It contained no vowels and could not easily incorporate foreign words and ideas. With the gradual expansion of Christianity, the need for a vocabulary able to express the new religious ideas also grew. The Egyptians took a revolutionary step: They freed their language from the limitations of the demotic script and adopted the Greek alphabet for writing. When they discovered that the

Greek alphabet could not provide for all the sounds in Egyptian words, they added six extra letters from the demotic. Thus the Coptic language was born to suit the new religion and its new philosophy. Their first achievement was to translate the Bible, which allowed Egyptians to read and enjoy the Holy Book in their own language. This undoubtedly contributed to the rapid expansion of Christianity among all classes of the population.

In Alexandria, however, individual secular philosophic schools survived despite the tragic events of the late 4th and early 5th centuries that destroyed the Mouseion and its membership. The rivalry between the old pagan and the new Christian schools persisted, and foreign students continued to come to Alexandria to study at institutions of both types.

One foreign student who came to Alexandria late in the 5th century was Severus of Antioch, still unbaptized, to study "the humanities," i.e. pagan learning. Many of his fellow students and friends came from outside Egypt, including Thomas the Sophist of Gaza, Zenodotus of Lesbos, Paralios of Caria and Zacharia of Gaza, the biographer. Zacharia gives us a vivid picture of how both professors and students were divided between pagan and Christian schools, and he tells about a student quarrel when Paralios of Caria converts to Christianity.

Many Egyptians also came to study in Alexandria in those days and ended up joining teaching staffs. An interesting example is Horapollon, the teacher of philosophy, who headed the pagan school whose students were involved in the Paralios quarrel. Horapollon was from Upper Egypt and was not the first of his family to go to Alexandria. The teaching profession, like others in

Byzantine times, tended to be hereditary, and Horapollon writes with pride that his father and other forebears had been professors and teachers in Alexandria.

Teaching in Alexandria at that time had a reputation that compared favorably with other centers of learning in the Mediterranean. Ammianus Marcellinus, the great Latin historian, draws a lively picture of Alexandria's intellectual life then:

Even now in that city the various branches of learning make their voices heard: For the teaching of the arts are still alive, the geometer's rod reveals hidden knowledge, the study of music has not yet completely dried up there, harmony has not been silenced and some few still keep the fires burning in the study of the movement of the earth and stars; in addition to them there are a few men, learned in the science which reveals the ways of fate. But the study of medicine … grows greater from day to day.

The students of ancient Alexandria, like their successors in major modern universities, felt special pride in their schools, and there seems to have been a kind of rivalry between universities as well. Alexandria's chief rival was still Athens, where students prided themselves on being attached to the places where Plato and Aristotle once taught. This rivalry between the two cities produced one of the most pleasant letters of Synesius, bishop of Cyrene. He lived in the trying times of the late 4th and early 5th centuries when paganism was being persecuted by every means. As a young man, he came to Alexandria and was privileged to study under the illustrious Hypatia, the pagan woman philosopher and martyr, whom he respected and admired greatly. Synesius was an intelligent man with a simple nature, a warm

character and strong attachments. The bishop's visit to Athens in later years aroused memories of his student days at Alexandria. He writes to his brother and amusingly describes his feelings:

I shall gain not only this by my voyage to Athens, an escape from my present evils, but also a relief from doing reverence to the learning of those who come back from Athens. They differ in no wise from us ordinary mortals. They do not understand Aristotle and Plato more than we do, and yet they go among us as demi-gods among mules, because they have seen the Academy, the Lyceum and the Poecile where Zeno gave his lectures on philosophy. However the Poecile no longer deserves its name, for the proconsul had taken away all the images, and has thus humiliated these men's pretensions to learning.

In another letter, he remarks:

Athens has no longer anything sublime except the country's famous names.... Today Egypt has received and cherishes the fruitful wisdom of Hypatia. Athens was aforetime the dwelling place of the wise; today the beekeepers alone bring it honor.

What happened to this great seat of learning at Alexandria and to the libraries that are estimated to have housed a half-million books? Evidence supports a scenario in which the entire Great Library, close to the harbor, was accidentally burned down during Caesar's Alexandrian War in 48 B.C. The Daughter Library satisfied the needs of scholars for four more centuries until it, too, was destroyed, along with the Serapeum, in 391 in accordance with the imperial decree to crush paganism. The 12th century story that Amr, the Arab general, destroyed the Royal Library after his conquest of Egypt, is no longer given much credence. It was probably a medieval fabrication by supporters of the new regime of Saladin.

Perhaps one of the most distinguishing features of Alexandrian intellectual life was its international character. Throughout a millennium, whether pagan or Christian, scholars were as mixed as its cosmopolitan population. This did not escape the acute observation of Strabo, who favorably compared Alexandria's academic life with other centers of learning: "The Alexandrians receive many foreigners but send out few of their own people to complete their training abroad."

The fact that an active international center of scholarship could function so well, in one place for so long, permitted a natural interchange of scientific experiences from diverse backgrounds. This probably explains much of the originality of ancient Alexandria's scholarly achievements.

Facing page:

A powerful forearm in marble holds a sphere. It must have originally belonged to a colossal statue either of an athlete or of an emperor holding the globe. Roman Period.
Graeco-Roman Museum, Alexandria

Following pages:

Two details from a large mosaic show, on the left, Nilotic scenes with a dwarf fishing and other flora and fauna; on the right, a family gathers beneath a canopy at a table laden with a variety of food while a dancer performs in front of them. Roman Period. Found at Thmuis (Tmai el-Amdid), Delta. Graeco-Roman Museum, Alexandria.

Alexandria:
French Expedition to the Modern Age

by Dr. Abdel/Azim Ramadan

Most historians agree that the golden age of Alexandria ended in 642 A.D. with the arrival of the Arabs, and that the city had a revival under Mohammed Ali (1805-1849).

But in the last three centuries of the first millennium and the first half of the second, Alexandria seemed to be just a large city with palaces. The Arabs did not value it as a defense line or a maritime trading center since they had no ships. Hence, their stay was rather fleeting, and their real influence on the city was minimal. Alexandria was mainly – almost purely – a Graeco-Roman city in Egypt, and the city's decline came with the end of the Graeco-Roman Period. The city went through a long period of stagnation and, apart from some sea and land battles fought there between the French, the British and the Ottomans, there would be little mention of Alexandria during this period in history books.

At the arrival of the French Expedition of 1798, Alexandria's strategic significance was no longer what it had been in Ptolemaic times when she was described as "the bride of cities," and was the center of world trade. Nor was it as important as during the Roman Empire, when she was the second greatest city of the world after Rome. Alexandria's stature declined after the Arab conquest of Egypt, when the country's foreign links turned from Europe (Greece, Rome and Constantinople) to Asia (the Arabian Peninsula, Damascus and Baghdad). Alexandria was no longer the capital of Egypt – the capital had moved to the inner part of the country, first to Fustat, then Qataii and finally to Cairo, all according to the succession of the ruling dynasty.

Nevertheless, Alexandria flourished up to the end of the 14th century. Then it began to steadily lose its importance due to two factors. First, in 1497, the Portuguese discovered the sea route to India via the Cape of Good Hope, and that resulted in most trade between Europe and India transferring from land routes to the Atlantic Ocean. Second, when the Ottomans conquered Egypt in 1517, the new invaders pursued a policy of isolationism. They were reluctant to re-activate trade with the West, fearing that trade would bring Western colonialism, and thus Western domination. The Ottomans went further and prevented European vessels from entering the Red Sea on the pretext that they would overlook the Muslim holy places in the Hejaz, a tradition that continued up to the end of the 18th century.

Nevertheless, Alexandria's strategic importance as a route into Egypt increased as France became convinced of the necessity to occupy Egypt and to open new areas in the East. This would compensate for its lost colonies in the West Indies and would control the land route – and ultimately the sea route – to India. It would also thwart the British advance in the Indian Ocean.

When the French troops landed, 18th century Alexandria was a small town located north of the old city. It sat on the peninsula between the Eastern and Western Harbors created when the island of Pharos was connected to the mainland by a narrow dike that was gradually widened by landfill.

At that time, the city had no buildings of importance. The 25 or 30 major mosques, the *Wikalat* (trade agencies) and public markets, as well as the houses and roadsides all had columns of limestone, marble, granite or alabaster. The columns, taken from ruined palaces in the old city, carried ancient inscriptions.

The city, according to the French historian Olivier, included 88 mosques – 36 were first-class mosques, and 42 were second class. More than 200 spinning mills made fine silk textiles for the rich, 400 mills made linen fabrics for the middle class and 50 others made rough woolen textiles for Bedouin Arabs. In addition, 50 factories made soap with oil imported from Greece, Crete and Syria. Red Marakishi leather and other high-quality leather work were also made in Alexandria.

The city's population at that time was about 8,000, according to Gratien Le Pere in *Description de l'Egypte*, and included Egyptians, Turks, Bedouins, Moroccans, Romans, Syrians and Jews, as well as some European Christians. However, by the time the French departed in 1801, Alexandria's population had decreased to about 7,000 because of the instability following the French invasion. The heavy fines and confiscation of property imposed on the citizens by the French, and the blockade of warships by the English,

compounded the city's problems. At the same time, the stagnation of trade and the outbreak of plague added to the city's miseries.

Napoleon Bonaparte's invasion of Alexandria started the night of July 2, 1798. The soldiers landed at Al Agami, 12 kilometers west of Alexandria. By 2 a.m., 5,000 soldiers had already reached the coast. They were divisions of Generals Kleber, Bon and Menou under the overall command of General Bonaparte. At 2:30 a.m. the troops marched parallel to the coast toward Alexandria. They reached the city walls at sunrise and began their siege.

The expedition consisted of 55 warships and 280 vessels carrying 36,826 soldiers as well as horses and guns. It was also accompanied by a large group of French savants who came to survey Egypt's economic and social culture.

Prior to the arrival of the French fleet in Alexandria, English warships led by Admiral Nelson came searching for the French. Nelson sent 10 of his officers to the city to meet Mohammed Kuraim, governor of Alexandria, and other city luminaries. The officers told the governor that the French might soon attack Egypt.

The French consul general slipped away and was brought by boat to meet Bonaparte as the French fleet neared Alexandria. He told Bonaparte about the governor's meeting with the British, and Napoleon decided to land his troops the night of July 2 – before the return of the English fleet, which was out searching for the French – and march on Alexandria before the town had enough time to organize its defenses. The troops reached the walls of the city at sunrise, and Bonaparte set up his command at Pompey's Pillar from which he watched the attack and issued orders to his generals.

Alexandria was the first

Egyptian city occupied by Bonaparte. It thus became the first Islamic Arab city belonging to the Ottoman State to be exposed to a European Christian military invasion in the modern age. Since the city belonged to an ancient Eastern civilization radically different from Europe's, Bonaparte was careful, even before his arrival in Egypt, to design a policy that would appeal to Alexandrians, and Egyptians in general, and draw them to his side. As early as June 27, he prepared a proclamation for the natives that was formulated into Arabic by the translators and Orientalists who accompanied him.

The proclamation was printed on the Arabic printing press aboard the commanding warship *L'Orient*; it was the first Arabic document produced by that press. It is noteworthy that before leaving Alexandria to occupy Cairo, Bonaparte gave orders to transfer the Arabic, Greek and French printing presses aboard *L'Orient* to the residence of the consul of Venice in Alexandria. He instructed that the machines were to be operational within 48 hours, and indeed, they produced 4,000 copies of the proclamation dated July 2, 1798, the day the French occupied the city. In it, Bonaparte proffered that he had come not to fight the Ottoman sultan, but to punish the *Sanagik* – the provincial Mamluk rulers – for their humiliation and disregard of the French and for their assault on French merchants. The proclamation reminded the Egyptians of the oppression of the Mamluks, who originally had been imported as slaves from Georgia and the Caucasus.

Bonaparte denied allegations that he had come to Egypt to eradicate Islam. "That is a flagrant lie," he stated. "Do not believe in it; tell the liars that I have come to retrieve your rights from the hands of the tyrants. I,

more than the Mamluks, believe in God and revere the great Prophet Mohammed and the Holy Quran."

Then he spoke in favor of the principles of the French Revolution. He stressed the equality of all people before God and said that what distinguishes one from another is only the mind, merits and knowledge. He mocked the Mamluks, saying, "There is a contradiction between them and the mind and virtues, and they have no qualifications to solely possess Egypt and to seize all the best things in it, from the beautiful slave girls and genuine horses to splendid houses."

He promised that Egyptians would have access to all these things: "From now on, no Egyptian should despair to be promoted to high positions or to reach noble ranks, that the scholars and virtuous and wise people will manage all matters, and in this way the conditions of the whole nation will improve."

Then he reminded the Egyptians of their ancient glory, saying, "In the past there were in the Egyptian land mighty cities and wide canals and prosperous trade; the injustice and greed of the Mamluks – nothing else – put an end to all that."

Nevertheless, circumstances in Alexandria did not go Bonaparte's way. Because of the state of war between France and England, the city was nearly strangled by a blockade, which thus antagonized the Alexandrians. Mohammed Kuraim led the resistance movement and was arrested and executed, but resistance against the French army spread throughout Egypt.

Although resistance ashore was widespread, the naval battle of Abu Qir in August 1798 was the main cause of the French expedition's failure. The conflict was fought between the French fleet, commanded by Admiral Brueys who was left behind by

Following pages:

Antique map shows Alexandria at the time of Napoleon Bonaparte's expedition around the turn of the 18th century. From the Description de l'Egypte, Etat Moderne, Vol. II.

M E R   M É D I

M E R

PHARE

Rayon du Marabou au Phare de

Fond de Roche

Passe des Djermes

Cap des Figuiers

Fort

ÎLE DU PHARE

Fort

Lac Salin

Moulin

S.te Chambre de q Constructions

Arsenal de la Marine

P O R T   V I E U X

Magasin de la Marine

Fond de l'arc et d'Herbe

Porte

Aiguade

Citerne

E N C E I

Mosquée des Septante

Porte des Catacombes

Fort

Rayon du Marabou à la Colonne de 10936.m o

Les Sondes des deux ports sont exprimées en Pieds.

Catacombes

Arcs

Mosquée

Catacombes

Cité

Côte

des

Arabes

la Tour

Mosquée

Catacombes et Temple souterram

Chemin

Cirque

Colonnes

Catacombes

Canal

1.er Pont

2.e Pont

d'Ale

L A C

Pl. 84.

MÉDITERRANÉE

TERRANÉE

le Diamant

Fond de Gravier

le Phare

Fond de Roche

Fond de Sable

Fond de Sable

Fond de Sable

Fond de Sable

Pharillon

Latitude

PORT NEUF

Côte couverte de Rochers

Môle ruiné

Santon

Canal ruiné

Tour des Romains

Vestiges d'un Canal

Murailles de Cléopâtre

Cimetière des

Chemin d'Aboukyr

Synagogue des Juifs

Citernes

Monastère Grec

ARABES

Porte de Rosette

DES

Mosquée (St Athanase)

Colonnes

Palais ruiné

Chemin de Rahmanyeh

de la Colonne

4e Pont

Aqueduc ou Souterrain

3e Pont

Môle ruiné

MARÉOTIS

MODERNE, ET DE LA VILLE DES ARABES.

Gravé par le Capitaine Cordier Adjudant de la place de Paris sous Mehuc.

Napoleon, and the British fleet, commanded by Lord Nelson. The battle was a disaster for the French – most of their ships were destroyed, and the rest were captured. More than 4,000 soldiers were killed, including Admiral Brueys and his best men. Abu Qir was the end of all French hopes to dominate the Mediterranean, and it was the strongest stroke against the French in Egypt.

After that, because of Alexandria's strategic siting on one hand, and the conflict between France and England on the other, Alexandria became a battleground between France and both England and Turkey.

In February 1799, an English warship bombarded Alexandria, and on July 14 an Ottoman army of 10,000, backed by the English fleet, landed in Abu Qir east of Alexandria and occupied the castle. A great ground battle took place in Abu Qir on July 25, 1799, which ended with the Ottomans' defeat. But that did not end the threat, for England decided to launch a big English-Ottoman expedition to expel the French from Egypt. The battle of Canop on March 21, 1801, left Alexandria under the siege of English troops led by General Hutchinson. The defeat and surrender of the French army in Cairo led to the agreement of June 27, 1801, and the subsequent departure of French troops in early August 1801. The position of the French troops in Alexandria was badly weakened, and on August 31 another agreement was concluded between the French and both the British and Ottomans that called for the withdrawal of French troops from Alexandria.

Throughout September 1801, ships left Alexandria carrying troops on their way back to France. Among them were 7,200 soldiers, 1,500 sailors, 1,400 diseased and 680 civilians. General Menou, who was infected with the plague during his last days in Egypt, was the last one to leave Alexandria, on October 18, 1801. His departure closed the book on the French expedition in Alexandria and all of Egypt.

After the French withdrawal, three forces maneuvered for power in Egypt: the Ottomans, the English and the Mamluks. In Abu Qir, nearly 6,000 Ottoman soldiers occupied sites adjacent to the Ottoman fleet's anchorage, and the British fleet was anchored in Alexandria's harbor. The Ottomans thought the time was opportune to make a move to restore their domination over Egypt, and conflict broke out between the Ottomans and the Mamluks in Cairo. The Mamluks, for their part, turned to the British for help. The popular revolution by the Egyptians that broke out in March 1804 ended this conflict, and the Egyptian leaders nominated Mohammed Ali, an Albanian officer in the Ottoman army, as ruler of Egypt. On May 13, 1805, the Ottoman sultan approved.

The English presence in Egypt during this time frame was reduced and restricted to Alexandria. Finally, England decided to pull out of the city completely. On March 14, 1803, General Stewart completed his preparations to leave. He delivered the towers and forts of Alexandria to Ottoman Governor Khurshid Pasha that same day. Two days later the English fleet sailed with 4,400 soldiers and put an end to the first English occupation.

Another British expedition, this one under Major General MacKenzie Fraser, began in March 1807 with orders to take Alexandria only, but not the rest of Egypt. The city's garrison was weak and Alexandria quickly capitulated under the threat of force. British troops advanced to Rosetta, but on March 31, in a fierce battle, they were defeated by its ruler, Ali Bey, with 170 killed, 250 wounded and 120 captured. The British retreated to Alexandria.

This expedition affected Alexandria's relationship with the rest of Egypt, which was cut off for seven years because the Supreme Porte – the Ottoman sultan's honored title – considered Alexandria a direct dependency of Istanbul and not under Egyptian rule. Pressures in Europe forced the British to withdraw from Alexandria, and on September 20, 1807, one day after the English withdrawal, Mohammed Ali entered the city in triumph for the first time and brought Alexandria back to the mother country.

The seizure of Alexandria by Mohammed Ali was another turning point in the city's history, and marked the beginning of the revival of a great city after several centuries of neglect. At first glance, Mohammed Ali recognized the importance of Alexandria, so he immediately laid foundations to ensure its development into the second city in Egypt after Cairo.

Mohammed Ali realized that the difficult travel and communications between Alexandria and the rest of the country would discourage any substantial development. Thus he proposed a canal to transport grain and other Egyptian products to Alexandria through the western tributary of the Nile. The work was finished in December 1820, and a great celebration was held in February 1821 to mark the arrival of Nile water at Alexandria. The new canal was named Al Mahmudiyah after the name of the Ottoman Sultan Mahmud II. It became the main route of transportation between Alexandria and the rest of Egypt. This canal was the starting point for the real cultural and social

development of 19th century Alexandria. The city's population rapidly grew to 60,000 between 1821 and 1840, and to 143,000 by 1848. By 1874, the population of Alexandria had reached 270,000.

Meanwhile, Mohammed Ali prepared Alexandria to be the safe harbor of his fleets. He completed a shipyard in 1831 thanks to several thousand workers and young technicians, including carpenters, ironsmiths, plumbers and mechanics. The new facility became one of Egypt's greatest military and naval establishments and an institute for educating and training Egyptian youth in the construction and repair of ships and marine equipment. And for navigation into and out of the harbor, a lighthouse was built on Ras El Tin Peninsula. It was one of the most beautiful constructions of the harbor.

After the completion of the Mahmudiyah canal, many European and Greek business and financial enterprises were established in Alexandria to develop the export and import trade. A great portion of the foreign community in Alexandria was made up of English subjects who immigrated to Egypt from Malta. In 1833, they numbered more than 3,000 people, or about 60 percent of the European community, followed by the Tuscans, most of whom were Jews, with 500 people; the Greeks, with 400; the French, with 300; and the Austrians with just under 300. Others came from Naples, Sardinia, Spain, Switzerland, Germany and Romania.

Mohammed Ali established a permanent committee for improving conditions in Alexandria. Its job was to develop the city and to promote cleanliness and public health. The committee also improved traffic control, supervised the construction of municipal buildings and

Following pages:

An 18th century view of what was then called the New Harbor. It is also known as the Eastern Harbor, and is seen from the old cemeteries on the isthmus that separate the Eastern and Western Harbors. To the far right is the Fort of Pharallion, of which nothing now remains, and to the left is Qayt Bay Fortress, which was just recently restored. From the Description de l'Egypte, Etat Moderne, Vol. II.

Cécile del.

VUE DU PORT-NEUF, PRISE DU CIM

CRE QUI LE SÉPARE DU PORT-VIEUX.

transferred all cemeteries outside the city walls.

Mohammed Ali's grandson, Abbas I, who succeeded him (1848-1854), was not a great builder like his grandfather. But, because he depended on England to support his regime, he signed a contract with an English company to build a railway from Alexandria to Suez. During his reign, the railway was completed as far as Kafr el Zayat, a distance of about 110 kilometers. The railway greatly increased Alexandria's importance, and the city continued to rapidly grow and develop.

His successor, Mohammed Said Pasha (1854-1863) was especially fond of Alexandria and lavished attention on the city. In his reign, the railway was extended all the way to Cairo, and the Mahmudiyah canal was greatly improved. He also connected Alexandria and Cairo with modern telegraph lines. Said built himself a lavish palace in the Kabbari District.

The next ruler, Ismail Pasha (1863-1879), wanted to modernize Egypt and Europeanize it. During his reign, Alexandria experienced even greater leaps in its development. The city expanded as internal and external trade grew, and there was an influx of immigrants who established foreign enterprises such as trade, transportation, shipping and navigation companies and some factories and banks. Trading activity in the harbor of Alexandria increased between 1863 and 1873 to constitute 94 percent of Egypt's total exports.

Ismail had new districts laid out and roads built. In the new Raml suburb, he built the Raml Palace. Ismail granted many plots of land in this district to Europeans who built scores of beautiful palaces. Among those was Count Zizinia, a Greek who was consul general of Belgium, after whom a part

of Raml is still named today.

Alexandria was one of the first Egyptian cities to build an underground sanitary sewer system. The first network began operating in 1878 and was gradually expanded as the population increased. During Ismail's reign, drinking water – taken from the Mahmudiyah canal and purified in a filtering station – was piped throughout the city. He also had several new streets constructed.

Inside the harbor, shipping docks and other marine facilities were built at a cost of more than three million Egyptian pounds during the years 1871-1879, a phenomenal sum at the time. Several lighthouses were also erected – the Agami Lighthouse in 1873, the Breakwater Lighthouse in 1876 and the Kabbari Lighthouse in 1877.

In 1863, Ismail inaugurated the railway running from Alexandria to the present site of Bolkley Station via Sidi Gaber Mosque. In the meantime, the Europeans became not only part of Alexandrian society, but also partners in the municipal administration that participated in the local executive authority. The police force included 50 foreigners, most of them Swiss. Theatres such as the Zizinia Theatre were also founded in the city.

That was the situation in Alexandria when the military revolution against tyranny and foreign control broke out in 1882, led by Orabi Pasha. Orabi was a *fellah*, or peasant farmer, himself, and was the first to rise from the ranks to become colonel of a regiment. He was thus able to mobilize the *fellaheen* and to threaten the position of the European powers in Egypt.

In response to the Orabi Revolution, both the English and French fleets arrived at Alexandria in May of that year ready to intervene if necessary. On Tuesday, July 11, Admiral Seymour gave his orders to open fire. The bombardment started at 7 a.m. and continued until 6 p.m. with only two short respites. The fleets' bombs fell randomly on all parts of the city, destroying its buildings and setting fires everywhere. Alexandria suffered greatly.

On July 12, the Orabians realized that the city would fall as soon as the fortifications were destroyed. They decided to retreat to the countryside to try to reorganize their resistance. In order to delay the advance of the British troops, the Orabi forces set fire to the city at the order of Soliman Dawood, commander of the Sixth Regiment. By that evening, Alexandria was aflame and continued to burn until the next day.

With the resistance put down, the British moved in and occupied Alexandria. They restored discipline to the city and commercial activity resumed. Under the British occupation of Egypt, Alexandria's cityscape became even more European and quite distinguished from any other city in Egypt.

As soon as the revolution was over, the Europeans returned to Alexandria in droves. According to the 1897 census, they accounted for 46,000, or 14.5 percent, of the city's population. That survey showed Greeks to be the biggest single ethnic portion with their community of 15,182 people. The Italians were next with 11,743 people; then the English, with 8,301; the French, with 5,221; and the Austrians, with 3,197.

During the first 25 years of the 20th century, the number of foreigners in Alexandria continued to increase. In 1917, their population was 84,705 – double that of 20 years earlier. In 1927, foreigners in Alexandria totaled nearly 100,000 people.

They controlled most of the city's economic activity through the flow of foreign capital and the "Capitulations" – treaties that applied European laws to European nationals living in Egypt. These were applied to Egypt as part of the Ottoman Empire and gave the Europeans enormous economic privileges.

Foreign communities in Alexandria were organized and effective. Each community celebrated its own national and social occasions, had its own chapel or synagogue, as well as clergy, schools, hospitals and cemeteries.

The Greeks constituted the biggest foreign community in Alexandria. In the 1947 census, they represented nearly 50 percent of the foreign residents in the city. Many Greeks said they felt like they were living in their own country; since it is the city of their compatriot, Alexander the Great, perhaps that is not surprising.

Greek families began moving to Alexandria in numbers in the period of Mohammed Ali. Since 1830, the Greek community has created its own services, projects, activities and educational schemes. When Greece became independent from the Ottoman State in the early 1830s, the Greek community of Alexandria acquired the privileges of the Capitulations and thus came under the protection of the newly born state; Greece's consuls general in Egypt became honored presidents of Alexandria's Greek community.

Over the course of a century, Greek financial institutions multiplied in the city. In the business community, names like Tozziza, Cozzika, Benachi and Salvago became familiar. The Greek community's cultural and informational activities also increased. Between 1862 and 1972, Alexandrian Greeks published 253 journals and magazines – most of them in Greek.

During the last hundred years,

Following pages:

Engraving shows Cleopatra's Obelisks along the Alexandrian shore of the Mediterranean at the end of the 18th century. The upright one now stands in Central Park in New York City. The fallen one, partially buried in the sand, now stands on the northern bank of the River Thames in London. From the Description de l'Egypte, Antiquités, *Vol. V.*

Cécile del.

Ballard Sc.

Egypt's Greeks published more than 5,000 books and booklets. Many Alexandrian Greeks studied the history, literature and linguistics of Egypt in general and Alexandria in particular. Moreover, many printing houses in Alexandria produced books by Greek authors dealing with Egyptian issues. A Greek-Arabic dictionary was published in 1898, and three Greek translations of the Holy Quran were published, one in Alexandria in 1879.

Italians made up the second largest community in Alexandria during the city's golden age of Europeans. Their population was estimated at 27,000 during the early 1930s. They founded a number of schools in the city, including what has become the Ras el Tin School and the Faculty of Agriculture in the University of Alexandria. They also built the Italian Hospital that was originally named for Benito Mussolini in the Al Hadarah District. *Il Messaggero Egiziano* was the Italian newspaper in Alexandria. In addition, the Banco di Roma, and the Commercial Bank are well-known financial institutions and there is an active Italian Chamber of Commerce.

The French were also an important community in Alexandria with their numerous and varied educational institutions. During the early 1930s, nearly a fifth of the more than 11,000 students in the 30 French institutes in Alexandria were French. Among these institutes were La Mission Laique, which owned and directed Le Lycee d'Alexandrie and the Frere des Ecoles Chretiennes which owned St. Marc and St. Catherine colleges in Muharram Bey and Bacchus.

Although the majority of the British community in Alexandria were Maltese, the English impact on Alexandrian society was evident. There were British schools, hospitals, charitable and humanitarian organizations, as well as social and commercial groups. In 1901, Victoria College in Azarita was founded. Following the pattern of English public schools, it accepted students of all nationalities. The school was moved to its present site at Victoria in 1909. St. Andrew's School was founded in 1859 and then moved to Silsilah in 1900. The Scottish School for Girls and the British Boys' School were founded in 1928. The English also established their medical, social, cultural and sportive institutions, such as the Anglo-Swiss Hospital, the British Book Club, the Sporting Club and the Union Club. The British Boat Club was founded in 1919, a boy scout troop was formed in 1912, and a girl scout troop followed in 1921.

In 1896, the influential British Chamber of Commerce was established in Alexandria. Its members were considered to represent British public opinion in Egypt. Up to 1930, the president of the Alexandria chapter also headed the British Chamber of Commerce in Egypt. The British also founded a Society for the Prevention of Cruelty to Animals in Alexandria.

Alexandria's Jewish community included several nationalities. As early as 1700, the Jews of Rosetta and Edku were attracted to Alexandria and lived east of the city. In the mid-18th century, Jews from Rosetta, Damietta and Cairo moved to Alexandria. Their numbers increased under Mohammed Ali, and in 1850, the Jewish community completed its Elidhou Hannabi Synagogue in Alexandria. Thanks to European charitable aid, Alexandrian Jews were able to organize their community and establish various educational, medical, sportive and social institutions in the city. At the beginning of World War I, more than 10,000 Jews emigrated from Palestine to Alexandria. Many of them were Russians. The Jews of Egypt issued in French the Zionist newspaper *La Liberté* which defended Egyptian national interests and was in close contact with the Egyptian majority party Al Wafd and its leader, Saad Zaghloul. Jews were also involved in Communist movements.

Throughout the period of the British occupation, Alexandria was a major base for the British fleet. Thus, the city played an important role in World War I as a Mediterranean base. During World War II, Alexandria became one of Britain's most important naval bases and an operations center for the war against the Axis forces in the African desert. Allied troops used the Alexandria railways, and the routes from Alexandria to Cairo and Mersa Matrouh were among the most strategic in the area. Consequently, Alexandria had to pay for its role, and the city became the target of German air raids that inflicted heavy damage. The victory of General Montgomery in El Alamein, however, saved the city from the Axis troops led by Field Marshal Rommel.

During the decades from 1922 to 1956, national independence in Egypt underwent three phases. Following the British declaration of February 28, 1922, a phase of incomplete independence laid the foundation for constitutional rule and established a government responsible before the parliament. The Treaty of Alliance concluded in August 1936 between Egypt and Great Britain inaugurated a new phase that terminated British occupation and transformed the occupation army into an allied army. The third phase began with the July 23 Revolution in 1952. Another agreement was signed on October 19, 1954, that provided for the complete evacuation of British troops from Egypt. That agreement,

however, was nullified by Britain's involvement in the triangle aggression against Egypt during the Suez Canal conflict of 1956.

As these three phases unfolded, Alexandria witnessed several great historical events. The Arab League was born there on October 7, 1944, after hard and long talks launched by Egypt with the Arab countries. The Arab Conference held at the University of Alexandria to discuss the terms of political unity issued the first Arab League document, known as the "Protocol of Alexandria."

In July 1952, the city witnessed the departure of King Farouk. Thus Alexandria saw the arrival of Mohammed Ali, the first ruler of modern Egypt in 1807, and also saw the last ruler in the Mohammed Ali dynasty fall 145 years later. Although Farouk lived in Al Muntazah Palace on the sea at the city's eastern end, and although the cabinet had its summer seat in the Bolkley area of Alexandria, the city soon declared its support for the Revolution. Naval forces joined the rebel troops, and a part of the army moved to Alexandria to put the city under its control. On Saturday, July 26, 1952, General Mohammed Naguib, general commander of the army, accompanied by Colonel Anwar Sadat (who later became a president of Egypt) went to the government's summer seat in Alexandria. They discussed with Ali Maher, the prime minister, the delivery of a message from the revolutionary command demanding that the king abdicate and leave the country that same day. Farouk signed the historical abdication document in Ras el Tin Palace, and left Alexandria forever for exile in Italy.

Another important event witnessed by Alexandria was the nationalization of the Suez Canal Company by Gamal Abdel Nasser on July 26, 1956. This event triggered the triangle aggression against Egypt by Great Britain, France and Israel that October. Anti-aircraft artillery in Alexandria played a key role in protecting the Egyptian navy from aerial bombardments.

While these political events unfolded, Alexandria underwent a new wave of construction and urban development. In 1925 Lake Al Hadara was drained and the suburb of Smouha was founded. In 1934, construction began on the 20-kilometer-long promenade and boulevard, known as the Corniche, that runs along the city's seacoast.

The Corniche and the long beaches beneath it have become one of Alexandria's most beautiful features. It has made the city Egypt's foremost summer resort, and tourism has become one of its most important resources. The city built bathing cabins along the beach, and tourist cafeterias and restaurants line the Corniche from Muntazah, Maamura and Abu Qir in the east to Agami, Hanoviel and Sidi Krir in the west.

Al Muntazah Palace, the summer seat of the former royal family was built on a plateau overlooking the most fascinating beach at the eastern end of the city. The palace was surrounded by vast gardens beside a man-made forest whose area together was about 370 *feddans*, which equals almost 384 acres. Both the beach and gardens of Al Muntazah were opened to the public after the Revolution. The small Salamlek Palace has become a tourist hotel, and in 1964, the impressive Palestine Hotel was built in the garden. Beautiful cabins and a marine cafeteria were built on the beach.

Modern Alexandria is also rich in wide, tree-lined roads such as Tariq Al Hurryiah, or Road of Liberty, that runs from Bab Sharq to the district of Victoria. Tariq Al Nasr, or Road of Triumph, connects the harbor to the city center, and the Suez Canal Road

provides a new approach to the city.

Alexandria also has a wealth of open public spaces. Khartoum Square, for example, is ornamented with statues and pillars. General Abdel Moneum Ryadh Square has a beautiful fountain and a clock made of planted flowers; the famous Raml Station Square provides a setting for the tram terminal; Saad Zaghloul Square has its statue of the great leader; and in the Silsilah area is the sculpture *Flying Sails*, by Fathy Mahmoud, that symbolizes an ancient myth about the birth of Alexandria.

In the center of the city there are several large gardens and parks such as Antoniadis Garden, the Zoological Gardens, the Rose Garden, the Open Park, Al Shallalat Garden and Al Muntazah Garden. Green areas are abundant in the streets and squares of the city and total 450 *feddans*, or nearly 467 acres.

Alexandria's harbors have kept pace with the city's growth. The famous, crescent-like Eastern Harbor, with Pharos Island at the western end and the Silsilah spur at the eastern end, is now used mainly by yachts and fishing boats. The Western Harbor is now the city's principal port anchorage for a wide range of large and small ships. It has several approaches from the city. The most important is the Passengers' Gate at the end of Al Nasr Street that connects the Maritime Station with Al Tahrir and Orabi squares in the heart of the city. The harbor includes the passenger terminal built in 1960 and newly renovated, a radio station, storage silos, refrigeration facilities, docks for oil tankers and 86 piers totaling more than 6.5 miles or about 10,500 meters of dockage. The port is able to receive and handle up to 65 ships at a time.

Meanwhile, Alexandria's shipyard – built in the era of

Pl. 95

VUE DE LA PLACE DES TOMBEAUX. 2 VUE DES TERRASSES D'UNE PARTIE DE LA VILLE.

Mohammed Ali – has been updated and developed into one of the most modern and highly regarded shipyards in the Mediterranean basin; its area totals 400 square kilometers, and with dock lengths of up to 1,000 meters, the yard can build ships of up to 30,000 deadweight tons. There are also two dry docks – the smaller serves ships with loads up to 10,000 tons and the larger, more modern one serves vessels with loads up to 85,000 tons.

During the last century, many historical and archaeological monuments dating back to Ptolemaic, Roman, Byzantine and Arab times have been discovered in Alexandria. In the Kom el-Shugafa District (site of the Pharaonic village of Rhakotis) the ancient Roman cemetery and catacombs were accidentally discovered in 1892. The Roman Amphitheatre was discovered in 1963 along with some Roman baths and Islamic tombs in Kom el Dikka. In Anfushi (the famous Pharos Island) an important Ptolemaic cemetery was discovered in 1901. It was restored by the Egyptian Archaeological Authority and is now one of Alexandria's most famous monuments. Some ancient cisterns used for reserving water still remain in the city. The largest is the Shallalat cistern. It is a three-story quadrate building located near Al Shaheed Salah Mustafa Street. The ancient cemetery of Chatby, which was discovered near the sea, north of Saint Mark's School, is considered one of the most important cemeteries of Alexandria. The famous Tanagra statuettes, now in the Graeco-Roman Museum, were found there. Many other discoveries were made recently such as the Mustafa Kamil tombs with their unique architecture, and the Isidor Temple, or the Temple of Black Head, founded by Isidor in the 2nd century A.D. as a gift for the Goddess Isis.

In a nutshell, after national independence Alexandria underwent cultural development and urban expansion not equalled even in the Ptolemaic age. It is now the second capital of Egypt, and an important cultural center with a respected university, numerous museums and galleries, and historical churches, cathedrals and mosques.

Alexandria's urban expansion is unprecedented in history. The city now runs more than 70 kilometers – nearly 45 miles – along the Mediterranean Coast in the northwest Nile Delta. It is bordered in the north by the sea and in the south by Lake Mariut. Eastward, the city reaches Abu Qir Bay and Edku, while the western limits reach Sidi Krir. According to the 1976 census, Alexandria covers more than 2,679 square kilometers. The urban center occupies about 100 square kilometers, including the old city and its new suburbs, King Mariut, Alamein and Sidi Abdel Rahman. The remaining area is about 40 percent croplands, 35 percent desert and 25 percent water from Lake Mariut.

Today, the most important part of this area is the new integral extension of the populated districts: Al Muntazah, Raml, Sidi Gaber, Bab Sharq, Muharram Bey, Attarin, Al Gumruk, Manshyiah, Al Labban, the Harbor, Karmouz, Mena Al Basal, Dekhailah and Ameryiah. The residents of these districts constitute the overwhelming majority of Alexandria's population that, according to the 1986 census, totaled 2,906,493 residents and 10,834 foreigners. As mentioned earlier, the total population of the city on the eve of General Bonaparte's arrival in 1798 was 8,000 people. A comparison between these figures reveals the incredible growth the city has witnessed through the modern age.